VIOLENCE IN LINCOLN COUNTY
1869–1881

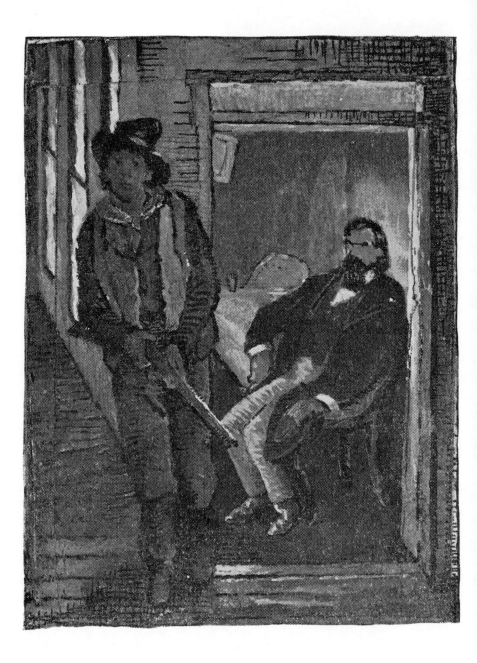

Violence in Lincoln County 1869~1881

a New Mexico Item

William A. Keleher

with a new introduction by
C. L. Sonnichsen

UNIVERSITY OF NEW MEXICO PRESS
Albuquerque

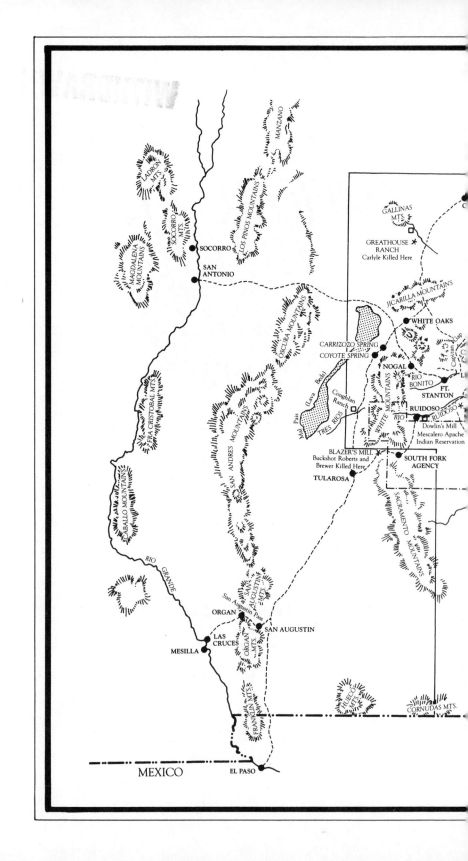

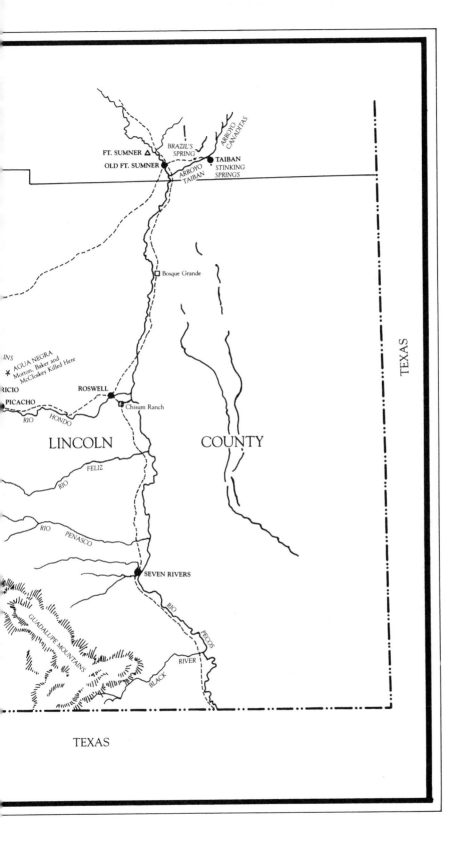

FT. SUMNER △
OLD FT. SUMNER ●
BRAZIL'S SPRING
ARROYO CANADITAS
TAIBAN ●
STINKING SPRINGS
ARROYO TAIBAN

☐ Bosque Grande

INS
★ AGUA NEGRA
Morton, Baker and
McCloskey Killed Here
RICIO
PICACHO ●
ROSWELL ●
☐ Chisum Ranch
RIO HONDO

LINCOLN   COUNTY

RIO FELIZ

RIO PENASCO

SEVEN RIVERS ●

GUADALUPE MOUNTAINS

RIO PECOS

BLACK RIVER

TEXAS

TEXAS

T 107684

Library of Congress Cataloging in Publication Data

Keleher, William Aloysius, 1886–1972.
  Violence in Lincoln County, 1869–1881.

  Reprint. Originally published: Albuquerque :
University of New Mexico Press, [1957] With new
introd.
  Includes bibliographical references and index.
  1. Lincoln County (N.M)—History.   I. Title.
F802.L7K4   1982   978.9'64   82-1984
ISBN 0-8263-0620-9   AACR2
ISBN 0-8263-0616-0 (pbk.)

CONTENTS

ILLUSTRATIONS

Frontis

Drawing by Ernest L. Blumenschein, Taos artist,
showing his visualization of the meeting between
Lew. Wallace and William H. Bonney (Billy the Kid).

Photographs between pages 304 and 305

Lew. Wallace in the uniform of a Major-General,
taken soon after the close of the Civil War.

Photostat of the verdict of the Coroner's Jury
which held the inquest on July 15, 1881,
on the body of William H. Bonney.

Milnor Rudulph, foreman of the Coroner's Jury.

Charles Bowdre, comrade of Billy the Kid, and his wife.

James J. Dolan.   John H. Riley.

Maj. Emil Fritz, Maj. Lawrence G. Murphy,
John H. Tunstall, Deluvina Maxwell.

The Palace of the Governors in Santa Fe
as it appeared in 1878.

Page 174

Reproduction of letter of March 9, 1877,
written to President Hayes by Lew. Wallace
with reference to a position in the State Department.

Will Keleher: Relentless Historian

Some twenty years ago I had lunch with Will Keleher at his house in Albuquerque, a comfortable, old-fashioned place with a small dining area in a well-lighted alcove where we ate crisp, nonfattening food and talked about history. After lunch the dialogue escalated into an argument, vigorously sustained on both sides, about the value of materials available to the local and regional historian. Mr. Keleher maintained that the only trustworthy legacy from the past was sworn testimony in a court of law. I held out for newspapers, county records, letters, autobiographies, and the recollections of people who were there, admitting that bias and misinformation and distortion of facts were to be expected and allowed for. Even sworn testimony, I insisted, can be as unreliable as newspaper accounts—sometimes more so. As I look back now, I realize that Will was trying to tell me that grassroots historians like myself were not spending enough time in county courthouses, and of course he was right.

We parted friends and kept up a cordial, if intermittent, relationship until his death. I learned meanwhile that he himself used every available historical source, just as I did—that he was unbelievably well acquainted with New Mexico newspapers, and that he had interviewed every old-timer he could find who might possibly have useful information. He was, in fact, an indefatigable, even a relentless, historical sleuth, seeking truth wherever he could find it.

His profession as a lawyer, however, did have a determining effect on his work—on the subjects he chose, on his methods and attitudes. His business was the law, and he was a historian only in the evenings and on weekends and holidays. "I observed the rule I had established," he says in his autobiography (pp. 273–74), "providing that no part of the work would be allowed to interfere with my regular law office practice hours. . . . Working late at night, getting to sleep late, and starting to work on the books soon after daybreak, made it possible for me to accomplish a great deal." The relentless historian was, in short, relentless first of all with himself.

His close acquaintance with New Mexico, its people, and its history began early. Born in Lawrence, Kansas, of Irish-immigrant parents, Will became a resident of Albuquerque in 1888 at the age of two. He grew up with the town and the Territory, working first as a telegraph operator, then as a reporter and city editor for two Albuquerque newspapers. Court reporting gave him the urge to become a lawyer. In 1913, even though he had been out of school for more than thirteen years, he began his legal studies. Two years later he graduated with a law degree from Washington and Lee University. For over fifty years he was active in Albuquerque politics, in public service, and in the successful practice of his profession. First of all he was a lawyer, and his legal studies provided his best contacts, gave him his best material, and shaped his career as a writer.

As a historian, he was self-taught—a convert—and like most converts he was an enthusiast, eager to go an extra mile for the faith. He did what historians do and then did a little more. It was this enthusiasm which made him relentless in his pursuit of truth, relentless in running down every bit of peripheral information that seemed to have any bearing on the matter at hand, relentless in reproducing every document in full in his printed books. Serious students raise their voices in praise of his achievement. Undedicated readers may throw up their hands in despair, not because Will Keleher tells them too little, but because he tells them more than they want to know.

The law, in the first place, gave Keleher his ideas for writing. Problems of land ownership, ever present in New Mexico, appealed to him from the beginning. Cases involving Spanish and Mexican land grants were often debated in New Mexican courts and provided some of the most colorful chapters in the state's history. His first effort at historical writing was a paper on "The Law of the New Mexico Land Grant," read before a joint meeting of the New Mexico and Texas bar associations at Amarillo, Texas, on July 5, 1929. The essay, published in the *Texas Law Review,* was favorably received, and this small success encouraged the author to immerse himself in the complicated and controversial history of the Maxwell Land Grant. It provided good material in the two areas which interested him most, offering "an interesting assortment of characters to write about and much important litigation to be considered." Thirteen years after the publication of his paper on land titles, *The Maxwell Land Grant: A New Mexico Item* was published.

The word *item,* used in the titles of three of his four historical works and in his autobiography, tells something about Keleher's habits of thought. He might as well have used the word *case.* His orderly mind works in compartments. He likes to break a major topic up into segments and consider them one by one. In *The Maxwell Land Grant* he provides a rough chronology and then takes a topical approach. Lucien B. Maxwell gets a chapter. The Indian-rights issue gets a chapter. The Spanish-American claimants get a chapter. The vigilantes get a chapter. A final section is devoted to "Steve" Elkins and "Tom" Catron, entrepreneurs par excellence. As a result, Keleher violates Aristotle's dictum that a composition must have a beginning, a middle, and an end; each chapter is an "item." Nevertheless he did his research with what he calls "lawyer-like precision" (*Violence,* p. 111) and was tireless in his pursuit of information.

Courthouses and archival collections were his primary hunting grounds. Next in importance was the testimony of witnesses and participants, and he traveled far and often to find them and record their stories. In many cases he did not have to find them since he had already made contact in the course of his activities as newsman and lawyer. Whether they were old friends or new, the qualities of his personality were such that they trusted him and helped him almost without exception. He was able to persuade reticent men to talk freely—men who had refused to open their mouths before—and he always made sure they approved his quotations.

The third leg on which his researches stood was newspaper reporting, and he was probably better acquainted with Territorial and state journals than any man in New Mexico. He tells in his autobiography (p. 258) of a visit to Hillsboro to consult the *Sierra County Advocate,* only to find that the unbound files were scattered about, unsorted and unprotected, in a concrete shed at the rear of the courthouse. Appalled by this "chaos," he was about to leave when he "stooped down and scooped up an armful of copies and was delighted to see that the scooped up newspapers, beginning with the issue of June 25, 1899, and for subsequent weeks, were the very issues which I needed most"—the issues dealing with the trial of Oliver Lee, Bill McNew, and Jim Gililland in the famous Fountain murder case. A few months later the entire file went up in smoke because it was too hard to move to a new courthouse.

Thoroughness is the first characteristic of the Keleher Method, as initiated in *The Maxwell Land Grant.* The second is completeness. The relentless historian always quotes his documents in full. Other historians may be satisfied to take a few key sentences from a legal document, a letter, or a newspaper story, but not Keleher! He leaves out nothing. This makes for some fatigue on the part of the undisciplined reader and for considerable repetition when two documents cover the same ground, but it removes all suspicion of selection, slanting, or concealment. Completeness also includes the reproduction of minor documents to fill out the record, for example, Bob Olinger's report of the successful transfer of Billy the Kid from Mesilla, where he was tried, to Lincoln, where he was to be hanged (*Violence,* p. 331):

> I hereby certify that I have completed the performance of the services herein required this 21st day of April, 1881.
>   Robert Olinger, Special Deputy Sheriff

Only at the end of his writing career does Keleher show a disposition to condense. Toward the end of *Violence in Lincoln County* he summarizes more than one document (pp. 284, 301, 233–34) and occasionally uses ellipses to indicate omission, but important quotations are still reproduced in full.

A conspicuous characteristic of the Keleher Method is voluminous documentation. As a lawyer he is used to citing cases and precedents in his legal briefs. As a neophyte historian he loves to explore the bypaths that lead to footnotes, endnotes, and appendices, and he rejoices in filling his notes with every bit of supplementary information in his files. He uses more pages for annotation than anybody since the Victorians. A two-page note is not unusual, and when an especially long one is carried forward at the bottom of successive pages, it may end three pages farther along. Supplementary information is placed at the end of each chapter in a section called "Profiles and Notes," the biographical "profiles" taking up perhaps half the space. These encyclopedic appendages seldom point to sources. Keleher likes to place his references in the text next to the passages quoted, and he consistently follows this practice with newspaper quotes—not often with other citations, an omission for which the academic historians take him to task. One usually looks in vain for any indication of the origin of biographical details, and an eager graduate student would give way to despair at Keleher's failure to pinpoint the location and title of specific documents. He explains his reasons in a section on sources at the beginning of *Violence* (p. xvi):

> It has not been considered necessary to identify the source of each individual Wallace item. . . . the originals of the Wallace personal correspondence and incidental items are in the Wallace collection in Indianapolis; and the originals of the official Wallace papers and documents are in the National Archives.

If the eager graduate student wants to know more, he can dig it out for himself.

In one final respect the Keleher Method differs from others. As a lawyer and as a person, Keleher is as much interested in causes and consequences as he is in actual events. He reports dramatic moments but does not stage scenes or strive for surprises or emotional impact. He presents the facts, all the facts, and nothing but the facts in most cases, leaving the development of suspense and emotional involvement to the novelists and popular historians. Quite naturally under these circumstances he strives for judicial impartiality, seeing both sides of every question, giving controversial individuals the benefit of every doubt, seldom betraying any bias of his own. In dealing with newspaper stories, of course, he is in the presence of violently partisan editors. When his journalistic sources are diametrically opposed, he quotes both sides (*Violence*, pp. 129–30).

Keleher improved and refined his method as time went on. Last and best of his works was *Violence in Lincoln County, 1869–1881,* published in 1957 by the University of New Mexico Press. It was badly needed. The Lincoln County troubles had been romanticized by a whole regiment of popular writers, with Walter Noble Burns in the lead, and Billy the Kid had been metamorphosed from a semiliterate outlaw on the fringes of the trouble to a heroic figure at the center. It was Keleher's mission, as he saw it, to put Lincoln County affairs in true perspective and reduce Billy the Kid to his proper dimensions. Using his familiar methods, Keleher succeeded admirably. The writing is always skillful and at times lively. The portraits are penetrating and just but always charitable. There were men on both sides, Keleher believes, "with malice and hatred in their hearts, envious and jealous of their fellows" (p. xiii), but "some men of great courage and integrity were anxious to act honorably under exceptional stress and strain. . . . Others died bravely" (p. xiv). In contemplating these flawed human beings, he sometimes betrays his own feelings. "Poor McSween," he remarks, "was in a state of resigned confusion" as "Judge Bristol and District Attorney Rynerson pursued him" (p. 140).

As before, Keleher resists all temptation to make high drama out of the events described. Walter Noble Burns could fictionalize, but not Will Keleher. William Bonney and Governor Lew. Wallace meet "face to face in dramatic fashion," he admits, during their famous encounter at Lincoln on March 17, 1879, but this meeting, which gets three pages of character analysis and invented conversation in Walter Noble Burns's romance, is covered by Keleher in one twenty-line paragraph. All documents and correspondence connected with the episode are, of course, quoted in full.

It should be obvious by now that the Keleher Method concentrates on a lawyer-like pursuit of facts and no-nonsense presentation. The image of the relentless historian comes through so strongly, in fact, that one may overlook Keleher's gifts as a writer. He does have an imagination. He does reach for the colorful phrase. He does smile at the ridiculous. Rev. Thomas Harwood in *The Maxwell Land Grant* is "a one-man army of the Lord" (p. 75). The Pioneer Saloon in White Oaks "sold three different grades of whiskey at different prices out of the same barrel, depending on which brand the customer called for, and since he always called for the same brand, there was never any complaint" (*Fabulous Frontier*, p. 40).

There is even a vein of poetry in him, seldom seen but occasionally in evidence. He quotes Eugene Manlove Rhodes's *Engle Ferry* (*Fabulous Frontier*, p. 168) with relish, and writes some good prose poetry of his own at the beginning of a chapter devoted to Pecos Valley developer James John Hagerman in which he offers a bird's-eye view of the upper drainage of the Pecos River. "Subterranean waters emerge from their hiding places," he begins. "Springs fed by the perpetual snow of mountain tops bubble from their depths. Here in northeast New Mexico, more than thirteen thousand feet above sea level, is the place of the headwaters of the Pecos River. . . . there are countless grassy meadows, bright with the color of wild roses, columbine, Indian paint brush, Shasta daisies, bluebells and black-eyed Susans. . . . The magic of the Santa Fe Mountains hovers over the spirit of the Pecos

River for more than forty miles from its source. Witness to the magic are the golden glow of eastern skies at daybreak and purple haze that tells of the setting sun just before twilight" (p. 180).

Obviously enjoying himself immensely, Keleher spends five pages on the Pecos and its tributaries and five more on the irrigation schemes of Pat Garrett and Charles B. Eddy. Hagerman has to mark time for ten pages before the author gets around to him.

He does not often take his eye off the ball in this fashion, but he is subject to occasional slips and errors in his first three volumes—slips that a vigilant editor should have caught. He is careless about paragraph transitions (*Fabulous Frontier*, p. 86). He has a weakness for the dangling participle (*Fabulous Frontier*, pp. 86, 300). He sometimes stretches a paragraph to cover more than one topic, gets proper names wrong (Numa Raymond for Reymond, Wayne Brazil for Brazel, the Harrold brothers for Horrell, Cesario Pedragon for Pedregon, Print Rhodes for Rhode). He has an awkward habit of telling what is in a quotation before he quotes. A good editor would have kept him from writing "script" for "scrip," from calling an Apache wickiup a "jacal," from describing Tom Catron as a "stormy petrol." In *Violence* he was, editorially speaking, much better served.

Considering his immersion in basic and peripheral facts and his neglect of the devices that promote reader interest, Keleher reads surprisingly well. His prose, clear and concise always, is uncomplicated but well finished, often graceful. The most critical reviewers of *Violence* agreed that the book was "highly readable" and some enthusiasts called it "graphic and enthralling" (*American Book Collector*, October 1957; *Tulsa World*, July 21, 1957). This was high praise for a work so largely composed of quotations, indicating that the quotations themselves were of exceptional interest.

All reviewers agreed that the volume was "a significant contribution to Southwestern history." W. H. Hutchinson in the *San Francisco Chronicle*, November 24, 1957, hailed it as "the most important work ever performed on the first and most violent of the Western range wars," though he expressed regret that Keleher remained impartial and refrained from voicing "his own considered opinions" about the episode. On the other hand Frederick W. Nolan, writing in the English Westerners' *Brand Book* (July 1957), praised him for refusing to "draw conclusions." Professional historians regretted the absence of "adequate citation" (*Pacific Historical Review*, February 1958), and some nonprofessionals found it "overlong" and "redundant" (*American Scholar*, Winter 1957–58; *True West*, September–October 1957). Negative opinions were rare, however, and most critics agreed with T. M. Pearce of the University of New Mexico, writing in *Western Folklore* (Summer 1957):

> W. A. Keleher's new book, *Violence in Lincoln County*, tells the complete story, making use of all previously known documents and drawing upon

legal records, newspaper files and unpublished writings (such as the Tunstall letters) not hitherto examined. The result is just as graphic a story as anyone has ever devised with the help of his imagination, and by far the most reliable account yet written. In his carefully dispassionate style, he manages to make the whole ranching world of vast Lincoln County come to life, and the business of trading, fighting, riding, running, capture, escape, death and survival, trial and punishment live for the reader as they have never done before.

The agreement seems to be general that Keleher, following his own lights, made a significant contribution to history and handled his materials with special skill.

It must be noted, however, that his supremacy in his own field has not remained unchallenged. The legend of Billy the Kid has begotten so much writing that two volumes have been devoted to nothing more than the bibliography of the subject, while numerous books and essays develop in detail one aspect or another of the Lincoln County saga. Lawrence Kelly, for example, has devoted a thick volume to the career of Tom Catron; Leon C. Metz has produced a full-length study of Pat Garrett; Robert N. Mullin, Philip Rasch, William V. Morrison and many others have considered aspects of the Billy the Kid story; Eugene Cunningham, Edwin Corle, Amelia Bean, and Frazer Hunt are four among many who use the war as material for fiction.

The primary source, however, in addition to Keleher, is Maurice Garland Fulton's *The Lincoln County War,* put together in 1968 from three manuscripts after Fulton's death by Robert N. Mullin. In many ways the two authors are alike. Both place Billy the Kid among the buck privates in McSween's little army and give him higher rank only in the final chapters of their books. Most of the time they use the same or similar documents and correspondence, though Fulton, writing later, found some sources unknown to Keleher. Since he lived at Roswell and was in closer touch with the people and lore of the country, he made some notable additions to the story, including the now generally accepted theory that José Aguayo placed a pistol in the outhouse at the Lincoln County jail where Billy could find it, thus adding a key fact to the standard account of the Kid's escape.

The men seem to have worked independently of each other, though Keleher acknowledges a considerable debt to the researches of editor Robert N. Mullin. Keleher is mentioned only once near the end of Fulton's book. It seems fair to say that both volumes are essential to a full understanding of the battles and background of the Lincoln County War. They may be regarded as twin monuments to the violence in Lincoln County which will always leave a blood-red stain on the history of New Mexico. Keleher, however, came first.

C. L. Sonnichsen

FOREWORD

FOUR EVENTS of major historical significance took place in New Mexico between the years 1846 and 1868: General Kearney's Arrival in Santa Fe with an Army of Conquest in 1846; the Confederate Invasion of the Territory in 1861; the Arrival of Carleton's California Column on the Banks of the Rio Grande in 1862; and the Long Walk of the Navajo Indians in 1863 from mountain hideouts near the Arizona-New Mexico boundary to the Pecos River, adjacent to the New Mexico-Texas boundary, and their triumphant and joyful return to their beloved Chuska mountains five years later.

During Territorial days, roughly the sixty-six years elapsing between the American Conquest in 1846, and the achievement of statehood in 1912, all policy decisions of importance were formulated in Washington, and executed and administered in New Mexico by federal officials holding office at Washington's pleasure. Of necessity federal policies relating to the administration of Territorial affairs were changed from time to time, to conform to the national political trends and the idiosyncrasies of department heads. The Territorial Legislature had authority to enact local laws, and to provide penalties and methods for their enforcement, but the Congress of the United States reserved the right, under the Organic Act establishing the Territory, to pass an act of nullification.

In *Turmoil in New Mexico* published in 1952 the present writer endeavored to portray something of the background of the conflicts, achievements and accomplishments of a number of early Territorial governors, among them Charles Bent, James S. Calhoun, William Carr Lane, David Meriwether, Abraham Rencher, Henry Connelly, and Robert B. Mitchell. A new era began for New Mexico with Governor Mitchell's

resignation in 1868. By 1868 the wild Indians had been pacified
to some extent, ending the actual shooting war that had been
fought between red men and white men on New Mexico soil
for generations. The cease-fire orders had resulted from a
makeshift program for placing the Indians on reservations in
lieu of lands wrested from them during the fighting.

Location engineers were surveying routes for proposed railway lines in various parts of New Mexico in 1868, while promoters of the projects were in Washington appealing for
government subsidies. The year 1868 saw a rush of migrants
into New Mexico, attracted by reports of rich discoveries in
precious metals. In the excitement which accompanied reports
of assured railroad construction, and development of mineral
resources on a large scale, the newcomers pushed and shoved;
speculated in Spanish and Mexican land grants on an unprecedented scale; traded and trafficked in gold and silver mining
claims and properties; bought and sold great tracts of timber
land that had been wheedled out of the federal government
under one pretext or another.

Although in 1868 the Gila Apaches continued to terrorize
southwestern New Mexico and adjacent Arizona, the Legislature in that year established the new county of Grant. In 1869
it established Colfax County in the Ute country of northeastern
New Mexico, and Lincoln County, the homeland of the Mescalero Apaches, in the southeastern part. To assure prompt passage of the bills establishing the new counties, they were given
appealing names: Lincoln, in memory of the martyred president; Grant, as a tribute to the then President of the United
States; and Colfax, in honor of Schuyler Colfax, at the time a
nationally known figure in the Republican party. It was inevitable that the establishment of the new counties would cause
further dislocation and dispersal of the Indian tribes inhabit-
ing the areas. The Indians, however, had no vote and no voice
in legislative matters. As a result, their demands for justice received scant consideration.

The act of 1869 establishing Lincoln County described indefinitely and uncertainly a vast area of country in southeastern
New Mexico, "embracing all that territory between the 34th
parallel of latitude on the north, the Texas boundary line on
the south, the 104° of longitude, or Pecos River on the east, and

the eastern slope of the San Andres mountains on the west." The new county of Lincoln, as described, contained hundreds of thousands of acres of unsurveyed public domain. Much of it was located in that part of the Territory marked "Staked Plains," on official maps. In the Staked Plains area of the new county, the Pecos River, with headwaters in the mountains between Las Vegas and Santa Fe, was a vital, significant stream, without which the surrounding country would have been of little value to the livestock industry. In good seasons the grass in some parts of the Pecos Valley grew stirrup high. West of the Pecos River, in the virgin timber country of the White and Sacramento mountains, there were many areas of surpassing scenic beauty. In the valleys, there was much land suitable for agriculture and horticulture.

Buffalo and antelope roamed the Staked Plains of New Mexico and the adjacent Texas Panhandle for generations before the coming of the white man, providing a happy hunting ground for the Comanches and other Plains Indians, supplying them generously with meat and skins. When United States troops rounded up the Indians and placed them on reservations in Indian Territory (now a part of Oklahoma), white hunters hurried into the country recently relinquished by the Indians and slaughtered buffalo by the thousands. The hunters were after buffalo skins. They had no use for the meat, considered by some frontiersmen to be more palatable and nourishing than beef. The carcasses of the wantonly killed buffalo were left where the animals were killed, food for wolves and carrion, the skeletons left to the disposition of wind and sun.

In the 1870's settlers poured into East Texas from the States, hungry for farming land. Gradually that country was fenced off. Pasturing great herds of cattle became impractical. Cattle drives became a thing of the past. Searching for grass for their herds, East Texas livestock men found it in the Staked Plains in New Mexico and the Panhandle of Texas, an ideal grazing country, vast in its dimensions, with good winter climate and plenty of water available for stock at all seasons of the year. In the late 1860's, a few Texas cattle were driven into the Pecos River country. During the early 1870's the cattle drives became a virtual stampede. In 1872, H. M. Beckwith reported that ninety thousand head of East Texas cattle had been driven up

the Pecos and tallied at crossings near Seven Rivers, Lincoln
County. In the following year, 1873, Beckwith reported that
sixty-three thousand head of Texas cattle had been tallied as
passing through Seven Rivers, of which between twelve and
fifteen thousand head wintered that year on the Pecos River.
The bulk of the cattle driven from Texas in the late 60's, 70's
and early 80's found a home in the Staked Plains and the
Panhandle.

The movement of cattle into the new country marked the
completion of a cycle. Domestic cattle had replaced the buffalo; the cowboy had replaced the Plains Indians. Some Plains
Indians, however, refused to submit meekly to the white man's
invasion and occupation of their country. Renegade Comanches, aided and abetted by unscrupulous white men, for some
years made life miserable for cattlemen in the Staked Plains
country of New Mexico, and in the Texas Panhandle. Cattle
thievery was a leading industry on the Texas-New Mexico border for many years. On April 13, 1871, the Santa Fe *New Mexican* reported:

We are informed that owing to the constant depredations by cattle
thieves in the vicinity of Bosque Redondo and Puerto de Luna, the
stockraisers in that country have organized a vigilance committee
and threaten vengeance upon the suspected parties. Hon. L. B.
Maxwell, since his residence at Fort Sumner, has already suffered
from cattle thieves to the extent of a thousand head.

Comanches ranged up and down the Pecos River, stealing
cattle almost at will, according to the *New Mexican* of May 30,
1871. That paper estimated that 1,000 people were at that time
engaged in the "trade," and that during recent months some
30,000 head of stock had been stolen in Texas by the Comanche
and other thieves, driven into New Mexico, and sold to Colorado buyers. When military aid was obtained, soldiers were
stationed at Portales with instructions to break up the wholesale thievery. Commenting on the situation, the *New Mexican*
said: "This damnable and outrageous traffic must be stopped,
and we cannot thank the military enough for their laudable
efforts in this direction." That the livestock stealing industry
in eastern New Mexico and west Texas was well organized and

adequately financed was evident from a story published in the Santa Fe *New Mexican* of June 1, 1878:

On May 28, 1871, Capt. James Frank Randlett, 8th Cavalry, captured a pack train of 23 burros loaded with powder, lead, cloth and trinkets, on the Staked Plains, enroute to the Comanche country. A Comanche squaw, who was guiding the outfit to the Comanche camp, and ten Mexican men, claiming to be from Santa Fe, San Miguel and Mora counties, were arrested. Next day, Randlett captured 510 head of cattle coming from the Comanche country in charge of traders. The burros were killed and goods destroyed. Those arrested were placed in jail in Fort Bascom.

An editorial note added:

This good work should go on until this nefarious trade is most thoroughly broken up. It has long been a disgrace to our Territory, and the cause of untold loss and suffering to the frontier settlers of Texas. Let the troops be kept in the field, and summary justice meted out to all traders found in the Indian country, and in a short time they will find out that the profits attending such unlawful expeditions will not compensate for the risks involved.

Between the years 1875 and 1880, the Panhandle of Texas developed rapidly as a livestock and agricultural country. Most settlers knew in a vague sort of way that a Potter County existed in that part of the state, but had little knowledge of or information concerning its boundaries or political organization. As late as August 10, 1878, the Las Vegas *Gazette* directed attention to an ideal situation: "There are no county officials in Potter county in the Panhandle of Texas. Better yet, in that county there are no state officers or emissaries to interfere with the unalloyed liberty which the inhabitants of that county enjoy. When any horse thieves or bad characters make their appearance they are strung up to the cottonwoods. Tascosa is the chief town."

There was no appreciable difference between the topography of the Staked Plains of New Mexico and that of the Panhandle. "The Law" had not yet caught up with the growth of that country; and as a result it offered unlimited opportunities for ambitious, capable, energetic cattle thieves. Rustlers were inclined to treat livestock owners on the boundary line impartially, stealing cattle in Texas and selling them in New Mexico; stealing cattle in New Mexico and selling them across the line in Texas.

The Lincoln County country, in some areas, had been settled up some years in advance of the settlement of the adjoining Panhandle country. Adventuresome Spanish-Americans, braving the hazards of Indian attacks, settled in a pleasant place along the Bonito River, first named Placitas, and later Bonito. In a moment of patriotic fervor, the Legislature of 1869 changed the name from Bonito to Lincoln. Whether known as Placitas, Bonito or Lincoln, the little town that became the county seat of Lincoln County appeared to be strife-prone from the very beginning. Death by violence was not unusual. Men seemingly went out of their way to stir up discord which at times ended in bloodshed. Marcos Estabrook and Elisha A. Dow, hopeful, perhaps, of causing some excitement during a dull period, threw the town into an uproar in 1875 by filing a homestead claim in the United States Land Office on the land on which the town of Lincoln was situated. The filing of the claim raised a doubt as to the validity of the title of every property owner in town. A Memorial by the Territorial Legislature in 1878, and a subsequent Act of Congress were required to cure the title defect.

Lincoln County held within its boundaries all the props, trappings and paraphernalia needed for staging an out-of-doors theatrical production of huge proportions. On the southwestern tip of the county there was located the Mescalero Indian reservation on which the remnants of the discontented Mescalero tribe huddled together miserably in poorly built *jacals,* the tribal leaders constantly blaming officials for poor rations of food and skimpy issues of clothing. To keep the Mescaleros subdued, there was Fort Stanton, located within a hard day's ride of the Agency. The attitude of the cavalrymen, stationed at Fort Stanton, toward the Mescalero Apaches, was influenced by a traditional distrust, dating back to 1855, at which time, it was claimed, the Indians had killed Capt. Henry W. Stanton, in whose memory the fort had been named.

In the flat country, along the Pecos and its several tributaries, there were hundreds of thousands of acres of unsurveyed public domain, affording grazing to great and small bands of cattle, watched over by owners and cowboys, many of them belligerent from their cradle days. The federal government purchased great quantities of beef, butchered and on the hoof, to fill the ration requirements of the Indians, and to feed the soldiers at Fort Stanton. The government also bought other supplies in great quantities for subsistence of man and beast at the Agency and the Fort. As the result of government purchases of vegetables, fruit, hay and grain, settlers farmed on unsurveyed public lands in the valleys of Lincoln County, producing crops which could be readily sold in the local market. Pending a survey of the public domain, and the establishment by the government of the means for acquiring a patent to a homestead, the settlers traded and trafficked in what became known as "Squatters' Rights," deeds and conveyances which in time became recognized in the county as evidence of ownership of property, out of the use of which developed feuds and fights culminating in violence.

In the late 70's, Lincoln County began to grow and develop, and prosper a bit, but the growth, development and prosperity were short lived, being retarded for a generation by the acts of a few men, some of them with malice and hatred in their hearts, envious and jealous of their fellows. This book is largely devoted to the telling of that story, with its many strange bypaths, and sometimes almost incredible ramifications.

As will be apparent from these pages, the Lincoln County War was a vast and complicated event, or series of events. Despite assertions made by some writers to the contrary, Texans had little or nothing to do with that war. It was a contest unique in the frontier life of America, fought to a finish between and among men from various parts of the globe—Ireland, Canada, Vermont, Massachusetts, New York, Michigan, and many other places. It was a young man's war, inaugurated and carried on, sometimes unwittingly, by men of strong and determined character, but distorted vision. Few participants were willing to give an inch of ground, or take a step toward the peaceful settlement of controversies.

The Lincoln County War of 1878 is seen only through the haze of years. Blurred figures appear on the horizon of history.

Men in high place, in civil and military life, schemed, connived and conspired to accomplish unworthy objectives; selfish men, ambitious for wealth and power, turned arrogant and hostile in their endeavors; ignorant men, acting in utter disregard of the rights of others, blindly followed stupid leaders along trails of dishonor which led to disaster. Some men of great courage and integrity were anxious to act honorably under exceptional stress and strain. Others bent on defying the law and following paths of crime charted their courses with reckless disregard of the rights of others. Some men inadvertently became fugitives from justice; others, who could have quietly left the country without being open to a charge of cowardice, elected to remain, and died bravely in blasts of gunfire accompanied by the whine and ping of bullets. Men, regardless of whether they were good men or bad men, and regardless of their motives, united in starting a conflagration which continued to illumine the skies of southeastern New Mexico for a generation after their day. Ghostly embers of that conflagration still exist in the recollection of descendants of Lincoln County pioneers. The scars it left on the countryside are apparent and visible today along the Pecos River, the Bonito, the Hondo, in the White Mountains and the Sacramentos.

Acknowledgments

Thanks and appreciation are due to many people for kind and generous cooperation in making this work possible. At the risk of unintentionally omitting the names of some to whom I am indebted, I wish to express my gratitude to a host of helpers and contributors. First and foremost I wish to thank Robert N. Mullin, of Chicago, formerly of Las Vegas and El Paso, for his generosity in allowing me to browse at will through his outstanding collection of New Mexicana, and providing me with typescripts and photostats of important items not otherwise obtainable. I wish to thank Ernest L. Blumenschein, of Taos, for drawing the frontispiece; Caroline Dunn, Librarian of the William Henry Smith Library of the Indiana Historical Society, Indianapolis, for furnishing me with microfilms from the Lew. Wallace collection; P. M. Hamer and staff of the National Archives, for photostats from the Samuel B. Axtell and Lew. Wallace official files; Gertrude Hill, Chief Librarian of the New Mexico Museum Library, and her assistants,

Ruth E. Rambo, Edna A. Medearns, Edith G. McManmon, for many courtesies extended over a period of several years; David Otis Kelley, Chief Librarian, and his assistants at the University of New Mexico; W. D. Bryars, Clerk, U.S. District Court of New Mexico; U.S. Senator Dennis Chavez and Charles Davis, his administrative assistant; U.S. Senator Clinton P. Anderson and Claude E. Wood, his administrative assistant; W. E. Bentley, Charlottetown, Prince Edward Island, Canada; Arlene Schlegel, University of Iowa Library; Adelina Jaramillo Welborn, granddaughter of Lucien B. Maxwell, Fort Sumner; Mrs. Odelia Bernice Finley Johnson, of Albuquerque, great granddaughter of Lucien B. Maxwell; Mrs. Laura H. Cahoon, Roswell; Rev. Neil C. P. Dukelow, Pastor, First Presbyterian Church, Atchison, Kansas; Wilbur Coe, of Glencoe, and John Boylan, of Lincoln, for drawing maps of old Lincoln County; Lorine W. Garrett, Historical Museum of Arizona, Prescott, Arizona; Constantia P. Chavez, County Clerk, Doña Ana County, Las Cruces, New Mexico; Geraldine S. Mathisen, District Court Clerk, Third Judicial District, Las Cruces; Mary M. Long, Deputy District Court Clerk, Sixth Judicial District, Silver City; F. R. Blackburn, Research Director, Kansas State Historical Society, Topeka; Herman Lindauer, Deming; Miss C. O'Callaghan, British Embassy, Washington, D.C.; Robert Ward, of Lovington, for a copy of *Thirty Six Years in New Mexico,* written many years ago by his father, the late Charles W. G. Ward; William J. Eaton, of Socorro; Betty Copeland, Free Public Library, Burlington, Iowa; Mrs. Leticia Grzelachowski Padilla, Puerto de Luna; T. R. Worley, Executive Secretary, Arkansas History Commission, Little Rock, Arkansas; Gilberto Espinosa, of Albuquerque; R. Stewart Kilborne, New York City; and Mrs. Elizabeth Warner, Northampton, Massachusetts.

In conclusion, I gratefully record here my thanks and appreciation to George Fitzpatrick, editor of the *New Mexico Magazine,* and my sister, Julia M. Keleher, of the University of New Mexico, for reading the manuscript; Ellis Neel, for typing, and Ilda B. Sganzini for indexing.

WILLIAM A. KELEHER

Albuquerque, New Mexico
January 31, 1957

SOURCES

Official records of the Axtell and Wallace administrations in the National Archives, Washington, D.C.

Lew. Wallace collection in the William Henry Smith Library, of the Indiana Historical Society, Indianapolis, Indiana.

Robert N. Mullin collection, Chicago, Illinois.

Official records in the United States District Court, Santa Fe, New Mexico, and in the District Courts of Lincoln, Doña Ana, Grant, Socorro and Santa Fe counties.

Personal interviews in 1910 with John W. Poe; in 1912 with Charles Siringo; discussions with George Curry, Andrew H. Hudspeth, Lucius Dills, George Ulrich, and others who had unusual opportunity to know the history of old Lincoln County.

Newspapers of the period, particularly the Las Vegas *Gazette* (abbreviated LVG), Santa Fe *New Mexican* and Lincoln County *Leader;* stray items from incomplete files of Mesilla *Independent,* Mesilla *News,* Grant County *Herald* and Cimarron *News and Press.*

Papers, documents and photographs in the Old Lincoln County Museum. (Courtesy of Mr. and Mrs. John Boylan, curators.)

It has not been considered necessary to identify the source of each individual Wallace item used or referred to in this book. Unless a citation indicates to the contrary, the originals of the Wallace personal correspondence and incidental items are in the Wallace collection in Indianapolis; and the originals of the official Wallace papers and documents are in the National Archives.

VIOLENCE IN LINCOLN COUNTY
1869–1881

CHAPTER ONE

IN RETROSPECT

IN 1868, the Territory of New Mexico was but one of several territories of the United States, all of them presumably entitled to equal rights, privileges, and protection under the law. Leading New Mexicans of the time, however, took the position that because New Mexico was conquered territory, it occupied an extraordinary place in the scheme of things politically and should be given preferential consideration. In some respects New Mexico did indeed occupy a status that was unique in the government of the United States. Although nomad Indians dominated in population, it was an inhabited country at the time it became American territory, and had been inhabited for hundreds of years along the Rio Grande and its tributaries by a civilized people. To this extent, New Mexico was different from other existing territories. As a result of its isolation and unique status, New Mexico was for many years looked upon by official Washington as an orphan among the states and territories. As early as 1852 Col. Edwin Voss Sumner submitted an official report to Washington recommending, among other things, that the government "return New Mexico to the Mexicans and Indians;" and as late as January 7, 1874, Gen. William Tecumseh Sherman, testifying before a senate committee, declared that "ownership of the Territory of New Mexico was not worth the cost of defense."

In the early years subsequent to the Occupation of 1846, it appeared that the federal government was reluctant to take the necessary steps to permit the Territory to function properly. On numerous occasions it was evident that Washington officials deferred action and decision indefinitely on simple requests, the granting of which would have benefited both Indians and non-Indians. Nevertheless, in 1868, it was obvious that the federal government had achieved a number of major objectives during the two decades of New Mexico's official existence. By payment of $10,000,000 to Texas in 1849, it had settled, by diplomatic means, the vexatious boundary dispute between Texas and New Mexico. Beginning with 1846, and continuing for many years, the federal government had expended annually great sums of money to police the wild Indians. In 1863, it had established the Territory of Arizona by cutting off the western half of New Mexico, and in the same year had authorized the straightening of the boundary between New Mexico and Colorado.

During the Civil War, from 1861 to 1865, the federal government had maintained troops in the Territory, at great expense, to repel invading Confederates. Between the years 1863 and 1868, Washington had financed the war against the Navajo Indians, which resulted in their imprisonment on the Pecos River in eastern New Mexico. The federal government had insisted, in 1868, upon the abolition of peonage, a long-established custom in the Territory, and upon the abandonment of martial law, in effect throughout New Mexico during the Civil War years.

From the earliest Territorial days down to the commencement of the Civil War, the office of governor of New Mexico was considered the patronage of congressmen from the Southern states. As a result, governor after governor was a Southerner. Immediately prior to the commencement of hostilities in 1861, there was good reason to believe that New Mexico would declare its allegiance to the South, and in due time become a Confederate state. The federal government, acting decisively, stifled the growth of Southern influence in the Territory.

Abraham Rencher, of North Carolina, lawyer and former congressman, believed to be a secessionist, an appointee of President Buchanan, served as governor of New Mexico from 1857 to 1861. When Abraham Lincoln was elected President, Rencher was relieved as governor, and Henry Connelly, a doctor, was appointed to succeed him. Connelly took the oath of office on September 4, 1861. On that particular occasion, the taking of the oath to support and uphold the Constitution of the United States was of greater significance than at any previous time in the history of the nation. Although born in Virginia and educated in Kentucky, Connelly was not a Southern sympathizer. He had been in and out of New Mexico and Chihuahua almost constantly since 1824, practicing medicine in emergencies, but devoting most of his time to the Santa Fe trade. At the time of the Occupation in 1846, Connelly was perhaps the most influential American in New Mexico, and he proved to be a loyal and faithful agent of the federal government during the trying years of the Civil War.

Robert B. Mitchell of Ohio, recently discharged from the Union army with the rank of brigadier general, became governor following Connelly's resignation. Mitchell took the oath of office on June 6, 1866. He failed to take his duties either seriously or with dignity. During the 1866-67 session of the Legislature, he affronted the members by leaving Santa Fe immediately after delivering the opening message, and absenting himself for several months without apology or explanation. The Legislature adjourned sine die, and ordered that all bills enacted during the session be forwarded to the Secretary of the Interior in Washington. Because the bills lacked the Governor's signature, the Congress on March 26, 1867, adopted a joint resolution approving them, subject to certain conditions and reservations. President Grant accepted Mitchell's resignation on March 25, 1869, and appointed William A. Pile, of St. Louis, to succeed him. Pile, a lame-duck congressman, one-time minister of the gospel and former army officer, took the oath of office in Santa Fe on August 16, 1869. The *New Mexican* introduced him to the people of the Territory:

William A. Pile arrived in Santa Fe last evening and will at once assume the duties and responsibilities of the executive office which, for several months, has been practically vacant—Gov. Mitchell having devoted his time exclusively to private business. Gov. Pile has been, for many years, a resident of St. Louis. At the beginning of the democratic rebellion, fired with patriotic enthusiasm, he resigned the pastorate of a church in that city, and hastened to the "tented field," to fight, as a private soldier, for principles he had long upheld by eloquent advocacy. In the army he rose by regular advancement to the rank of Brigadier General, with the brevet of major general, and in every grade and command did his country good service and dealt the enemy sturdy and effective blows. At the close of the war he was elected by the Republican party as one of the representatives of St.

Louis in the 40th Congress, in which he served with marked ability and such fidelity to his constituency that he was renominated in 1868 with but little opposition. He made a gallant fight for the succession, but the frauds of the rebel democracy defeated him by a majority of less than one hundred. Intelligent, energetic, thoroughly radical in politics and wholly western in character, feeling and experience, our new governor can hardly fail to administer the Executive Department of our Territorial government to the satisfaction of our people, and give them abundant reason to be pleased with the change.[1]

New Mexico politicians did not know just what to think or say about Governor Pile. He was the exact opposite in character, temperament and disposition from Robert Mitchell, his predecessor. The new governor was a sincere advocate of prohibition in a day in New Mexico when excessive drinking of whiskey, brandy and native wine was not considered unusual. Soon after becoming governor, he invited the people of Santa Fe to attend a series of Sunday evening lectures. On November 30, 1869, the Governor lectured on "The Worth of Men Shall Praise Thee," a text taken from the Psalms. On Christmas Eve, 1869, he delivered a temperance lecture at the Good Templar's Hall; and on January 30, 1870, in the Presbyterian Church, under the auspices of the Santa Fe Bible Society, he lectured on the subject, "Courage, the Measure of Man's Power." On July 17, 1870, the subject was "Fictitious Narrative as a Means of Instruction—Its Uses and Abuse." On August 19, 1870, when the Reverend D. F. McFarland, Pastor of the Presbyterian Church, was absent in Fort Wingate, Governor Pile occupied the pulpit and preached in his place.

Educated to think in terms of philosophy and theology, Governor Pile found it difficult at times to cope with politicians widely experienced in the arts of knuckle-down, no-holds-barred politics. He was thrust into several serious jousts with New Mexico politicians. One such engagement, which assumed serious proportions, revolved around what appeared in the beginning to be a routine administrative matter in which Pile, Attorney General Catron, and Territorial Librarian Ira M. Bond, all from Missouri, played the leading parts in a drama that became known as "The Battle of the Archives."

Catron had been an officer in the Confederate army, and to

that extent was vulnerable as a member of the Republican party. Bond had been a captain in the Union army during the Civil War. After the war he had been active in Missouri politics, supporting Lincoln and Grant in their campaigns for the Presidency. After being defeated in a contest for election as chief clerk in the Missouri House of Representatives, Bond became a resident of Santa Fe. Through Pile's influence he was appointed Territorial Librarian; and on March 1, 1870, was admitted to the New Mexico bar by Chief Justice Palen.

There was every reason to assume that Captain Bond's stay in New Mexico would be pleasant and profitable. However, Bond had been Territorial Librarian only a few weeks when a storm broke over Santa Fe. It was reported that he had "sold, thrown out and given away," many valuable papers and documents, part of New Mexico's priceless collection of archives. In an interview in the Santa Fe *New Mexican* on April 5, 1870, Bond explained and defended, protesting against what he described as "a false and malicious article," published in the Santa Fe Weekly *Post* of April 2. Tom Catron, it appeared from Bond's explanation, had looked over the rooms occupied by the Library, and decided that he wanted to use one of them as additional office space. There was only one drawback to the immediate use of the room. It was packed almost from floor to ceiling with old papers and documents, some of them yellowing with age. Bond explained in his interview:

Attorney General Catron obtained permission, as I supposed, from the Secretary of the Public Buildings, to fix up and clean the room for an office, at his own expense, then called on Gov. Pile and asked if he had any objection, to which the Governor said he had none. Gov. Pile took me to the room and instructed me to preserve the papers that were valuable, and store the others in an adjoining room to the rear.

Before disposing of the papers and documents, Bond said that he had consulted two prominent Spanish-American citizens, both of whom had carefully examined them and passed upon their value from the historical standpoint. Bond consistently maintained that he had not "thrown out anything of value," but notwithstanding this he caused the publication of a notice in the *New Mexican* of April 21, which read: "All persons having any of the papers recently removed from the Palace in their possession, are notified that they were removed by mistake as to their value; and all such persons are requested to return them at once to the Territorial Library."

The "Battle of the Archives" was enthusiastically seized upon by a number of political leaders of Santa Fe, both Republicans and Democrats. It afforded them a long-awaited opportunity to commence a full-dress political war on Governor Pile, with the object of forcing his resignation, a fate which had befallen a number of his predecessors.

On April 16, a large mass meeting of citizens was held in Santa Fe, at which inflammatory speeches were made denouncing Pile for "his outrageous conduct" in connection with the archives, and lambasting him because of other alleged political stupidities. Under the leadership of Judge Kirby Benedict, resolutions were adopted at the meeting, replete with resounding rhetoric. One resolution declared that the actions of the Governor, Bond and Catron, in dealing with the archives, "had no precedent in recorded history excepting the barbarous burning of the library of Alexandria." The meeting went on record as declaring:

> That the Governor was the prime cause of the sale and destruction of archives of the Territory, a portion of which are more than 200 years old, under peremptory instructions to the Librarian; that he has proven himself unworthy of the confidence of the people.
>
> That the president of the United States be and hereby is respectfully solicited to remove William A. Pile from the position he now occupies as Governor of the Territory of New Mexico, which office he is not capacitated to fill, and which he has by his conduct, disgraced.

Attorney General Catron wrote long letters of explanation, in regard to the Library episode, absolving Governor Pile from any responsibility, and in turn the Governor wrote a number of letters to the newspapers stating his position, among them a long letter to the editors of the Republican *Review* in Albuquerque, which was published on April 28, 1870. In that letter, the Governor said among other things:

A few soreheads have attempted to raise a great howl against me about the removal and sale of some old documents and papers by the Territorial Librarian. A packed meeting was held here recently and violent resolutions were adopted. I am enclosing herewith affidavits and statements proving the whole thing false and malicious.

Complying with the Governor's request, the *Review* published the text of reports, affidavits and other material, dealing with charges and countercharges, adding further to the already existing confusion surrounding the facts and circumstances of the unfortunate incident.

Although the charge of unlawful destruction of archives formed the basis of the attack on Pile, his enemies found it advisable to tack on other charges to the resolutions adopted on April 16. Among the additional charges, the Governor was accused of retaining Thomas B. Catron as Attorney General of the Territory, well knowing that Catron was "an unreconstructed rebel," and of conspiring at a recent Territorial Republican convention, with Diego Archuleta and other political leaders, in anticipation of statehood for New Mexico, to divide among members of a certain clique of Republicans, the two United States senatorships and other federal patronage appointments. Defending himself against the charge of retaining Catron as Attorney General, Pile said in an interview:

Mr. Catron, since the close of the war, has supported the reconstruction policy of the government; he has been an able, faithful and efficient officer. He was Attorney General when I came to New Mexico. He was recommended to me by J. Francisco Chaves, Delegate in Congress, S. B. Elkins, United States Attorney, and J. G. Palen, Chief Justice of the Territory.

Pile brushed aside as "rubbish," the charge that he had conspired with any one concerning political matters predicated upon the possibility that New Mexico might become a state of the Union. Besides defending himself against political accusations, Governor Pile found it necessary to make official visits to many parts of the Territory. On April 17, 1871, he hurried to the scene of rioting in and near Elizabethtown, the outgrowth of an attempt by the Maxwell Land Grant Company to drive miners and prospectors off Grant lands. Returning to Santa Fe, Pile issued a proclamation urging all parties to the rioting to "cease and desist," and asking them to submit their controversies to the courts.

When President Grant on May 24, 1871, offered Pile an appointment as Minister Resident to the Republic of Venezuela, he gladly accepted it. He advertised in a Santa Fe newspaper his willingness to swap a "very fine piano," for a "good ambulance and a span of mules." Having made the trade, William A. Pile left Santa Fe for Denver and the East, via Conejos and Fort Garland. The *New Mexican* paid him a farewell tribute: "In leaving New Mexico, Gov. Pile leaves many warm friends who regret his departure. If he leaves any enemies, they are those who have been unable to wield the governor as their tool and instrument, and therefore regard him with feelings of spite and spleen."

President Grant, on August 4, 1871, appointed Marsh Giddings of Michigan as Pile's successor.[2] Giddings qualified as governor on August 31, 1871. The first few months of the Giddings administration passed without serious incident. The military band serenaded the new governor on the evening of September 25, and he shook hands with hundreds of people at the reception following the band concert. Kind advisers, Thomas B. Catron among them, helped Giddings prepare his message for the Legislature, which began its session on December 7, 1871. Dealing with education, railroads, Territorial finances, public lands and Indian affairs, the message was "well received" by the legislators, according to the *New Mexican*.

It became apparent, however, soon after the opening day of the Legislature, that its members were not particularly interested in adopting a statesmanlike attitude toward major problems of government. They were anxious to achieve objectives immediately at hand, one of which was to arrange for the transfer of Chief Justice Joseph G. Palen from the First Judicial District, with headquarters in Santa Fe, to Mesilla, the headquarters of the Third Judicial District. As a result, the Legislature passed a law which banished the Chief Justice from Santa Fe, and assigned him to duties in the southeastern part of the Territory. In a strong message, Governor Giddings promptly vetoed the law, expressing the view that courts should have and retain the inherent right to assign judges in their discretion. The Democrats in the Legislature were particularly anxious to get Chief Justice Palen away from holding court in the First Judicial District. Biding their time, preparing for a coup, they secretly arranged for the printing of a number of bills, which they proposed somehow to enact into law. On January 10, 1872, the Democratic minority was ready for action. Milnor Rudulph, Speaker of the House (later on July 15, 1881, to serve as foreman of the coroner's jury at Fort Sumner which held an inquest over the body of William H. Bonney), pounding his gavel, declared the legislative day ended.

To the surprise of those not identified with the conspiracy, John R. Johnson, a Democrat, mounted the Speaker's rostrum, with a gavel in his hand, and pounded for order. In less than two minutes Johnson had entertained a motion by a member of the House to declare the Speaker's chair vacant, and declaring Johnson as Rudulph's successor. Johnson immediately declared the motion seconded and carried. Milnor Rudulph, already on his way out of the chamber, called upon the Sergeant-at-Arms to clear the House, but that officer was either unable or unwilling to do so. Rudulph then demanded that Carlos M. Conklin, perennial sheriff of Santa Fe County, who was present as a spectator, assist the Sergeant-at-Arms. Sheriff Conklin, a veteran politician, a survivor of many political wars, pleaded that he had no authority under the law to act, and asked to be excused from participating in the imbroglio.

Assuming, for the purpose of the record, that they had control of the House, the Democrats continued with their maneuvering, and in short order, behind closed doors, declared that vacancies existed in the seats of four Republican members— Buena Ventura Lobato, Juan Antonio Sanchez, Antonio Tircio Gallegos, and Antonio de Jesus Sisneros. The House then seated four Democrats—Jose Cordoba, Mateo Romero, Juan B. Gonzales and Francisco Antonio Montoya, all of whom were present, ready to be seated. The rump Legislature then passed a number of bills, among them one transferring Chief Justice Palen from Santa Fe to Mesilla. The new Speaker, John R. Johnson, ordered his newly selected Sergeant-at-Arms to arrest and hold until the further pleasure of the House, the Hon. Milnor Rudulph, "former Speaker of this House," and Julian Montoya and Juan Cristobal Chavez, two of his most outspoken supporters. Thereupon the House recessed until nine o'clock the following morning.

The unexpected maneuvering in the House of Representatives created tremendous excitement and confusion among politicians in Santa Fe. In a matter of hours the officialdom of the Territorial and federal governments swung into action. Milnor Rudulph, signing himself as Speaker of the House, managed to get a letter through to Gen. Gordon Granger, commanding the United States military district for New Mexico, asking for help. Governor Giddings also appealed to Granger, claiming that a state of anarchy and rebellion existed. Chief Justice Palen enlisted the support of United States Marshal John Pratt, who agreed to cooperate with General Granger in restoring law and order in the Legislature. Attorney General Catron sued out a writ of habeas corpus in the Supreme Court, alleging that Rudulph, Montoya and Chavez were being unlawfully deprived of their liberty. On January 11, 1872, when time came to call the House to order, with "Speaker" Johnson presiding, he was prevented from proceeding by a squad of soldiers from General Granger's command at Fort Marcy, reinforced by United States Marshal Pratt, and several deputies. Milnor Rudulph was escorted to the Speaker's chair, and the House suspended further deliberations until January 22, when the Supreme Court, through Judge Hezekiah S. Johnson, announced the court's decision in the habeas corpus proceedings, entitled *U. S. on the Relation of J. Bonifacio Chavez* vs. *John R. Johnson, Alejandro Branch, H. Clay Carson and Daniel Tappan*. The court held that the attempt by the Democrats to take over the House of Representatives was "unauthorized, illegal, revolutionary and void." The Democrats were critical of Judge Johnson, declaring that "he was but a puppet of Judge Palen." The Supreme Court having laid down the law, with United States soldiers and the forces of the United States Marshal's office standing by to see that there was no interference, the House resumed its work. The Republican majority, by resolution, expunged from the record and nullified all proceedings had and taken under the direction of the now-discredited "Speaker" Johnson.

On January 7, 1874, Governor Giddings offered a reward of $500 for the capture of Zacariah Crompton, E. Scott, and "three other persons by the name of Harrold," who on the night of December 20, at Placitas (Lincoln) had killed Isidro Patron, Isidro Padilla, Dario Balazar and Jose Candelaria, and wounded Apolonio Garcia and Pilar Candelaria. The notice authorized payment of $500 for the capture of all five men, or $100 for the capture of any one of the five. The reward notice focused attention on a desperate situation which had developed in and about the town of Lincoln. For weeks the lives and property of the people there had been jeopardized because of the acts and threats of men from Lampasas County, Texas, who had settled in the Ruidoso country. Among the newly arrived settlers were five brothers—Samuel, Thomas, Martin, Benjamin and Merritt Harrold, recent participants in a bloody feud with the Higgins family in Texas. The Harrold brothers started a private war in New Mexico after Brother Ben had gone to Lincoln, where he was shot and killed following an altercation with a deputy sheriff. The four surviving Harrold brothers, accompanied by grim-looking neighbors and friends, hurried to Lincoln and belligerently demanded that "the law" investigate the killing. An investigation was refused on the ground that Ben Harrold had been lawfully killed while resisting arrest. The Harrolds planned revenge. Juan Patron, county clerk of Lincoln County, gave an eyewitness account of the retaliation, published in the Santa Fe *New Mexican* of January 9, 1874:

An assault was committed about midnight on a house on Dec. 20, 1873, where the people had assembled to attend a wedding dance. The doors were broken open, fire was opened through the windows and doors with guns and pistols. In the firing four men were killed and two wounded.

On January 20, 1874, the *New Mexican* gave a report on a mass meeting held in Lincoln on January 3, at which steps were taken to protect the people of the community. Notices of the meeting had been posted and handed out, reciting "that the Probate Judge of the County and the Justice of the Peace of the Precinct had fled, and gone elsewhere to reside in this hour of our need, when their services were so imperatively required in the preservation of peace and to restore to the distracted people a sure guarantee of peace, order and protection." L. G. Murphy presided at the mass meeting. J. J. Dolan was elected secretary. By unanimous consent L. G. Murphy, Jose Montano and William Brady were appointed by the meeting "to act and determine in any case or cases, that may arise in which the citizens of the county are concerned, clothing them with all the powers and functions now conferred by law on Judges of Probate and justices of the peace, by the statutes of New Mexico, and so much more power as they may deem necessary to exercise, to preserve peace and good order, and protect the people in all the rights inherent in them as free citizens of this glorious, grand Republic."

While Murphy, Montano and Brady organized a vigilance committee to act in the emergency, the countryside prepared for war. The *New Mexican* of January 27 gave the latest available news from the front:

A private letter of the 21st inst. which has been shown us from Placitas, county seat of Lincoln County, gives the following concerning the unfortunate war between the Texans and Mexicans: "All here is war and rumors of war. The sheriff left here yesterday with sixty men to arrest the Harrolds and from a courier just returned we learned a fight was going on last night. A general distrust prevails throughout the whole section. Every man met is armed to the teeth. Up and down the Rio Hondo a number of ranches have been deserted, and now many fine places could be purchased for a song, their owners and occupants being determined and anxious to depart from a place where the reign of peace and order will not apparently, be re-established for a long time to come."

By February 2, 1874, the troubles in and about Placitas showed no signs of abating. On that day Sheriff A. H. Mills and County Clerk Juan Patron met with Governor Giddings and General Granger, in command of federal troops in New Mexico, and appealed to them for help. As a result of the meeting, letters were sent to the President of the United States, the Secretary of War, and the Secretary of the Interior, delineating the emergency, and asking for assistance. Federal intervention became unnecessary when the Harrold brothers and their supporters voluntarily left Lincoln County, and returned to Texas, leaving behind them a pattern of gunfire and sudden death which was to become familiar in Lincoln County in days to come.

Both before the coming of the Harrold brothers to Lincoln County, and after their return to Texas, the ordinary citizen of the county was fearful of becoming involved in arguments, disputes or controversies of any kind. Any misunderstanding, however slight and harmless it appeared to be in its inception, might well end in gunplay, with a fatality on one side or the other. Many factors contributed to the inherent possibilities of gunplay: the apparently irresistible urge and impulse of some men to kill without justification or reckoning; the universal habit of carrying firearms; the widespread custom of drinking intoxicating liquor to excess; the trait of misinterpreting the intent of a man's chance remarks, and taking offense where none was intended.

Two things, however, above all others seemingly contributed to the violence of the day: the over-generous consumption of hard liquor, and the widespread practice of too hastily resorting to the use of improved deadly weapons. In the 70's and 80's there appeared to be available in every town, village and hamlet in the Territory an ample and continually replenished supply of whiskey and brandy. Double Anchor and Pike's Magnolia, each rectifying ninety proof, were two of the most popular whiskies then distributed throughout New Mexico. These brands were sold at wholesale for $2.50 the gallon, including the United States Internal Revenue tax of ninety cents. When dispensed at retail over the bar, a gallon of liquor averaged a gross profit of from $18.00 to $20.00.

It was not until the 70's that improved weapons were introduced and offered for sale generally in New Mexico. Liquor and guns ordinarily were sold in the same establishment. From and after 1870, any man carrying a gun in most parts of the Territory, whether bad man or good man, was obliged to arm himself with a new-style weapon of a type developed as one of the by-products in the final months of the Civil War. The new guns were in almost every respect vastly superior to the old weapons. The ammunition for use in the new guns, encased in a cartridge, eliminated any possibility of wet powder, and the bullet or other projectile was almost certain to be propelled in a given direction when the trigger of the weapon was pulled.

Fixed ammunition and greater fire reliability eliminated the bluffing that had been possible by users of old-style guns. With new-fangled weapons available, one man pointed a gun at another at his own risk. There was every reason to believe that he meant business, and was staking his life that he was going to kill or be killed. The new styles in guns compelled users to revise their techniques, to practice drawing quickly, to attempt to improve their marksmanship, and to prepare generally against any contingency possible in gunplay. With the increased popularity of new weapons, the office of precinct coroner assumed greater importance and significance in many communities. In any event, whether a man was drunk or sober, whether he was using a new gun or an old one, killing was not considered a particularly heinous offense in early days in Lincoln County, or elsewhere in New Mexico, if justification real or fabricated could be pleaded. There were many examples of violence following the general use of new, high-powered weapons, in a number of which hard liquor was a contributing factor.

On October 21, 1874, Lyon Phillipowsky, a Lincoln County deputy sheriff, while shopping in the L. G. Murphy & Co. store in Lincoln, became involved in an argument with Clerk William Burns, invited him outside to "shoot it out." In the duel to the death in the street in front of the Murphy store, Phillipowsky, who, it was claimed, had been drinking, was mortally wounded. He died the next day. A coroner's jury returned a verdict of justifiable homicide.

The summary execution of Jose Segura, an alleged horse thief, by a band of masked men, was deplored by many who believed that even horse thieves were entitled to a trial under the law. On July 18, 1876, Segura was arrested in Lincoln and arraigned before Justice of the Peace J. B. Wilson. Evidence was introduced tending to show that Segura was afflicted with a passion for running off with other men's horses. The *New Mexican* of July 24 told of Segura's fate:

Had the Judge held a trial, no doubt, according to the evidence, Segura would have been convicted, but the examination having been merely preliminary, he was committed in default of bail in the sum of $1,000 to await the action of the grand jury. Armed with a commitment from Judge Wilson, Sheriff Baca, with a guard of three men, started with the prisoner for Fort Stanton. When within three miles of the fort, the Sheriff and guards were overpowered by seventeen masked men who took the prisoner into their custody. Shots were heard shortly afterward.

Frequently the defense to a killing was fabricated to meet the situation which confronted a murderer after the "deceased" was no more. The needless and uncalled-for killings disturbed the right-thinking, God-fearing people of the entire area. Included in that category were the killings of Robert Casey, Paul Dowlin, and a sergeant from Fort Stanton, all separate incidents.

Robert Casey came to New Mexico in 1867 from Mason County, Texas, bought a ranch two miles from Picacho on the Rio Hondo, in territory that was at the time part of Socorro County, on which he thereafter ran cattle and operated a grist mill. Casey (whose cattle brand K C prompted cow thieves to convert it into B O and other like brands) was shot and killed in Lincoln by William Wilson on August 2, 1875, while attending a political convention.

At two o'clock in the afternoon, from behind an adobe wall, Wilson fired two shots at Casey as he walked along the main street. There were two versions of the killing: one was that Casey's political enemies had employed Wilson to kill him, the other that the men had a dispute over settlement of an eight-dollar debt.

William Wilson was tried before a jury and convicted of the Casey murder. He had the doubtful honor of being the first man to be legally hanged in Lincoln County. The hanging, attended by a large crowd of invited guests, took place on December 10, 1875.

Remnants of Casey's cattle herds were sold many months after his death to John H. Tunstall, through arrangements made by Alex. McSween. Some of Casey's friends and neighbors, who had expected to buy some of the Casey cattle at favorable prices, did not relish the fact that Tunstall, a stranger, had come into the community, with plenty of ready money, and paid higher prices for the stock than they were prepared to pay.

The gruesome details of the hanging of William Wilson for

the Casey murder, were given in a story written by "a special correspondent," published in the Santa Fe *New Mexican* on December 21, 1875. Apparently quite an elaborate program, with due deference to protocol, had been arranged for the occasion. Reflecting life in the raw in a frontier community, the story was as follows:

On the day appointed for the execution of William Wilson, before daybreak, the carpenters were at work erecting the gallows, and even at that early hour strangers, men and women, and even children, were pouring in from the adjacent country. At eleven o'clock the prisoner, in an ambulance, accompanied by Captain Stewart, Commander of the post at Fort Stanton, Dr. Carballot, and Rev. Lamy, of Manzano, preceded by Company G. 8th U. S. Cavalry, under the command of Lieut. Gilmore, arrived in Lincoln and proceeded to the residence of Sheriff Baca. The prisoner then arrayed himself in his funeral clothes and the procession moved to the gallows. Before mounting the platform, Wilson shook hands with several whom he recognized, and mounted the scaffold, calm and collected. The escort was drawn up in line fronting the gallows while four men dismounted and kept back the crowd which by this time had increased considerably. While on the scaffold the death warrant was read first in English and then in Spanish, after which the dying declaration was read and translated; Wilson then received the Extreme Unction, and the merciful Sheriff declared that the execution would be stayed for half an hour. However, the leading men of the town, actuated by pity for the poor unfortunate, entered such a vigorous protest against such barbarous proceedings, that the Sheriff proceeded with the execution. The priest descended from the scaffold, the black cap was adjusted and the prisoner with hands tied behind and the noose around his neck awaited his doom. The Sheriff descended from the scaffold and in an instant justice so long outraged was avenged, and the perpetrator of one of the foulest murders which has ever disgraced a civilized community was no more. After hanging 9½ minutes, the body was cut down and placed in the coffin, when it was discovered that life was not yet extinct. A rope was then fastened around Wilson's neck and the crowd drew the inanimate body from the coffin and suspended it from the gallows. When it hung for twenty minutes longer, it was then cut down and placed in the coffin and buried.

On February 20, 1876, the Grant County *Herald,* critical of the bungling at the Wilson hanging, blamed Judge Bristol for alleged prejudicial rulings during the trial of the case. The Silver City *Herald* hurried to Bristol's defense, saying that if error had been committed "it was competent for the aggrieved party to appeal to a higher tribunal." The negligent manner in which Wilson had been executed resulted in considerable adverse comment in the Territorial press, prompting the Santa Fe *New Mexican* to note on March 3, 1876, that before signing the Wilson death warrant, Governor Axtell had discussed the case with Judge Bristol, the district attorney and defense counsel; and that they had agreed that Wilson had been given a fair trial and was not entitled to executive clemency.

Capt. Paul Dowlin, unarmed at the time, was shot and killed by Jerry Dillon, a former employee, on May 5, 1877, at Dowlin's mill, six miles from Fort Stanton over a short cut trail through the mountains. According to witnesses, Dillon fired two shots at Dowlin with a carbine, then shot him with a revolver. When Dillon began shooting, Dowlin kept advancing toward him. As Dillon continued to shoot, Dowlin begged: "Stop for God's sake, and listen to reason." Dowlin lived long enough to give an account of the shooting. Jerry Dillon "lit out for Texas," according to the Santa Fe *New Mexican* of May 15, 1877, and was never heard from again. Dowlin was an old-timer in the Territory. He served as a captain in the New Mexico Volunteers during the Civil War, after which he became Post Trader at Fort Stanton. Dowlin also represented Lincoln, Doña Ana and Grant counties during one session of the Legislature. At the time of his death he owned a flour mill, sawmill, ranches, livestock, a store, and other property in the area.

A week after the Dowlin killing, on a quiet Sunday afternoon, May 12, 1877, John S. Chisum and George Hogg, cattlemen, were visiting in A. A. McSween's house in Lincoln. Frank Freeman, formerly of Alabama, and Charles Bowdre, both of whom had been drinking, rode up to McSween's house and demanded that Chisum step outside. When he refused, Freeman and Bowdre fired twenty to fifty shots at the house, shattering windows and splintering doors. Through with the sport of shooting at McSween's house, Freeman went to a nearby restaurant where he shot and killed a sergeant from Fort Stanton without provocation. Sheriff Brady and a posse arrested Freeman following a fight in which Brady knocked Freeman down in the street with a pistol. When Freeman got to his feet, he knocked Brady down with a blow from his fist. When Charles Bowdre attempted to interfere in the melée, John H. Riley, with a gun in his hand, held him at bay. Subdued and arrested at last, a squad of soldiers, in charge of Sergeant Keith, started with Freeman for Fort Stanton. On the way from Lincoln to the fort, Freeman managed to "escape."

NOTES AND PROFILES

[1] William Anderson Pile was born near Indianapolis, Indiana, February 11, 1829. He accompanied his parents to Missouri as a small child. After preparatory studies, he studied theology, and became a minister of the Methodist Episcopal Church, and a member of the Missouri conference. He enlisted on the Union side in the Civil War, was commissioned a chaplain of the First Regiment, Missouri Light Infantry, promoted several times in rank, until on April 9, 1865, he was brevetted a major general "for gallant and meritorious services in the siege and capture of Fort Blakeley, Ala." Mustered out of the military service on August 24, 1865, Pile went into politics and was elected as a Republican to the Fortieth Congress, serving from March 4, 1867, to March 3, 1869. He was defeated for re-election to the Congress in 1868. Pile qualified as governor of New Mexico on August 16, 1869, and served until on or about July 1, 1871. Upon leaving New Mexico, Pile was appointed Minister Resident to Venezuela, serving from 1871 to 1874. Returning home in 1876, Pile acted as a confidential agent of the Venezuelan government in the United States, with offices in Philadelphia. Later Pile moved to Monrovia, California, where he died on July 7, 1889.

[2] Born in Litchfield County, Connecticut, in 1816, Marsh Giddings moved to Kalamazoo, Michigan, in 1831. Admitted to the Michigan bar, he practiced law in that state for thirty years. For many years prominent in Republican politics, Giddings served eight years as probate judge in his home county, was a member of the Michigan State Constitutional Convention, and a Presidential

elector in 1864. President Grant offered to nominate Giddings to be Consul General to India, but he declined the offer. Grant then appointed him governor of New Mexico. The appointment was confirmed August 31, 1871, and Giddings qualified on August 31.

On or about March 1, 1875, Governor Giddings became seriously ill. He had hoped to recover sufficiently to return to Michigan, where he was anxious to spend his last days. By June 2 the Governor had sold his household furniture, an ambulance had been loaded with the family baggage, and was waiting at the door of the Palace of the Governors, for the Governor to become a passenger. Because of his feeble condition, Giddings abandoned plans for the trip. He died the next day; and the ambulance took the body East for burial. Funeral services were held in Santa Fe on June 4, conducted by Rev. George G. Smith, of the Presbyterian Church.

CHAPTER TWO

SAMUEL AXTELL, GOVERNOR

SAMUEL BEACH AXTELL of Ohio, a political soldier of fortune, became governor of the Territory on July 30, 1875. He was described by a contemporary as "a rather handsome, distinguished looking man." Some two years later, on February 2, 1877, the Santa Fe *Gazette* was to describe him as "a man somewhat advanced in years, who wears a clean shaved face, which shows many marks of care." The Santa Fe *New Mexican* of November 6, 1877, referred to him as "a gentleman of rather rotund figure, and a very agreeable conversationalist." Taking an oath as governor of a territory was not a new or novel experience for Axtell. Only a few months before, on January 6, 1875, he had taken the oath in Washington, D. C., as governor of the Territory of Utah before the Hon. Stephen J. Field, Associate Justice of the Supreme Court of the United States. Although he qualified as Utah's governor on January 2, Axtell did not begin the duties of the office until February 2, 1875.

Assuming the governorship of Utah, Axtell inherited a political squabble of no mean proportions. As of January 1, 1875, George L. Woods, a Republican, was governor of Utah. For weeks prior to that date, Woods had been involved in a bitter political quarrel with George Q. Cannon, a member of the Church of Jesus Christ of Latter Day Saints, who, on the face of the returns, had been elected on the Republican ticket as delegate-in-congress from Utah, at the election held on November 6, 1874. Notwithstanding Cannon's election, Woods stubbornly refused to deliver him a certificate of election, without which he could not be seated in Congress. Woods realized, when it was too late perhaps, that his superiors in Washington had methods at hand to counteract his stubbornness. When the

Secretary of the Interior asked Woods to resign as governor, he declined to do so. In a personal letter to President Grant, he asked him to intercede on his behalf. Woods reminded the President of their long years of personal friendship; and urged him not to forget that he, Woods, "had been a devoted follower and a staunch Republican," and had "stood up for Grant when no one else did." In his letter to the President, Woods expressed his views concerning the action taken by the Congress in 1874 in amending an existing law which had authorized the governor of the Territory of Utah to veto legislation. The amendment of 1874, of which Woods complained, provided that the Legislature by a two-thirds majority vote could overrule the governor's veto. Woods "could not endure being governor," he told Grant, unless the Congress would repeal "that obnoxious law." President Grant considered the Woods letter as a resignation, and promptly nominated Samuel Beach Axtell to be governor of Utah. The Senate confirmed Axtell's nomination on December 21, 1874, with the proviso that it would not become fully effective until February 2, 1875.

Following his appointment, Axtell remained in Washington during the holiday season of 1874, shaking hands with old friends and political cronies who had served with him in the Congress when he had represented a California district. He left for Utah late in January, 1875. On February 2, a reception committee, traveling in a private car, met him at Farmington, a junction point of the Union Pacific and the Utah Central railways. The committee formally welcomed Axtell to Utah and escorted him to Salt Lake City. He registered at the Townsend House, his official residence while in the Territory. In all probability the new governor had been well instructed before leaving Washington as to the manner in which he should initially conduct his official duties. Consequently, on February 5, 1875, three days after arriving in Salt Lake City, Axtell delivered to George Q. Cannon a certificate of election as delegate-in-congress from Utah Territory.[1]

No sooner had Axtell delivered the certificate to Cannon than he was accused by the non-Mormon press and some political leaders of the Territory of being subservient to the Mormon wing of the Republican party in Utah. The Salt Lake *Evening News* of February 7, however, praised Axtell for his courage in a political crisis, and was critical of Woods, the retiring governor:

That gentleman is gone from our gaze; snuffed out like a candle, and we have not heard nor seen the first man, woman or child manifest the slightest expression of sorrow at his official decapitation.

Shortly after his arrival in Utah, Axtell made a tour of the principal towns of the Territory, for the purpose, as he announced in the press, of meeting the people and learning about their problems at first hand. At a reception in Ogden on February 20, he told an audience of his background:

Twenty years ago last August I was selected as first District Attorney of a county formed in California. I served the people of that County for six years. Afterwards I had the honor to represent, in Congress, one of the most populous districts in California, and subsequently to be reelected to that position. . . . During all this time, and for all the success I have enjoyed in public life, I have been indebted to the common people, the laboring men of the country. . . . I come to Utah, appointed by the government of the United States as the chief executive of the Territory . . . determined to be a governor, not of a section, but of the whole people.

Axtell shortly discovered that being governor of Utah was a hazardous occupation. Before long he found himself the central figure in a vicious fight between the leaders of the Mormon and anti-Mormon factions of the Territorial Republican party. The San Francisco *Chronicle* of March 8, 1875, published a story from Salt Lake City, which told of the attacks upon Axtell:

There have been published in this city for the last thirty days incessant attacks upon Governor Axtell, the newly appointed governor, who has been in the Territory about that length of time. Also charges have been telegraphed to the press in regard to him, which he asserts are false in every particular. It is not believed there is any dissatisfaction among the public with regard to his course.

The Salt Lake Evening *News* of March 12 defended Axtell:

We have not heard a single citizen of good repute express any dissatisfaction with the course of the Governor, nor have we heard of any citizen having done so. The Governor has not had much official business to attend to since he came, consequently, there could have been but little to express dissatisfaction about had he done everything ill. There is, however, a small but boisterous clique of persons, essentially bad in the grain, who would recklessly slander and villify the very best federal officers that could be sent here, if they would not stultify themselves by adopting the narrow, selfish, undermining, rascally, ruinous policy of said clique.

A Washington dispatch to the San Francisco *Chronicle* on March 16, 1875, told of alleged prejudice on the part of the Salt Lake "agent" of the Associated Press:

There is a general complaint here against the agent of the Associated Press in Salt Lake, who is accused of transmitting false and partisan reports to the press. The sensational reports circulated by the Associated Press from Salt Lake with reference to Governor Axtell are generously denounced, and are charged to the instigation of a political ring, which desires to overthrow Axtell, who nevertheless retains the confidence of the administration.

Axtell's political enemies in Utah contended that by associating himself with the "Mormon" wing of the Republican party, he had alienated all "good and true Republicans in Utah," and was wrecking the organization in every part of the Territory. Many telegrams and letters were sent to Washington, demanding that the President remove Axtell immediately. Axtell's supporters hastened to defend him. Fortunately for the Republican party, locally and nationally, circumstances developed which made it unnecessary for the President to make a choice between the Axtell and anti-Axtell forces. Marsh Giddings, governor of the neighboring territory of New Mexico, died at an opportune time for all concerned, on June 3, 1875, making it possible for Washington to extricate Axtell from a situation which was becoming increasingly serious.

Quick to perceive a political opening and to make the most of it, Axtell went from Salt Lake to Washington, interviewed influential friends, talked about political expediency and party policy. In a few days, Columbus Delano, Secretary of the Interior, told Axtell that the President had decided to appoint him to the governorship of New Mexico. Axtell wrote to Delano thanking him for the appointment, asked him to "thank the President in his name for this distinguished mark of his confidence," and promised that he would use his utmost endeavors to discharge the duties of the trust according to law.[2]

Sworn in as governor of New Mexico on July 30, 1875, Axtell soon realized that the office was one which would demand serious and diligent attention. Although New Mexico had no political problems stemming from religious differences of the type he had encountered in Utah, the Territory had a host of other pressing problems.

It could hardly be expected that Samuel Axtell would have any understanding or appreciation of New Mexicans and their problems. Undoubtedly he was obliged to accept and tolerate, to some extent, conditions as he found them. Exaggerated tales of Axtell's ninety-day tenure of the Utah governorship were quickly circulated in New Mexico. Professional politicians in Santa Fe began a campaign to embarrass and discredit him by spreading reports that he had been accepted in Utah as a member of the Church of the Latter Day Saints, and that in secret he was a Mormon bishop; that he had remained in Utah only long enough to complete plans for the conversion of the people of New Mexico to the Mormon faith. Within a few weeks after his arrival in Santa Fe, the new governor was known throughout the Territory as "Obispo," Spanish for "Bishop," a name that stuck to him as long as he remained in the Territory. Statements containing denials came from both the Mormons and the Governor.

From Salt Lake City, on June 13, 1877, Brigham Young wrote a letter to Secretary Carl Schurz, in Washington, in which he declared that Axtell had not been baptized in his faith, and denied that he had ever been a bishop. The letter was one of the last letters Brigham Young ever penned. On August 27, 1877, he died. In his letter to Washington the great apostle of the church wrote:

I am informed that Mr. Charles M. Howard, Register of the Beaver Land office, in this territory, has published a card in the New

York Sun of June 27th, in which he states that I told J. W. Barnes, late Receiver of the Land Office at Beaver, that I had baptized Gov. Axtell, formerly of this Territory, and now of New Mexico, in the Mormon church. I understand that he states further that this conversation with Mr. Barnes took place at the residence of Bishop John R. Murdock. I did meet Mr. Barnes at Mr. Murdock's residence while I was passing through Beaver last fall. Our conversation was in the presence of several gentlemen, and I wish to give an explicit denial to this statement concerning Governor Axtell. I have much pleasure in stating that Gov. Axtell presented himself here as a gentleman and the governor of the people of this territory, and not of any sect, party, clan or ring, and the statement that he is a Bishop in the Church of Jesus Christ of Latter-Day Saints, or that he has been baptized into the church is entirely without foundation in truth.

On June 14, 1877, Axtell wrote a letter to Schurz denying that he was a convert to the Mormon faith, or a secret agent of Brigham Young:

I am not a convert to the Mormon faith, nor do I know, except in a general way, what the Mormon faith is. I am not, and never have been either secretly or otherwise, an agent of Brigham Young, and have no connection or correspondence of any character with him. It is true, that I wrote some letters to the Salt Lake *Herald* over the signature of "El Obispo," and some one had facetiously styled me "the Bishop," and in writing to the press, I have some times adopted "El Obispo," the Spanish for "the Bishop," as a nom de plume. My letters were written for the entertainment of friends and for my own amusement, and had no political significance. . . . I am not and have not been engaged in preparing the way for an exodus of the people known as "Latter Day Saints," from Utah to New Mexico. I have no knowledge of any such movement.

Governor Giddings' prolonged illness had rendered him unable to contribute to any significant extent toward solving New Mexico's most pressing problems. As a result, when Axtell became governor, he found himself facing an accumulation of difficulties. Nothing in Axtell's experience during his adventuresome years in California's gold fields, as a congressman from California, or in his brief tenure as Utah's governor, had prepared him to cope adequately with existing perplexities in New Mexico, and there were several. Crime was rampant in many parts of the Territory in 1875. Axtell was asked almost every day to extend assistance toward the capture and punishment of criminals even though he had little authority to furnish help in such emergencies. When called upon to assist in connection with the apprehension of the guilty in particularly atrocious murder cases, Axtell offered the traditional $500 reward for "the arrest and conviction" of the culprits, trusting to the generosity of the next Legislature to make the reward money available. There were few arrests in criminal cases in the 70's and even fewer convictions. Jurors were reluctant to find defendants guilty, sometimes because of fear of reprisal, at other times because of the influence of political lawyers.

Conditions were particularly serious in Lincoln County, the vast area in the southeastern part of the Territory, established by the Legislature on January 16, 1869.[3]

NOTES AND PROFILES

[1] George Quayle Cannon, long-time prominent citizen of Utah, was born in Liverpool, England, January 11, 1827, died in Monterey, California, April 12, 1901. Cannon came to the United States with his parents in 1842, lived in Nauvoo, Illinois, located in Utah in 1847, learned the printer's trade, became editor of the Deseret *News*.

Cannon, a Republican, was elected as delegate-in-congress from Utah to the Forty-Third and two succeeding Congresses (March 4, 1873-March 3, 1879); served as a director of the Union Pacific Railroad, and many other important financial and industrial corporations. Frank Jenne Cannon, a son, served as a congressman from Utah from March 4, 1895, to January 4, 1896, and as United States senator from January 22, 1896, to March 3, 1899.

[2] Samuel Beach Axtell was born near Columbus, Franklin County, Ohio, on October 14, 1819. He attended the local schools and Oberlin College; was graduated from Western Reserve College, Hudson, Ohio; studied law and was admitted to the bar in 1842. He practiced law in Mt. Clemens, Michigan, from 1843 until 1851, when he went to California and engaged in mining. He was

elected prosecuting attorney of Amador County in 1854 and served until 1860, when he went to San Francisco and practiced law until he was elected as a Democrat to the Fortieth and Forty-First Congresses (March 4, 1867, to March 3, 1871). He became affiliated with the Republican party during the Grant administration. President Grant appointed Axtell governor of Utah Territory, an office he held from February 2, 1875, until on or about June 20, 1875. After he resigned as governor of Utah, President Grant appointed him governor of New Mexico. He took the oath of office on July 30, 1875, and served as governor until his forced resignation became effective, September 30, 1878, when Lew. Wallace succeeded him.

During the legislative session of 1878, Axtell became involved in a bitter quarrel over a bill entitled "An Act to Incorporate the Society of the Jesuit Fathers of New Mexico." The fight for the passage of the bill was led by Rev. Donato Maria Gasparri, S.J., Superior of the Jesuits in New Mexico. When the bill passed despite Axtell's opposition, he returned it to the Legislature with a veto message containing a blistering attack on Gasparri, whom he described as an "Italian adventurer." The Legislature again passed the bill, overriding Axtell's veto, but it was later nullified by Act of Congress.

Gasparri died in Albuquerque on December 18, 1882, at the age of forty-eight. When the Santa Fe railway experienced difficulty in obtaining rights of way into Albuquerque, Gasparri assisted its agents in persuading land owners to sign deeds of conveyance on reasonable terms. Donato Maria Gasparri's nephew was Pietro Cardinal Gasparri, renowned Papal diplomat, who died in Rome November 18, 1938.

On August 1, 1882, Axtell was appointed chief justice of the Territory of New Mexico, an office he held until May 11, 1885, on which date his resignation was accepted by President Cleveland. Several Ohio political leaders did not hold Axtell in high regard. Active opposition developed when it became known that President Garfield proposed to appoint him to the New Mexico Supreme Court. On March 12, 1881, A. L. Conger, vice president of The Whitman & Barnes Mfg. Co., of Akron, wrote a strongly worded letter to Garfield: "I see by newspapers, and learn by rumors and from other sources that ex-Gov. S. B. Axtell of Summit county, Ohio, is seeking for some executive appointment at your hands. . . . I have good reasons for not believing him to be an upright man and do not believe he could be elected to any office within the gift of the people of this county. . . ."

On March 18, 1881, J. A. Long, George T. Perkins, Thomas F. Wildee, George W. Crouse and others, wrote Garfield from Akron, protesting against any political patronage being bestowed upon Axtell: "Mr. Axtell is a comparatively late resident of this county, for while his family may have been domiciled here, he for the greater part of the last 20 years has been absent, and a part of that time and even during the years of the Rebellion, represented a district of California in the House of Representatives as a Democrat. . . . Without going into any extensive discussion as to Mr. Axtell's acts while holding positions under former administrations, it is sufficient to say, that his reputation as a politician in this community is unsavory to the greatest degree. . . . His local record as a member of the party shows him to be a rank and selfish disorganizer, a man who never acts in the party's cause, until he first ascertains how it will affect him personally, and who is prepared to tear down the party organization unless it is made subservient to his own selfish ends."

Axtell continued to live in Santa Fe after leaving the bench. He died while visiting relatives in Morristown, Morris County, New Jersey, on August 6, 1891, and was buried in the Morristown First Presbyterian church cemetery.

[3] On February 15, 1878, almost ten years after the establishment of Lincoln County, the Legislature ran a new division line between Doña Ana and Lincoln counties, and enlarged Lincoln County by providing that all of the then existing Doña Ana County east of the intersection of parallel twenty eight degrees thirty minutes west of Washington (following the parallel southwardly to the intersection of the line separating Doña Ana County from Texas) should be annexed to and become a part of Lincoln County. (See Chap. 34, Laws of 1878.) As of 1878, bounded on the east and south by Texas, Lincoln County contained 27,000 square miles, or 17,280,000 acres, and was probably the largest county unit in the United States. Measuring 180 miles in extreme length and 160 miles in extreme breadth, the county was divided from north to south by the Pecos River. Among the tributaries of the Pecos River were the Peñasco, Ruidoso, Bonito, Hondo, Seven Rivers and Black River.

The town of Lincoln lost much of its old-time glamor and prestige on August 17, 1909, when the voters cast their ballots 900 to 613 to move the county seat to Carrizozo, a new town on the El Paso and Northeastern Railroad (now Rock Island—Southern Pacific), thirty miles to the west. In litigation following the election, Judge Edwin Mechem on June 10, 1910, sustained Carrizozo's claim to the county seat. His decision was affirmed by the Territorial Supreme Court on September 22, 1910.

CHAPTER THREE

EMIL FRITZ, JOHN CHISUM, ALEX. McSWEEN

I N THE FIRST MONTHS of the Civil War, a body of Union troops, known in history as the California Column, arrived in New Mexico from the Pacific coast for the express purpose, as it was widely heralded, of "saving the Territory from the invaders." The advance guard of the Column reached the Rio Grande on July 4, 1862, followed at twenty-four hour intervals by detachments of infantry and cavalry.

A total of two thousand men, commanded by Col. James Henry Carleton, camped north and south along the banks of the river, prepared, according to Carleton's announcement, "to offer any sacrifice, and to die if necessary, in defense of their country's flag."

The Column had heroically endured the heat and burden of many days in crossing over the desert country of California and Arizona, their days and nights of discouragement being brightened from time to time by Carleton's dramatic proclamations promising the opportunity for the achievement of fame and glory on New Mexico battlefields fighting against Confederates. However, the Confederate troops, most of them Texans, anticipating the arrival of Union reinforcements from California, had discreetly abandoned New Mexico as a theater of war and had crossed over the border into Texas before the first trooper of the Column washed his hands in the muddy waters of the Rio Grande. No doubt the California Column was an outstanding military organization, composed almost entirely of volunteers: big, strong men, considerably above the average in intelligence. Most members of the Column had signed the muster rolls in the gold-mining camps of northern California.

With the Confederate troops in retreat, the California Column was deprived of the opportunity to engage in combat. Some units were reorganized and assigned by Carleton (by this time promoted to brigadier general) to serve with New Mexico troops in a war against the Apache and Navajo Indians. Upon completion of their military service, scores of veterans of the California Column remained in New Mexico and became prominent in business, the professions, and public life. Among them was Emil Fritz, a German-American, who, when he took out a policy insuring his life, started in motion a chain of circumstances which reached the lives of many people.

Born in Stuttgart, Germany, Emil Fritz emigrated to the United States as a young man. He was mining for gold in California at the outbreak of the Civil War, and volunteered for service in the Union army at Camp Merchant, California, on August 16, 1861. Having had military experience in Germany, he was made a captain, and helped to organize Company B, First Regiment of California Cavalry. After months of drills and maneuvering, Fritz came to New Mexico with Carleton's California Column in 1862. When Company B's term of service expired on August 1, 1864, it was reorganized at Fort Sumner, and Fritz re-enlisted. He served in the reorganized unit until it was mustered out in Albuquerque on September 16, 1866. Fritz' honorable discharge papers read that he had left the service with rank of brevet lieutenant colonel of U. S. Volunteers. During the Civil War Fritz served at Fort Stanton and other military posts in New Mexico. After being discharged from military service, he became a partner in L. G. Murphy & Co. in Lincoln.[1] He was a frugal, thrifty, hard-working man, with business acumen. There was every reason to believe that the business of L. G. Murphy & Co. would continue to prosper. During the year 1873, however, it became apparent that Fritz was seriously ill. After consulting the post surgeon in Fort Stanton, he went to Santa Fe for further medical treatment. On May 22, 1873, Fritz started on the return trip to Fort Stanton, "very infirm physically," according to the Santa Fe *New Mexican*. Discouraged over his condition, Fritz left the fort on June 10, 1873, and began the long and tiring stagecoach trip to the railroad in Kansas City, traveling from there on the cars to New York, where he embarked for Germany. On September 5, 1873, Fritz wrote a letter from Bad Niederau, Wurtemburg, Germany, to Manderfield & Tucker, of the daily *New Mexican,* which was published in that paper on October 6. In his letter Fritz told of his arrival in Europe, of the condition of his health, and expressed the hope that he would "get home in December." Fritz' letter in part:

DEAR FRIENDS: I write you a few lines just to let you know that I still live. Today is the first day I am out of bed since August 14th, and have had more doctors and physic than would kill a dozen men, but now they say (the doctors) I should recover, so from this, you may see I have not had time to see anything of the old world. I landed July 28th in Cherburg, France, and the same night went to Paris very sick. There I was with my sister, but never went out of the house as I was very sick. . . . August 9th I arrived at Stuttgart at my father's house, very sick, where I found four of your papers. The cholera is making terrible havoc all over Germany and is also close here, but in the Black Forest I think we will be safe. Regards to all my friends—I hope to get home in December.

Emil Fritz died in his father's house in Stuttgart, almost within sight of the Black Forest, on June 26, 1874. It was believed at first that he had left a last will and testament, and that it had been deposited for safekeeping with Murphy & Co., in Lincoln. Searchers failed to find an Emil Fritz will in Murphy's safe, or elsewhere.

After a lapse of many months it was decided to administer Fritz' estate on the assumption that he had died intestate, in which event it was recognized that the assets would be distributed among surviving relatives in accordance with the New Mexico laws of descent and distribution. It appeared that Fritz had lived and died a bachelor, and that he had been survived by his father and other relatives in Germany, and by a younger brother and sister, Charles Phillip Frederick Fritz and Emilie Fritz Scholand, both of whom lived in Lincoln County.[2]

On April 25, 1876, almost two years after his death, Lawrence G. Murphy, probate judge of Lincoln County, and managing partner in L. G. Murphy & Co., in which Emil Fritz was a co-partner, appointed William Brady of Lincoln, as administrator of Emil Fritz' estate. Brady had served with Murphy in the New Mexico Volunteers during the Civil War.

In undertaking to administer the assets of the estate, Brady was confronted with a number of vexatious problems. Important among them was the necessity for taking the required steps to collect the proceeds of a policy of insurance on Fritz' life. Collection of the proceeds from the policy proved difficult because the company which had issued it was in receivership. There was a further complication: Spiegelberg Brothers, of Santa Fe, contended that Fritz had assigned the policy to them as security for a debt. Then the question arose as to whether the Spiegelberg debt was Fritz' personal obligation, or the debt of the Murphy & Co. partnership. Brady explained the difficulties he had encountered in a petition in the Probate Court:

> That among the assets of the said Fritz estate is a policy of insurance on the life of said Emil Fritz, deceased, issued by the Merchants Life Insurance Company of the City of New York; that said insurance company refuses to pay said sum or any part of it, and is now in the hands of a receiver; that it is necessary in order to realize anything from said policy to appoint an agent and attorney in said City of New York to collect said policy and to this end it is necessary to make a reasonable outlay and to give said agent and attorney when appointed, full and unreserved power to compromise by part payment or bring suit as such agent and attorney will deem proper and for the benefit of said estate.

The Probate Court authorized Brady to obtain assistance in collecting on the policy. On August 22, 1876, he filed a report, reciting that Levi Spiegelberg[3] of New York City had been appointed ancillary administrator of the Fritz estate in New York, with authority to compromise the claim, if necessary, and collect the proceeds. Brady resigned as administrator of the estate on September 19, 1876. Emilie Fritz Scholand and Charles Fritz, sister and brother respectively of Emil Fritz, were named to succeed him, and furnished a $10,000 surety bond. Their bondsmen were James J. Dolan,[4] a partner in L. G. Murphy & Co., and Alexander A. McSween, a Lincoln attorney employed by Brady as his counsel while serving as administrator.[5] The newly-appointed administrators continued McSween's employment.

In an effort to collect the money on the life insurance policy, Alex. McSween went to St. Louis, where he consulted lawyers and bankers, who referred him to Donnell, Lawson & Co., bankers in New York City. McSween then went to New York and talked to Levi Spiegelberg, in whose hands the policy had been placed for collection. McSween and Spiegelberg had a dispute about the amount of money that should be collected. Spiegelberg washed his hands of the entire business, but asked $700 in payment for services rendered and expenses incurred. McSween consulted Donnell, Lawson & Co. That firm advanced him the $700 to pay Spiegelberg, and advised him not to settle for less than the full amount of the policy with interest from date of death. By December 14, 1876, McSween had returned to Lincoln, on which date he wrote a letter to Charles Fritz, setting out in detail the negotiations carried on in the East. Apparently Fritz had done some talking about the business during McSween's absence. In his letter McSween told Fritz:

I understand you are very mad at me; I would like to know why. Come at your earliest convenience and let me know the cause of your discontent. I cant chase the wind nor idle tales, but if you really distrust me I want to know; then you can give, doubtless, your reason and I'll be satisfied. When I see you and state the facts, I think you'll change your mind. I know I worked in good faith and supposed you had the requisite amount in me. . . . Whoever tells you I am trying to get that money for Mrs. Scholand states something of which he knows nothing—something manufactured by himself. Both of you made a contract with me in behalf of the estate, and not in behalf of either or both of you. I regret that you should mistrust me when I was working for you in good faith, spending even my own funds in further cause of the interests you represent. If you entertain any fears, you can have an order for the proceeds when collected. I excuse you on account of the pressure that may have been brought to bear upon you.

Month after month passed and the Fritz insurance money had not yet reached Lincoln. Probate Judge Florencio Gonzales and Charles Fritz joined in writing a letter on August 1,

1877, to Donnell, Lawson & Co., instructing that firm as to disposition of the money, when collected, and countermanding any instructions previously given by McSween:

Certain misunderstandings and irregularities having arisen in regard to the disposal of moneys collected or to be collected by your firm in regard to the life policy of Emil Fritz, deceased, and in the matter of which A. A. McSween, as attorney of Administrator of the estate of said deceased gave you directions, the undersigned Judge of Probate for the County of Lincoln and Territory of New Mexico, on application of the administrator of said estate, herewith instructs and directs you that after deduction of your fees for collection you deposit the amount remaining at the First National Bank at Santa Fe to the credit of Charles Fritz, administrator of the estate of Emil Fritz, deceased, and subject to the order of the Probate Court of the County of Lincoln and the Territory of New Mexico, as previously ordered by the said Probate Court and agreed upon and understood by all the parties, any documents and directions sent to you by A. A. McSween notwithstanding, and such directions and documents are hereby revoked and amended.

Judge Gonzales and Charles Fritz had not been timely in writing to the New York bankers. The proceeds from the policy had been placed to McSween's credit, probably in a St. Louis bank, by Donnell, Lawson & Co., on July 19, 1877. Having collected the Fritz insurance money, McSween was now anxious to examine the L. G. Murphy & Co. books of account in order to determine the value of the Fritz estate interest in that business. Such an examination presented difficulties because of the dissolution of L. G. Murphy & Co., and the formation of a new partnership known as Dolan, Riley & Co.[6] Dolan refused to allow McSween to examine the books of the old partnership, whereupon McSween filed a petition in the Probate Court asking the court to compel Dolan to permit the examination. The court issued such an order, and appointed Ivan B. Patson, Morris J. Bernstein and Alexander A. McSween as the examiners. Dolan persuaded Emilie Scholand and Charles P. Fritz, the administrators of the estate, to join him in resisting the request for an examination of the books, and as a result McSween filed a petition in the Probate Court on August 1, 1877, setting forth his side of the controversy, and asked that he be released from further liability on the Scholand-Fritz bond. McSween's petition in part:

Your petitioner, A. A. McSween, represents that he is one of the sureties named in and who executed a bond for $10,000 in favor of the Territory of New Mexico, with James J. Dolan as co-surety, and Emilie Scholand and Charles Fritz, administratrix and administrator of the estate of Emil Fritz, on Sept. 19, A.D. 1876. Your petitioner represents that said Emilie Scholand has not been a resident of said county for the past nine months, having removed therefrom in November last; that your petitioner has written her to return and do and perform her duties as administratrix as aforesaid; but that she has failed and refused to do so; that neither the said Emilie Scholand nor the said Charles Fritz has taken any effective steps such as could and should have been taken toward closing the said administration of said estate and making a final report; that when your petitioner signed and executed the said bond with the parties aforesaid he was employed by said Emilie Scholand and Charles Fritz as attorney for said estate, and that he signed and executed said bond relying upon the representations of said Emilie Scholand and Charles Fritz to the effect that they would proceed with such administration as your petitioner as such attorney would counsel and the law direct; but that they nor either of them have performed their duties as your petitioner advises, and the law directed, that they and each of them are incompetent to administer on the assets of said estate; that your petitioner has good reason to believe and does believe that any monies received by said administrator and administratrix will be misapplied and will not be forthcoming to answer the orders of your honorable court in the premises.

McSween admitted that he had collected the life insurance money:

That your petitioner, as attorney as aforesaid, has collected the amount of a policy of insurance upon the life of said deceased for ten thousand dollars in the Merchants Life Insurance Company of the City and State of New York #1058, dated July 12, A.D. 1871, and that he is satisfied from information from reliable sources that if said money is paid to the said Emilie Scholand and Charles Fritz, or either of them, such will be misappropriated by them, leaving said bondsmen or sureties to make good their defalcation and maladministration, neither of them having property whereof any sum or sums adjudged against them as such administrator or administratrix could be made. Your petitioner therefore prays that your honor may cause said Emilie Scholand and Charles Fritz to give an account of their administration of the said estate, and that when such is done and a decree setting forth such settlement entered on the records of said court, your said petitioner may be relieved from further responsibility in the premises and the said bond so far as your petitioner is concerned may be declared null and void and of no force or effect, your petitioner hereby expressing his willingness to comply with any order your honor may make on the premises touching such settlement and making good any breach of said bond that may have occurred or may occur until the first day of the September 1877 term of said court.

Judging from all appearances, Alex. A. McSween was a fairly well-to-do lawyer and business man in 1877. He had been busy and industrious during a residence of several years in Lincoln County. The Las Vegas *Gazette* of August 4, 1877, told of McSween's ambitious plans to build a new dwelling place and business building in Lincoln, and to go into the banking business there in association with R. D. Hunter, of St. Louis, and John S. Chisum. Although the *Gazette* failed to mention the name of John H. Tunstall in connection with McSween's proposed business ventures, it was an open secret that Tunstall, a comparatively recent newcomer, and McSween were to be associated together in retail merchandising in Lincoln under the firm name of Tunstall & Co.

John Henry Tunstall, new-found friend, and now a business associate of Alex. A. McSween, was an odd character in a frontier country. Born and reared in England, he had been attracted to America by the reported possibilities for making substantial returns on risk and semi-risk investments. With the single exception of the Scottish Loan & Mortgage Co., financed by Scottish and English capital, there was at the time no concern of any consequence making loans in sizeable amounts on land and livestock in New Mexico. Consequently, a man from abroad, with capital to invest in the Territory was a rarity; and there was every indication that Tunstall would be welcomed with the proverbial outstretched arms.

Tradition has it that McSween became acquainted with Tunstall in Santa Fe, and induced him to visit Lincoln County. Tunstall had been on a grand tour in British Columbia; and then had looked for land and livestock investments in the Pacific Northwest. In California, Tunstall heard that land could be bought cheap in New Mexico, and that handsome profits, in some years as high as eighteen percent, could be realized from livestock operations. As a result he came to New Mexico from northern California, and was looking about in Santa Fe, when he met McSween.

Tunstall was barely twenty-three years old at the time he went to Lincoln County with McSween in November, 1876. Tunstall had told McSween and had let it be known in Lincoln that he had money to invest and could get more money from England to invest in the "proper" kind of an enterprise. With such an introduction it was not long before Tunstall was credited throughout Lincoln County as being "a wealthy Englishman." This impression was rather unfortunate for the young man. Because of his reputed wealth, outlaws had little hesitancy in stealing livestock from him as soon as he became established in ranching. McSween sponsored Tunstall in Lincoln. He advised Tunstall concerning prospective business ventures, pointed out bargains in ranch properties. When Lawrence G. Murphy and James J. Dolan tried to interest Tunstall in a ranch property of their own, McSween warned him away from the deal, claiming title to the property was fatally defective. Gradually McSween assumed management of Tunstall's business affairs. He helped him invest available funds, mostly furnished by Tunstall's father and other relatives in England. The business to be known as Tunstall & Co. was to be only one of a number of enterprises Tunstall and McSween had in mind for the future.

That McSween would no longer confine himself exclusively to the practice of law, but would compete with them in business through financing by Hunter, Chisum and Tunstall, was startling news to James Dolan and John H. Riley. Only recently they had obligated themselves for the payment of substantial sums of money borrowed to purchase the interest of L. G.

Murphy in L. G. Murphy & Co. In buying out Murphy, both Dolan and Riley had relied upon the possibility of being allowed to operate the business for some years to come without serious competition. Dolan and Riley watched McSween's expansion moves with keen interest. They had always considered McSween in the role of an attorney and counsellor-at-law, and not as a prospective competitor in business. In fact, McSween had occasionally represented L. G. Murphy & Co. in court, and from time to time had done legal work for the firm of rather a confidential nature.

In late August of 1877 there was tangible evidence that Tunstall and McSween were about to commence business in Lincoln. A stock of merchandise purchased in St. Louis began to arrive in wagon-train shipments from Las Vegas. Tunstall bought lumber and employed carpenters to build a storeroom. It was understandable that Dolan and Riley should view with apprehension and alarm the invasion by McSween and Tunstall of the mercantile business in Lincoln. The new store, apparently backed by English money, would cut deeply into Dolan-Riley profits. It was to be expected that John S. Chisum might bid more aggressively than ever on beef contracts for army posts and Indian agencies, and that the new bank, by making loans to farmers, settlers and small livestock operators, at lower rates of interest and longer maturities might easily divert many Dolan-Riley customers.

While McSween was making preparations to invade the business and banking field in Lincoln, his August 1 petition, demanding an accounting in the Fritz estate, remained on file in the Probate Court. On December 7, 1877, Administrator Charles Fritz filed a petition asking the Probate Court to order McSween to deposit the proceeds from the insurance policy in the court fund:

The undersigned administrator of the estate of Emil Fritz, deceased, respectfully shows to the court: That A. A. McSween has acted as attorney in said estate, and particularly for the purpose of collecting an insurance policy on the life of said Emil Fritz, deceased, for the sum of ten thousand dollars or thereabouts. That the undersigned is informed and believes that the said A. A. McSween has collected said amount, and he requests the court to make its order directing the said A. A. McSween to deposit or so place said sum of money so that it will be subject to the order of the court and for such further order in said matter as the court may deem expedient for the protection of the estate or to insure its speedy and final settlement.

Alex. A. McSween was badly mistaken if he expected Dolan and Riley to stand idly by while he and his associates competed for the trade of Lincoln. Encouraged to do so by Dolan, Charles Fritz and Emilie Fritz Scholand, the latter at the time a resident of Doña Ana County, signed a complaint with District Attorney Rynerson's approval, in Judge Bristol's court in Mesilla, on December 27, 1877, charging McSween with embezzlement. Mrs. Scholand alleged in support of the criminal charge:

Emilie Scholand, being first duly sworn, on oath says that she is informed and believes and verily does believe that Alexander Mc-Sween has committed the crime of embezzlement by embezzling and converting to his own use the sum of ten thousand dollars belonging to the estate of Emil Fritz, deceased, to wit, at the county of Lincoln on the tenth day of December in the year of our Lord one thousand eight hundred and seventy seven in the Territory of New Mexico, and in the 3rd Jud. Dist. said Ter'y.

Based on the Scholand affidavit, Judge Bristol authorized the issuance of a warrant for McSween's arrest. On the day the warrant was issued, the McSweens were on their way from Lincoln to Las Vegas; and by prearrangement, John S. Chisum was on his way to Las Vegas from his South Spring Ranch. The McSweens and Chisum met at Anton Chico, on the Pecos River, and traveled together to Las Vegas, reaching there on Christmas Eve, December 24, 1877. They had planned to spend Christmas in Las Vegas, and leave the following day for St. Louis, on what Chisum subsequently described as "a business trip." McSween and Chisum were arrested in Las Vegas on December 27, 1877, by the sheriff of San Miguel County upon the telegraphed request of Attorney Thomas B. Catron of Santa Fe.

James J. Dolan assumed responsibility for McSween's arrest,

in an affidavit signed on June 17, 1878, in the presence of Special Investigator Angel. It appeared from the affidavit that the matter of distributing the Fritz insurance money had been discussed with McSween in Probate Court. The Dolan affidavit in part:

The court adjourned till the first Monday in January, 1878, at which time Mrs. Scholand was to be present, she being notified by the Clerk of the Court, and the money paid over. McSween was to be present and turn over the money. He made no objection nor did he say that he was going away or could not be present. That before the meeting of the court said McSween left for St. Louis, as every one believed, never to come back. That I went to Mesilla and communicated the facts to Mrs. Scholand, and whereupon McSween was arrested at Las Vegas and brought back to Mesilla on the charge of embezzlement. The only interest I had in this money was to have the court decide to whom it belonged, whether it belonged to us or whether the estate should keep it.

Chisum had nothing whatever to do with the alleged embezzlement by McSween of the Fritz insurance money. In his telegram to the sheriff, Catron promised to file a petition in court in connection with pending litigation, asking for the issuance of a writ of ne exeat against Chisum, and gave assurance that a warrant would be forwarded forthwith in McSween's case charging him with embezzlement. The Grant County *Herald* told the story of Chisum's arrest in one sentence: "Chisum tried to leave the Territory, but Catron headed him off at Las Vegas with a writ of ne exeat."[7]

There is no need to speculate on the happenings incident to the arrest of Chisum and McSween. On January 16, 1878, and succeeding days, Chisum wrote a narrative which told the story from his standpoint:

In December, 1877, I started for St. Louis, Mo., on some business and got to Las Vegas on the night of Dec. 24. Upon arriving there I found that T. B. Catron had telegraphed to Las Vegas to know if Chisum and McSween had passed Las Vegas yet. The Sheriff commanded us not to leave the city. I was traveling in company with McSween and his wife, all going to St. Louis on business, and of course in a hurry, as all travelers are. So the McSweens and I waited for forty eight hours and no warrant came for the arrest of either one of us. The Sheriff held us as long as he could without papers. So we hitched up our horses to an ambulance and started for St. Louis two days after Christmas. After going some half mile, we were over-taken by the Sheriff and stopped on the public highway. The Sheriff had thirty or forty men with him, some armed with pistols, some with rocks, some with clubs, but all making a desperate charge upon us and surrounding the ambulance we were traveling in. I was jerked out head foremost and fell upon my face on the hard road. I was then seized by the throat by one of the Sheriff's men until I said to the Sheriff: "Will you please be so kind as to loosen the grip of this man?" The Sheriff spoke and the man loosened his hold. So I breathed once more of the fresh air of New Mexico that they brag so much about. McSween was also jerked out of the ambulance and dragged by a lot of the gang. Mrs. McSween was left sitting all alone crying in the ambulance without a driver or even protection. The Sheriff and his party were somewhat excited; McSween was some-what confused; I was laughing and cool. I looked the gang over and noticed one young man that had on a clean shirt, who had just arrived at the scene of the excitement. I asked him if he would be kind enough to drive Mrs. McSween to the hotel, and the young fellow consented to do so and drove her there.[8]

Arresting officers took Chisum and McSween to the court-house in Las Vegas. McSween was placed in the jailor's sleep-ing quarters for safekeeping. Chisum was held incommunicado on a charge of resisting an officer in the discharge of his official duties, but was released from custody for the night upon fur-nishing cash bond. Arraigned before a justice of the peace the next day, Chisum was formally released on a $500 bond. Mc-Sween was detained in the jailor's quarters for four days and nights pending the arrival from Doña Ana County of a warrant for his arrest on a charge of embezzlement. Upon receipt of the warrant, McSween was taken to Mesilla by Deputy Sheriff A. P. Barrier, for arraignment before Judge Bristol.

On or about January 5, 1878, carrying out Tom Catron's instructions, the Sheriff of San Miguel County asked Chisum to pay the amount claimed due on a judgment obtained against him in a suit filed by Alexander Grzelachowski of Anton Chico.

When Chisum told the Sheriff that he "was not prepared to pay," the Sheriff locked him up in jail and kept him there for several days. While in jail, Chisum wrote to Governor Axtell in Santa Fe, protesting against the acts of the officers in holding him in jail for a civil debt. Axtell's reply was of little consolation to Chisum: "I cannot pardon you. You have the right to habeas corpus."

While held prisoner in Las Vegas, papers were served on Chisum in three lawsuits in which he had been named a defendant in the district courts of Bernalillo and Santa Fe counties. In the Santa Fe County suit, in which attorney R. H. Tompkins was the plaintiff, he asked judgment against Chisum for $1,500 for legal services rendered. In his Las Vegas narrative, Chisum wrote that he had employed Tompkins for a brief time to defend him in a suit brought against him by William Rosenthal in which he sought judgment on promissory notes involved in the tangled affairs of an alleged partnership known as Wilber, Chisum and Clark. In the other suits, Van C. Smith, of Roswell, and Charles W. Lewis, of Albuquerque, both asked judgments against Chisum, alleging that he owed them money on partnership debts.

John S. Chisum had been considered by most people in New Mexico and Texas to be a well-to-do, perhaps a wealthy man, for many years prior to December 27, 1877, the day on which he was arrested in Las Vegas. Besides being considered prosperous in his business affairs, Chisum was looked upon as a man of integrity, and reputable in his business dealings. For years he had been a colorful figure in the livestock industry of the Territory, grazing thousands of his cattle on hundreds of thousands of acres of public domain, extending for many miles east and west, north and south, along the Pecos River and its tributaries in southeastern New Mexico. Since he was privileged to graze his livestock on land free of rent or taxes, there was every reason to believe that John S. Chisum had profited substantially by his operations. It was generally thought that he had made money on contracts to furnish beef to military posts and Indian reservations; and it was known that in good years his cows and calves brought top prices in overland drives to Texas and Kansas markets.

However outward appearances proved to be somewhat deceptive. Actually, Chisum's affairs had been in a critical condition for some time as the result of a complicated business transaction in which he had become unwittingly enmeshed, and which eventually precipitated his almost total financial downfall. A persuasive Arkansas promoter was the villain who lured Chisum into a scheme which eventually spelled the end of his supremacy as a cattle king. In his narrative of January 16, 1878, Chisum told how he happened to become involved in a transaction which, with its many ramifications and side issues, exposed him to great financial liability, and caused him endless trouble and much anxiety in the last years of his life.

In writing the narrative in Las Vegas, John Chisum used both the first person singular, and the fiction of a purported interview in which an imaginary newspaper reporter asked the questions, and a victimized person gave the answers.

Chisum's recital of a bizarre promotion scheme, disregarding the alternate styles adopted, may be summarized as follows: In March, 1867, while living in Denton County, Texas, a Mr. Wilber called on Chisum, introduced himself, and told him that he and a Mr. Clark were planning to go into the beef-packing business in Fort Smith, Arkansas; that both he and Clark were extremely anxious to have Chisum become associated with them in the proposed business venture "because he was a stockman." At the first interview Chisum flatly refused even to consider the proposal. However, Wilber was a man who was not easily put off, being both persistent and insistent. During a subsequent interview, Chisum weakened and suggested a basis on which he might go into the business: "I finally agreed that if he and Clark would raise $66,666.66 and invest it in a packing house, salt and barrels, and other fixtures necessary for the packing of beef, then when I saw that this was done I would furnish $33,333.33 in beef at cash price, provided they would agree not to pack over 5,000 beeves the first season." In order that there might be no room for a misunderstanding as to "what I proposed to do and what I proposed for them to do," Chisum and Wilber wrote out and signed a rough outline of the proposed venture, each keeping an exact copy.

Suspecting, when it was too late, that he had signed a paper which might cause him trouble, Chisum wrote to a friend in

Arkansas and inquired about Clark's background, character and financial standing. To quote from Chisum's narrative: "The answer was, 'Clark has got nothing and let him alone.' This settled the matter with me, and if Wilber had written to me as he had agreed to do, it would have made no difference to me. I should have refused to have anything to do with them from that day to this. I have never seen Wilber since, and I never did see Mr. Clark in my life."

John Chisum remained in Denton for some three months after Wilber left: "But having not received a line from him nor Clark, I of course came to the conclusion that all idea of the packing business was abandoned under my proposition to them."

In June, 1867, Chisum left Denton and went to Concho County, Texas, some two hundred miles west; and in the following July, "started for New Mexico with a herd of beef and got to New Mexico in August, 1867." Remaining in New Mexico until April 5, 1868, Chisum then returned to Texas, arriving in Coleman County on May 8, 1868. Upon arriving there, Chisum heard disconcerting news: "Then and not until then did I learn that Wilber and Clark had been packing beef at Fort Smith in the fall of 1867 under the name of Wilber, Chisum and Clark; one of my brothers heard that such a firm was packing beef at Fort Smith, three hundred miles distant, and knowing where I was and fearing something was wrong, he went to Fort Smith and found out that what he had heard was true. They were in the mercantile business and a large sign over their store as well as over their packing house, proclaimed that the business was conducted under the name of Wilber, Chisum & Clark. Even on their bottles of cocktails were labels, 'Wilber, Chisum & Clark,' which they had made in New York. One of my brothers exposed the whole thing that evening, and the next day they were closed up and the swindle exposed."

Sensing danger in the situation that had developed and anxious to obtain legal guidance, Chisum left for Austin on May 10, 1868. At the state capital he called upon his old and trusted friend, Gov. Elisha M. Pease, and showed him the agreement he and Wilber had signed, "and asked him if that made me a partner of those men. He said, 'No,' and asked me the circumstances. I stated them and he then said that if I had been in the country, and, knowing that these men were using my name and by so doing were getting other people's property, I had not let it be known that I was no partner then the law would make me responsible; but that if I had been out of the state and did not know all this, then the law would not make me responsible. But he said, 'You yet have a duty to perform; you should publish those men and let it be known that you were not a partner and therefore would not be responsible for contracts they had made or might make hereafter.' This I did in three newspapers, one in Arkansas and two in Texas."

At the time the purported and pretended firm of Wilber, Chisum & Clark suspended business in Fort Smith, it owed between $80,000 and $90,000 on promissory notes. Owners and holders of promissory notes employed lawyers, who in turn notified Chisum, the only solvent member of the supposed partnership of Wilber, Chisum and Clark, that they looked to him for payment: "I was sued upon some of these notes before I left Texas to return to New Mexico. The courts decided I was no partner of the said pretended firm and was not responsible for contracts made by them. I remained in Texas over four years after the maturity of these notes and by the Texas law these notes were barred by the Statute of Limitation."

In New Mexico, some ten years after he had signed the agreement with Mr. Wilber, concerning what he believed to be a proposed or contemplated business deal, the Wilber, Chisum & Clark note obligations began to bob up in John S. Chisum's thoughts by day and to disturb his rest at night: "After those old forged notes had been lying around for years, William Rosenthal of Santa Fe notoriety, sent to New York and other places and gathered up this commercial paper, as he called it, and got the owners to transfer it to him, so he became the owner of the notes. If I were to undertake to explain all of the underhand advantages that have been taken in this matter, it might reflect on some of the big ones. So we will just let that pass as it is too bad to tell. We will just say Willie Rosenthal complained and because he did so, I was put in jail."[9]

In his narrative of January 16, 1878, Chisum failed to make any reference whatever to an important and significant business transaction which, when discovered by his New Mexico creditors, became a matter of grave concern to them. On or about November 15, 1875, the Las Vegas *Gazette* reported in a matter-of-fact way, that John S. Chisum had sold to Col. R. D. Hunter, of St. Louis, Missouri, and Medicine Creek, Kansas, for a consideration of $319,000, his ranches and range rights in the Bosque Grande country, together with the Chisum brand, and an estimated twenty to thirty thousand cows, calves and bulls.

On or about March 8, 1876, some ninety days after the Chisum-Hunter deal had been completed, Alexander Grzelachowski, of Puerto de Luna, through Attorney Catron, filed suit against Chisum, in the District Court of San Miguel County, asking judgment against him for $3,000, plus interest. Grzelachowski's suit was based on a promissory note which it was alleged, Chisum had endorsed, but had refused to pay at maturity. In his Las Vegas narrative Chisum referred to Grzelachowski in several places as "Chowski" and wrote of him in a not unfriendly way, saying, among other things, that "he was a Polander by birth and a merchant by profession, a very nice gentleman, very polite and nice in his manner and well educated."

In defending himself in the Grzelachowski suit, Chisum pleaded failure of consideration, and other niceties of the law, but the court rendered judgment against him on August 17, 1876, for the full amount sued upon. In an effort to collect on the judgment, Grzelachowski's attorney, Tom Catron, filed an affidavit alleging that Chisum had transferred his property to Hunter without adequate consideration, with intent to hinder, delay and defraud creditors. It was on the basis of this affidavit that Catron, while Chisum was in Las Vegas at Christmas time in 1877, had asked the court to issue against Chisum the writ of ne exeat ("let him not go out of the Kingdom"), a remedy of the early common law of England.[10]

True to his standard procedure, John Chisum fought back vigorously in the court proceedings in which he found himself involved through Tom Catron's attempt to obtain a writ of ne exeat against him in the Grzelachowski lawsuit. On or about June 18, 1878, Judge Samuel C. Parks sustained a motion filed by his attorney, Thomas F. Conway, asking for a dismissal of Catron's petition. Judge Parks held that New Mexico had adopted the English common law and that a court of equity in

New Mexico had the authority to issue the writ, but that Catron had failed to allege or prove facts sufficient to justify its issuance against Chisum.

As an aftermath of his arrest on December 27, 1877, the grand jury of San Miguel County indicted Chisum on March 10, 1878, for "resisting arrest at the hands of an officer of the law." Attorney Conway pleaded not guilty for his client, and Chisum was released on $250 bond. On March 6, 1879, the Attorney General of the Territory moved to dismiss the indictment and Chisum was thereupon permitted to "go hence without day."

The question of John S. Chisum's liability on the Wilber, Chisum & Clark notes literally followed him to the grave. On April 23, 1884, Catron, Thornton and Clancy, joined by William Breeden and H. L. Waldo, all prominent Santa Fe attorneys, filed an omnibus suit in the District Court of Lincoln County (before that county was dismembered) against John S. Chisum, Pitzer Chisum, James Chisum and William Robert, son-in-law of James Chisum, in which the court was asked to set aside certain alleged fraudulent transactions between and among the defendants. The suit was filed on behalf of ten plaintiffs, all seeking the same relief. The complaint, consisting of a dozen or more typewritten pages, alleged that each plaintiff had obtained individually a judgment against John S. Chisum; that all such judgments appeared to be uncollectible, the names of the plaintiffs and the amounts of the judgments being described as follows: John Ayers, administrator of the estate of William Rosenthal (who died in 1880), owner of judgments recovered by Rosenthal in his lifetime on October 6, 1877, in Bernalillo County, in the sum of $2,370.68; and on February 26, 1881, in Santa Fe County in the sum of $18,000; Luis M. Baca, of Socorro, owner of a judgment recovered on October 20, 1876, in Socorro County in the sum of $4,161.83; William Babb, of Texas, owner of a judgment recovered on November 24, 1877, in Doña Ana County in the sum of $7,510; Van C. Smith, of Arizona, and Aaron O. Wilburn, of California, owners of a judgment recovered on February 24, 1877, in Santa Fe County in the sum of $1,957.83; Charles W. Lewis, of Albuquerque, owner of a judgment recovered on October 24, 1876, in Socorro County in the sum of $1,982.40; James P.

Chase, of Socorro, owner of a judgment recovered on October 27, 1877, in Socorro County in the sum of $426.50; Jose Ynes Perea and Moses Zickerberg, of San Miguel County, owners of a judgment recovered on March 10, 1877, in the sum of $437.88; Alexander Grzelachowski, of San Miguel County, owner of a judgment recovered on August 17, 1876, in the sum of $3,456.75.

Among other things it was alleged in the complaint: that about the year 1877, "John S. Chisum was the owner of a large herd of cattle, situated in Lincoln County, New Mexico, and in the edge of Texas, numbering about thirty thousand head;" that the plaintiffs were informed and believed that "the said John S. Chisum in 1877 transferred his entire herd of cattle and all horses and personal property owned by him, and all real estate and ranches claimed and occupied by him, to Hunter and Evans;" that the conveyance to Hunter and Evans was "partly for the purpose of paying a debt to them, and partly for the purpose of preventing plaintiffs and other creditors of John S. Chisum from recovering their indebtedness, and with the secret understanding upon the part of John S. Chisum and Hunter and Evans, that after Hunter and Evans had been re-paid the money due them by the said John S. Chisum, the re-mainder of said property should be held in trust for the said John S. Chisum, to be reconveyed to him, or to such parties as he might direct."

The complaint further alleged that Hunter and Evans re-tained possession of Chisum's property until they had disposed of enough of it to satisfy all their claims, and that thereafter in 1880, John S. Chisum directed Hunter and Evans to convey and transfer the remainder of the property, including large herds of cattle, to his brothers, Pitzer Chisum and James Chisum. Continuing, the complaint alleged that "Pitzer Chisum and James Chisum were insolvent at the time, and were not possessed of any property with which to pay for the cattle, and did not in fact, pay to Hunter and Evans one dollar in consideration of the transfer to them;" and that Pitzer and James Chisum and the defendant, William Robert, son-in-law of James Chisum, "had confederated together in furtherance of a secret trust," being at all times "but tools and employes in the hands of John S. Chisum." With great particularity and minute attention to detail, the plaintiffs set forth and alleged the manner in which the defendants had conspired together to defeat their claims.

Stricken by a fatal malady, John S. Chisum was unable to appear in court, or otherwise perpetuate his testimony in the lawsuit that had been brought against him by his judgment creditors. On November 14, 1884, a decree was entered by the trial judge, finding the issues for the plaintiffs, holding that the conveyances and transfers of property by Chisum had been to the prejudice of creditors. Under the decree, P. L. Vanderveer was appointed as special master with instructions to sell sufficient of the property to make $57,030.86, which when recovered was to be paid to the plaintiffs. John S. Chisum was unaware of the final decree of the court. He died on December 20, 1884, eight months after the suit had been filed.

Some thirteen years after Chisum's death another entry was made in the docket in connection with the litigation. On August 23, 1897, Judge H. B. Hamilton, upon considering the petition of Attorney W. T. Thornton, ordered the clerk of the court to have the record show that the decree of November 14, 1884, had been fully complied with and ordered that the real estate of the defendants in Lincoln and Chaves counties be free from the judgment lien.[11]

NOTES AND PROFILES

[1] Lawrence Gustave Murphy, founder of L. G. Murphy & Co., was born in Wexford, Ireland, emigrated to America in young manhood. He died in Santa Fe on October 20, 1878, after a long illness, at the age of forty-seven years. Murphy received a classical education in Ireland, and for a time may have studied for the Roman Catholic priesthood in Maynooth College and Seminary.

Murphy enlisted in the United States Army, served in Utah under troops commanded by Albert Sidney Johnston in 1859. He was in New Mexico at the outbreak of the Civil War. Following the President's proclamation of May 31, 1861, Murphy enlisted in the First Regiment, New Mexico Volunteers, on July 27, 1861, at the time being organized by Col. Ceran St. Vrain and Lt. Col.

Christopher Carson. Murphy was commissioned a captain and regimental quartermaster, and was later promoted to be a major.

After being mustered out of the service in 1866, Murphy became sutler at Fort Stanton, a post he relinquished three years later, following a controversy with Commanding Officer Clendenning. In 1869, Murphy moved from Fort Stanton to Bonito (Lincoln), a Spanish-American village nine miles away, where he established a general merchandise business known as L. G. Murphy & Co., in which Major Emil Fritz later became a partner.

On December 28, 1874, there was published in the Santa Fe *New Mexican* a legal advertisement dated August 29, 1874, reading: "Death having dissolved the partnership heretofore existing between L. G. Murphy and Emil Fritz, under the style and title of L. G. Murphy & Co., it is requested that persons having claims against said firm will present them for settlement within thirty days from date, and all persons indebted to said firm will please settle within that time or have their accounts placed in the hands of an attorney for collection. (Signed) Lawrence G. Murphy." In the same issue there was another notice: "From and after this date the firm of L. G. Murphy & Co. of Lincoln, in the county of Lincoln, will consist of L. G. Murphy and J. J. Dolan. Dated August 31, 1874."

Murphy formally severed his connection with L. G. Murphy & Co., as of April 20, 1877, according to the Santa Fe *New Mexican* of that date, and thereafter the business was continued by the two remaining partners, James J. Dolan and John H. Riley, under the name of Jas. J. Dolan & Co.

Besides merchandising in Lincoln, Murphy had substantial investments in ranching and livestock operations in Lincoln County. In the Grant County *Herald* of February 16, 1878, Murphy offered to sell his interest in a pretentious ranch property, a vast expanse of open country some twelve miles south of White Oaks: "Desiring to leave Lincoln County, I offer for sale, cheap for cash, all my right, title and interest in the best Cattle Ranch in New Mexico, known as the 'Carisosa.' It secures twenty miles square of first class pasturage, and abundant water for ten thousand head of stock. There is also about 600 head of cattle of different ages, but mostly composed of young cows, with 14 young Durham bulls. Also, a residence, corrales, outhouses, library, poultry, choice hogs, horses, wagons, young orchard and many other advantages and inducements which can only be appreciated when seen. I would add, further, the Extensive Range forms a natural corral, having but one open entry on the north and an exit on the south, where a house has been built for a guard."

After Murphy's death, the ranch was acquired by Thomas B. Catron of Santa Fe, who sold it in October, 1882, to an English syndicate, represented by J. A. Alcock. Emerson Hough described the ranch in an article published in the *American Field* of August 18, 1883: "The range is about forty miles by fifteen; the buildings are of the usual low, single story adobe class, but are good of their kind, the main house a model of comfort. The house is furnished throughout with a luxuriousness and elegance of style which is utterly astonishing to one accustomed to the scant comforts of the ordinary ranch. There is no lady to preside over the household. The Steinway piano stands silent; the fine engravings are not too often dusted; the cowboys make their beds upon the nicely carpeted floor." At the ranch Hough became acquainted with the man who helped William H. Bonney make his get-away from Lincoln after killing Bell and Olinger: "An old German by name of Gauss, who came here thirty years ago as a United States soldier, is the presiding deity of the kitchen. He himself is a walking volume of incident. He tells with pride how Billy the Kid once made him saddle a horse for him under cover of a rifle, after Billy had killed the two sheriffs at Lincoln. We had had enough of Billy, and asked the old gentleman to give us a relief, which he did in a choice variety of hunting stories."

² Emilie Fritz had married William Scholand, from whom she was divorced by a decree signed by Judge Warren Bristol in the District Court of Lincoln County on April 18, 1876. Mrs. Scholand was given custody of the two children born of the marriage, Emilie, four years old, and Anna, two and one-half years old. Emilie Fritz was nineteen years old when she arrived in Lincoln County. Her brother, Emil, had left Germany before she was born.

³ Levi Spiegelberg, one of the six fabulous Spiegelberg Brothers: Jacob, Elias, Levi, Emanuel, Lehman and Willi, all of whom engaged in merchandising and freighting on the Santa Fe Trail in New Mexico at one time or another, was a colorful character, particularly well known in Santa Fe and Albuquerque. Jacob Spiegelberg came to Santa Fe with Kearny's troops in 1846; Lehman came to the Territory in 1858. Levi Spiegelberg was one of the organizers of the Bank of New Mexico, chartered by the Legislature January 29, 1863. Other organizers included Ceran St. Vrain, Sigmund Seligman and Jose Manuel Gallegos, all noted characters in their day.

One by one the Spiegelberg brothers, with the exception of Elias, who was accidentally killed in Santa Fe, January 16, 1879, drifted to New York City, where they engaged in business, beginning in the late 60's and early 70's. Levi Spiegelberg had an exciting experience several days after the battle of Valverde, fought between Union and Confederate troops on or about February 22, 1862. Captured by a Confederate patrol near Socorro, while enroute to Chihuahua with a train of merchandise, Spiegelberg was taken before a board of inquiry at Socorro, charged with being a Union spy. Fortunately for Spiegelberg, he was recognized by Col. A. M. Jackson, of General Sibley's staff, one-time Secretary of the Territory, who had lived in Santa Fe before the war. Jackson gave Spiegelberg a pass for him and his train to return to Albuquerque. The pass read: "All guards, patrols, or other forces of this Army, will respect this order in full, and afford reasonable necessary protection to the persons named." One of the conditions attached to the pass required Spiegelberg to be out of Socorro within one hour. Afterward Spiegelberg related that he and his men had the wagon train on the road to Albuquerque and almost out of range of Confederate guns within thirty minutes after receiving the pass.

⁴ James J. Dolan, born in Laughrea, County Galway, Ireland, on May 2,

1848, accompanied his parents when they emigrated to America, and was employed at the age of twelve years in a New York City dry-goods store. He continued in that employment until 1863, when he enlisted in Company K, Seventeenth Regiment of the New York Zouaves. Discharged in 1865, Dolan enlisted in the regular United States Army in 1866 and served at several military posts in New Mexico. In the early 70's Dolan was employed as a clerk for L. G. Murphy & Co., post traders at Fort Stanton. Three years later he was made a member of the firm, which, in the meantime, had started business in Lincoln.

On May 9, 1877, Dolan became involved in an unfortunate altercation in Lincoln with Hilario Jaramillo, a twenty-year-old employee. Dolan claimed that Jaramillo attacked him with a knife, and that he was obliged to shoot him, inflicting a fatal wound, in order to save his life. The Santa Fe *New Mexican* of May 22, reported: "Dolan gave himself up, but was discharged, as he killed in self defense."

When L. G. Murphy withdrew from the L. G. Murphy & Co. partnership in 1877, Dolan formed a partnership with John H. Riley, which was dissolved in 1880. On July 13, 1879, Dolan was married to Miss Caroline Fritz, daughter of Charles Phillip Frederick Fritz.

The Lincoln County War wrecked Dolan's business and crippled him financially. After the Lincoln County troubles had subsided he engaged in ranching and mining. At one time he owned a fractional interest in the famous Homestake Mine in White Oaks. In 1883 Dolan was elected Treasurer of Lincoln County, and held that office until 1888, when he was elected to the Territorial Council, representing Grant, Doña Ana, Sierra and Lincoln counties. On June 3, 1889, Dolan was appointed Receiver of the United States Land Office in Las Cruces. James J. Dolan died on February 26, 1898, at his ranch home on the Feliz River. According to the White Oaks *Eagle* of March 3, 1898, death was caused by "hemorrhage of the bowels." Dolan gave his version of the trouble in Lincoln County in a communication to the editor of the Santa Fe *New Mexican,* in two published columns on May 25, 1878.

[5] Little is known of the background of Alexander A. McSween, one of the principal characters in the Lincoln County War. There is some reason to believe that his full name was Alexander Abraham McSween. He came to New Mexico on March 3, 1875.

The records of Atchison County, Kansas, show that Alex. A. McSween, age twenty-nine, of Eureka, Kansas, was married to Sue E. Homer, age twenty-seven, of Atchison, Kansas, on August 23, 1873. The daily *Champion* of Atchison, of Sunday, August 24, 1873, noted the marriage, "at the Presbyterian Manse by Rev. Edward Cooper, D.D., on the 23rd inst., of Alexander A. McSween, Esq., of Eureka, and Miss Sue E. Homer of this city." The *Champion* continued: "Eureka has reason to be proud of this prize it has taken from us. May she blossom in the fair southwest and cast the same genial glow around the home of her husband she did to the friends she leaves behind her. Selah! Roll up your sleeves, Mac, and pitch into business now; no more excuses old boy."

McSween was between thirty-five and thirty-six years old on July 19, 1878, the date of his death, which would fix 1843 as the approximate year of his birth. McSween's friends in Lincoln believed that he had been born in Charlottetown, Prince Edward Island, Canada; had studied for a time for the Presbyterian ministry, for the law in St. Louis, and had resided briefly in Kansas. Through the courtesy and assistance of Mr. W. E. Bentley, a barrister of Charlottetown, efforts were made by the present writer to learn something of McSween's identity and background, a formidable task because of the nearly eighty years since his death in Lincoln. Through Mr. Bentley's efforts, Murdock McSween, sixty-four years old, a member of the only McSween family in the entire area, was located in Brookfield, eleven miles from Charlottetown. Murdock McSween's grandfather, also named Murdock McSween, emigrated to Prince Edward Island from Scotland about 1830, and adopted a child named "Aleck" and looked after him until he was a grown man, when he left the Island for the United States. No information was available as to Aleck's family name or background. Presumably, "Aleck," the adopted son of Murdock McSween, was Alex. A. McSween, the lawyer of Lincoln, New Mexico. Rev. Lawrence E. Blaikie, Presbyterian minister at Brookfield, searching the church archives in 1955, found no record of the baptism of an "Aleck" or "Alex." McSween, or certification by the Presbytery of any McSween to preach. A search of the files of *The Patriot* and *The Examiner,* Charlottetown newspapers, from the period, July 19, 1878, to September in that year, failed to disclose any information in regard to McSween.

In the Santa Fe *New Mexican* of June 8, 1878, there was published a communication concerning McSween, signed "El Gato," of Fort Stanton, which said among other things: "Of McSween's ability there can be little doubt and although the means he has employed to accomplish his ends would disgrace the most uncivilized cannibal that ever devoured a missionary, success, as is usually the case, carries with it the adoration and respect of the multitude."

"El Gato" continued to say that "King" Alexander McSween had recently taken a trip along the Ruidoso, and while there had issued a proclamation reading: "We by the grace of God, King of Lincoln, Lord of the Pecos, etc, etc, to all whom it may concern, Greeting: Whereas, it has pleased a kind Providence, ably seconded by some of our devoted and loyal subjects, to remove from our path sundry obstacles, to wit: the former Sheriff of this county, Wm. Brady, and a large number of his friends, therebefore, be it known, that in consideration of the valuable assistance rendered by our loyal subjects to this kind Providence in fulfilling our dearest wishes, we by the advice of our ministers in council assembled, do hereby grant a full and unconditional pardon to all offenders against the laws of neighboring states who may have been employed as instruments of Providence in destroying our enemies. May an adobe wall ever protect our loyal subjects. Given at our Palace at Lincoln, this 1st day of May in the year of Our Lord, 1878, and of our reign the first. Alexander I. God Save the King."

[6] John H. Riley, who became a partner in Dolan, Riley & Co., also known as Jas. J. Dolan & Co., following the withdrawal of L. G. Murphy in 1877, played a minor role in the Lincoln County War. He was born on Valentia Island, near Dingle Bay, Ireland, on or about March 19, 1841. When he was twelve years old, Riley's parents emigrated to America.

In the gold fields of California seeking his fortune at the outbreak of the Civil War, John Riley enlisted in the Union army at Marysville, California, on August 17, 1861, and came to New Mexico with Carleton's California Column. He saw service in various parts of New Mexico until mustered out at Fort Union on August 31, 1864. Following his discharge from military service at Fort Stanton, Riley worked as a clerk for Murphy & Co. On or about September 20, 1875, according to the Santa Fe *New Mexican* of September 21, Riley shot Juan B. Patron with a rifle, following a quarrel in Lincoln, inflicting dangerous wounds near the spine and in the bowels. It was at first believed that Patron had been fatally wounded, but he survived. At a preliminary hearing before a Justice of the Peace, Riley pleaded self-defense and was discharged from custody.

Riley depended upon his fists instead of a gun in another encounter, according to the Mesilla *News* of June 12, 1878: "J. H. Riley and J. S. Crouch came near getting into a fist fight, lately, in Mesilla, while talking over the Lincoln county troubles. There is something manly in that kind of an encounter. Any scrub can shoot another opponent down, but it takes some courage to face the music and give and take punishment, according to the rules practiced by the late John Morrisey."

When Dolan & Co. became insolvent and suspended business as the result of the Lincoln County War, Riley moved from Lincoln to Las Cruces, where he was active for a time in politics. In 1885 Riley moved to Colorado and worked there for several years on railway construction projects. Returning to Las Cruces, he was elected assessor of Doña Ana County in 1889, and participated to some extent in county and Territorial politics. In the 90's Riley moved to Colorado Springs, Colorado, where he remained until his death from pneumonia on February 10, 1916. Burial was in Denver.

For twelve years before his death Riley lived at the El Paso Club in Colorado Springs, and made weekly visits to his cattle ranch near Fowler. (Colorado Springs *Evening Telegraph*, February 11, 1916.)

Riley's version of the difficulties in Lincoln County was published in the weekly Santa Fe *New Mexican* of April 20, 1878. Among other things Riley said of Sheriff Brady: "Poor Brady! After an honorable record of twenty years as a soldier and an officer, a greater portion of which was served in the War of the Rebellion, to be assassinated by cowardly, sneaky tools of an unprincipled and ambitious man. Who in New Mexico can say aught against Sheriff Brady? As an officer he was respected and feared by the citizens of our county, and as such was in the way of Alex. McSween. Brady leaves a wife and nine children to mourn his untimely death."

[7] Thomas Benton Catron was born near Lexington, Missouri, on October 6, 1840; was graduated with a B.A. degree from the University of Missouri on July 4, 1860. He studied law in Missouri, but laid aside Chitty and Blackstone to enlist in the Confederate army in which he served throughout the Civil War. Catron came to New Mexico in 1866. He was admitted to the Bar of the Territory on June 15, 1867; served as district attorney of the Third Judicial District, became attorney general for the Territory on January 1, 1869; later served as United States district attorney for New Mexico.

Catron served an apprenticeship of many years' duration in public life. He was elected four times to the Territorial Legislature; was for years a member of the Santa Fe town Board of Education; he served as mayor of Santa Fe. On March 27, 1912, Catron achieved a long-time ambition when he was elected to the United States Senate, in which he served until March 4, 1917. Senator Catron died in Santa Fe on May 21, 1921. No man was better acquainted than Tom Catron with the details of the so-called Lincoln County War. As a banker he had financed the firm of L. G. Murphy & Co.; as United States attorney, and in private practice, he had filed a number of suits against John S. Chisum.

Despite the fact that he was in a position to talk about the troubles in Lincoln County, Catron preferred not to reminisce. From Catron's viewpoint, the Lincoln County War was of no great significance or importance when contrasted with the bloody fighting he had experienced, and the sudden death that had come to so many men under his command in battles fought during the Civil War. In the words spoken many years ago by a sage New Mexican, now adopted by the present writer: "No man ever lived in New Mexico who bored with a bigger auger than Tom Catron."

[8] For many years the original John S. Chisum narrative was in the possession of Chisum's niece, Sallie Chisum Robert. Sallie Chisum Robert and Lillian Casey Klasner (daughter of Robert Casey, killed in Lincoln on August 2, 1875) were intimate friends for many years. The two women visited Santa Fe together to look after land matters on or about September 1, 1904, and while there discussed a plan to collaborate in writing their recollections of early days in Lincoln County. The project was never completed. For a time Mrs. Klasner had possession of fragments of the narrative.

Mrs. Klasner was born on the Casey home place, in southern Lincoln County, which was mapped as Section 16, Township 11 South Range East. But for the Casey homestead rights, this area would have been a public school section under Act of Congress.

[9] William Rosenthal was a resident of Cimarron as of the first of July, 1870. Later he became a United States assistant internal revenue collector, and still later a livestock broker. He lived in Santa Fe for several years after leaving Cimarron. On May 25, 1871, Rosenthal was married in Santa Fe to Josefa, daughter of Hon. Jose Manuel Gallegos, long-time delegate-in-congress for New Mexico.

The Grant County *Herald* of July 13, 1878, noted: "Wm. Rosenthal, of

Santa Fe, is in Silver City looking after his interests in the beef contracts of southern New Mexico and Arizona."

[10] Alexander Grzelachowski, merchant and livestock man of Puerto de Luna, was widely known in the Pecos River country in the 70's and 80's. Born in Poland in 1832, he came to the United States when a young man, died on May 24, 1896, after a colorful and eventful life, most of which was spent in New Mexico.

Easily one of the best educated men of his day in New Mexico, Grzelachowski excelled as a linguist. He joined the Union army in Santa Fe on February 3, 1862, and served throughout the Civil War as a Roman Catholic chaplain with the Second Regiment of New Mexico Volunteers. After the war, Grzelachowski established a general merchandise business in Puerto de Luna, for many years an important trading center, and engaged in large-scale operations in ranching, cattle and sheep production. He made use of his superior education by asserting leadership in Pecos River irrigation projects of importance to the community, and pioneered in helping to establish water rights for the people in the area.

Grzelachowski's store was one of Billy Bonney's favorite hangouts. He was one of the store's best customers. Clerks were under orders to give him unlimited credit. Bonney had a number of close friends in Puerto de Luna, among them Cleto Chavez, strong man of the countryside, who wrestled with Bonney and won a championship belt hung up as a prize by Grzelachowski; and Andres Coronado, who on several occasions took over Bonney's pistol when he threatened to become obstreperous at dances.

[11] John Simpson Chisum, pioneer Texas and New Mexico cattleman, was born in Madison County, Tennessee, August 15, 1824, died in Eureka Springs, Arkansas, December 20, 1884. Chisum came to New Mexico from Paris, Texas, in 1867, driving hundreds of cattle, many of them picked up on Texas and New Mexico ranges, and branded in his brand under powers of attorney executed by the owners. Chisum grazed his cattle in the Pecos River country in New Mexico, a vast area of public domain, with good grass, and plenty of water. The grazing lands appropriated by Chisum, located in the "Staked Plains" country, previously buffalo country, had been used by the Comanches and other Plains Indians for grazing horses and stolen cattle.

Within a few years after coming to New Mexico, Chisum had built up a great cattle outfit. Bills of sale for livestock were virtually unknown in early-day New Mexico, and much confusion existed over cattle brands and ownership. Contracting to furnish beef for reservation Indians and military posts in New Mexico and Arizona was a profitable enterprise during early Territorial days. Chisum got his fair share of beef contracts.

His name appeared frequently in connection with minor litigation in the early days of Lincoln County. On April 21, 1875, A. J. Fountain, acting district attorney for the Third Judicial District, sued Chisum for $2,614, claimed to be due the Territory for taxes. A. A. McSween represented Chisum in court.

On October 26, 1875, the case was settled. Thomas B. Catron, U. S. District Attorney, filed several minor suits against him in the federal court, mostly for small amounts claimed to be due on license and tobacco taxes.

On January 27, 1876, at two o'clock in the morning, as the stage from Silver City to Mesilla was slowly going uphill in Cook's Canyon, three masked men stepped from behind big boulders and compelled the driver and express messenger to get down. Only two passengers were in the coach, John S. Chisum and Thomas F. Conway, his attorney, both asleep. Chisum had $1,000 in currency on his person, but managed to conceal all of it but $100, which he gave to the highwaymen, together with his watch and chain. Conway contributed $25 and his watch and chain. The robbers also took $4,000 in silver bricks consigned to Kountz Bros. in New York, and rode away.

On May 19, 1877, Chisum became seriously ill with the smallpox, but recovered in a few weeks.

In 1877, one of Chisum's brothers, James S. Chisum, of Hardeman County, Texas, became associated with him in the ranch business in New Mexico. Sallie L. Chisum, James Chisum's daughter, was married to William Robert in Anton Chico on January 26, 1880, Rev. J. A. Annin, a Presbyterian minister, of Las Vegas, performing the ceremony.

Frank H. Howell, of Pleasanton, California, son of Major March Howell, early-day Pecos Valley surveyor, related by marriage to E. A. Cahoon, pioneer Roswell banker, was a frequent visitor to the William Robert home on the Chisum ranch in the early 80's. Writing to Mrs. Laura Cahoon, widow of E. A. Cahoon, on March 29, 1954, Mr. Howell recalled with nostalgia: "The old Chisum ranch was such a wonderful place, very pretty, fine orchard and garden, big house (the front porch 144 feet long), beautiful alfalfa fields and, best of all, such good, kind, generous people."

Frank Howell told Mrs. Cahoon of a romance that flowered, and then withered in girlhood for Sallie Chisum Robert: "I think Sallie Chisum was born about 1860. She loved a man named Will Ford, who came up with John Chisum from Texas, I think, in 1868. The family strongly objected to the match so Will Ford left. In 1903, I met him in Boise, Idaho. He was well to do, unusually personable, excellent reputation, well established, and associated with the big cowmen of that region. I had considerable business with him. Of course, we soon discovered that we had the mutual tie of knowing the Chisums. I told him that I had heard Sallie say that he was the man she loved. It was a great shock to him. He said that it was the same with him, that it was the disappointment of his life—that he could never get over it. Then, every time I saw him, he wanted to talk about 'what might have been.'"

CHAPTER FOUR

CHARGES OF CHICANERY

IT WAS COMPARATIVELY EASY for John S. Chisum to extricate himself from the perplexities of the law in San Miguel County by giving bond for his future appearance. However, officers had been instructed to hold Alex. McSween without bond, and he was taken from Las Vegas to Mesilla by Deputy Sheriff Adolph B. Barrier. Fortunately for McSween, as it later developed, Barrier was not an experienced officer, but a painter and paper hanger by profession. His card in the Las Vegas *Gazette* advertised that he would do "gilding, frescoeing, graining, glazing, marbling, calcimining, paper hanging and painting."

When arraigned before Judge Bristol, in Mesilla, McSween pleaded not guilty. Bristol fixed his appearance bond at $8,000. Unable to furnish sureties on a bond acceptable to either Judge Bristol or District Attorney Rynerson, McSween was remanded to Barrier's custody, with instructions from the court to deliver him to Sheriff Brady in Lincoln. The Las Cruces *Eco* published a story purporting to give the background of McSween's arrest. The Santa Fe *New Mexican* clipped the *Eco's* story, and published it on January 19, 1878:

Alexander A. McSween, who was recently arrested at Las Vegas upon the charge of embezzling the funds of the late Col. Fritz' estate, was a practicing attorney in Lincoln County. His arrest was made upon a warrant sued out by Mrs. Scholand, an heir of the estate, from Judge Bristol's court. McSween was employed by the administrators (Charles Fritz and Mrs. Scholand) to collect the policy money on the life of Col. Emil Fritz, amounting to $10,000 and interest, which he became possessed of some months since and which he drew in his own name and kept there ever since. It appears that

L. G. Murphy was also a claimant for the money as surviving partner of the firm of Murphy & Fritz. . . . McSween, it is charged,
has hitherto refused to account for this money to the administrators,
but being pressed for a settlement, agreed to repay the amount at
the next session of the Probate Court which was to meet in Lincoln
County early next month. In the meantime he faded from Lincoln
and was arrested in Las Vegas while on his way to the States and is
still in custody of the officers of the law.

The Grant County *Herald* of February 9, 1878, commented
on McSween's arrest on its editorial page:

Considerable interest has been manifested throughout southern
New Mexico in regard to the case of A. A. McSween, a practicing
attorney of Lincoln County, who was arrested at Las Vegas some
weeks since on a charge of embezzlement preferred by parties in
Dona Ana county. Mr. McSween was on his way to the States at the
time, and offered to furnish bonds in the sum of $20,000, condi-
tioned for his appearance before Judge Bristol within ten days, which
offer was declined by the sheriff of San Miguel county, who it appears, was under instructions to present his prisoner before the judge
of this district without unnecessary delay. This duty the sheriff discharged, and on Monday last, the preliminary hearing was held before Judge Bristol at Mesilla; as a result of which Mr. McSween
was held to answer in the sum of $8,000.

The *Herald* summarized its understanding of the McSween
difficulty:

The Las Cruces *Eco* of Jan. 24 published a communication from
Mr. McSween wherein that gentleman explains the circumstances
which led to his arrest. He states that in October 1876 he was retained under a general power of attorney by the administrators of
the Estate of Emil Fritz, deceased. That in January 1877 his account against said estate amounted to nearly four thousand dollars.
That in August 1877, acting in his capacity as attorney for the
estate, he collected in New York some seven thousand dollars, proceeds of the policy of insurance upon the life of the said Emil Fritz.
That he immediately notified the administrators of such collection,
announcing his readiness to settle with them. And that subsequently

$280 of the money was paid by order of one of the administrators. Mr. McSween further states that his journey to the east in December last was undertaken upon private business, and that he had given ample notice of his intention to leave, as well as of the length of time to which his absence would probably extend.

Upon the other hand, one of the administrators states that the power of attorney given to Mr. McSween was executed in blank, and that it was not given until about the time he started for New York; that the administrators were prevailed upon to sign the paper only after the most urgent solicitation upon his part; that McSween went to New York at his own instance and upon private business and pleasure, and then demanded that the estate should pay all his expenses; that McSween paid the custodian of the policy, Mr. Spiegelberg of New York, the sum of $700, in order to obtain possession of the same, when there was no warrant for any such charge nor any authority for paying it; that the allowance of $2,150 to Donnell, Lawson & Co. for collecting $9,300 on a life insurance policy of $10,000 bears on its face the evidence of fraud; that McSween was long since notified that at least one of the administrators had employed another attorney and no longer required his services; and that finally, notwithstanding repeated efforts, they have been unable to bring Mr. McSween to a settlement.

The *Herald* added its own appraisal of the situation:

We have been unable to ascertain what evidence was elicited upon the preliminary examination, but the fact that the accused was held on $8,000 bond would seem to indicate that the prosecution had made out a strong case. An indictment will doubtless be found at the next term of court for the county having venue, and we may reasonably anticipate that the case will be marked by continuances, changes of venue and all kinds of dilatory proceedings to the utmost limit of the law's indulgence.

Following Judge Bristol's instructions, Deputy Sheriff Barrier started from Mesilla to Lincoln with Alex. McSween as his prisoner, fully intending to deliver him to Sheriff William Brady upon arrival, but on the way to Lincoln, McSween, always a persuasive talker, induced Barrier to disobey the order of the court. Upon arriving in Lincoln, McSween was permitted to "escape" and Barrier continued on to Las Vegas without paying his respects to Sheriff Brady. The Las Vegas *Gazette* of May 4, 1878, published the sequel to the story:

Mr. Barrier, who took Mr. McSween to Lincoln County last January was arrested here yesterday for contempt of court. He promptly gave bond for his appearance at court in the third district next October and was discharged. Barrier is charged with contempt in not delivering McSween over to Sheriff Brady in accordance with the order of the court at Mesilla. Barrier claims that he found such a condition as would endanger McSween's life in delivering him and therefore retained him in his custody until assurances were given that he would not be killed.

Judge Bristol was prejudiced against McSween and lectured him upon arraignment in Mesilla, according to an affidavit signed by Deputy Barrier in Las Vegas on June 28, 1878:

At the suggestion of Judge Bristol, McSween's examination was continued to District Court on account of the absence of Juan B. Patron and Florencio Gonzales, two witnesses whom McSween wished subpoenaed. The conduct of Judge Bristol during said examination convinced me that he was very much prejudiced against McSween. After the examination was continued and the amount of the bail fixed, the Judge delivered a lecture to McSween, which was very unbecoming and in which he showed himself to be a bitter partisan. He ordered that the bond should be approved by W. L. Rynerson. On the 5th day of February, the judge delivered to me an instrument of writing by which I was required to take McSween to Lincoln and deliver him to the Sheriff of said county. On the 6th of Feb. I started to Lincoln from Mesilla with Tunstall, Wilson, Shields and McSween.

On January 18, 1878, John H. Tunstall, client, friend and confidante of Alex. McSween, apparently lacking the judgment and discretion which would have restrained him from doing so, wrote a letter from Lincoln to the editor of the Mesilla *Independent,* published on January 26, in which he insinuated that Sheriff Brady had manipulated Lincoln County tax collections for the use and benefit of Dolan and Riley. Tunstall took as the text for his letter a few words from Governor Axtell's recently delivered message to the Legislature in Santa Fe, in which the

Governor had touched on the delinquent tax situation in Lincoln County. As subsequent events demonstrated, Tunstall's act in writing the letter to the *Independent* was a tragic mistake. In submitting the letter for publication, Tunstall, to all intents and purposes, sentenced himself to death. He was a marked man from January 26 on. His letter, including the *Independent's* headlines, follows:

FROM LINCOLN COUNTY
A TAX-PAYER'S COMPLAINT

Office of John H. Tunstall,)
Lincoln, Lincoln Co., N. M.)
January 18, 1878)

"The present sheriff of Lincoln County has paid nothing during his present term of office."

Governor's Message for 1878

———

Editor of the Independent:

The above extract is a sad and unanswerable comment on the efficiency of Sheriff Brady, and cannot be charged upon "croakers." Major Brady, as the records of this County show, collected over *Twenty-five hundred dollars,* Territorial funds. Of this sum Mr. Alex. A. McSween Esq., of this place paid him over *Fifteen hundred dollars* by cheque on the First National Bank of Santa Fe, August 23, 1877. Said cheque was presented for payment by John H. Riley Esq., of the firm of J. J. Dolan & Co., this last amount was paid by the last named gentleman to Underwood and Nash for cattle. Thus passed away over *Fifteen hundred dollars* belonging to the Territory of New Mexico. With the exception of thirty-nine dollars, all the Taxes of Lincoln County for 1877 were promptly paid when due. Let not Lincoln County suffer for the delinquency of one, two or three men. By the exercise of proper vigilance the tax payer can readily ascertain what has become of that he has paid for the implied protection of the commonwealth. It is not only his privilege but his duty. A delinquent tax payer is bad; a delinquent tax collector is worse.

J. H. T.

Sheriff Brady, James J. Dolan, John H. Riley, and their supporters were angered by Tunstall's letter. They were quick to claim that McSween had prompted Tunstall to write it, and had procured its publication. On January 29, 1878, the *Independent* published a reply to Tunstall's letter, written by James J. Dolan. Charging that McSween "was one of the smallest taxpayers in Lincoln county," Dolan contended that Brady's tax accounts were in good order:

In answer to a communication in reference to taxpayers of Lincoln county published in your issue of the 26 inst. and signed J. H. T., I wish to state that everything contained therein is false. In reference to Sheriff Brady I will state that he deposited with our house Territorial funds amounting to nearly $2,000, subject to his order and payable on demand. Owing to sickness in the family of Sheriff Brady he was unable to be in Santa Fe in time to settle his account with the Territory. This I hope will explain satisfactorily how the Gov. in his message had our county (Lincoln) delinquent. If Mr. J. H. T. was recognized as a gentleman, and could be admitted into respectable circles in our community, he might be better posted in public affairs. For my part I can't see the object of Mr. J. H. T.'s letter unless it is to have the public believe that A. A. McSween is one of the largest taxpayers in our county, when in fact he is one of the smallest. Sheriff Brady is ready and willing at any time to show uneasy taxpayers what disposition he has made of the money paid by them. He can also show clear receipts from the Territorial Treasurer of his account.

Corroborating Dolan's assertion, Antonio Ortiz y Salazar, of the Territorial Treasurer's office, issued a statement, published in the Santa Fe *New Mexican* on February 9, 1878, declaring that Brady's tax accounts had been properly kept and that no money had been misappropriated.

Smarting from the public humiliation he had suffered as the result of being arrested and jailed in Las Vegas and abused, as he contended, in Judge Bristol's court in Mesilla, Alex. McSween wrote a long tattletale letter on February 11, 1878, to Secretary Schurz of the Department of the Interior. On the letterhead, below the firm's name and address, "McSween & Shields, Law Office, Lincoln County Bank Building, Lincoln,

New Mexico," there was inserted on McSween's behalf a special notice:

My correspondents are requested to address me at Roswell Post-office, N. M. as my mail is put in a special sack and left at my office, putting me in possession of it several hours before the general mail is distributed at Lincoln Post-office, thus enabling me to reply to all letters on the day on which received.

PLEASE BEAR THIS IN MIND.[1]

It was well known in Lincoln that McSween had arranged with Postmaster Ash Upson,[2] at the hamlet of Roswell, some fifty-six miles to the east, to have his mail placed in a separate sack and delivered by the mail carrier to McSween's office in Lincoln. This arrangement was not for the purpose of expediting a reply to letters, as McSween's sticker on his stationery indicated, but to prevent James Dolan, Lincoln postmaster, from learning too much about McSween's business affairs.

In his letter to Schurz, McSween complained about many things. He cited instances of alleged cheating and crookedness in connection with the performance of army contracts. He contended that traders and Indian agents conspired and connived to defraud the government. He recommended that Major F. C. Godfroy,[3] Agent for the Mescalero Apaches, be suspended from office. The McSween letter to the Secretary, related a sordid story of alleged chicanery, deception and double-dealing:

SIR: Your commendable efforts to improve the working of your department induces me to write to you in relation to the management of the Mescalero Apache Indian Agency in this county; and in doing so, I am not without the hope that you may give the subject matter immediate attention.

Before stating particulars I may mention that Maj. Godfroy, the present agent, boasts of the fact that the Commissioner of Indian Affairs sends him a copy of all letters of complaint and accusations; if he should be favored with a copy of this no possible good could result from this letter, for whenever you forewarn you forearm.

It looks as though the agent were the property of J. J. Dolan & J. H. Riley, known here as J. J. Dolan & Co. For the past two years these men have had the flour and beef contracts (as sub contractors

I think) and have delivered articles unfit for use. Sprouted half rotten wheat has been mashed and turned in as first rate flour. The flour for this agency is principally ground in a Mexican mill without a bolt or smutter—in other words, the wheat is mashed. Frequently bran has been bought and turned in as flour. Occasionally these fellows patronize a good grist mill situated within 18 miles of the agency. For example, when Gen. Vandeveer was here inspecting, the Clerk of the Agency under direction of the agent, placed a few sacks of good flour at different points. Into these the General placed his knife and was, of course, highly satisfied with the flour!

These fellows are also Indian traders. At their store they receive "surplus," by an underground railroad process. Frequently they load wagons with Indian coffee and sugar and send over here to sell—these same men have a store here.

The beef they furnish is of the poorest quality. The cattle they kill are frequently too poor to walk to the butcher pen and have to be killed on the range and carted to the issue house. They *never* kill the number reported, nor do they feed the number of Indians they report.

Indian blankets have been given or sold to citizens. It's well known that these men deal in stolen cattle and thus encourage stealing—the agent is certainly aware of this.

M. J. Bernstein, clerk, kept books for said J. J. Dolan & Co. during six months of the past year, during which period he received a salary, we believe, from the government. The Indians are continually depredating on citizens owing to the fact that the Agent fails to give them what the government has allotted to them.

I suggest that you send a detective here who will ferret this matter; he'll find things as I have stated them. Or you might suspend the Agent until an investigation was had. If this course were adopted, the Agent should know nothing of it until the temporary agent should present the papers to take charge, so that there could be no putting in order, of "fixing up," for, certainly, if the Agent gets word, the object of an investigation will have been to a great extent defeated. *A thorough search will disclose fearful villainy* on the part of all concerned.

I can furnish unimpeachable affidavits in support of the hints given herein should you require them.

Should you appoint a temporary Agent, I would recommend Robt. A. Weidemann of this place as a competent and responsible man who would discharge his duty without fear or favor. For my responsibility I refer to Soule, Thomas and Wentworth, 208 S. 4th Street, St. Louis, Mo., and Col. R. D. Hunter, Nat. Stock Yards, East St. Louis, Ill. *In confidence.*

Some nine months after McSween's letter to Secretary Schurz, Indian Agent Godfroy was removed from office. In attempting to justify his conduct at the Agency, Godfroy wrote a joint letter on November 21, 1878, to E. A. Hoyt, Commissioner of Indian Affairs, and Secretary Schurz, naming John S. Chisum, whom he described as "a noted horse and cattle thief," and McSween, whom he described as "an unprincipled petty fogging lawer," as the men responsible for much of the trouble in Lincoln County. The Godfroy letter in part:

There has been, during the past year, a great deal of murder and robbery in this county, which has greatly unsettled my Indians, and made them very hard to manage, consequently, I had to place a great deal of confidence in my employes, one of whom, I have been informed, abused my confidence. In this county there was a ring, or clique, (headed by one John S. Chisum, a noted horse and cattle thief) who at the time he was stealing horses from the Indians, put in a claim against the government for over $45,000 as shown by evidence taken by Inspector Watkins and Special Agent Angel, this ring being formed for the overthrow of all the principal officeholders in this Territory. This ring has been the cause of all the troubles in this county. My character, among the others, was attacked and my removal determined upon by the Ring, to make room for one of their favorites. My principal traducer was an unprincipled petty fogging lawyer by the name of Alex. A. McSween, who has since been killed while resisting the Sheriff of the county, also, one Rev. T. F. Ealy, who claimed to be a missionary, but judging from his actions and connection with the outlaws and murderers was everything else than what he represented himself to be.

Godfroy claimed that several attempts had been made to kill him:

This ring and their hired assassins declared that they could not only ruin my character but would take my life. The latter has been attempted several times and it is almost a miracle that I have escaped. On the 5th August last a party of these outlaws (numbering 25 to 30) rode up to the issue room and attacked us. As there were very few Indian warriors present we had all we could do to resist their attack. They succeeded in killing the agency clerk. I was afterwards informed that this attack was instigated by Mrs. McSween who (desirous of carrying out her husband's plans) had said she would not leave the county until I was killed. This of all Indian agencies is not an enviable one but as I came here determined to do my duty and use every endeavor to carry out the wishes of the government in civilizing the Indians, to that end I have used all of my energies and am happy to say that I now have under fair control what was at one time the worst tribe of Indians in the southwest. The military, anxious to find some shortcomings, have not only in many instances been discourteous, but have shown petty malice and endeavored to annoy me in every manner possible, which annoyances every unprejudiced mind will own that I have borne with patience.

Subsequent events demonstrated that Indian Agent Godfroy was mistaken about the circumstances surrounding the death of Morris J. Bernstein, the Agency clerk, who was killed on or about August 5, 1878. The Las Vegas *Gazette* of September 14, 1878, published an article which gave support to the contention that Atanacio Martinez had fired the fatal shot under circumstances which justified the killing. Sheriff Peppin contended that Bernstein had been killed as the result of an attack on the Agency by "an armed body of men headed by Scurlock, Bowdrie, French and Kid, in all twenty or more."

Peppin, as well as Godfroy, was mistaken as to the facts in the case. Agent Godfroy notified Colonel Dudley at Fort Stanton of Bernstein's death. On August 6, 1878, Dudley wrote Godfroy saying that he had sent Lieutenant Goodwin, with a detachment of fifteen men, with plenty of ammunition, and five days' rations, "for the purpose of arresting Scurlock and his party, who, it is alleged, killed your clerk, Mr. Bernstein. Lieut. Goodwin has orders to pursue these outlaws, and capture them if possible. . . . I shall either come, or send an officer tomorrow and investigate this murderous affair." The Las Vegas *Gazette* of September 21, 1878, commented on Godfroy's resignation:

James A. Broadhead, of New York, has been appointed agent for the Mescalero Apaches, in place of Major Godfroy. According to all reports, Godfroy was a pious old fraud and deserved decapitation.

The Mescalero Apache reservation, carved out of a portion of public domain in Lincoln County, was established as the result of an intolerable situation which had developed because of the government's inept handling of remnants of the Mescalero tribe. During and subsequent to the Civil War years, hundreds of Mescaleros were confined at the Bosque Redondo under the direction of Gen. James H. Carleton. The Mescaleros objected to being penned up with the Navajo captives. Singly and in groups they ran away from their Bosque Redondo guards, and returned to their former haunts in the White and Sacramento mountains. In an attempt to remedy the situation the government, on May 29, 1873, established a reservation for the Mescaleros, and compelled them to live on it. According to the Las Vegas *Gazette* of July 3, 1873, the boundaries of the reservation, as originally established, were as follows:

Commencing at the southwest corner of the Fort Stanton reduced military reservation and running thence due south to a point on the hills near the north bank of the Rio Ruidoso, thence along said hills to a point above the settlements, thence across said river to a point on the opposite hills, and thence to the same line upon which we start from Fort Stanton, and thence due south to the 33rd degree of north latitude; thence to the top of the Sacramento mountains and along the top of said mountains to the top of White mountains; thence along the top of said mountains to the head waters of the Rio Nogal, thence to a point opposite the starting point, and thence to the starting point.

The establishment of the Mescalero reservation in 1873 ended the uncertainty and speculation concerning the location of a home for the Indians, and resulted in a rush of settlers to Lincoln County. The Las Vegas *Gazette* of July 24, 1875, noted: "Eleven wagon loads of emigrants from near Fort Smith, Ark., numbering fifty men, women and children, passed through Las Vegas yesterday enroute to the Fort Stanton country."

Reflecting the tempo of the times, the Las Vegas *Gazette* of October 23, 1875, commented:

The country in the vicinity of the Mescalero reservation is filling up rapidly with white settlers. Roman, chief of the Mescalero Apaches, was recently given a silver medal in recognition of his faithful and efficient services in the interest of peace. Roman helped suppress an outbreak of Mescaleros who threatened to retaliate for depredations committed upon their stock by whites in the vicinity.

The Indian Agency at Cimarron in Colfax County, which the government had maintained for many years, was discontinued on July 18, 1878. The Utes remaining in that area were removed to the Southern Ute Agency in Colorado, and the remnants of Mescalero Apache bands which had been receiving rations at Cimarron were relocated on the Mescalero reservation in Lincoln County. (Annual Report of the Commissioner of Indian Affairs, 1878.) S. A. Russell (formerly of Des Moines, Iowa) who had been Indian Agent at Abiquiu, was transferred to the Mescalero Agency, where the facilities were anything but pretentious. Discouraged with conditions he found at the Agency, Russell wrote to Washington on August 11, 1879:

The shanty occupied by the agent and the adjoining storerooms are built of pine slabs, set on end in the ground and covered with long planks. When it begins to rain (and that is nearly every day for about two months of the year) we commence moving furniture and goods and placing vessels to catch the drippings (some time pourings,) from the roof, and for three months in the spring (when the wind is constantly blowing,) the name of the agency can be written in the dust any hour and in any part of the building.

The Mescaleros were not particularly interested in stock-raising, according to Russell:

The time may come when these Indians can be trusted with stock, and will engage in stock raising. What the result would be if supplied with stock at present may be judged from a circumstance which I will relate. They have a great many "feasts," some more important than others. One of the latter occurred some weeks ago, lasting several days and nights continuously. They insisted that I should give them a certain number of cattle and other supplies for the feast. I refused to do so. After importuning me for several days and reducing the quantity asked for from time to time, and still being refused anything more than their usual rations, they said to me that they would kill their horses and eat them. I remonstrated and finally said to them that they must not do so. They claimed their horses were their own, and they had a right to kill them, but finally said that if I would give a specified number of them their usual rations, (except beef,) a few days in advance of the regular time and consent to their trading horses for cattle they would do so, and I compromised with them on these terms.

Concerning the personal conduct of the Mescalero Indians, Agent Russell wrote:

Although they do not cheerfully yield to restraint, it is not difficult to govern these Indians when sober, but when drunk (and they are much given to drinking,) they are wild and reckless.

Victorio, a famous Apache, in a peaceful mood for the moment, joined the Mescaleros, according to Russell:

I have felt much gratified at my success in getting Victorio and his band of Warm Spring Indians to come in and locate on this reservation, and also with the action of the Indian Department in assuring them that their families, now at San Carlos, will be sent to them. I feel confident it will end the long contest between them and the Army, in which so many lives have been lost.

The Mescalero reservation, in Russell's opinion, was a poor place for the government to undertake to civilize the Indians:

This reservation is well suited to wild, roving Indians, but a more unfavorable locality for an Indian reservation could not have been found in the whole country if selected with reference to civilizing the Indians and encouraging them to become self supporting by engaging in agriculture. The reservation is a large one for the number of Indians, being 40 miles square, (perhaps larger,) and yet there is perhaps less than 600 acres of land, (exclusive of that owned by white men,) within the reservation that can be brought into cultivation. Is not this statement the strongest possible argument in favor of their removal to the Indian Territory?[4]

For a time the government attempted, without much success, to induce the Jicarilla Apaches to join their Mescalero brethren on the Mescalero reservation. On May 10, 1879, the weekly Santa Fe *New Mexican* published an item from the Cimarron *News and Press* which revealed the situation:

San Pablo, the head chief of the Jicarilla Apaches, who left here last year for the reservation near Fort Stanton, paid Cimarron a visit last Saturday and Sunday. He says that he remained on the Stanton reservation but two weeks; that the country was not what it was represented to his people and that the few who accompanied him there were dissatisfied and would prefer to depend upon their guns for subsistence rather than to draw rations at that point. He stated that his people were scattered all through the mountains west of Cimarron, and that they would go down into the buffalo country soon.

NOTES AND PROFILES

[1] The daily *New Mexican* of May 25, 1872, published one of the first references to Roswell, as a place: "Van C. Smith has named his place on the Rio Hondo, in Lincoln county, 'Roswell,' which address should be placed upon all mail matter directed to him, for if simply directed to Rio Hondo, it may be carried to any point upon the stream, and cause great delay and inconvenience."

[2] Marshall Ashmun (Ash) Upson, early-day printer and newspaperman, deserves more than a footnote to New Mexico history. Upson filed a claim against Alex. A. McSween's estate on January 15, 1879, for $68.89 for "attending private mail sack between Roswell and Lincoln from Aug. 20, 1877 to Aug. 27, 1878, at $1.50 per week, for 400 three-cent postage stamps and like items." The Santa Fe *New Mexican* of October 16, 1877, noted that "Upson has received his appointment as Postmaster at Roswell and also as notary public." Born in

Wolcott, Connecticut, on November 23, 1828, the son of Samuel Wheeler Upson and Sally Maria Stevens Upson, Ash Upson died in Uvalde, Texas, on October 6, 1894.

Upson wrote a letter to his sister, from Roswell on September 25, 1878 (made available through the courtesy of Don Lathrop, a nephew, of Long Beach, California), in which he referred to the money McSween owed him: "You must, none of you borrow trouble about me. I am in no danger, though, now the danger is over, I will tell you that for months I was surrounded with a crowd, even the family I lived in, who would have taken my life in a moment if they dared. They and many others of their class, are fugitives now. Yet, pecuniarily I am considerably loser by this fight. One man alone, banker, lawyer and merchant at Lincoln, owed me over $200. He was shot and killed in his own house. The house burned and no administrators yet appointed on his estate, and no prospects of getting my money until his estate is settled. He had collected school money forms, and owed $1.50 per week for running a private mail sack for him for over one year."

Just why Upson came to New Mexico has never been satisfactorily explained. There is reason to believe that before traveling to the West, he was a reporter on the New York *Tribune.* Although a capable printer, Upson worked for a time when he first came to New Mexico as a purser or conductor on stage coaches. Later he owned or worked on newspapers in Elizabethtown, Cimarron, Las Vegas, Albuquerque, Mesilla, and other places. The Las Vegas *Gazette* of March 3, 1877, said of him: "During the summer of 1870, Ash Upson and John Bollinger concocted a plan to start a weekly in Las Vegas. . . . Ash, as he is familiarly called by everybody in the Territory, had some experience in the publication of journals in New Mexico, having been 'boss devil and inkslinger' on the Albuquerque Semi Weekly *Review,* and other papers of Elizabethtown and Fort Stanton. . . . Ash talked William D. Dawson, of Elizabethtown into selling him a printing outfit for $900.00, but Upson never paid for the same, but moved it to Las Vegas. . . . Ash in Las Vegas kept up his old licks of 'digging everybody in the ribs' in semicomical style, but prosperity for the paper was the ruination of Ash . . . and he left Las Vegas after seven weeks."

Ash Upson achieved literary immortality in New Mexico by ghosting for Sheriff Pat Garrett "The Authentic Life of Billy the Kid, the Noted Desperado of the Southwest, Whose Deeds of Daring Have Made His Name a Terror in New Mexico, Arizona and Northern Mexico," published by the Santa Fe *New Mexican* Printing Co. in 1882. Sold at time of publication for $1.50, a copy will now sell for $250, with few copies offered for sale at any price.

Upson made statements in the book concerning the place and date of William H. Bonney's birth and boyhood years, which later writers have never been able to verify by record or documentary evidence. About the time "The Authentic Life" was to be published, the Mora *Pioneer* (reprinted in the Las Vegas

Gazette, October 22, 1881) commented: "Sheriff Pat Garrett has written a 'Life of the Kid,' which will soon be published. Every citizen should purchase at least ten copies of the work, to assist the writer. Mr. Garrett, as sheriff, took the life of a noted desperado, and the people have rewarded him. This would have satisfied some men. We can see no pressing necessity for the work he is to have printed, and can only look on it as the means of reaping a further harvest from a lucky shot. By all means let the people buy the book, and thus encourage literature and the performance of duties by public officers."

Seven years after they had published "The Authentic Life," Pat Garrett and Ash Upson abandoned literature for the real estate business. The Santa Fe *New Mexican* of July 12, 1889, noted that the two men "had entered the real estate field, under the firm name and style of Upson & Garrett."

For an extensive reference to Ash Upson's background, see two-page article written by Maurice Garland Fulton, published in the Roswell *Record* of October 7, 1937. Among other things, the article contains excerpts from a number of Upson's letters to relatives in Connecticut. Major Fulton's comment: "It is a misfortune that Ash Upson did not write more about his life in New Mexico. His knowledge of what was going on must have been unparalleled."

[3] Frederick C. Godfroy, son of James Jacques Godfroy and Victoria Godfroy, was born in Monroe, Michigan, in 1828, died at Plattsburgh, New York, on June 15, 1885, and was buried in Buffalo, according to information obtained by Robert N. Mullin from surviving members of the Godfroy family.

Frederick C. Godfroy attended a parochial school in Monroe. It was his father's ambition that Frederick study for the Roman Catholic priesthood. However, young Godfroy entered the University of Michigan at Ann Arbor and partially completed a course of studies. After leaving the University, he clerked in Charles G. Johnson's dry goods store, and in the Wing & Johnson bank in Monroe, later working for Mitchell & Waldron, bankers in Hillsdale, Michigan. In 1876 Godfroy was appointed agent for the Mescalero Indians in New Mexico. He began his duties at a time when the Indians of the Agency were disturbed over the activities of the white settlers in Lincoln County. Governor Wallace asked Godfroy's assistance in quelling the disturbances. The Governor wrote to Godfroy from Lincoln on March 12, 1879: "You can be of the greatest possible help to me in the effort now being made to catch the thieves and murderers in this part of the Territory, by allowing the military, through whom I am trying to operate, the assistance of some of your Indians, as guides to detachments—say ten men in all."

[4] Annual Report of the Commissioner of Indian Affairs, 1879.

CHAPTER FIVE

OFFICIALS CONNIVE
WITH FATAL RESULTS

FEUDING AND FIGHTING between the Dolan-Riley and McSween factions expanded in scope and intensity during the last months of 1877 and first months of 1878. The legal skirmishing in which the two factions had engaged in the Probate and District courts was preliminary to future warfare. It was well known in Lincoln that Charles Fritz and Emilie Fritz Scholand were now following the advice of James J. Dolan in all matters concerning the administration of the Emil Fritz estate. McSween was now convinced, if he had ever had any doubt, that his enemies were planning and conspiring to cripple him financially and drive him out of the country; that his arrest in Las Vegas on an embezzlement charge had been the first calculated step taken in a campaign to crush him and his friend and associate, John H. Tunstall.

On February 5, 1878, Attorney S. B. Newcomb, representing Emilie Scholand and Charles Fritz, reverting to the Emil Fritz insurance money claim, filed a suit against McSween in the District Court of Lincoln County. The plaintiffs asked judgment against McSween for ten thousand dollars, "together with such other sums of money as might be found due them," alleging that he had received for them and on their behalf various sums of money "which he had then and there faithfully promised to pay them." Notwithstanding such promise to pay, it was alleged that McSween, "disregarding his several promises and undertakings, but contrary and fraudulently intending craftily and subtly to deceive and defraud the plaintiffs in this behalf, hath not as yet paid the several sums of money to them, the said plaintiffs." The plaintiffs petitioned for a writ of attachment, based on an affidavit signed by Charles Fritz which declared:

And this affiant further says that the said Alexander A. McSween fraudulently contracted said debt, and incurred the obligation respecting which this suit is brought, and obtained said credit from the said Charles Fritz and Emilie Scholand by false pretenses; and that the said Alexander McSween is about to remove his property and effects out of this Territory; and has fraudulently concealed and disposed of his property and effects so as to defraud, hinder and delay his creditors.

Judge Bristol authorized the issuance of the writ of attachment and fixed the amount of the bond at $16,000, which was furnished and approved by the court, with Emilie Scholand and Charles Fritz as principals and James J. Dolan and W. L. Rynerson as sureties. After the writ of attachment had been issued, Dolan took it from Mesilla and delivered it to Sheriff Brady in Lincoln, according to an affidavit Dolan made for Special Investigator Angel on June 28, 1878. In the affidavit, Dolan declared that he had become angry because Tunstall had written a letter to the Mesilla *Independent,* and had attempted to provoke Tunstall into a quarrel:

I brought the attachment papers against McSween's property in the suit of Charles Fritz and Emilie Scholand from Mesilla and delivered them to Sheriff Brady. I left Mesilla on the 5th of February, 1878. At San Augustine on my way I heard McSween, Tunstall, Barrier, Shield and Wilson were there. I went to their camp next morning to see Tunstall. I heard about a letter he had written to the *Independent.* It was untruthful and as to his attempt to injure us and these facts made me very angry. I was armed. I talked to Mr. Tunstall in a very severe manner. He acted in a very childish manner. I tried in every way to see if he was a man. He made no resistance although he was armed. I did not drop my carbine on him. I threw it over my shoulder with the butt toward him.

McSween failed to answer or plead to the Fritz-Scholand attachment suit in his lifetime. On August 15, 1881, Sue E. McSween, administratrix of the estate of Alexander A. McSween, deceased, filed an answer, through Attorney Leonard, denying the allegations of the complaint and alleging that at the time of the commencement of the suit, the two plaintiffs were and "still are indebted in a large sum of money, to-wit, in the sum of ten thousand dollars for work, labor and services done and performed by the said Alexander A. McSween for the said plaintiffs and at their request and for money by the said defendant before that time lent and advanced to and paid and laid out and expended for the plaintiffs at their request and for money by the said plaintiffs before that time had and received and for the use of the plaintiffs; and for money due and owing from the said plaintiffs to said defendant upon accounts stated between them."

Notwithstanding that he had been sued in the District Court on February 5, 1878, and knowing that a writ of attachment had been placed in the hands of the sheriff for service against his property, McSween filed a supplemental pleading in the Fritz estate in the Probate Court, in which he reasserted his original contentions and defenses, and again asked the court to rule in his favor. McSween's pleading was apparently intended to be a complete defense to the accusations made against him by his opponents. Among other things, he alleged that the administrators of the Fritz estate were wasting and mismanaging the assets by commencing and maintaining a suit against him for monies collected by him and belonging to said estate; that he had offered time and again to settle the same and had always been ready and willing so to do but that the administrators had failed, neglected and refused to settle with him, and by their course were creating and making great expense for the estate to pay and thereby wasting its assets, all at the request of James J. Dolan, "who is striving to obtain possession of said money and who is not entitled thereto as petitioner believes." McSween made a further important and significant allegation:

That one of the securities on the administration bond, viz., *Jas. J. Dolan,* did on the 19th day of Jan'y, 1878, sell, assign and mortgage all of his property in the territory of New Mexico to one Thos. B. Catron; that he has not only mortgaged and assigned his own property, but fraudulently and without authority has attempted to assign all interests, both legal and equitable, which are due and owing the estate of Emil Fritz, deceased, from the late firm of L. G. Murphy & Co., and is consequently, as petitioner believes, insolvent.[1]

Charles Fritz, according to McSween, was looking after his own interests:

That the said Charles Fritz, administrator as aforesaid, in violation of his oath of office, did on the 14th day of January, 1878, order and direct the undersigned petitioner (who was and is attorney for said estate) not to commence a suit against L. G. Murphy for the money due said estate, viz: $23,376.10, as he intended to compromise same and look out for his own interests, and that he did not care for the absent heirs and did not propose to work for their benefit.

McSween asked the court to require the administrators to furnish a new bond, and to make an accounting of the affairs of the estate, or to revoke the Letters of Administration previously issued to them:

Your petitioner prays that the said administrator and administratrix be required to make, execute and deliver a new bond sufficient in amount and in proper form to secure said estate from waste and mismanagement and that your petitioner be relieved from future responsibility on account of the liability as security as aforesaid and further that the said administrator and administratrix be required to account with the said probate court during March 1878 term thereof and that unless such bond as mentioned above is executed and delivered during said term the letters heretofore granted them as such administratrix and administrator will be revoked and for such other and further relief as may be just and equitable.

The writ of attachment issued in the Scholand-Fritz suit at Mesilla on February 7, 1878, directed the Sheriff of Lincoln County, "to attach the goods and chattels, lands and tenements, moneys, effects and credits of Alexander A. McSween as will be sufficient to make $8,000, to answer the complaint of Charles Fritz and Emilie Scholand." The bond, in double the amount of the judgment prayed for, was sufficient, in theory at least, to protect McSween, the Sheriff and the Sheriff's bondsmen against any loss or damage which they might sustain as the result of a wrongful attachment. It was more or less a routine task for the Sheriff to levy the attachment against McSween's property. The Sheriff, however, had been instructed to attach Mc-Sween's interest in Tunstall & Co., whatever this interest might be, and this presented a problem. It is quite likely that Sheriff Brady had little knowledge or information concerning the extent of McSween's ownership, if any, in Tunstall & Co. How could he attach McSween's intangible interest in Tunstall & Co., without at the same time placing Tunstall's interest in jeopardy? Ordinarily, it would have been difficult for the Sheriff to make a decision on the method of procedure.

There was no necessity, however, for Brady to be apprehensive about technical matters in undertaking to serve the writ. He had District Attorney Rynerson's blessing and full official and unofficial support and advance approval in regard to all things that might be anticipated in making the service. Rynerson had a twofold interest in the proceedings; he was both district attorney of the district in which the attachment suit had been filed and a co-surety with James J. Dolan on the attachment bond. Anxious to cooperate in every way possible, as an official and as a friend, Rynerson, on February 14, 1878, wrote a rather remarkable letter to Riley and Dolan. In the letter Rynerson referred to previous communications, and gave detailed instructions for levying the attachment. According to a story told in Lincoln at the time, Dolan read Rynerson's letter hastily and then lost or mislaid it; later, it was picked up and handed to McSween. Another version was to the effect that the letter had been stolen from Dolan's coat pocket and given to McSween. In any event, the contents of the letter became public property in Lincoln at a critical time. The original letter was produced and offered in evidence at the Dudley Court of Inquiry. The letter, as written, punctuated as in the original, follows:

LAW OFFICE OF
WILLIAM L. RYNERSON

DISTRICT ATTORNEY, 3RD JUDICIAL DISTRICT, N. M.

Las Cruces, N. M. Feb'y. 14th, 1878

FRIENDS RILEY & DOLAN
    Lincoln N M

I have just received letters from you mailed 10th inst Glad to know that you (Dolan) got home OK and the business was going on OK If Mr. Weidman interfered with or resisted the Sheriff in discharge of his duty Brady did right in arresting him and any one else who does so must receive the same attention. Brady goes into the store in McS' place and takes his interest Tunstall will have same right then he had heretofore but he neither must not obstruct the Sheriff or resist him in the discharge of his duties If he tries to make trouble the Sheriff must meet the occasion *firmly* and legally. I believe Tunstall is in with the swindles with the rogue McSween. They have the money belonging to the Fritz estate and they must be made to give it up. It must be made hot for them all the hotter the better especially is this necessary now that it has been discovered that there is no hell. It may be that the villian Green "Juan Bautista" Wilson will play into their hands as Alcalde If so he should be moved around a little Shake that McSween outfit up till it shells out and squares up and then shake it out of Lincoln. I will aid to punish the scoundrels all I can Get the people with you Control Juan Patron if possible You know how to do it Have good men about to aid Brady and be assured I shall help you all I can for I believe there was never found a more scoundrely set than that outfit.

Yours &c
W. L. Rynerson[2]

Guided by the instructions and relying upon the assurance contained in Rynerson's letter, Sheriff Brady proceeded to perform his official duties. The writ of attachment came to his hand on February 9, 1878, and on that day Brady levied an attachment against all the merchandise in the Tunstall & Co. store in Lincoln, inventorying scores of items of men's and boys' wearing apparel and country-store merchandise. On February 10, Brady levied the attachment against "one house and lot occupied as a dwelling house by A. A. McSween; one building and lot used and occupied by store, bank and law office by A. A. McSween & Co., together with corral, outbuildings and appurtenances." The Sheriff also attached all the furniture and furnishings in McSween's home, including "one parlor organ, with one lot of music."[3]

Having completed the work of levying on what he conceived to be McSween's property and property interests in the town of

Lincoln, Sheriff Brady delegated to his deputy, J. B. Matthews, a Dolan-Riley employee, the duty of levying the attachment against McSween's property elsewhere in the county. On February 18, 1878, Deputy Matthews, accompanied by a posse, attached whatever interest McSween owned in Tunstall's ranch and livestock in the Rio Feliz country, some fifty miles from Lincoln. According to his return, Matthews' attachment included 110 cows, 31 yearling calves, 45 two-year old calves, 2 bulls, all branded S fresh with an X; 55 cows, 25 yearling calves, 22 two-year old cattle, all branded X and "some branded with other brands in addition," and 18 cows branded arrow slash, 3 bulls branded slash on the side, 8 head of cattle, brands not distinguished, 8 head of horses and cow ponies, one set of good harness, 2 blacksmith anvils, one crowbar and one long-handled shovel.

After Tunstall's ranch and livestock had been attached, several members of the Sheriff's posse waylaid John H. Tunstall as he was riding horseback toward Lincoln, at a place some eleven miles from there. One of these men, or more than one, shot and killed Tunstall.[4] Surrounding circumstances indicated that he had been killed in cold blood. Justice of the Peace John B. Wilson, of Precinct No. 1, Lincoln County, empaneled a coroner's jury, composed of five of the most prominent citizens of the precinct, and conducted an inquest. After having viewed Tunstall's body and heard the testimony of witnesses, the jury returned its verdict:

We, the undersigned Justice of the Peace and jury who sat upon the inquest held this 18th day of February A.D., 1878, on the body of John H. Tunstall, here found in Precinct (No. 1) number one of the County of Lincoln and Territory of New Mexico, find that the deceased came to his death on the 18th day of February, A.D. 1878, by means of divers bullets shot and sent forth out of and from deadly weapons, and upon the head and body of the said John H. Tunstall, which said deadly weapons then and there were held by one or more of the men whose names are herewith written: Jesse Evans, Frank Baker, Thomas Hill, George Hindman, J. J. Dolan, William Morton, and others not identified by witnesses that testified before the coroner's jury. We the undersigned to the best of our knowledge and belief from the evidence at the coroner's inquest believe the above statement to be a true and impartial verdict.

Geo. B. Barber
John Newcomb
Sam'l Smith
Frank Coe
Benj. Ellis

John B. Wilson
Justice of the Peace in and for Precinct No. 1,
Lincoln County, Territory of New Mexico.[5]

Robert A. Widenmann, for a time a United States deputy marshal, under Marshal John S. Sherman, Jr., made a written report on the Tunstall killing within five days after it occurred.[6] According to Widenmann, he, together with Tunstall, Richard M. Brewer, William Bonney, and John Middleton, driving a bunch of horses ahead of them, left Tunstall's ranch for Lincoln on February 18, 1878. Widenmann's statement, based in part on hearsay, because he was not an eyewitness to the Tunstall killing, is as follows:

We started from Tunstall's ranch about 8 o'clock A.M. and traveled slowly. About 5 o'clock P.M. (February 18th) while Tunstall, Brewer and I (Widenmann) were driving the horses, Middleton and Bonney were about 500 yards in the rear, a flock of wild turkies rose near the trail. Brewer and I had gone some 50 or 100 yards from the trail, when we heard a noise in our rear. Turning in our saddles we saw a body of horsemen coming over the hill at a gallop. No sooner did these men see us than they turned in our direction and commenced firing at us. There were 18 men in the party. We saw at once that we had no chance against such odds on the ground we were on and therefore made for the opposite hill which was covered with rocks and timber. On our way there we were met by Middleton and Bonney and we took our stand on the top of the hill. Middleton at once said that Tunstall had been murdered, that he had tried to induce him to come our way, but Tunstall evidently excited, did not understand him and rode up to the attacking party. It was afterward ascertained that Tunstall rode up to the party, that Morton commenced cursing him and ordered him off his horse, and when on the ground, Jesse Evans shot him through the chest, which shot felled him to the ground. Morton then jumped from his horse, drew Tunstall's pistol from its scabbard, shot Tunstall through the head, shot Tunstall's horse in the head with the same pistol, returned the pistol to its scabbard and then mashed Tunstall's skull with the butt of his (Morton's) gun. We kept our position, the murdering party, after killing Tunstall, rode partly around us and then disappeared behind another hill, not coming within range of our rifles. It was also ascertained that the sheriff's posse had, while on the Penasco, plotted to kill Tunstall, Brewer and myself. We made the best of our way to town, where we arrived about 10 o'clock P.M.

Needless to say, the killing of John Tunstall proved a sensation in Lincoln and Doña Ana counties, and caused considerable comment throughout the Territory. Three days after the killing, Lt. Daniel M. Appel, Assistant Surgeon of the United States Army, stationed at Fort Stanton, conducted a post-mortem examination of Tunstall's body. On July 1, 1878, Appel signed an affidavit as to his findings, in which he volunteered conclusions and theories as to the cause of death. Lieutenant Appel's affidavit follows:

On or about Feb. 21, 1878, I made a post-mortem examination of John H. Tunstall. I found that there were two wounds in his body, one in the shoulder passing through and fracturing the right clavicle near its centre, coming out immediately over the superior border of the right scapula passing through in its course the right sub clavicle artery. This wound would have caused his death in a few minutes and would have been likely to have thrown him from his horse. It would not have produced immediate insensibility. The other wound entered the head about one inch to the right of the medio line almost on a line with the occipital protuberance of the left orbit. There was a fracture of the skull extending around the whole circumference from the entrance to the exit of the ball and a transverse fracture across the middle portion of the base of the skull extending from the line of fracture on one side to that of the other. In my opinion the skull both on account of its being very thin and from evidence of venereal disease was likely to be extensively fractured from such a wound and the fracture in this case resulted entirely from said wound. A wound of this kind would cause instantaneous death passing as it did through the most vital portion of the brain. There were no marks of violence or bruises on the body except the two above wounds nor was the body or skull mutilated. The cap of the skull was not at all fractured. It is my opinion that both of the wounds could be made at one and the same time and if made at the same time were made by different persons from different directions and were both most likely made while Tunstall was on horseback inasmuch as the directions of the wounds were slightly upwards.

There being no powder marks on the body to indicate that the wounds were made at a short distance and the further fact that the edges of the wounds of exit were not very ragged, I am of the opinion that they were both made by rifles. Powder marks would be shown on the body if the gun or pistol was fired within about six feet of the body.

Placed on the defensive by the uproar that followed the killing of John Tunstall, Sheriff Brady wrote a letter to District Attorney Rynerson on March 4, in which he attempted to justify his actions. Originally published in the Mesilla Valley *Independent,* the letter was published in the Las Vegas *Gazette* of April 13, 1878, almost two weeks after Brady, its author, had been killed. The letter follows:

SHERIFF'S OFFICE, LINCOLN CO., N. M.
March 4, 1878

W. L. RYNERSON, ESQ.
   Dist. Atty. 3rd Judicial Dis.
     Las Cruces, N. M.
SIR:
   Deeming it my duty, I beg to submit for your information the following report of events which have transpired within the county since the receipt of attachment papers on property of A. A. McSween of this place, on the night of February 8 last. On the following day I proceeded to the store of A. A. McSween, or of J. H. Tunstall & Co. and levied the attachment in conformity with law, and, with the assistance of two others, commenced taking an inventory of the stock, etc. During the whole of this time, I was met at every step by insult, vituperation, and obstacles of every degree, and I am justified in believing that while inventorying the property in the private residence of McSween, an accident alone saved me from assassination.

On the 10th I deputized one of my assistants to proceed to the Rio Feliz distant some 50 miles from this point, where the company herd of cattle and horses were held, to attach the same. He took with him four men and on his arrival he found there one Wiedimann in charge of some 15 armed men, and some men against whom the same Wiedimann claims as Deputy U. S. Marshal to have warrants of arrest. These men he invited to partake of his hospitality while the posse were not allowed to approach the house.

After the reading of the attachment said Wiedimann informed my deputy sheriff that he could not make the attachment, and the threatening attitude of the armed men around him convinced my deputy that the destruction of himself and party would speedily follow any attempt to enforce the attachment, and he wisely returned to report. I then increased his posse to about twenty-four of the best citizens procurable and again sent him to enforce the attachment which he did, except as to the horse herd, which they attempted to run off, and while a portion of the posse were in pursuit of the party J. H. Tunstall fired on the posse and in the return fire he was shot and killed. It has been falsely averred that attached to my deputy's posse were men against whom U. S. warrants had been issued. To disprove this, I present you a letter which reached him before he attached, and in addition to my minute verbal instructions:

LINCOLN, N. M. FEB. 15TH, 1878

J. B. MATTHEWS,
   Deputy Sheriff

DEAR SIR: You must not by any means call on or allow to travel with your posse any person or persons who are known to be outlaws. Let your Mexicans round up the cattle and protect them with the balance. Be *firm* and do your duty according to law and I will be responsible for your acts.

I am sir, Respectfully yours,

WILLIAM BRADY, Sheriff, Lincoln Co.

When I had completed the inventory I placed three men in charge of the property attached. On return of Wiedimann and his party he was joined by another party of reckless men, and by stating to the military authorities that one of the men (Evans) against whom he had a warrant was closeted with the men I placed in charge, he obtained possession, arrested the men in charge on trumped up charges, and by force retook all the property I had attached, and for all I know still has possession, unless, as I incidentally learn, the Probate Judge has placed in charge of the store a Mr. Ellis as administrator of the estate of the late J. H. Tunstall. Anarchy is the only word which would truthfully describe the situation here for the past month, and the quiet and order now prevailing I fear very much that this condition of things will not last.

I regret to say that our Justice of the Peace J. B. Wilson became a willing instrument in the hands of the leaders of the mob, and at their instance and without a shadow of justice issued warrants of search and arrest indiscriminately against my posse, and all who in any manner countenanced us against the mob. I was myself arrested by his warrant and on examination before him was held in two hundred dollars bond. Private houses were entered under cover of these search warrants, and the inhabitants robbed and insulted by his so called constables. I trust that the law will not be found powerless to punish such violation of it in his person.

I await further instructions as to obtaining repossession of the property I attached.

Very Respy, Yr. Obt. Servt.

WM. BRADY

Sheriff, Lincoln Co.

W. G. Koogler, editor of the Las Vegas *Gazette,* was not willing, under the indicated circumstances, to accept Sheriff Brady's explanation as adequate. In an editorial note, Koogler said:

The foregoing letter from Major William Brady, Sheriff of Lincoln County to Col. W. L. Rynerson, District Attorney, has been handed us for publication. We regard Sheriff Brady as an honest, well meaning man, who has been most shamefully abused by men in whom he had reposed confidence, and who are now trying to sacrifice him in order to cover their own iniquities. Having said this much we will, perhaps, not be misconstrued when we call attention to that portion of the Sheriff's letter in which he speaks of having written to his deputy (Matthews), directing him not to call on, or allow to travel with his posse, any person or persons known to be outlaws. Why did Sheriff Brady find it necessary to instruct his deputy not to select "known outlaws," as a posse? Why did he permit a man to act as his deputy to whom it was necessary to send such instructions? And how does it come that notwithstanding the sheriff's written order, we find these "known outlaws" not only traveling and acting with the posse, but brutally murdering Tunstall under cover of the deputy sheriff's authority! These are matters which must be cleared up.

There was reason to believe that both Brady and Matthews were quite familiar with the character and reputation of the men Matthews had chosen to help in levying the attachment against Tunstall's property. On November 24, 1877, more than two months before the Tunstall killing, the Las Vegas *Gazette* told of the imprisonment by Brady of Baker, Evans and other desperadoes in Lincoln:

The prisoners, Evans, Baker, Hill and Davis, now in jail in Lincoln, charged with many deeds of outlawry, stealing horses, cattle, etc., were heavily ironed on the 4th inst. by Sheriff Brady. Their place of imprisonment is literally a hole in the ground, where candles are constantly burning to enable the prisoners to recognize each other. Rumors are rife of proposed attempts to release them by force, and the town is constantly in a state of excitement. There is no doubt that a large band of desperadoes are in the mountains, armed friends of the self confessed culprits, but what their designs are is a matter of speculation. Some say that they anticipated that the authorities would take the prisoners to Mesilla for trial and proposed a ransom on the road. Others again assert that they intend to make a bold attack upon the Lincoln jail to effect that purpose. Their force is variously estimated at 20 to 60 men. Whatever their numbers or design, they will meet with determined resistance, as Major Brady will do his duty as he has heretofore done, faithfully and well, in the case of these dangerous characters.

N. B. Since setting up the foregoing in type, Evans, Baker, Hill, and Davis and others held for horse stealing, were rescued by an armed force of 32 men. The doors of the jail were not even found locked.

In a long letter to his parents in London, written from Lincoln on November 29, 1877, less than ninety days before his death, John H. Tunstall had told in detail the incidents leading up to the capture of Evans, Baker, Hill and Davis, referred to in the Las Vegas *Gazette* article of November 24. While Tunstall was on a trip to St. Louis, thieves had stolen two of his best horses, and "a pair of magnificent mules" from his ranch, and had also stolen several of Dick Brewer's horses. Tunstall told his parents in his letter that Brewer and two men took up the trail and overtook the thieves, who agreed to surrender Brewer's horses, but wanted to keep Tunstall's animals as pay for their trouble. This being refused, Brewer went to Las Cruces, where he failed in his attempts to interest the authorities in going after the criminals. Upon returning to Lincoln, Brewer was commissioned a deputy sheriff. Organizing a posse of fifteen men, Brewer started after the thieves, following them for two days and two nights. Finally the posse, "in the grey dawn," to quote Tunstall, surrounded a house in which the thieves were hiding. An extract from Tunstall's letter:

It was a strong place called in this country a *choza,* (that is a house built over a hole in the ground in such a way that when you are inside, there is as much of the house under, as over the ground.) A good many shots were fired. Jesse Evans said he couldnt tell how he failed to hit Dick Brewer as he had three fair, square shots at him and he was saving his shots for him alone. The bullets struck within 4 or 5 inches of him each time. Jesse Evans seemed as cool as if he was not interested; the end of it was that some men in Dick Brewer's party who know those fellows well, told them they meant taking them, dead or alive and they surrendered.

When the men came out of the *choza* with their hands up, Brewer arrested "Jesse Evans, the captain of the desperadoes, Frank Baker, his lieutenant, Tom Hill, who is the hardest nut in all the gang, and a young Texan named Davis." Tunstall met the Brewer posse and the prisoners enroute to Lincoln. Possemen and prisoners alike exchanged greetings with Tunstall. Davis quipped: "By jove, Dick Brewer doesnt know if he has got us, or we have got him." Tom Hill then said to Tunstall: "Well, have you got any whiskey, Englishman?" "Merely a dram," replied Tunstall. "If you knew me you would know that I dont need any to keep my blood warm, but if you met me in Lincoln I would soak you if you wished."

Hill said: "Well, we'll be in the jug by then. You get back and you can soak us there if you like."

Dick Brewer made a prediction to Tunstall: "They will get out of gaol as sure as fate. They have more friends in the country than enemies & you mark me, those chaps will get let out. Brady (the Sheriff) will let them go for sure." Tunstall visited Evans, Baker, Hill and Davis in the Lincoln jail:

I went to see the boys one Sunday and chatted with them for awhile; I got them pretty mad over a few things I told them that were too true to be palatable, but I never was notorious for "rubbing the right way," & the people here know that I usually say about what I think and take the chances on how it suits the audience. They asked me if I remembered promising them some whiskey. I said, "Yes," and they chaffed me about my two mules, told me they were sold to a priest down in Old Mexico. They saw that I could joke as well as they could & we laughed a good deal. Some time after that I sent them a bottle of whiskey.

In the same letter, Tunstall told his parents that "Dick Brewer was as brave as a lion," and how pleased he had been to shake "Brewer's great paw," upon meeting him again after an absence of several weeks.

Shortly after Tunstall's death, Sheriff Brady wrote a letter to United States District Attorney T. B. Catron, giving him the details of the killing. The letter was almost identical to one Brady had written to District Attorney Rynerson on the same subject. Catron referred the letter to Governor Axtell, with the suggestion that he notify the President of the United States of the condition of affairs in Lincoln County, and ask him to use his good offices in having federal troops ordered to the scene of the trouble, to assist Territorial officers in serving legal process and maintaining the public peace. Acting upon Catron's recommendation, Axtell telegraphed a summary of Brady's letter to Washington, and left for Lincoln, his first trip to that section of the Territory since becoming governor.

It was apparent from Axtell's actions and associations during his sojourn in Lincoln and Fort Stanton that he was prejudiced against the McSween crowd; and that, if opportunity offered, the weight of his official influence would be given to the Dolan-

Riley faction. The Governor made a brief call at McSween's house, but his hostility to McSween was manifest. It was common gossip in Lincoln at the time that Axtell was under obligation to the Dolan-Riley crowd because he had borrowed money from John H. Riley. Many months later, Special Investigator Angel was to comment on this subject:

The facts are that in 1876 Gov. Axtell borrowed of Mr. Riley $1800, which sum was probably repaid in November, 1877. I do not believe, however, that Gov. Axtell received the money to directly influence his action. It was some time before the troubles actually commenced in Lincoln County. However, they were brewing at the time. The only influence this transaction could have on the action of Gov. Axtell was that as Riley had befriended him, to return the compliment, and certainly his official action lays him open to serious suspicion that his friendship for Murphy, Dolan and Riley was stronger than his duty to the people and the government he represented.

Some months after his visit to Lincoln, Governor Axtell gave his version of the background of events at Special Investigator Angel's request:

When I arrived at Fort Stanton, on the fourth day after leaving Santa Fe, I was informed by Col. Purington, commanding the post, that my request for help had been granted, and that he had orders to assist the civil authorities. He also informed me that there appeared to be a dispute as to who were civil officers. The Sheriff of the County had certain writs issued out of the District Court. A Deputy Sheriff of San Miguel County had McSween in charge and declined to deliver him to Brady. Wilson, Justice of the Peace, had issued warrants against the Sheriff and his deputies, and a deputy U. S. Marshal for Lincoln County claimed the right to direct the movement of the troops. Under these circumstances, Col. Purington asked my advice as to whom he should render assistance. I told him that Wiedderman's appointment as Deputy Marshal had been revoked; that Wilson had been appointed Justice of the Peace by the County Commissioners, and that the appointment was good for nothing—that a Justice of the Peace must be elected, could not be appointed, that it was so established by our Territorial Constitution, the Organic Act. Col. Purington went with me to Wiederman's office

and saw him, and he admitted that his appointment had been revoked. We also went to the office of Wilson, Justice of the Peace, and
informed him what was the law in his case. He said he would not act
as Judge any more, and bundled up his papers and retreated in good
order into his bar room. I did not remove him from office—he was
not in office. Col. Purington asked me to put these facts in writing
for the information of the people. I did so. This is my proclamation
of March 9, 1878. If it makes anybody an outlaw the fault is in the
facts not in me.

There was room for doubt and argument about the sound-
ness of Axtell's contention that Justice of the Peace Wilson "was
not in office," at the time of the Governor's visit to Lincoln.
Actually a regular meeting of the Board of County Commissioners of Lincoln County was held on February 14, 1877, at
which the following action was taken:

James H. Farmer, Justice of the Peace of Precinct No. 1, of this
County and Territory, having resigned, giving as reasons for so
doing the distance of his residence to the seat of the precinct, and
occupations that incapacitate him to faithfully discharge his duties
as Judge, his resignation was accepted, and John B. Wilson was appointed in his place, and the Clerk is authorized to issue his commission to that effect to said John B. Wilson.

The charge made at the time that Axtell acted arbitrarily
and illegally in declaring Wilson's appointment "illegal and
void" was strengthened by the fact that Axtell as governor had
placed his signature to a bill passed by the Territorial Legislature on January 13, 1876; which provided:

In the event that any vacancy exists now in any county office, or
that hereafter may occur in any county, precinct or demarcation in
any county by reason of death, resignation or removal or of any
other manner, the county commissioners of said county shall have the
power to fill such vacancy by appointment until an election be held
as provided by law.

Governor Axtell's proclamation of March 9 declared that

only Judge Bristol and Sheriff Brady had the right to enforce law in Lincoln County. The text of the proclamation follows:

PROCLAMATION

TO THE CITIZENS OF LINCOLN COUNTY.

The disturbed conditions of affairs at the county seat brings me to Lincoln County at this time. My only object is to assist good citizens uphold the laws and to keep the peace. To enable all to act intelligently it is important that the following facts should be clearly understood.

1ST.

John B. Wilson's appointment by the County Commissioners as a Justice of the Peace was illegal and void and all processes issued by him were void and said Wilson has no authority whatever to act as Justice of the Peace.

2ND.

The appointment of Robert Widenmann as U. S. Marshal has been revoked. And said Weidenmann is not now a peace officer nor has he any power or authority whatever to act as such.

3RD.

The President of the United States upon application by me as Governor of New Mexico has directed the Post Commander Col. George A. Purington to assist Territory civil Officers in maintaining order and enforcing legal process. It follows from the above statements that there is no legal process in this case to be enforced, except the writs and processes issued out of the Third Judicial District Court by Judge Bristol and there are no Territorial civil officers here to enforce these except Sheriff Brady and his deputies.

Now, therefore, in consideration of the premises, I do hereby command all persons to immediately disarm and return to their homes and usual occupations under penalty of being arrested and confined in jail as disturbers of the public peace.

Up to the time of the proclamation of March 9, 1878, no one had been killed except Tunstall, according to Axtell's statement to Angel:

Up to March 9, 1878, no man had been killed except Tunstall.

I conversed with all the citizens of Lincoln County I could meet. I advised them to seek peace and pursue it, to be in earnest to uphold the law. I told them I would use my best exertions to have every man who was present when Tunstall was killed, and who took any part whatever against him, indicted and tried, and as they claimed to justify as officers resisted in the discharge of duty, they must make this claim good on their trial and in open court. I told them Judge Bristol would be with them in about three weeks, and would organize a grand jury, and investigate all the facts. There were four men said to have been in the Sheriff's party spoken of by what is called the McSween party, as outlaws, said to be very bad men. It was feared by the McSween men that Sheriff Brady would not be active in their arrest. I talked to Col. Purington about this, and I told him I would give him a request in writing to arrest these four men and to keep them in his guard house till the court should sit. We did not think best to inform any one of this for fear it might thwart our purpose.

Axtell's statement to Inspector Angel conflicted sharply with statements contained in an affidavit made on June 11, 1878, some ninety days after Axtell's visit to Lincoln, by D. P. Shields, brother-in-law and law partner of McSween. In his affidavit, sworn to before Probate Clerk J. Felipe Baca, of San Miguel County, Shields told of the happenings on the occasion of Axtell's appearance:

On the 9th day of March 1878, Gov. S. B. Axtell, together with George H. Purington, Captain of the 9th Cavalry, Commanding at Fort Stanton, called at the house of A. A. McSween in Lincoln. Robert A. Wideman, Deputy U. S. Marshal, Rev. T. F. Ealy and myself were present. The Governor informed us what he proposed to do in regard to the situation. Some one present requested that he should ascertain the true situation of affairs from the citizens. The Governor's reply was: "God deliver me from such citizens as you have here in Lincoln." To which Mr. Wideman replied: "The citizens are right, but God deliver me from such executive officers." Governor Axtell said he had all the information he wanted and that he would act upon it. On the following day in company with Mr. Isaac Ellis, a merchant of Lincoln, I called upon Gov. Axtell at Fort Stanton. His attention was called to the situation of affairs in Lincoln County; he was informed of the character of the men constituting the Sheriff's posse, and told that those men were charged with having murdered Mr. Tunstall; that the people desired these men should be ousted and the charges against them investigated. He said Mr. Wilson was not a legal justice of the peace and that he could not act. The Governor was informed that there were other justices in the county and the investigation could be had. His reply was no, the same could be left until the District Court. He was informed that the citizens would be in danger of being murdered as Tunstall had been while such men were acting as the Sheriff's posse. His attention was called to the celebrated letter written by William L. Rynerson, District Attorney, to Riley & Dolan. The Governor remarked that Mr. Rynerson could stand upon that letter. He was reminded also of the conduct of Rynerson in refusing to approve the bond offered by McSween, to which he replied that McSween was a fugitive from justice.

Montague R. Leverson,[7] in Lincoln County to further a land colonization scheme, wrote to President Hayes, on March 16, 1878, urging him to suspend Axtell, appoint a governor pro tem, and to suspend the District Judge and the District Attorney of the Third Judicial District, "by whom the District Judge is used as a tool." Leverson's letter:

I have come here to select, in this garden of New Mexico, a suitable location for a colony from Old and New England. Whether such colony will be formed will depend on the restoration of peace, and life and property being made secure in this distressed country; the insecurity of life and property and the disturbed condition of affairs being caused by United States officials. I have made a careful inquiry from both sides into the base and brutal murder of Mr. Tunstall and I solemnly assure you that a real investigation will prove conclusively that the murder was plotted and contrived by the District Attorney of the third judicial district, by whom the District Judge is used as a tool. I deeply regret to add that Governor Axtell has illegally and despotically exerted his power to screen the murderer. I think it probable that the conduct of the Governor has been influenced more by weakness and want of intelligence than intentional criminality. . . . The assassins of Mr. Tunstall assert that he was killed while in the act of resisting the Sheriff's posse. The statement is wholly false. . . . He was murdered by a shot from his own pistol, none of whose chambers had ever been fired off, after he had given it up without being asked to do so; his skull was then broken in, and his murderers were men who had escaped jail, but had been joined to the Sheriff's posse for the express purpose of murder. Mr. Tunstall was a British subject.

Richard M. Brewer, chosen by destiny to play a leading part in the Lincoln County War, was greatly affected by John Tunstall's death. A Vermonter by birth, Brewer was reared from childhood to manhood in Wisconsin. The girl he loved in Wisconsin married the other man, and Brewer left home at the age of twenty-five years, hoping to heal the hurt of lost love, and anxious to hide himself in the most isolated spot he could find. He found the place in a small ranching property on Los Feliz River in Lincoln County, New Mexico.

Here, divorced from most things pertaining to the outside world, he worked hard, generally from daybreak until after sundown. He was slow to place confidence in people or to form close friendships. He asked nothing more than to be let alone, and allowed to overcome obstacles in his own way. Gradually, Brewer took his rightful place in the scheme of things in a new country, in which the nearest neighbors lived miles away. A big man, with great arms and huge, strong hands, Brewer was a capable man on a ranch. He loved the land and knew how to handle livestock. He was intelligent, fearless and able to hold his own in any ordinary encounter.

In 1876, John H. Tunstall, on Alex. A. McSween's recommendation, bought a ranch not far from Brewer's property. Brewer and Tunstall became acquaintances, and then close friends, primarily because of a common interest in horses and horse-breeding. On occasions when Tunstall was absent from his ranch, he employed Dick Brewer to look after the place for him.

Dick Brewer had watched at fairly close range the unfolding of events immediately preceding the killing on February 18, 1878, of Tunstall, his friend and neighbor. He had been sufficiently close to the maneuvering to permit him to recognize the participants, most of whom fled and scattered to the four winds soon after the killing. In fixing responsibility for Tunstall's death, the coroner's jury had named Jesse Evans, Thomas Hill,

Frank Baker and William Morton, among others, as the murderers. Of the four named, Evans and Hill were believed to have formerly lived in Texas. Baker was reported to have been a former resident of Syracuse, New York, and Morton was from Virginia.

Sheriff Brady "sat out the dance," according to Brewer, and did nothing to arrest the men suspected of killing Tunstall. The reason for Brady's inactivity was apparent. Tunstall had been killed by members of a posse acting under his authority in attaching Tunstall's property. As day after day went by, and officers failed to make any move toward arresting Tunstall's murderers, Brewer became more and more impatient and dissatisfied. He was particularly anxious to learn the whereabouts of Tom Hill. One eyewitness to the killing had reported that Hill was the man who had fired the shots that caused Tunstall's death. With the "law" sitting idly by, Brewer decided that he would go after the killers, with others, if others were willing to go, or alone, if necessary.

On March 4, more than two weeks after Tunstall's death, Brewer received word that if he would ride down the Pecos River toward Chisum's South Spring Ranch, he might expect to run into some of the men he was looking for. Deputized as a constable, with warrants in his hands issued by Justice of the Peace John B. Wilson and accompanied by a posse of several men, Brewer left Lincoln for the Pecos. Near San Patricio, he picked up William Bonney, who had been at the Tunstall ranch shortly before Tunstall was killed.

The Las Vegas *Gazette* of March 16, 1878, published a story from Roswell dated March 9, 1878, which told of the arrest of Frank Baker and William S. Morton. Signed "Pecos," a nom de plume used on a number of occasions by John S. Chisum, the *Gazette* story was as follows:

A party of men headed by Richard Brewer, who was armed with warrants and duly deputized, arrested two of the party charged with the killing of J. H. Tunstall early this week, on the Pecos, nearly opposite the crossing of the Penasco. Their names are Frank Baker, and Wm. S. Morton. They were brought to Chisum's ranch, South Spring River, where they remained on Thursday night and started to Lincoln on Friday morning. This capture was not made until after a chase of more than six miles, in the bottom of the banks of the Pecos. No one was hurt and but few shots were fired.

Brewer's posse was in a quandary as to what to do with Baker and Morton. Should they be taken back to Lincoln and handed over to Sheriff Brady? If that was done, would Brady turn them loose, with or without bond, so that they would once again be free to fight their enemies to the death?

Frank Baker and William Morton were now, to all purposes and intent, prisoners of war. They had good reason to believe that they might not live to see Lincoln Plaza again. Morton was apparently a foresighted man, and a courageous one. On the supposition that his life might be taken, Morton wanted the outside world to know his side of the story. As a result, he wrote a letter from Chisum's South Spring Ranch, on March 8, to his cousin, H. H. Marshall, of Richmond, Virginia, which he handed to Postmaster Ash Upson upon the arrival of the posse in Roswell on March 9. Morton requested Upson to mail the letter if he heard "bad news" within the next few days, otherwise to destroy it. Morton was entirely justified in being apprehensive.

On either March 9 or 10, Frank Baker and William Morton were shot and killed by one or more members of the Brewer posse, near Steel Springs, some twenty-five miles from Roswell and eight miles from the mouth of Bluewater Canyon. William McCloskey, presumably a loyal member of Brewer's posse, but under suspicion of secretly being a friend of Morton, was shot and killed at the same time. District Attorney Rynerson, Sheriff Brady, and other public officials, described the killing of Baker, Morton and McCloskey as first-degree murders.

When Postmaster Upson learned of the killings, he mailed Morton's letter, and in due course it reached its destination in Virginia. In calm, matter-of-fact style, Morton had named the men in Brewer's posse, and recited the facts, from his viewpoint, of the events culminating in the Tunstall killing. The Morton letter:

Some time since I was called upon to assist in serving a writ of attachment on some property wherein resistance had been made against the law. The parties had started off with some horses which should be attached, and I as deputy sheriff with a posse of twelve men was sent in pursuit of same. We overtook them, and while attempting to serve the writ our party was fired on by one J. H. Tunstall, the balance of the party having ran off. The fire was returned and Tunstall was killed. This happened on the 18th of February. The 6th of March I was arrested by a constable's party, accused of the murder of Tunstall. Nearly all of the sheriff's party fired at him, and it is impossible for any one to say who killed him. When the party which came to arrest me, and one man who was with me, first saw us about one hundred yards distant, we started in another direction when they (eleven in number) fired nearly one hundred shots at us. We ran about five miles, when both of our horses fell and we made a stand. When they came up they told us if we would give up, they would not harm us.

After talking awhile, we gave up our arms and were made prisoners. There was one man in the party who wanted to kill me after I had surrendered, and was restrained with the greatest difficulty by others of the party. The constable himself said he was sorry we gave up as he had not wished to take us alive. We arrived here last night enroute to Lincoln. I have heard that we were not to be taken alive to that place. I am not at all afraid of their killing me, but if they should do so, I wish that the matter should be investigated and the parties dealt with according to law. If you do not hear from me in four days after receipt of this, I would like you to make inquiries about the affair.

The names of the parties who have me arrested are: R. M. Brewer, J. G. Scurlock, Chas. Bowdre, Wm. Bonney, Henry Brown, Frank McNab, "Wayt" Sam Smith, Jim French (and two others named McClosky and Middleton who are friends). There are two parties in arms and violence is expected. The military are at the scene of disorder and trying to keep peace. I will arrive at Lincoln the night of the 10th and will write you immediately if I get through safe. Have been in the employ of Jas. J. Dolan & Co., of Lincoln for eighteen months since the 9th of March '77 and have been getting $60.00 per month. Have about six hundred dollars due me from them and some horses, etc., at their cattle camps. I hope if it becomes necessary that you will look into this affair, if anything should happen, I refer you to T. B. Catron, U. S. Attorney of Santa Fe, N. M. and Col. Rynerson, District Attorney, La Mesilla, N. M. They both

know all about the affair as the writ of attachment was issued by
Judge Warren Bristol, La Mesilla, N. M. and everything was legal.
If I am taken safely to Lincoln, I will have no trouble, but will let
you know.

If it should be as I suspect, please communicate with my brother,
Quin Morton, Lewisburg, W. Va. Hoping that you will attend to
this affair if it becomes necessary and excuse me for troubling you
if it does not.

With Frank Baker and William Morton dead and accounted
for, the Brewer posse began to consider ways and means of proceeding against Jesse Evans and Tom Hill. The Mesilla *Independent* of January 26, 1878, reported that Hill, Evans and
other outlaws had stolen a bunch of horses in the lower
Mimbres country, in Grant County; that the thieves had been
overtaken and the stock recovered; that in the fight that followed, Hill had been killed, or seriously wounded, and Evans
had been shot in the groin. Susequent events proved that neither
Hill nor Evans had sustained serious injury. If they had been
injured, they were well enough, and strong enough, to ride with
the Matthews posse on February 18, 1878, and from reliable accounts, mean enough to play leading roles in the Tunstall killing on that day.

On or about March 1, 1878, less than two weeks after the
Tunstall killing, Tom Hill (known in Texas, according to William H. Bonney, as Tom Chelson) was shot and killed while
attempting to rob a sheep camp near Alamo Springs, Doña Ana
County. The *Independent* of March 23 told the story of Hill's
death:

Mr. Wagner, a sheep driver, had made a camp near Alamo
Springs. He left the camp to water his sheep, leaving an employee,
a half breed Cherokee in charge. During Wagner's absence, Jesse
Evans and Tom Hill entered the camp for the purpose of robbery.
They drew their pistols on the Cherokee and told him they wanted
some money that was contained in a trunk in the wagon. They told
him to keep quiet, and proceeded to saddle a horse and pack mule
belonging to Wagner. They then broke open the trunks that were in
the wagon and commenced scattering the contents. The Cherokee
picked up a Winchester rifle standing near and objected to this.

When the two robbers opened fire on him, he dodged and ran. They shot after him until he fell, shot in the leg, some distance from the wagon. The robbers evidently believing they had finished him, proceeded with their work. While they were rummaging the wagon, the Cherokee crawled up to within a short distance of the robbers, unobserved and opened fire on them. He first shot and killed Hill. Then he went for Evans, who having received a wound in his wrist, dropped his rifle and pistol, sprang on Wagner's horse and decamped. Hill is dead and buried. There is no mistake about it this time.

Although he was a prisoner in the county jail in Mesilla in midsummer 1878, charged with the attempted robbery of Wagner's sheep camp and under indictment for the Tunstall murder, Evans had no particular reason to be worried or apprehensive over his prospects in life. James J. Dolan, influential in official affairs, was his friend and protector; and District Attorney Rynerson was anything but hostile toward him. Restless because of his confinement in jail, Evans filed a petition, through his attorneys, S. B. Newcomb and W. T. Jones, asking a writ of habeas corpus in the District Court of Doña Ana County, alleging that he was being unlawfully detained as a suspect in the Tunstall case. District Attorney Rynerson represented the Territory at the hearing before Judge Bristol on July 2, 1878. According to the Mesilla *News* of July 6, 1878, Robert A. Widenmann was the Territory's principal witness. He testified that he, Tunstall, Dick Brewer, John Middleton, and William Bonney, driving a bunch of horses, were on their way from Tunstall's ranch to Lincoln, between 5 and 6 o'clock P.M. on February 18, 1878:

We saw a large party coming after us, fifteen to twenty strong. We started to run to get out of their way. When within 300 yards of us they fired at us. I looked back and recognized Jesse Evans, Frank Baker, J. J. Dolan, Tom Hill, Geo. Hindman, A. L. Roberts and Billy Morton. I ran into a ravine to the left of the mountain. Tunstall ran into a ravine to the right of the mountain. The party followed Tunstall. I had run some distance when I heard shots, on the other side of the mountain.

Judge Bristol questioned Widenmann sharply:

Mr. Widenmann: You say you were running horseback, dust fly-
ing, balls whistling around, yet you could casually look back, see a
large party of 15 or 20 coming at full speed 300 yards behind; that
you recognized Mr. Dolan in the party, when everybody knows that
a number of reliable witnesses swear positively that Mr. Dolan was
25 miles from there at the time. Mr. Widenmann, your testimony in
this matter will be taken with a good deal of allowance.

Widenmann could not testify that he had seen Tunstall shot,
and could not name the man or men who had shot him; and was
forced on cross-examination to admit that he had not seen Tunstall's body after the shooting. Called to testify in his own behalf, Evans established an alibi for James J. Dolan, and denied
any first-hand knowledge of the crime. Evans declared under
oath that he had seen Dolan on the morning of February 18,
1878, at a place twenty miles from the place where Tunstall's
body had been found; that he, Evans, had not seen Tunstall on
the day he was killed; that he had had nothing whatever to do
with the shooting; that he and Frank Baker rode together; that
they were not with the Sheriff's posse on the day of the killing.
District Attorney Rynerson recommended to the court that
Evans be allowed to furnish bond for his future appearance.
Thereupon Judge Bristol fixed the bond at $5,000, and ordered
E. H. Wakefield, a special deputy, to take Evans to Lincoln.[8]
    The Santa Fe *New Mexican* did not esteem Robert A. Wid-
enmann's reputation for truth and veracity. The Grant County
Herald of August 8, 1878, published an editorial which had
recently appeared in the *New Mexican:*

Our attention has been called to the testimony of R. A. Weideman
given before Judge Warren Bristol in the habeas corpus case of Jesse
Evans as detailed in a late number of the Mesilla *News.* We are
neither surprised nor disappointed, as we have long since pronounced
him an unmitigated liar and scoundrel. He is also a cowardly murderer. His conduct in Lincoln County shows him to be in every way
a villain; and how with all the crimes surrounding him, he has been
permitted to escape to Silver City, is more than we can understand.
It looks to us as though it was putting a premium on crime. Since this
man Weideman made his advent amongst us he has made it his business to earn for himself the character of a first class liar and fraud,

and concluded his successful efforts with perjury in the testimony referred to. We warn the good people of Grant County that he is a
dangerous man, and they cannot be too well guarded against his cheek
and plausibility. He "done" many persons in Santa Fe by mythical
remittances from Europe, which of course, never arrived. To be fore-
warned is to be forearmed.

NOTES AND PROFILES

[1] On January 12, 1878, James J. Dolan and John H. Riley executed a
mortgage deed conveying to Thomas B. Catron forty acres of land in Lincoln,
"upon which the dwelling house and store of said Dolan & Riley is situated,"
together with their personal property. (See Book B of Contracts, page 116,
et seq.)

On June 10, 1878, John H. Riley and James J. Dolan executed what was
known at the time as a "shirttail mortgage," by which they conveyed to the
Second National Bank of New Mexico, at Santa Fe, all their real and personal
property in Lincoln County, including dwelling house, store building, storerooms, stock of goods, hardware, groceries, shoes, hats, caps and general merchandise of every description, "including all the book accounts of L. G. Murphy
and E. Fritz, of James J. Dolan and John H. Riley, and all the notes belonging
to said firms, or either of them, and all the grain and hay which the said John
H. Riley and James J. Dolan may have on hand at their place of business or at
other places in the Territory of New Mexico; also fifteen hundred head of
cattle classed yearlings, two year olds, three year olds, and cows all branded
←——⟨, and marked with an under slope on both ears; thirty-five head of
horses branded with the letters J. J., the last J. marked on the left shoulder;
twelve head of mules branded the same as the horses, all of which stock is ranging
on the Rio Pecos near Black River, except those in use by said Dolan and
Riley." The mortgage deed was given to secure a debt of $16,000, "advanced
by the bank to Dolan and Riley on their notes of hand." The mortgage deed
was recorded in Lincoln County on June 21, 1878.

[2] William L. Rynerson, a principal actor in the Lincoln County War, was
born in Mercer County, Kentucky, February 22, 1828; died in Las Cruces,
New Mexico, July 4, 1893. A student for a time at Franklin College, Indiana,
Rynerson went to California in 1852 in search of gold. He enlisted in Company
C, First Regiment of California Infantry, in Amador County, California, on
August 18, 1861, and marched to New Mexico with Carleton's California

Column in 1862. Rynerson was mustered out of the military service in Mesilla on November 3, 1866, with the rank of brevet lieutenant colonel.

Elected to the New Mexico Legislature in 1867, as a representative from Doña Ana County, Rynerson introduced a resolution censuring John P. Slough, chief justice of the Territory. Slough resented the insinuations contained in the resolution, and had made some remarks about Rynerson. The two men met in the billiard room of La Fonda (the old Exchange Hotel) in Santa Fe on Sunday, December 17, 1867. In a matter of a few seconds, Rynerson shot and killed the Chief Justice.

At the preliminary hearing Rynerson was defended by famed Kirby Benedict, one-time judge of the New Mexico Supreme Court, and by Stephen B. Elkins, law partner of Thomas B. Catron. (Elkins in later years married a daughter of Henry Gassaway Davis, of West Virginia; became Secretary of War in Benjamin Harrison's cabinet; served in the United States Senate from West Virginia from 1895 to 1913.) Rynerson's lawyers pleaded the tried-and-true self-defense, and he was acquitted. The preliminary hearing, held to determine whether or not Rynerson should be bound over to the grand jury, lasted several days. Judge Joab Houghton sat as a committing magistrate. R. M. Stevens, an eyewitness, testified that he heard angry words as the two men approached each other, and that Rynerson had said to Slough: "I want you to take it back." Slough said: "What did I say?" Rynerson answered: "You called me a s-n of a b--ch and a thief." Judge Slough said: "I dont take it back," or "I wont take it back." Rynerson then drew his Colt pistol, according to Stevens, and said: "If you dont take it back, I'll shoot you." Slough said: "I dont propose to take anything back." The shooting followed. (Santa Fe *Gazette*, January 3, 1868.) The Chief Justice, mortally wounded, died in a short time.

Friends of the two men claimed that Rynerson had been induced to introduce the resolution in the Legislature by one of Slough's political enemies. It also developed that Rynerson and Slough were only casual acquaintances. Rynerson's act in killing Slough caused a great sensation throughout the Territory. Colonel of Volunteers in the Union army, Slough led Colorado troops on forced marches into New Mexico at the time of the Confederate invasion, and participated in the skirmishes which culminated in the routing of the invaders at the battle of Glorieta, east of Santa Fe, on March 27, 1862.

In 1870, Rynerson was one of the promoters of Ralston City, a silver mining camp in Grant County. In the same year Governor Pile appointed him adjutant general of the Territory. Rynerson was admitted to the bar of New Mexico on November 1, 1870. On January 21, 1878, Governor Axtell appointed Rynerson as district attorney of the Third Judicial District to succeed himself.

³ The writ of attachment of February 7, 1878, was found on Sheriff Brady's body on the day he was killed. Brady's return to the writ was amended by John N. Copeland, who succeeded Brady briefly as sheriff. As of April 12, 1878, Copeland wrote: "Received the within writ this 12th day of April 1878, as found on the body of the late William Brady, deceased." Apparently Sheriff

Brady had failed to serve McSween personally with a summons incidental to the writ of attachment, at or about the time he levied on the McSween-Tunstall property on February 9 and 10.

Consequently, Sheriff Copeland made an amended return, which read: "Received this writ on April 24, 1878, but on instructions of Charles Fritz, one of the Plaintiffs, said writ was not served until the 27th of May 1878, on which date in Lincoln County, New Mexico, the same was served by me by reading the within to the within Alex. A. McSween, and by attaching the property of said Alex. A. McSween, a list of which is hereto attached."

Copeland listed 550 laws books, valued at $3,000; 1 stove, $15.00; 1 writing desk, $20.00; 12 chairs, $24.00; 3 book cases, $24.00; 1 letter press, $5.00; 2 waste paper baskets, $1.00; office carpet, $40.00. McSween's private residence, with corral attached, was appraised at $1,200 by George B. Barber and Jose Montano. A carpenter shop was valued at $50; 5 cows at $60, and 4 saddle horses at $200. McSween's one-half interest in the store, office and bank, was appraised at $1,000. The total appraised value of the property attached by Brady and Copeland was $7,379.50.

[4] John Henry Tunstall was not yet twenty-five years old at the time of his death. As the result of long-continued efforts, Robert N. Mullin, on July 1, 1956, received from England a certified copy of the birth record showing that John Henry Tunstall was born March 6, 1853, at No. 14 Liscombes Cottages, Dalston, District of Hackney, County of Middlesex. His father, John Partridge Tunstall, was described as a commercial traveler. For many years comparatively little was known about young Tunstall's background in England, or his travels in America.

In 1952 a chance meeting occurred in Oxford, England, between Tony Long (son of Haniel Long, Santa Fe poet), his wife, Leslie Murphy Long, and Hilary Tunstall-Behrens, a British lecturer, up for another degree at the University. Inquiry disclosed that the John Henry Tunstall killed in Lincoln on February 18, 1878, was Hilary's great uncle, and that the Tunstall family had saved the many letters he had written home from America. Subsequently, the letters were made available to the late Maurice Garland Fulton, of Roswell, New Mexico, and others for study and consideration.

[5] Las Vegas *Gazette*, March 23, 1878. On February 25, 1878, Isaac Ellis filed a petition in the Probate Court of Lincoln County, saying that Tunstall died on February 18, 1878, leaving an estate consisting of dry goods, groceries, evidences of indebtedness, cattle and horses; that J. P. Tunstall, age not known, residing in London, England, was the lawful heir of the decedent.

On May 23, 1878, Otero, Sellars & Co., of El Moro, Colorado, filed a claim, verified by Jacob Gross, against the Tunstall estate for $1,268.19. On February 5, 1878, Fort Stanton furnished a military escort to Constable Emil Bower, upon his request, which helped him round up about 275 head of stolen cattle, which he had located near Pope's Crossing on the Pecos River. After the roundup, Bower asked all stockmen on the river to go through the herd as it was being driven north, and cut out their stock. Most of the cattle had been stolen from Tunstall's ranch, and from the Hunter and Evans herds. Constable Bower was told that the cattle had been driven along the river by "John Jones, Jim Jones, Tom Jones, alias George Davis, and Tom Cockner."

On March 5, 1878, soldiers under Capt. Henry Carroll, commanding Company F, Ninth Cavalry, drove into Lincoln 138 of the cattle which were stolen from Tunstall's ranch after Tunstall had been killed. The cattle were delivered to Susan E. McSween. (Cimarron *News and Press*, March 13, 1878.)

On January 11, 1879, Susan E. McSween was appointed administratrix of Tunstall's estate. She gave notice in the Golden *Era*, White Oaks, each week from July 21, 1881, through September 1, that the estate would be settled on the first Monday in September, 1881. Later she sold all Tunstall estate assets at public sale for $332, after having filed a petition in the Probate Court in which she said that she "had endeavored to collect notes and accounts, but without success; that many of the parties against whom they are have left the country and those remaining have nothing and are unable to pay; that from the circumstances surrounding this estate, the greater part of which was destroyed during what is known as the Lincoln county war; and the general disturbance that affair has made in the financial condition of the people has made the claims worthless." Mrs. McSween filed a final report in the estate on March 5, 1883, saying that "due to what is known as Lincoln County War, there was no balance for distribution."

[6] Robert Adolph Widenmann, who had more than one opportunity to die the death of a hero during the Lincoln County War, was born in Ann Arbor, Michigan, on June 24, 1852, and died in Haverstraw, New York, April 15, 1930, according to the research of R. N. Mullin. In Lincoln County, where ability to use a six-shooter was of much greater importance than ability to spell correctly, Widenmann's name was spelled with many variations. (Widenmann is correct.)

According to Mr. Mullin's careful investigation into Widenmann's background, "Bob" Widenmann, son of the Bavarian Consul in Ann Arbor, attended the Lutheran parochial school in his native city, then went to Stuttgartin, Germany, where he lived for several years with a grandfather, who was postmaster there. Returning to America, Widenmann lived for some time in New York City, then drifted West, finally arriving in Lincoln in mid-February, 1877. In Lincoln, Widenmann became acquainted with McSween, Tunstall and other McSween sympathizers. Through his father's acquaintance with German-born Carl Schurz, Secretary of the Interior, Widenmann received a commission as United States deputy marshal from United States Marshal John Sherman, Jr. He also was employed briefly as a clerk in the store of Tunstall & Co., and as a helper on the Tunstall ranch. While living in New Mexico Widenmann wrote many letters to relatives in Michigan describing the lurid life of the frontier.

After the troubles in Lincoln County had subsided, Widenmann went to

England, and lived for a time with the Tunstall family in London. Widenmann failed in his efforts to get John Partridge Tunstall in London to advance him money for promotional schemes. Widenmann was married to Albertine Seiler-Lemke, in Philadelphia, on November 23, 1881, and thereafter lived in Ann Arbor, where he was associated for a short time with his father in the hardware and general merchandise business. Widenmann retained recollections of his wild West days for many years. In the family orchard, on Whitmore Lake, Widenmann frequently practiced the fast draw and pistol shooting.

Because of his father's friendship with Secretary Schurz, young Widenmann found it possible to carry on a correspondence with Schurz regarding Lincoln County affairs. That Widenmann was not a man who could cope with and overcome the hazardous conditions existing in Lincoln County at the time, was apparent from the not too charitable appraisal of his character written to John Partridge Tunstall in London, by Alex. A. McSween, a few days after John H. Tunstall's death: "I have nothing against him (Widenmann) more than his laziness, youthful pomposity, lack of discretion so indispensible now and in the language of the country, poking his nose where it does not belong."

[7] Montague R. Leverson was described by Robert A. Widenmann in a letter written from Lincoln on March 20, 1878, to H. C. Beeten, Windsor Hotel, New York, as follows: "Mr. Montague R. Leverson, an Englishman of education and refinement, who is thoroughly acquainted with western manners and customs, and who is at present visiting this section, would be eminently fitted for appointment on a commission to investigate John Tunstall's death, as he would assure thorough honesty in the investigation."

The Santa Fe *New Mexican* did not share Widenmann's views. On January 18, 1879, that newspaper commented: "That dead beat and tramp, Montague R. Leverson, of Leverson's Ranch, Douglas County, Colorado, notorious throughout this section for his ignorant and presumptuous interference in our local affairs, has now turned his attention to state affairs in Colorado, and is before the legislature in that state with a memorial asking to be allowed to revise the Code."

[8] Mystery surrounds the life and career of Jesse Evans. Where was he born? Where and when did he die? Was "Jesse Evans" an assumed name? These and other questions have puzzled writers and researchers for many years. Ed Bartholomew, author of "Jesse Evans, a Texas Hideburner" (Frontier Press of Texas, Houston, 1955), picked up the trail of Jesse Evans after his footprints had become obliterated in New Mexico, and followed it diligently.

Bartholomew succeeded in tracing down some facts authenticated by court and prison records. Among other things, he developed that Jesse Evans had been on the dodge on a robbery charge, and with several other outlaws had engaged in a pitched battle with Texas Rangers near Cibola Creek, eighteen miles north of Presidio, Texas, on July 3, 1880, in which Ranger George R. Bingham was killed. Evans was arrested for murdering Bingham and tried before a jury in the District Court of Presidio County, on October 9, 1880. Convicted of murder in the second degree, he was sentenced to ten years in the penitentiary. The record shows, according to Bartholomew, that Evans was entered as a prisoner at the Huntsville Penitentiary on December 1, 1880, and given the number 9078; that he was twenty-seven years of age at the time, having been born in 1853; that his height was 5 feet 5 and ¾ inches, weight 150 pounds; complexion fair, eyes grey, hair light; two large scars on his left thigh, a bullet scar above and below his left elbow.

In accordance with the law at the time, Evans was "leased" out to a contractor, escaped from him on May 23, 1882, and was never recaptured. After his escape the life history of Jesse Evans became enveloped in the will-o'-the-wisp of time.

CHAPTER SIX

SHERIFF BRADY ASSASSINATED

O N APRIL 1, 1878, William Brady, Sheriff of Lincoln County, was shot and killed in broad daylight on the main street of Lincoln. Deputy Sheriff George Hindman, walking with Brady, was killed in the same blast of gunfire. Brady and Hindman were killed some forty days after the murder of John H. Tunstall, on February 18, and less than three weeks after Governor Axtell's visit to Lincoln for the announced purpose of investigating conditions in the county. As a result of Axtell's investigation, he had taken drastic action in several directions, including the issuance of proclamations declaring that Justice of the Peace John B. Wilson had no authority to act; announcing the revocation of a United States deputy marshal's commission previously held by Robert A. Widenmann; and pointing out that the law in Lincoln County was to be administered solely by Judge Bristol and Sheriff Brady.

The assassination of Sheriff Brady caused a sensation throughout the Territory, and produced violent repercussions in Lincoln County.[1] J. B. Matthews, chief deputy sheriff under Brady, in charge of the posse, a remnant of the one which had killed John Tunstall, had a narrow escape from death while walking near Brady and Hindman. Hindman, one of the victims of the April 1 shooting, had been a member of the posse which killed Tunstall. John Middleton, Hendry Brown and William Bonney were quickly accused of having fired the shots which killed the two officers; and it was claimed that Frederick Wait and James French were accomplices. Eyewitnesses said that the assassins had been concealed behind an adobe wall in the rear of the Tunstall store, which afforded a view of the street.

Men told different stories in regard to the events of April 1, 1878, in Lincoln. No doubt but that the day was one of extraordinary excitement. D. P. Shields, brother-in-law and law partner of Alex. A. McSween, made an affidavit before Probate Judge J. Felipe Baca in Las Vegas, on June 11, 1878, in which he gave some sidelights on the events of some seventy days before:

On the 1st day of April William Brady, the Sheriff, was killed, about 9 o'clock in the morning. On the afternoon of that day George H. Purington, Commanding Officer at Fort Stanton, together with Lieut. Smith and a number of soldiers were in Lincoln. Purington permitted Geo. W. Peppin and others who were with him to make arrests and search houses without producing any warrant or authority. Peppin said Purington had authorized him to do so. McSween called the attention of Purington to the statement made by Peppin. Purington said Peppin could do as he pleased. About that time Dr. M. R. Leverson came up and called the attention of Captain Purington to that part of the Constitution of the United States which provides for the security of persons and property from seizure or search without warrant. The reply of Purington was: "Damn the Constitution and you for a fool."

Following the killing of Sheriff Brady, curious people hurried into Lincoln from the surrounding country to learn about the shooting. Among the visitors was Calvin Simpson, who went to Lincoln from Las Vegas, a three-day trip one-way. After remaining in Lincoln for several days, Simpson described the situation as he saw it in a letter to the Las Vegas *Gazette,* published on April 13:

Killing people in Lincoln is the leading industry at the present time. They kill anybody, native or stranger, with or without cause according to circumstances and inclination.

Editor-Lawyer W. G. Koogler, publisher of the Las Vegas *Gazette,* born and reared in the Shenandoah Valley, Virginia, who had built up an immunity to feud killings as the result of long residence in the mountain country of his native state, noted with alarm in his paper on April 13, 1878, the killing of Tunstall, Morton, Baker, Roberts, Brady, Hindman, and other Lincoln County citizens. He summed up the situation with lawyer-like precision:

It seems to an outside observer from the drift of events since the murder of Tunstall, that one party has determined to execute vengeance on all whom they suppose have been directly or indirectly, instrumental in his death. We are loath to believe that Sheriff Brady had been in any way connected with the death of Tunstall. He had ever borne a reputation of an honest man and good officer, but he must have been greatly overreached and misled in the character of the posse he was sending after Tunstall, or else, if cognizant of its personnel, he was greatly wrong. They should have been incarcerated, at least, after disobeying the spirit of his instructions. The papers are full of criminations and recriminations by correspondents, which tend to keep alive, rather than allay, the excitement, and breed further lawlessness, rather than lead to justice. This lawless condition has grown out of a matter, the determination of which would seem to be more proper for the calm determination of a court of justice than the arbitrament of the rifle and shotgun. It was simply a question of $8,000 or $10,000 between McSween on one side, and Dolan & Co., upon the other side. The former collected it and claimed to hold it in trust for the heirs and administrators of the estate of Emil Fritz. The latter claim to be creditors of the Fritz estate, and wanted their accounts settled. The charge of embezzlement against one, and fraud against the other, have been freely made. It was simply a question to be calmly decided by the courts between the two claimants; but by violent and precipitate action it has assumed the proportions of a bloody and destructive feud in which several good men have been killed, as well as several bad ones. The death of Tunstall, compassed as it was, through the aid of lawless men, goes far to condone, in the public mind, though it should not, much lawlessness on the part of his friends. Tunstall was no desperado. He was an inoffensive man, and the development of facts, thus far, does not appear to show clearly that he stood seriously in the way of an attachment of the property of McSween. He seems to have been killed, against the direct instructions of Sheriff Brady, out of pure cussedness. Yet, no legal steps were taken to arrest those who did the deed, and violent and lawless revenge has followed as a consequence. The assassination of Sheriff Brady will be equally hard to

justify. He was not an outlaw. His character and standing were sufficient guaranty that in case he was guilty of any wrong, directly or
indirectly, he could be reached by the law. He was a man to face any
tribunal, and the rectitude of his intentions no doubt led him to be
careless in exposing himself to an attack, which resulted in his death.
Violence should be stopped and the court should have an opportunity
for untramelled action. The wrongs, or injustice merely done to
property rights, by the law's delay, are not comparable to the injustice of taking human life.

Editor Koogler's calm, logical and dispassionate appraisal
of the Lincoln County troubles found support, and resulted in
comment in several other Territorial papers. When the Mesilla
Independent published an editorial in somewhat similar vein,
James J. Dolan wrote a letter to the Santa Fe *New Mexican*
from Lincoln on May 16, 1878 (published on May 25), in an
attempt to justify his position as an active participant in some
of the difficulties. Referring to the *Independent's* recently published editorial, Dolan charged that there was an "unholy alliance" between A. A. McSween and John S. Chisum, and said,
among other things:

McSween, with what little brains he has, aided by ten thousand
dollars he has embezzled from the Fritz family, and a few willing
tools, has defied the law, and ruined one of the best counties in the
Territory, for no other purpose than to enable him to cover his robbery and other foul acts. . . . McSween wants to keep the ten
thousand dollars collected from the Fritz estate and he knows he
can't do it as long as Mr. Riley and myself live. Therefore he desires
to have us assassinated.

In regard to Chisum, Dolan said: "Mr. Riley and I are in
Mr. Chisum's way, because our business conflicts. He wants to
control contracts in New Mexico as well as in Arizona; in this
we have bothered him."

The killing of Sheriff Brady and Deputy Hindman, alleg-
edly by William H. Bonney, Hendry Brown, Fred Wait, John
Middleton and James French, or some one or more of them,
was preliminary to further killings in the immediate future.
Within a matter of hours after Brady and Hindman had been

killed, two more men lost their lives in a duel to the death at Blazer's Mill, located within the exterior boundaries of, but technically not a part of, the Mescalero Apache Indian reservation.

Following the death of Brady and Hindman, the county commissioners of Lincoln County at a special meeting authorized a reward of $200 each for the arrest of the slayers of Brady and Hindman, to be paid to the person who arrested and delivered any of the fugitives to officers of the law, "dead or alive." News of the reward was of particular interest to Andrew L. Roberts, otherwise known as "Buckshot" Roberts, a comparative newcomer in the Ruidoso Valley who apparently considered it in the same category as a bounty for killing catamounts. Roberts told curious neighbors that he was from Texas, but because his speech did not possess the twang common to most Texans, there were those who claimed that he was not a real Texan, but that he was from the deep South. People in the surrounding country were uncertain as to just how to classify Roberts. Some said that he had formerly been a Texas Ranger; others that he had shot it out with the Texas Rangers, and had killed one or more of them; still others claimed that Roberts had left Texas for New Mexico as fast as he could travel on a certain day, propelled on his journey by a round of buckshot, fired from a double-barrelled shotgun, as a result of which he was thereafter known as "Buckshot" Roberts. Few doubted that Roberts had been a member of the Matthews posse which had hunted down and killed John Tunstall on February 18, 1878. That he was even suspected of having been with the posse was sufficient to justify the McSween crowd in being on guard in dealing with him.

On April 4, 1878, Roberts rode from his home to Lincoln, where he obtained official assurance and confirmation of the report he had heard in the mountains that the county had offered to pay $200 for the arrest of each of the several men suspected of having killed Sheriff Brady and Deputy Hindman. Officers in Lincoln told him that Dick Brewer, Billy Bonney and other suspects might be located in the vicinity of Blazer's Mill. Within a matter of hours, Roberts rode into Blazer's on a mule, a conspicuous figure in a country where there were many horses and only a few mules.

Armed with rifle, pistol, and plenty of ammunition, it was only too apparent that Roberts was not on a mission of peace or an errand of mercy. At Blazer's, Roberts was met by what might be called an informal reception committee: Richard M. Brewer, George Coe, Frank Coe, John Middleton, Charles Bowdre, William H. Bonney and others of the McSween faction. In fact, Brewer and some of his men had been on the lookout for Roberts and George Kitt, also reported to have been with the posse that had killed Tunstall. When Bowdre sighted Roberts, he drew his gun on him, and shot him instantly upon his refusal to surrender. Fatally wounded, Roberts managed to get in a last, desperate shot which killed Dick Brewer,[2] who died almost instantly. In the exchange of shots, George Coe received a bullet wound in the hand; John Middleton sustained a slight wound in the breast. Brewer's death was considered by the anti-McSween crowd as avenging the deaths of Frank Baker and William S. Morton, who had been shot and killed on March 9 or 10, 1878, less than thirty days before the shooting at Blazer's Mill. Dr. J. H. Blazer, an eyewitness to most of the events preceding the shooting of Brewer and Roberts, supervised the burial of both men.

News of the shooting of Dick Brewer and "Buckshot" Roberts was slow to penetrate to the outside world, and only meager details were currently published. The Cimarron *News and Press* of April 18, 1878, published an article signed "Stanton," quite possibly written by Alex. A. McSween, which told of the trouble at Blazer's Mill:

Yesterday Richard M. Brewer and some other citizens were at Blazer's Mill. There they met one of the famous Jesse Evan's gang, now known as A. L. Roberts, one of the Sheriff's posse, who so foully and brutally murdered Tunstall. Since the perpetration of that inhuman deed, he has been in the employ of Murphy, Dolan & Riley. It appears that Roberts expressed himself as being sorry for what had happened; that having found out the composition of the outfit he intended to abandon it. He had his six shooter and carbine. Some one asked him to give up his arms, that they had a warrant for him, whereupon he drew his revolver; but before he could use it, the men who demanded the surrender shot him in the stomach. He then pulled down a mattress on the floor, dragged it to the door, and laid upon it. He now began to shoot indiscriminately. Mr. Coe was the first to receive a shot, being badly shot in the hand; the next, John Middleton, being shot in the chest. Brewer was about 100 yards from the room occupied by Roberts when the shooting commenced. He fired only once. When raising up the second time, Roberts shot him in the head, killing him instantly. The wounds of Coe and Middleton are not considered dangerous. At last accounts Roberts was dying. Dick Brewer died young—27 years of age. His father and family live in Wisconsin.

The *News and Press* correspondent was not entirely satisfied with the accuracy of the story of the double killing, but there is no doubt that he was a great admirer of Richard Brewer:

The above account may not be correct, but I give it as I received it from an eye witness. Whether correct or not I want to say a few words concerning Mr. Brewer.

Richard M. Brewer was one of nature's noblemen. Physically faultless; generous to a fault; a giant in friendship; possessing an irreproachable character and unsullied honor; kind, amiable, and gentle in disposion, he had fallen early into the "three by six," promised him eighteen months ago.

Outside the Murphy-Dolan-Riley faction, no one knew Mr. Brewer but to respect him. He was a young man without vices of any kind. Had he been content to enslave himself, he would, no doubt, be living now, but to a man of his kingly nature, existence would be intolerable under the conditions sought to be imposed.

Murderers and horse thieves hated him; their friends hated him. But the *people*, Mexicans and Americans, held him in the highest possible esteem. He had a fine ranch on the Rio Ruidoso, which he had been cultivating the past four years. It was his intention to make Lincoln county his permanent home.

"Stanton" preached an eloquent funeral sermon in the concluding paragraph of his story:

Peace to your ashes, Dick! as you were familiarly called. Sweet and pleasant be your slumbers. Ever green and fresh be your memory. Some will malign you, but that will not disturb you for when the mist has cleared away and the horizon of truth is clearly seen, even they will be shamed to silence. Death has deprived your father and mother of an obedient and loving son; your sister and brother of the prince of brothers; the county of Lincoln of one of her best, most industrious, sober, upright and honest citizens.

In the Cimarron *News and Press* of May 2, 1878, there was published an "In Memoriam" for Dick Brewer, reflecting the sentiment of an important segment of the community and emphasizing the circumstances surrounding his death:

We the undersigned residents of Lincoln County, in the Territory of New Mexico, deeply deplore the loss our county sustains by the death of Richard M. Brewer, a young man of irreproachable character, who commanded the respect and admiration of all who knew him. Some of us have been acquainted with him over eight years and none ever knew his name to be associated with anything of a questionable character. He was a hard working, generous, sober, upright and noble minded young man. Cattle thieves and murderers and their "kid gloved" friends hated him, and promised him a violent death years ago. In good faith, he went as special constable to arrest the murderers of John H. Tunstall by virtue of a warrant issued by John B. Wilson, a justice of the peace in the town of Lincoln. Before he could make his return thereon, Governor Axtell issued a proclamation to the effect that Wilson was not a legal J. P., although the act of our Legislature, by virtue of which said Wilson was appointed justice, was approved by his Excellency. Mr. Wilson had acted as such justice for over a year without having his authority questioned. Immediately after the issue of that proclamation our late sheriff, and those who were interested in screening the murderers, obtained warrants against Mr. Brewer and *posse* for having made an effort to execute the warrant issued by Wilson. Brewer and *posse* knew well that if the late sheriff arrested them they would be murdered, so they took to the mountains.

We tender our heartfelt sympathy to the aged parents of the late Richard M. Brewer, and other relatives in Wisconsin, and we beg to assure them that while they have lost a good son and relative, we feel that our county has lost one of her best citizens.

One hundred fifty citizens signed the "In Memoriam." John

S. Chisum was the first signer, followed by J. Ellis & Sons, Merchants; G. B. Barber, Surveyor and C. E.; J. B. Patron, Speaker of the House of Representatives; Jose Montano, Merchant; McSween and Shields, Attorneys; J. N. Copeland, Sheriff; J. Newcomb; T. F. Ealy, M.D.; Dow Brothers, Merchants; R. M. Gilbert, A. Wilson and W. Fields, members of the 1878 grand jury.

Close witnesses to the Roberts and Brewer killings included David M. Easton, clerk and bookkeeper for Blazer, Frederick G. Godfroy, superintendent of the Mescalero Agency, and Andrew Wilson. Easton gave his testimony concerning the killing many months later before the Dudley Court of Inquiry at Fort Stanton. His testimony was substantially as follows: That at the time of the shooting he was standing in front of Blazer's house, talking to William Bonney; that Roberts rode up, dismounted, spoke to Frank Coe, and then went and sat on the porch of the house; that Charles Bowdre, John Middleton and Hendry Brown came around the corner of the house and asked Roberts to surrender, firing at him at the same instant; that the bullet that killed Roberts came from Charles Bowdre's gun.

During Territorial days, grand and petit juries in New Mexico acted in a dual capacity. The same grand jury was qualified to consider and indict in cases involving violation of either Territorial or federal laws; and petit juries heard the evidence and returned verdicts in both Territorial and federal cases. The district judge also acted in a dual capacity, sitting in cases in which the Territory or the federal government was a party. On the United States side of the court, however, the United States district attorney presented federal cases to the grand jury and tried them before the petit jury; and on the Territorial side of the court, the district attorney of the judicial district represented the Territory before the grand and petit juries. One clerk kept the books and records for both sides of the court.

At the spring term of court in Lincoln County, which began on or about April 14, 1878, Judge Bristol empanelled a grand jury, which began its deliberations in an atmosphere charged with excitement and muttered threats of violence. Dr. J. H. Blazer,[3] of Blazer's Mill fame, was quite appropriately elected foreman of the grand jury. A combination dentist and sawmill operator, Dr. Blazer knew all about the shooting of Dick Brewer and "Buckshot" Roberts on April 4. He had been present.

The Lincoln County grand jury of 1878 transacted considerable business. A number of murder charges were sifted; many witnesses were examined under oath. In some instances, the grand jurors already knew quite a bit about the killings, had a good idea of the identity of the killers and of the reasons which had prompted them to kill. Judge Bristol delivered his charge to the grand jury on the opening day of the term, offering his understanding of the underlying causes of the unrest in Lincoln County, urging the diligent investigation into alleged offenses, and the finding of true bills, if necessary, without fear or favor. In the charge, published in part in the Mesilla *Independent* of April 20, 1878, Judge Bristol devoted considerable time to a recital of the troubles between two warring factions in the county:

In regard to the troubles now existing in this county I propose to address you in very plain and unequivocal language. There seem to be two principal parties, standing somewhat in the background and under cover, who are the real authors and instigators of these troubles. Mr. McSween and his adherents on one side, and Messrs. Murphy, Dolan and Riley with their adherents, on the other. It is my duty as Judge, it is your duty as jurors, to act with the utmost impartiality as between these parties and their followers. If the partisans on either side have committed crimes, then they ought to be indicted, tried, convicted and punished. I propose to have something to say upon both sides. In regard to the McSween case I am able to speak with some definiteness, because he has been before me on a charge of embezzlement, when a large amount of testimony was taken. In regard to the other side very serious charges are and for a long time have been floating through the community, but no evidence has been presented to me as to their truth or falsity. I can speak of them only as rumors, and charge you to inquire into them, and find out, as far as you can, the real truth.

Bristol then outlined for the jury the alleged misconduct of Alex. A. McSween, reciting the history of the Fritz life insurance transaction; of the efforts the Fritz heirs had made to compel McSween to pay over the money; of the efforts he had made to avoid payment; of the steps McSween had taken in and out of court to thwart and circumvent the law; of the killing of Tunstall; of the killing of Sheriff Brady and George Hindman:

Here we have a notable instance of a man starting out wrong, in defiance of what he knows to be the law, with a grip of iron holding on to money that does not belong to him, and instead of leaving the case to the peaceful adjustment of the law permits open resistance that finally culminates in bloodshed and murder. . . . Now, the trouble with McSween seems to be an attempt on his part to usurp the functions of administrator, of Judge, Court, jury, witness, and probably the heirs to the Fritz estate. We have seen what it has led to.

Turning to possible charges of illegal acts on the part of Murphy, Dolan and Riley, Bristol said:

The mildest charge brought against Murphy and Dolan, by McSween and his partisans, is that they are seeking by unfair and fraudulent means to get hold of and appropriate this identical insurance money now in McSween's hands; and they claim that if this money is paid over to the administrators, Murphy and Dolan in some way will get hold of it. This, if true, is no justification for McSween's extraordinary conduct in the premises. As a lawyer, he knows perfectly well that there were and are several speedy and effective remedies in law for preventing any misappropriation of this money. In a proper case the equity side of the court would intervene and put this money in safe hands, if any danger really existed of a misappropriation prejudicial to the interests of other parties, if any, pending the settlement of disputes, if there are any disputes. There is no difficulty about this matter.

Bristol's charge to the grand jury was weighted against McSween, being pitched more on the plane of a summing up by a prosecuting attorney in an effort to convict McSween before a petit jury, than an impartial attempt to direct a grand jury into the path of an unbiased investigation.

On the United States side, the grand jury having completed its labors, returned an indictment against Charles Bowdre,

"Dock" Scurlock, Hendry Brown, Henry Antrim, alias Kid, John Middleton, Stephen Stevens, John Scroggins, George Coe and Frederick Wait, for the murder of "Buckshot" Roberts. The indictment charged that on April 4, 1878, "Charles Bowdre, aided, assisted and abetted by others, with a gun in both hands, then and there held to, against and upon the said Andrew L. Roberts, then and there of his malice and afore-thought unlawfully . . . upon the left side of him, the said Andrew L. Roberts, inflicted a mortal wound, of which the said Roberts then and there instantly died." Besides Blazer, Andrew Wilson, David Easton and Frederick Godfroy had testified before the grand jury.

The Roberts murder case was docketed as *No. 411, United States of America* vs. *Charles Bowdry, et al.* The indictment charged that Roberts had been murdered on property under the exclusive jurisdiction of the United States of America, to-wit, the Mescalero Apache Indian reservation. Dr. Blazer, foreman of the grand jury, was probably aware that the Blazer Mill property was not located on the reservation, but on privately owned land. Frederick C. Godfroy, superintendent of the Mescalero Indian Agency, a witness before the grand jury, also presumably knew the boundary lines of the reservation. The indictment in the United States court, instead of the District Court of Lincoln County, may have been for the purpose of enlisting the powerful assistance of the federal government in rounding up outlaws, with the knowledge that at a future time the question of jurisdiction might be decided adversely to the government, as proved to be the case when Henry Antrim, alias Kid (William H. Bonney) was arraigned before the court when Case No. 411 was called for trial at Mesilla on March 30, 1881.

The report of the Lincoln County grand jury presented on April 18, 1878, by Foreman J. H. Blazer was almost a complete repudiation of Judge Bristol's recommendations and an absolute exoneration of Alex. A. McSween from suspicion of wrongdoing. In his charge to the grand jury, Bristol had devoted two-thirds of his time to an argument by which he sought to prove that McSween had been guilty of embezzlement. By contrast Bristol had spoken only briefly, and rather casually, in referring to the Tunstall murder. The grand jury refused to

adopt Bristol's viewpoint. It not only declined to indict Mc-
Sween, but gave him a clean bill of health. It characterized the
Tunstall killing as "a brutal murder." The report, published in
the Cimarron *News and Press,* of May 2, 1878, is in part as
follows:

The grand jury for the April 1878, term of the District Court of
Lincoln County, deeply deplore the present insecurity of life and
property though but the revival and continuance of the troubles of
past years.

The murder of John H. Tunstall, for brutality and malice, is
without parallel and without a shadow of justification. By this inhuman act our county has lost one of our best and most useful men;
one who brought intelligence, industry and capital to the development
of Lincoln County. We equally condemn the most brutal murder of
our late sheriff, William Brady and George Hindman. In each of
the cases, where the evidence would warrant it, we have made
presentments.

Had his excellency, S. B. Axtell when here, ascertained from the
people the cause of our troubles, as he was requested, valuable lives
would have been spared our community; especially do we condemn
that portion of his proclamation relating to J. B. Wilson as J. P.
Mr. Wilson acted in good faith as such J. P. for over a year. Mr.
Brewer, deceased, arrested, as we are informed, some of the alleged
murderers of Mr. Tunstall by virtue of warrants issued by Mr. Wilson. The part of the proclamation referred to virtually outlawed
Mr. Brewer and *posse.* In fact, they were hunted to the mountains
by our late sheriff with U. S. soldiers. We believe that had the governor done his duty while here, these unfortunate occurrences would
have been spared us.

The report mentioned the stealing and pilfering at the Mescalero Agency:

Under the impression that stealing the property of the United
States was a crime against our Territory, we heard evidence in regard
to the administration of affairs at the Mescalero Apache Indian
Agency in this county; but we are now informed by the District Attorney that crimes of the character thus investigated by us, are not
indictable in this court. We have, however, ascertained by evidence

that the Indians are systematically robbed by their agent of a large and varied assortment of supplies. We mention this here for the reason that it will explain why the Indians are migrating marauders, and steal from and murder our citizens. The witnesses by whom these facts can be proved are residents of this town and neighborhood, and a list of them has been furnished by us to the United States District Court Clerk.

Concerning the McSween embezzlement charge, the report said:

Your honor charged us to investigate the case of Alex. A. McSween, Esq., charged with the embezzlement of $10,000 belonging to the estate of Emil Fritz, deceased; this we did, but we were unable to find any evidence that would justify the accusation. We fully exonerate him of the charge, and regret that a spirit of persecution has been shown in this matter. . . . Your honor, too, charged us to investigate the charge of cattle stealing, etc., against Messrs. Dolan and Riley. This we did and the result is a matter of record.

Rynerson was given a meed of praise:

We acknowledge the punctuality and earnestness of Dist. Attorney Col. W. L. Rynerson in attending the grand jury during its arduous and responsible labors; and most respectfully request from your Honor to be discharged from further duties as grand jurors.

The Lincoln County grand jury having indicted John Middleton, Hendry Brown and William Bonney for the murder of William Brady, Bonney appeared in court on April 19, 1878, and pleaded not guilty to the indictment. Three days later, on April 22, 1878, a warrant was issued for Bonney's arrest, citing him to appear before the court on October 1, 1878. Bonney had left Lincoln, however, after his court appearance on April 19, and the warrant was not served on him until almost a year later. On April 14, 1879, Sheriff George Kimball made a return on the warrant: "This writ came to hand the 1st day of Feb. 1879 and was executed by arresting the body of said Bonney and I have him now here in court this 14th day of April 1879." The Sheriff's mileage charge was $2.00.

Although Bonney had been arrested, and was before the

court on the Brady charge in Lincoln for the spring term of 1879, the Territory was not anxious to try him before a jury in Lincoln County. On April 21, 1879, District Attorney Rynerson filed a motion for a change of venue, alleging:

That justice cannot be done said Territory on the trial of the said defendant, William Bonney, alias Kid, alias William Antrim, in the county of Lincoln, for the reason that jurors in attendance and all those liable to be summoned for the trial of said defendant by reason of partisanship in the late and existing troubles and lawlessness in said county, have so prejudiced the said jurors that they cannot fairly and impartially try the said defendant; and for the further reason that said jurors in said cause are so intimidated by lawless men in said county of Lincoln by fear of violence and lawlessness against their persons and property on the part of said lawless men that the said jurors and witnesses cannot fearlessly and justly perform their respective duties at said trial in Lincoln county.

Insofar as the record shows, Bonney had no attorney present in court to resist Rynerson's motion. On April 22, 1879, Judge Bristol granted a change of venue to Doña Ana County. The Territory's witnesses, Isaac Ellis, B. F. Baca and Jacob B. Matthews, were required by the court to furnish bond of $1,000 as assurance that they would be in attendance in Mesilla when the case was to be tried. Bonney left Lincoln soon after the court had granted the change of venue in his case. A year later, on April 23, 1880, when Sheriff Kimball was asked to serve a warrant on Bonney, ordering him to appear before the District Court in Doña Ana, on September 1, 1880, Kimball made a return to the effect that he had been unable to find the defendant, "after having made diligent search."

What about Billy Bonney during the interim between his arraignment before Judge Bristol in Lincoln on the Brady murder charge on April 19, 1878, and his rearrest on the same charge on April 14, 1879? S. R. Corbet, a clerk in Tunstall's store during Tunstall's life, threw some light on his movements in a letter written from Lincoln on February 3, 1880, to John Middleton, then in Barber County, Kansas, in which Corbet told of happenings since Middleton had left Lincoln County nearly two years before:

Bill Bonney is still here in the county—still on the lookout. He and Tom O'Folliard are both here. Tom was indicted for stealing Fritz's horses. Stood his trial and come clear, and then stayed around here until he got into trouble again trying to clear a friend of his, and was indicted for perjury. Bill Bonney shot and killed a man at Fort Sumner not long since by the name of Grant. Do not know the cause. He made friends with Dolan and outfit the night poor Mr. Chapman was killed. The reason he had he was tired of fighting and wanted to stand his trial and did not want to run from the Dolan outfit and the civil officers also. He gave himself up for trial at court April '79 and his case was changed by the prosecuting attorney to Doña Ana county. He stayed here in town until court at Mesilla, then gave the Sheriff the dodge and since has been stopping at Fort Sumner until he killed Grant.

For twenty-seven days after Brady's death on April 1, Lincoln County was without a sheriff. The town of Lincoln was an armed camp. Every man in the county, by virtue of necessity, was a sheriff in his own right.

Finally, after much talk and many informal conferences, the county commissioners held a special meeting on April 27, 1878, at which they appointed John S. Copeland to succeed Brady. The appointment was entirely unpalatable to Dolan, Riley and other anti-McSween people, who claimed that Copeland would be controlled in all his official actions by McSween's advice and counsel. The Dolan-Riley contingent did not propose to sit idly by and allow Copeland to take over the sheriff's office. James Dolan and his influential friends hurried to Santa Fe and complained to Governor Axtell. Exactly thirty-one days after Copeland's appointment, the Governor removed him from office by letter, and issued a proclamation appointing George W. Peppin as sheriff of Lincoln County. The Dolan-Riley people rejoiced; McSween and his followers were dejected.[4]

Axtell's letter notifying Copeland that he had been removed from office, dated May 28, 1878, was as follows:

SIR: It having been shown to my satisfaction that you have failed to comply with the law in relation to the qualification of Sheriff (See Acts of Legislative Assembly, 22d Session, page 49) in that you have failed to file your bond as collector of taxes and that more than thirty days have elapsed since you have been acting as Sheriff, it be-comes my duty to remove you from office. See Sec. 7 of said act.

In compliance with said law I do hereby remove you from the office of Sheriff of Lincoln county and require you to turn over to your successor in office George W. Peppin, Esq., all books, papers, processes and all and singular all property and effects whatsoever pertaining to the office of Sheriff of Lincoln County, or held by you or your deputies as I have appointed George W. Peppin, Esq., Sheriff of Lincoln county, to hold said office till the next election. Expressing my personal esteem for you as a citizen, I have the honor to remain.[5]

> Yours truly,
> S. B. AXTELL
> Governor

Axtell's proclamation, dated May 28, 1878, removing Cope-land and appointing Peppin as sheriff of the county, declared:

For the information of all the citizens of Lincoln county I do hereby make this public proclamation:

First—John N. Copeland, Esq., appointed Sheriff by the County Commissioners, having for more than thirty days failed to file his bond as Collector of Taxes, is hereby removed from the office of sheriff, and I have appointed GEORGE W. PEPPIN, Esq., Sheriff of Lincoln county. This has been done in compliance with the laws, passed at the Twenty Second session of the Legislative Assembly, relating to Sheriffs.

Second—I command all men and bodies of men under arms and traveling about the county to disarm and return to their homes and their usual pursuits, and so long as the present Sheriff has authority to call upon U. S. troops for assistance, not to act as a sheriff's posse.

And, in conclusion, I urge upon all good citizens to submit to the law, remembering that violence begets violence, and that they who take the sword shall perish by the sword.

Months after Axtell had removed Copeland as sheriff, Spe-cial Investigator Angel commented in an official report:

Copeland was an honest, conscientious man. Perhaps he was not the strongest man in character that ever existed—but I am yet to hear of any arbitrary act on his part—any murder, robbery or arson in which he had been a party or of his being supported while in office by a band of notorious outlaws and non residents. He was, on the contrary, surrounded by and had the confidence of a majority of the residents of the county—one of the County Commissioners having offered to be his bondsman. By the laws of the Territory, he was ex officio tax collector. The bonds as collector have to be fixed by the County Commissioners after they have ascertained the amount of taxes to be collected. Copeland had nothing to do with this—and owing to the troubled state of affairs in the county, the Commissioners could not find the amount of taxes to be collected. The Governor immediately seized the opportunity to aid Murphy, Dolan & Riley. He this time acts strictly within the law, and would that I could say the intent of the law and non partisan. He removes Copeland and appoints G. W. Peppin, one of the leaders of the Murphy, Dolan & Riley party, who comes from Mesilla accompanied by John Kinney and his murderous oufit of outlaws, as a bodyguard to assist him in enforcing law and order. Again we have an unusual number of murders, robberies, accompanied by arson. After Kinney and his party have accomplished their mission of murdering McSween and robbing and stealing all they can, they retire on their laurels and return whence they came, and Sheriff Peppin without the confidence of the people or even confidence in himself retreats to Fort Stanton, at which place he is under the safe protection of the soldiers.

Axtell defended himself against Angel's accusation in regard to Kinney's aid to Peppin:

If John Kinney acted with Peppin at any time, it was against my express orders. Later on, when the troops were withdrawn from the sheriff, and he was left to his own resources, I cannot blame him, if when attacked he took into his service all who offered. I am informed that Kinney and his band have returned to Mesilla, and I believe if Sheriff Peppin is sustained, he will rid Lincoln county of all thieves, assassins and desperadoes.

In attempting to justify his action in removing Copeland, and appointing Peppin, Governor Axtell complained in a statement given to Angel that the people had failed to follow the advice given to them on the occasion of his visit to Lincoln on March 8 and 9:

My advice to the people of Lincoln was not followed; but instead, a vigilance committee or band of regulators was organized to resist Sheriff Brady and override and violate the law. Murder followed murder with sickening rapidity. Finally, Sheriff Brady, with one of his deputies, was shot down in the open day, in the public street. After his death the County Commissioners, as they had a right to do, appointed John N. Copeland, sheriff. Col. Dudley informed me by letter that Copeland was daily in company with noted desperadoes for whom he had warrants, and that he failed, and refused to arrest them. Copeland also failed to give bond as Collector of Taxes, and the law makes it my duty in such case to remove him, and appoint a Sheriff. This I did and appointed George W. Peppin. He was highly recommended by Col. W. L. Rynerson, the District Attorney for the Third Judicial District, which includes Lincoln County. He is a married man; a resident and property holder in the town of Lincoln; is industrious and strictly sober, and came to the Territory as a soldier with the California Volunteers; he has given both his bonds, and they have been approved. . . . Peppin is redhot against Brady's murderers, and means to ride day and night, and to use all possible means to bring them to justice. He has been called a partisan. If this be partisanship, I pray God that Peppin and all good men may grow more partisan every day till this good work is accomplished. I have been informed by Col. Dudley and others that Peppin has been vigilant, active and courageous. I know his life is in danger, but I want to thank him for accepting this dangerous appointment, and for the brave and prudent manner in which he has executed his arduous duties.

George W. Peppin, Axtell's appointee as sheriff of Lincoln County, had been a witness to the events that had taken place in connection with the levying of the writ of attachment by Sheriff Brady on McSween's interest in the Tunstall & Co. store in Lincoln. Peppin signed an affidavit on April 18, 1878, eighteen days after Sheriff Brady had been killed, which told of his participation and observation:

George W. Peppin being first duly sworn deposes and on oath says: That about the first days of the month of February A.D. 1878 he, said affiant, was summoned as one of a posse to assist Sheriff William Brady to keep the peace and assist in serving the annexed writ of attachment. That he, said affiant, was present and saw Sheriff Brady attach all the right, title and interest of Alex. A. McSween in and to the goods chattels effects and premises pertaining to the store of Tunstall & Co., in the town of Lincoln, Territory of New Mexico, and the houses of A. A. McSween. That the annexed inventory exhibits the property attached and taken into possession by said sheriff William Brady under said writ of attachment. Said affiant further says that soon after said property was so attached and in possession of said William Brady, a number of armed men Atanacio Martinez, Richard Brewer, Doc Scurlock, John Middleton, William H. Antrim alias "Kid," Samuel Smith, Samuel Corbett, ———— Wayt, ———— McNab, ———— Edwards, Frank Coe and George Coe, George Washington (colored), George Robinson (colored), Ignacio Gonzales, Jesus Rodriguez, Esiquio Sanchez, Rowan Burgan and other persons whose names are to affiant unknown entered the said store and said Martinez by virtue of what purported to be a warrant arrested this affiant and all persons placed in charge by said William Brady of said goods chattels and premises and took the keys of said store and premises from Sheriff William Brady's men so placed in charge of said property and took said last named persons out of said store. Subsequently this affiant and others who were in charge of said goods and store as aforesaid, to wit: Jack Long, James Longwell, Charles Martin and John Clark (colored) were released and this affiant applied for some property belonging to him this affiant left in said store and premises; and was told that the keys were down at McSween's house (the defendant in attachment suit) and Mr. Corbett went after them and after bringing keys and taking out some of this affiant's property (blankets) from said store, proceeded to the house of said Alex A. McSween and there and then this affiant saw said Corbett deliver said keys to said Alex A. McSween. The sheriff's posse in charge of said goods and store as aforesaid were by the said Martinez and party disarmed. Sheriff Brady was also subsequently arrested and since said Brady was so dispossessed he has not been in possession of said property. Further affiant saith not.

Two days later, on April 20, 1878, Peppin signed another affidavit, apparently designed to remedy an omission in the first one, which had not given any reason for Brady's failure to use the authority of his office to retain or regain possession of the property attached on February 9 and 10, and which Peppin, in his first affidavit, declared had been taken by McSween's men from Brady's custody and control. The second affidavit follows:

George Peppin being first duly sworn, deposes and says: That Sheriff William Brady to whom the annexed writ of attachment was directed and who was dispossessed of property, goods and chattels as stated in annexed affidavit made by this affiant, was killed on the first day of April 1878. This affiant knows of no reason why the said sheriff did not retake possession of said property, before his (Brady's) death, unless he the said sheriff was unable so to do without bloodshed which the said William Brady informed this affiant he was anxious to avoid.

Feuding and fighting in southeastern New Mexico in the 70's and 80's was not the province only of livestock thieves, highway robbers and other transgressors of the law on the one side, and peace officers on the other. Even newspaper editors of the day lost their tempers at times, and on occasion expressed their feelings and sentiments rather frankly and vehemently. Since Lincoln County was without a newspaper in the 70's, the people throughout that entire area relied almost entirely upon the Mesilla *News* and the Mesilla *Independent* for information about the outside world.

The *News* was published by Ira M. Bond, a newspaperman of the old hand-press school who had grown up in printing offices, could set his own type, do the presswork, and compose his editorials direct from the case. In his day Ira Bond had been a "swift" and always proud of that distinction.

Albert J. Fountain, soldier of fortune, and lawyer, who had marched into the Territory with Carleton's California Column in 1862, was editor of the *Independent*. Fountain knew nothing of the practical side of newspaper work, but he was fearless and at times wrote editorials with a pen dripping blue vitriol instead of ink. The Las Vegas *Gazette* of September 8, 1877, told of the cat-and-dog fight in which Bond and Fountain were currently engaged. Bond, it appeared, had recently written an editorial complaining that Fountain "had threatened to make a mangled corpse of him on the streets of Mesilla." Bond, always considered a mild-mannered, gentlemanly, soft-spoken individual, ended his editorial on a fighting note: "The editor of this paper is willing to meet Fountain in the middle of the street at any time, day or night, and fight it out with either bowie knives or six shooters."

Months later Bond and Fountain became enmeshed in an acrimonious editorial debate over the Tunstall and Brady killings. The *News* of June 15, 1878, accused the *Independent* of being partial to the Tunstall cause:

It has been a cause of considerable comment all over the Territory, about the manner in which the *Independent* has acted in regard to the death of two men, Major Brady, Sheriff of Lincoln county, and Mr. Tunstall. We give way to no one in our desire to punish crime, and have often advocated the most stringent measures of the law to punish criminals.

Major Brady was a brave officer, and an upright official as sheriff or legislator, a kind husband, an affectionate father, and a warm hearted friend; and honored and respected by hosts of friends throughout the Territory. Mr. Tunstall was a gentleman but lately from England, of whom we know but little. But, what was Tunstall to the *Independent,* or the *Independent* to Tunstall, that it should howl itself hoarse, sick, and all but crazy about punishing persons for killing Tunstall, (some of whom it would punish not being within twenty miles at the time,) while it fairly shudders to even publish the names of the assassins and murderers of Sheriff Brady and Deputy George Hindman as they were walking quietly down the street to the courthouse on official business. It probably would shield their names and persons from the public by a cloak or wall, similar to the adobe wall near McSween's residence, from which the corral squad fired upon Brady and party. If not, why does it not howl for the punishment of these assassins? Has it done so, or will it do so? No danger of it. It is not paid to do that. It will probably howl to punish those who are not of "its sort." "Oh! Consistency thou art a jewel!"

Bond with the Mesilla *News,* and Fountain with the *Independent,* managed to continue publication despite many obstacles, such as shortage of money and an annoying frequency in the shortage of newsprint. The newspaper situation in Mesilla became a bit more complicated when S. H. Newman started a third paper named *Thirty Four.* The Santa Fe *New Mexican* of April 5, 1879, noted progress:

S. H. Newman, of *Thirty Four,* and Ira M. Bond, of the Mesilla *News* recently had a difficulty on the street in Las Cruces. No blood spilled, and only one black eye.

Despite the signs which foretold that war was inevitable in the Pecos River country, Governor Axtell, after he had named George W. Peppin as sheriff of Lincoln County, was apparently satisfied to remain in Santa Fe, and continued to maintain a "hands off" policy. The time came, however, when even Sheriff Peppin became annoyed with Axtell's attitude. On August 24, 1878, the Santa Fe *New Mexican* published a copy of an affidavit, signed by Peppin, criticizing Axtell for his lack of cooperation:

Deponent declares that he accepted the appointment of high sheriff of Lincoln county only on the understanding that he would be legally supported by the military force at Fort Stanton.[6] That he immediately entered upon the discharge of his duties, not only with a conviction that the position was an honorable one, but that he would be sustained in the discharge of his duties by the authorities appointing him. That notwithstanding he (deponent) has reported to General Dudley, commanding the post at Fort Stanton, the results of all his official acts, all of which information to his personal knowledge has been reported by General Dudley to his Excellency, the Governor, and to the District Commander, from the date of his appointment to the present hour, he, (deponent) has never received the scratch of a pen from his Excellency, the Governor, or his Secretary. Affiant further deposes that since his appointment he has visited every town, settlement or stream where parties would be likely to camp accompanied with two or three exceptions by the principal stock owners of the county, and that during his term of service as Sheriff of Lincoln County, and special deputy U. S. Marshal his experience has convinced him that it is wholly impossible to restore order and peace in Lincoln County without the strong arm of the military.

Sheriff Peppin was convinced that the McSween crowd had killed M. J. Bernstein, clerk at the Mescalero Apache Agency:

Deponent further deposes that on the 5th day of August last an armed body of men headed by Scurlock, Bowdrie, French and Kid, in all twenty or more, attacked the Mescalero Apache Agency, killing the chief clerk of said agency, one M. J. Bernstein, robbing him of his arms and contents of pockets; that these parties are personally known to him, but he is powerless to arrest them without the aid of the military. Affiant further deposes that in his belief unless some steps are taken to prevent a recurrence of such or similar attacks on the Indian agency a general Indian war is inevitable. Deponent further states that during his term of service he has never received any complaint of the Mescalero Apache Indians having committed any depredations within the county, but that there has been evidence submitted to him that depredations have been committed by the lawless bands on the Indians and numbers of horses stolen from them.

Attached to Peppin's affidavit was Colonel Dudley's personal confirmation and endorsement:

I have carefully examined Sheriff Peppin's affidavit and do not hesitate to state that I believe it to be a plain, unvarnished picture of the present state of affairs in this county, and one that is spreading and increasing daily. New parties have arrived within the last six days. One of them yesterday dismounted a citizen, a farmer on the Rio Hondo, stripped him of his clothing and forty dollars in money. Then they proceeded to the vicinity of the Pecos, and stole some ten head of horses.

The raids they have commenced on the Mescalero Apache Indians, in my opinion, in less than sixty days will result in an Indian war, which will devastate not only Lincoln county, but ranches in the vicinity. I have written so much on this matter, without effecting anything, that at first I refused to forward the enclosed document, but Sheriff Peppin assured me that it was the last favor of the kind that he would solicit at my hands.

Axtell forwarded the Peppin affidavit and Dudley's endorsement to Washington, according to the Santa Fe *New Mexican:*

Governor Axtell has forwarded their petitions to the President of the United States with a strong request, as Governor of the Territory, for assistance from the United States, to protect the people from domestic violence. If the Governor's request is not granted it will probably become his duty to convene the legislature.

On September 14, 1878, the Las Vegas *Gazette* questioned the accuracy of some statements in Peppin's affidavit:

How is this? Sheriff Peppin, in his affidavit to Governor Axtell, positively asserted that the Indian Agency was attacked by a mob, who not only killed the chief clerk, but also stole a lot of reservation animals. Gen. Dudley endorsed this statement. Now comes the Mesilla Valley *Independent,* which says:

"It is positively asserted that Bernstein was killed by a Mexican who was with a party going from San Patricio to Tularosa to assist in recovering a lot of stolen stock in the possession of Frank Wheeler and others then at San Nicolas. When the Mexicans reached the water at the Agency, they stopped to water their horses. Bernstein saw them and probably supposing them to be a party of 'Regulators,' attacked them with a party of Indians; he rode up on one Mexican and fired two shots at him; the man took shelter behind a tree. Bernstein still advancing, rode close to the tree and fired again at the man, who returned the fire and killed Bernstein. The Mexican says he acted strictly in self defense, and will at any time give himself up for trial. His name is Atanacio Martinez."[7]

NOTES AND PROFILES

[1] Born in Covan, Ireland, in 1825, Brady emigrated to America when a young man, enlisted in the Second Regiment of New Mexico Volunteers on August 19, 1861, served throughout the Civil War. While serving with the First New Mexico Cavalry, he was promoted to major October 27, 1865, for gallantry in action against the Navajo Indians on July 1, 1865. Brady was a long-time member of Montezuma Lodge No. 1, A. F. & A. M., in Santa Fe. His death was officially reported to the Lodge on May 3, 1878, and Thomas B. Catron, Max Frost and David J. Miller were named on a committee to draft resolutions of regret.

[2] Richard M. Brewer, killed at Blazer's Mill on April 4, 1878, by a bullet from the gun of "Buckshot" Roberts, was a New Englander by birth. R. N. Mullin, patient and painstaking researcher on men and events connected with the Lincoln County War, followed many clues over a long period of years before tracking down Brewer's background.

As the result of his investigation, Mr. Mullin established the following facts: Richard M. Brewer (sometimes called Bruer in Lincoln County items) was born in St. Albans, Vermont, in 1852, moving with his Vermont-born parents Renselaer Brewer, father, and Phebe Brewer, mother, to Richland County, Wisconsin, shortly before July 28, 1860, the date of a federal census. The Brewers settled on a farm four miles south of Boaz, in Dayton Township, Wisconsin.

When about eighteen years old, Richard Brewer left his Wisconsin home, and eventually made his way to Lincoln County, New Mexico, where he arrived about 1870, and began farming on the Rio Feliz. On April 6, 1878, Alexander A. McSween wrote to J. P. Tunstall, father of John H. Tunstall, in London, to tell him of Dick Brewer's death, and gave his age at that time as twenty-seven years. For some time prior to Brewer's death he had been employed as a foreman on young Tunstall's ranch. Tunstall, according to McSween, "was passionately fond of horses." It was a common interest in breeding horses that first brought Brewer and Tunstall together.

James J. Dolan gave his appraisal of Brewer in a communication published in the Santa Fe *New Mexican* of May 25, 1878: "I always considered Brewer an honest man and treated him as such until he became contaminated with Mr. McSween, his legal adviser."

[3] Dr. Joseph H. Blazer was a close witness to many exciting events of the Lincoln County War. Born in Allegheny County, Pennsylvania, in 1828, he studied dentistry, served throughout the Civil War with the First Iowa Cavalry. After the war he traveled extensively in Texas and Mexico.

In 1867 Blazer drifted into Lincoln County and traded a freighting outfit for a sawmill at Mescalero, known thereafter as Blazer's Mill. The mill had been operated even prior to the Mexican War of 1846. Lumber from the mill was used in the construction and repair of buildings at Fort Davis and Fort Bliss, Texas, and Fort Selden and Fort Stanton in New Mexico. Although Blazer placed a value of $20,000 on the mill, a board of three army officers appraised the improvements at $1,237 in 1884. (Report of the Commissioner of Indian Affairs, 1881.)

In the early 70's the government conceded that Blazer was entitled to a patent for the mill site because of his occupancy prior to the Executive Order of May 29, 1873, establishing the Mescalero Indian reservation. Blazer's Mill has a permanent place in New Mexico history because it was the scene of the killing of "Buckshot" Roberts on April 4, 1878. Dr. Blazer died in 1898. Twenty years before he had been foreman of the Lincoln County grand jury which indicted John Middleton, Hendry Brown and William H. Bonney for the murder of Sheriff William Brady on April 1, 1878.

[4] Through with the strife and trouble attached to the office of sheriff of a frontier county, George W. Peppin eventually went to work in the prosaic occupation of Post Butcher at Fort Stanton. The Lincoln County *Leader* of March 17, 1883, commented: "Long may Peppin wave his bloody apron." Peppin died in Lincoln on September 18, 1904. On September 23, 1904, the Capitan *News*

in telling of Peppin's death, said he had lived in Lincoln County for forty years. In the Lincoln cemetery a granite stone over Peppin's grave is worded: "Geo. W. Peppin, Co. A., 5th Cal. Infantry."

[5] Under New Mexico law in 1876, and for some years thereafter, the sheriff of a county was ex-officio tax collector. The act of January 10, 1876, under which Axtell removed Copeland, required the sheriff, as tax collector, to execute and file a bond "in a sum which shall not be less than double the amount of money to be collected by such collector." No doubt Axtell acted in an arbitrary manner in removing Copeland. The law under which he acted could have been construed to be permissive instead of mandatory. (See Chap. XVI, Laws of 1876.) It was Copeland's contention that he did not furnish bond because he had no way of estimating the total amount of taxes he would collect, and consequently, did not know the amount of the bond that would be required.

[6] Fort Stanton, for many years an important military post, was located nine miles from Lincoln and thirty-six miles from the Mescalero Apache Indian Agency. Established on April 11, 1855, the fort was dedicated to the memory of Capt. Henry Whiting Stanton, killed by Apache Indians in the Sacramento Mountains on January 19, 1855. Born in New York, Stanton entered West Point on September 1, 1838, was commissioned a second lieutenant on July 1, 1842, promoted to captain on July 25, 1854.

Gen. John Garland, Commanding the Military Department of New Mexico, authorized the establishment of the fort on a site selected by Gen. Nelson A. Miles. Secretary of War Jefferson Davis approved the establishment on April 11, 1855, and the surrounding area was made an official military reservation by Act of Congress on May 12, 1859. When established, Fort Stanton was in the heart of the Apache Indian country. As the years passed, the Apaches became less troublesome and the importance of the fort diminished. Occupied by Union troops at the outbreak of the Civil War, Fort Stanton was abandoned and evacuated on August 12, 1861, on orders of Col. B. S. Roberts, then commanding officer, and two companies of infantry marched to Albuquerque. Texas troops commanded by Col. John R. Baylor then took possession of the fort, but soon abandoned it because it had no strategic value. Gen. James H. Carleton, of California Column fame, reactivated the fort in 1863.

In the early years Fort Stanton depended entirely on the Bonito River for water. As the country settled up, trouble resulted when ranchers and livestock men attempted to take water from the Bonito on which the military claimed priority. In 1878 the army built a dam and reservoir on the Bonito five miles upstream at a cost of $17,000. These facilities were enlarged and improved in 1884. Abandoned as a military post in 1899, Fort Stanton was thereafter used as a hospital for the treatment of American merchant marine patients suffering from respiratory ailments. In the 1950's the government closed the hospital and relinquished the buildings and a tract of land surrounding them to the State of New Mexico. At present writing (1956) no disposition has been made of the thousands of acres of land comprising the military reservation. The Mescalero Indians have asked that the government relinquish the land to them, the former owners.

[7] Before working for the government at the Mescalero Agency, Morris J. Bernstein was employed as a bookkeeper by Spiegelberg Brothers in Santa Fe. In his spare time, Bernstein wrote poetry. When the Mescalero Indians complained that white men had stolen horses from the reservation, Bernstein, who held a deputy sheriff's commission, helped the Indians round up some of the stolen stock. According to the Santa Fe *New Mexican* of August 14, 1876, Bernstein and Indian trailers, on one trip up the Pecos River, recovered seven horses in Puerto de Luna and one in Fort Sumner.

CHAPTER SEVEN

DEATH COMES TO LINCOLN TOWN

J ULY 19, 1878, was a day of wrath and reckoning in Lincoln. For several days preceding that dread day, scores of mounted men, carrying a tried-and-true weapon, whether six-shooter, rifle or shotgun, and armed with all available ammunition, rode toward Lincoln, the county seat of Lincoln County. No need to ask the name of the place of rendezvous, or to inquire into the purpose of traveling toward a common destination. Instinctively, each man seemed to know that the objective was Lincoln; and that there would be fighting after reaching there. Men crossed rivers and climbed up and down mountain passes, hurrying toward Lincoln from almost every direction. They came from Mesilla on the Rio Grande, one hundred fifty miles to the southwest; from the Socorro County cattle range country, more than one hundred miles to the west; from Pecos River ranches and farms from distances ranging from fifty to one hundred miles to the southeast. Work on ranch and farm was left undone; bawling calves, hungry and famished for water, got no succor from hired hands; cows unfortunate enough to become mired in water holes were abandoned to their fate. Everybody seemed to know, without being told, that the time had come for a showdown between the McSween and Dolan and Riley forces.

On June 1, 1878, the Las Vegas *Gazette* published an editorial reflecting the opinion that the trouble in Lincoln County was local in nature, and if let alone, would die down. *Gazette* readers were advised to "ignore all correspondence from and concerning Lincoln County and see how quickly the troubled waters will sink." The editorial:

The newspapers are warming up over the Lincoln County troubles. Bitter speeches and harsh epithets are in order. Keep your temper, gentlemen. Exercise charity, practice Christian patience and don't allow yourselves to be drawn into this whirlpool of violent words and still more violent deeds. A disgraceful, lawless local feud should not be allowed to spread through the whole Territory, like the small pox. Just let it die down within the limits of Lincoln County. It really concerns only a few persons, who, if left to themselves, are not likely to injure each other by violence. It has been a constant interference by outside parties which has raised hell. Better quickly ignore all correspondence from, and concerning Lincoln County, and see how quickly the troubled waters will sink to rest.

The *Gazette* of June 15, however, described the unrest among settlers and impressment of citizens:

When one party or the other, gets in close quarters in Lincoln County, they send out couriers to warn the people to come in and aid in the fight. These riders are kind of press officers, and make them turn out, whether they want to or not. The quiet class of citizens are getting tired of fighting other people's battles and are leaving their farms, stock and growing crops and are seeking other and safer localities. It is fight, fight, or die, and most of the people prefer the first. The war in Lincoln County has done that section infinite harm. Such wholesale slaughter creates terror in the mind of good, law abiding people, and those who contemplated emigrating hither will hesitate long before venturing their lives and property in so reckless a community. Bad men, on the other hand, will seek it as an asylum and hiding place from crime.

As of June 22, the *Gazette* reported the imminence of hostilities:

Reports from Lincoln County indicate a renewal of hostilities between adverse factions; both parties are in the field and a collision is imminent. If they should succeed in completely destroying each other the result would be hailed by all good citizens.

That a crisis was approaching was apparent from a letter written by John S. Chisum from Bosque Redondo on July 1, 1878, to Irwin, Allen & Co., which was published in the Kansas City *Commercial Indicator* and other papers. The Pecos River country, according to Chisum, was being cleared of cattle. Chisum's letter, in part:

Hunter & Evans have up to this date, started from Col. Hunter's range on the Pecos river, to Kansas, 8,068 head of mixed cattle, and has now about 4,000 more ready for the road. In about another month they will start another herd of 4,000. I think I may say one half of those cattle will be put on the market, and the remainder will be kept on their range. No other cattle will be driven from the Pecos to any market. There are but few cattle on this river except R. D. Hunter's.

The *Gazette* of July 20, 1878, reported the progress of events:

About July 1, a party of 12 or 13 men arrived on the Pecos from Seven Rivers. They were accompanied by T. B. Powell, deputy sheriff, who had warrants for the parties charged with the murder of Major Brady. Alex. McSween, with a party of 14 to 18 men, was at the ranch of John S. Chisum. About the 4th Powell and his friends invested the Chisum ranch and continued the attack all day and all night. Not succeeding in reducing the camp, the siege was raised and Powell's party left. Then McSween's party also started up the Pecos. Powell had been reinforced by Marion Turner and some 12 or 14 men, making about 35 in all; Turner was also deputized to make arrests. The two parties combined pursued the fugitives. They found a break up the river was a blind, as the McSween crowd had left the river and struck off by the Capitan in the direction of Lincoln. Turner, Powell and their friends pursued, and word was given out that they were between Lincoln and Capitan on the morning of July 10th. At that time McSween's forces were at San Patricio with 40 men. The danger of a severe battle is imminent. Before the parties went down the Pecos, three fights occurred in San Patricio in one day; one man was severely wounded and several horses were killed.

Sheriff George Peppin, seeking support from any and every available source, had the benefit of the advice and counsel of James J. Dolan. Peppin sent riders to all parts of the county with an urgent plea for help, promising a deputy sheriff's commission to all who would volunteer to fight on his side. Dolan had taken the precaution to engage the services of John Kinney, and some fifteen hired gunfighters from Doña Ana and Grant counties. Kinney and his men rode into Lincoln from the Rio Grande at a critical time and placed themselves at Peppin's disposal. Peppin gained the support of Henry Beckwith,[1] and his two sons, John and Robert, from the Seven Rivers country, after he had sent word to them that he was desperately in need of their help in a fight against their common enemy, John S. Chisum.

The battle of July 19 was inevitable, and could not have been avoided except through cowardice on one side or the other. Leadership in the crisis, by the logic of events, had been thrust upon Lawyer McSween. Hounded and harassed by citations and writs issued out of Judge Bristol's court, the result in part of District Attorney Rynerson's maneuvering, poor Mr. Mc-Sween gave every evidence, in the last days of June and early days of July, 1878, of being in a state of resigned confusion. He recognized the hopelessness of trying to remain in the Lincoln country, and attempting to carry on the fight against the combined power of Bristol and Rynerson. Hopeful of finding a way out of his difficulties, McSween had traveled horseback to South Spring Ranch, and sought the advice of John S. Chisum. After talking to Chisum, McSween reached his decision. He began the return journey to Lincoln, convinced that he had no alternative but to stand his ground and fight. Some of John Chisum's most trusted cowboys, acting as a bodyguard, accompanied McSween on the return trip. As he rode north along the Pecos River, and turned in the direction of San Patricio and Lincoln, McSween was encouraged from time to time to note that men began to ride along with him, some from the Pecos, others from the Feliz, the Peñasco, the Hondo, the Bonito, still others from far off mountain tops and remote valleys of the upper country. Some of the men who joined McSween were ordinary farmers and ranchers, none hankering for a fight; others were well-known gunfighters. McSween would have been the first man to admit that he was not a fighting man, and that he had no stomach at all for the panoply of war.

Riding from the South Spring Ranch toward Lincoln, Mc-Sween's thoughts in all probability revolved around his own lack of ability for leadership in the enterprise in which he found himself unwillingly and fatefully committed, an enterprise demanding an inherent love of combat, a native, instinctive, animal-like knowledge of how to attack and when to go in for the kill. McSween realized that affairs in Lincoln County had now reached a point where no man's life or property could be said to be safe or secure, either day or night; that no prudent man dared venture in the open, even at high noon, without a gun in hand.

There was no doubt but that McSween and his supporters were standing at the crossroads. As he neared Lincoln, McSween undoubtedly realized that he was a marked man, and that for him death lurked in every turn of the road. But there was no turning back now, no way by which he might honorably avoid the ordeal confronting him. By the time he reached Lincoln, about sundown on July 15, McSween found himself the fateful captain of an army of forty-one men. Some rode along in high spirits, as if bent on a crusade of righteousness, fearless and anxious for a showdown fight; others were silent and apprehensive of things to come. Upon reaching the outskirts of the town, McSween deployed his forces. He took ten men to his own home; others were billeted in the Ellis and Montano homes; some made camp on the banks of the Bonito and in the hills beyond, north of town.

Sheriff Peppin had not been idle during the two days it had taken McSween and his followers to ride from Chisum's ranch to Lincoln. Peppin had commandeered and recruited about forty men, and true to his promise, had commissioned each and every one a deputy sheriff. Among leaders ready to fight on Peppin's side were: Joseph Nash, Henry, Robert and John Beckwith, Robert and Wallace Olinger, Andrew Boyle, John Hurley, J. B. Matthews, James J. Dolan, "Buck" Waters, "Buck" Powell, John Chambers, John Kinney, Tom Jones, Jesse Evans, Pantaleon Gallegos, Marion Turner, John Long, Jose Chaves y Baca, Sam Perry, James Reese. Peppin placed his men at strategic points in and about Lincoln. The Peppin forces were called the "Sheriff's Party," and their opponents were known as the "McSween Crowd." If Peppin's forces included Jesse Evans, one of Tunstall's alleged slayers, there was no denying that McSween's forces had the assistance of several notorious characters, among them William H. Bonney, one of the alleged slayers of Sheriff Brady and Deputy Hindman.

During all hours of the day and night of July 16, 17 and 18, it was not safe for man, woman or child to be on the streets of Lincoln. Bullets occasionally whizzed and whined through the air, but whether from poor marksmanship or otherwise, surprisingly few casualties resulted. Unfortunately for McSween's crowd, a stray bullet on July 16 hit and slightly wounded Benjamin Robinson, a soldier from Fort Stanton. Robinson claimed that while walking along the main street of Lincoln, peacefully and unarmed, four shots had been fired at him from the vicinity of McSween's house, and that he had narrowly escaped being killed.

As of daylight on July 19, the battle between the McSween and anti-McSween forces had reached a stalemate. Neither the Sheriff nor any of his deputies had succeeded in arresting, or serving warrants on any of the men barricaded in McSween's house. There was every indication that the military, nine miles away at Fort Stanton, would maintain neutrality. On July 7, 1878, R. C. Drum, Assistant Adjutant General in Washington, had issued General Orders No. 49, directing the attention of all army officers to the provisions of an Act of Congress approved June 18, 1878. These orders forbade the use of federal troops in assisting civil authorities as a posse comitatus, or in executing the laws, except in conformity with the provisions of the Constitution of the United States, or pursuant to an Act of Congress. In a word, federal troops could not be used in civil matters in the Territory, without the express permission of the President, obtained through military channels. (Text of order in LVG, August 17, 1878.)

Notwithstanding Drum's General Orders, Sheriff Peppin asked for help from Commanding Officer Dudley at Fort Stanton, writing him a politely worded letter on July 16:

GENERAL: I have the honor to respectfully state that mostly all the men for whom I have United States warrants are in town, and are being protected by A. A. McSween and a large party of his followers. They are in the houses of A. A. McSween, Ellis Sons, J. B. Patron and Jose Montano. They are resisting, and it is impossible for me to serve the warrants. If it is in your power to loan me one of your howitzers, I am of the opinion the parties for whom I have said warrants would surrender without a shot being fired. Should it be in your power to do this, in favor of the law, you would confer a great favor on the majority of the people of this county, who are being persecuted by a lawless mob.

Acknowledging Peppin's note, Dudley promptly expressed regret because of his inability to furnish the howitzer as requested without instructions from Washington. Sheriff Peppin at once wrote another note to Dudley:

GENERAL: I have the honor to acknowledge the receipt of your very kind favor of date; am very sorry I cant get the assistance I asked for, but I will do the best I can. The McSween party fired on your soldier when coming into town. My men on seeing him tried to cover him, but of no use. The soldier will explain the circumstances to you. I take this opportunity of thanking you for your kindness in the name of all my people.

Peppin's second letter disclosing the fact that one of Dudley's soldiers had been fired on, gave him a reason to interfere. Calling a meeting of his staff officers to consider the situation, he told them of Sheriff Peppin's communications, and read to them a letter from Saturnino Baca of Lincoln, urgently requesting that enough soldiers be sent to Lincoln to protect women and children. Dudley's staff promptly agreed unanimously that troops be sent to Lincoln for the sole and only purpose, as Dudley later expressed it, of protecting "helpless woman and children." The parade of Lieutenant Colonel Dudley and his troops into Lincoln on July 19, proved an impressive spectacle: sixty cavalrymen, one lieutenant colonel, three captains, several lieutenants, one Gatling gun, one howitzer, and an ample supply of arms and ammunition. The arrival of the military, as subsequent events demonstrated, marked the beginning of the end for the McSween side. In a matter of hours, the tide of battle began to veer toward the Sheriff's party.

Soon after reaching Lincoln, Dudley's staff officers convinced a reluctant justice of the peace, John B. Wilson, that he would be justified in issuing warrants for arrest of Alex. A. McSween and others on a charge of assault with intent to kill upon the person of Benjamin Robinson. With Judge Wilson's warrants in hand, Peppin and his deputies lost no time in making plans to arrest the men against whom they had been issued, knowing that they would be protected under the law for any killing done in event of resistance.

About dusk on July 19, McSween's house was set on fire. Deputies Marion Turner and Robert Beckwith called upon the inmates to surrender, but they refused. In the shooting that followed, Vicente Romero, Harvey Morris, Francisco Zamora and Alex. McSween, of the McSween forces, were killed, and Robert Beckwith was killed on the Peppin side. William Bonney ran from McSween's house in a desperate attempt to reach Tunstall's store. Soldiers fired at him, compelling him to swerve in his course. Running toward the Bonito River, Bonney escaped in the gathering darkness.

A coroner's jury, made up of Felipe Miranda, Jose Garcia, Marciamiano Chavez, Octaviano Salas, Felipe Maes, and Jose Serna, held an inquest on July 20 over the bodies of the five dead men. Viewing the remains, the jury noted the number and location of the bullet wounds: McSween, five; Romero, three in the body and leg; Harvey Morris, and Zamora, one each; Beckwith, two in the head and one in the wrist. The jury returned a verdict finding that McSween, Romero, Morris and Zamora "came to their deaths by rifle shots fired from the hands of the Sheriff's posse, while they, the above named persons were resisting the posse with force and arms"; and that Beckwith "came to his death by two rifle shots from the hands of the above named McSween, Morris, Zamora and others, and while they were resisting the Sheriff's posse, and while Beckwith was a deputy sheriff, acting in the discharge of his duties, trying to arrest the parties for whom he had warrants."

The Grant County *Herald,* of August 3, 1878, published one version of the encounter between McSween and Beckwith:

We learn McSween said after a hard fight that they would surrender. Beckwith said as he was a deputy sheriff he would go to the door; that they could surrender to him and he would protect them. As Beckwith approached the door, McSween and party jumped to the door and fired; it appeared that they expected more were coming and that they would kill all that were with him. Bob's gun failed to work; he received a ball in the corner of the left eye and fell dead. With a cry of "Revenge Bob Beckwith," no time was lost by the

Sheriff's posse in firing with effect. McSween said: "Oh, my God!
and dropped dead. . . . Mrs. McSween never went to see McSween
after he was killed and did not attend the funeral. Beckwith was
buried with honors at Fort Stanton.[2]

Justice of the Peace John B. Wilson wrote an eyewitness
account of the happenings of July 19, 1878, at the request of
Gov. Lew. Wallace:

I was ordered by Col. Dudley, Commanding Fort Stanton in New
Mexico, on or about the 19th of July, 1878, to take the affidavits
of Col. Purington, Capt. Blair and Dr. Appel accusing A. A. Mc-
Sween and others that were in his house on July 16th, 1878, of having
committed an assault on the person of one Benj. Robinson, a soldier
of Ft. Stanton by having shot 4 or more shots at him with intent to
kill as they had been informed and believed. I told Col. Dudley that
I was not certain whether it was lawful for me to issue such an order
or not and I thought it was the duty of a United States Commissioner
to issue it, as there was a soldier concerned in it. He got very angry
at me for refusing to issue it on that ground. He told me if I did not
take the affidavit and issue the warrant forthwith that he would report me to the governor. He called me a coward and said many other
bad words to me. I then went to my office and took the affidavits of
the named officers and after they signed and swore to them I issued
the warrant to the Sheriff of Lincoln county for the arrest of A. A.
McSween and others that were in the house on the 16th day of July,
1878, as per the affidavits and gave it to George W. Peppin to serve
returnable forthwith. The warrant has not been returned into my
office up to this date by Peppin or any one for him. I did not issue the
warrant by my own will but by the peremptory order of Col. Dudley.

Isaac Ellis, a Lincoln merchant, in an unsigned statement
corroborated Judge Wilson's recollections:

On or about the 17th of July 1878 Sheriff Peppin and posse attacked the town of Lincoln and kept up firing from the neighboring
hills until the morning of the 19th when Lieut. Col. N. A. M. Dudley,
with Capt. George A. Purington, Capt. Blair, Lieut. Goodwin and
Dr. Appel of Fort Stanton with a company of soldiers and 2 pieces
of artillery arrived here and went into camp about the center of

town and sent for me. When I arrived at the camp Dudley seemed
to be greatly excited. When I was informed by Col. Dudley that if
a gun was fired out of mine or any house in town he would immediately tear it to the ground regardless of women and children. While
at the camp of Col. Dudley the so called Sheriff George W. Peppin
came riding into camp with 3 soldiers, I think Peppin was riding a
government horse. After talking a short time with Dudley, Dudley
ordered the soldiers to go back with Sheriff Peppin. I then returned
to my house. Dudley set one piece of artillery about 200 feet from
and pointing towards my house. In a short time Peppin together
with about nine men came from the direction of the camp of Dudley
and came in my house and ordered me to give them coal oil for which
they stated they intended to use in setting fire to the house of A. A.
McSween. They further stated that they had him in the house and
intended to burn him out. They took the coal oil with them and went
back. When opposite the camp, Dudley came out and they, Dudley
and Peppin talked for some time. They then went on towards the
house of A. A. McSween and in a little while firing commenced
around McSween's house and we saw some smoke arise from the
house and firing was kept up until about nine o'clock at night. The
following morning McSween with two others were found dead in the
yard riddled with bullets and the house and contents were totally
destroyed by fire. The same morning the store of John H. Tunstall,
dec'd was broke open and robbed of about six thousand dollars worth
of goods. After the store was robbed Col. Dudley broke up camp and
returned to Fort Stanton.

On July 25, 1878, McSween's widow, signing herself "Mary
McSween," wrote to John Partridge Tunstall in London, to tell
him of her "dear, dear husband's death." Why Susan McSween
used the name "Mary," in writing to Tunstall is not known.
After giving some details of McSween's death, the widow in
her letter touched rather lightly, but pointedly, on a debt of
"four or five thousand dollars," which she said his son, John
Tunstall, owed McSween:

Oh, it is painful indeed that I am at last left to convey to you the
sad news of my dear, dear husband's death. He was killed on the
evening of the 19th. at home, and the house and everything in it,

burned to ashes. Was not able to save even a change of clothing for myself. Oh, that day was the most horrible sight that could be imagined. He was murdered even worse than poor John. Those thieves and murderers gathered around the house, set it on fire, and commenced shooting in at every door and window. When he found there was no chance of escape, he begged them not to shoot him, but that availed nothing. I buried him by the side of your dear son; that was always his wish. You cannot imagine the love he bore your son. I would have written before this, but the subject was so painful, and now it is only more painful. Oh, how can I survive all this, do pray for me. Mr. McSween was not himself from the day of your son's death, he has not left a thing undone to prove that he was a murdered man, and I fear, too, that Mr. Widenmann is killed; he started for Mesilla about four or five weeks ago, and we have not heard from him for about three weeks, and whilst those men were here they swore they would kill him. Others said we would never see him again; now we do not know what to think about it.

After those men killed my dear husband, they broke into the store [Tunstall's] and dressed themselves up from head to foot, and invited all others to help themselves, which many did; they broke into the office, and rummaged through the papers, took what they wanted of them, opened the trunk and took all his clothing. Oh, but it pained me to see this done. John had given me many little keepsakes that I prized very highly, but they too, had to burn up with the balance of my things. They have also threatened my life; because I have defended both Mr. McSween and your son, and many believe that I am really in danger. I will write you more particularly when I recover from the shock. I hope you will pardon me for speaking of a matter which is not entirely business, but as I am left entirely destitute, with not even a change of clothing, I deem it necessary to speak of the matter; but I was aware of your son owing Mr. McSween about four or five thousand dollars and also knew he had asked you to pay it. Now I fear you have sent it, and somebody will find it. They are beginning to claim small debts already. Can you not pay it for me, or could you not send some small portion of it to me, that I may have something to depend on for awhile at least. Nothing can be done yet about Mr. McSween's business. Nearly every man has left town and gone to the mountains to save their lives. I will write you again, soon, am very sad at present. I am of a very nervous disposition, and cannot stand under too much; excuse this for I scarcely know what I am doing.

The shooting, killing and pillaging in Lincoln in mid-July, 1878, resulted in a virtual stampede of people and livestock from all parts of Lincoln County. The Las Vegas *Gazette* of August 16, told of removal of cattle:

Col. R. D. Hunter is moving every hoof of cattle he has on the Pecos across the Staked Plains to the Panhandle. He will take them to Colorado and the remainder to Wyoming. The move is occasioned by the Lincoln County War. Mr. Coggins will also send the eight thousand which he bought from Hunter across to the Panhandle. In a few weeks there will not be a hundred head of stock on the Pecos. So much for a war, a county depopulated and industry banished.

Many settlers had been forced to leave the county, according to the *Gazette:*

Six wagon loads of emigrants from North and South Spring River in Lincoln county passed through Las Vegas Tuesday going north. They were driven out by the lawless element of that section. They had tried hard to take no part in the contest and preferred to leave rather than take either side. About twenty horses had been stolen from them. A deputy sheriff rode up with a posse and demanded that they take up arms and go with them and fight. This they refused to do and loaded up and left the country. They left their houses, lands, standing crops, gardens and everything pertaining to comfortable homes. They will seek work on the railroad. No new country can well afford to lose so industrious and law abiding class of people.

Alex. A. McSween's enemies claimed that he had dreams of becoming wealthy in Lincoln County. Apparently he failed to accumulate any great wealth, assuming that the assets belonging to his estate were accurately inventoried. His widow, Susan E. McSween, was appointed administratrix of his estate shortly after his death. The inventory and appraisal, completed April 22, 1879, listed twenty-seven head of cattle at $270, several thousand dollars in accounts receivable, one-half interest in a store building, $800, desert land on Rio Feliz, $250, George Van Sickle ranch, $250. After the inventory had been completed, a notation was added:

Since the above and foregoing inventory was made what might have been assets of his estate were blown to the four winds during the Lincoln County troubles.

What became of the net receipts from Emil Fritz' insurance money? No doubt but that Attorney McSween collected the face of the policy; from which he claimed he was entitled to deduct $700 paid Spiegelberg Bros. in settlement of their claim, and some $2,700 paid to Donnell, Lawson & Co. of New York for services rendered, and to reimburse himself for travel and incidental expenses. No adequate accounting was ever filed by McSween in the Probate Court in the Fritz estate showing the receipts and expenditures of the insurance money, and Susan McSween failed to account for any balance on hand in the administration of her husband's estate.

Susan Homer McSween carried on the Lincoln County War after his death to the best of her ability. In many respects she was a remarkable woman. Born in Gettysburg, Pennsylvania, in 1845, before her marriage she lived for a time in Atchison, Kansas, coming to the Territory with her husband on March 3, 1875. She lived in New Mexico until her death in White Oaks on January 3, 1931. Her grave is in Cedarville Cemetery in White Oaks. On July 19, 1879, Mrs. McSween observed the first anniversary of her husband's death by filing a suit in the District Court of Lincoln County asking judgment against Colonel Dudley for $25,000 damages, alleging defamation of character. The complaint, prepared by Attorney Leonard, was written on twelve pages of foolscap.

Mrs. McSween alleged, among other things, that she had requested Governor Wallace in the fall of 1878 to provide a military escort for her from Santa Fe to Lincoln, being fearful of bodily harm if she traveled by ordinary conveyance; that the Governor referred her request to General Hatch, who in turn forwarded it to Dudley. Instead of complying with her request, Mrs. McSween alleged that Dudley "procured and forwarded to the Department of Military District Headquarters at Santa

Fe ... and from there transmitted to Lewis Wallace, Governor of New Mexico," affidavits attacking her character; that Dudley had wickedly and maliciously induced Saturnino Baca, a long-time resident of Lincoln, to sign an affidavit containing many false statements, in which he had declared that "Susan McSween had threatened to have him and his entire family killed"; and "that during the months of May, June and part of July, 1878, the McSween house was occupied at times by a gang of well known murderers and horse thieves, not fewer than twenty, and even as high as thirty at a time;" and that he, Saturnino Baca, had "seen the gang, all fully armed, in the yard at the McSween residence, among the number the notorious 'Kid,' alias Antrim, Jim French, Scurlock, Stephen Stephens, Bowdry, Waite, and others of similar reputation, coming and going at all hours of the night"; that Mrs. McSween "had threatened so many times to have him and his entire family murdered, that he had appealed to Dudley for protection; that Dudley furnished him with a guard of three soldiers at his home in Lincoln, but he was finally obliged to move to Fort Stanton and seek protection of the flag of the garrison."

Mrs. McSween further alleged in her complaint against Dudley that he had maliciously procured a false affidavit from George W. Peppin, sheriff of Lincoln County, "in which Peppin swore that he had been in Lincoln County for fourteen years; that he had served in the U. S. Volunteers during the Civil War; that he was a mason by trade; that his family resided in Lincoln until the recent disturbances in the county forced him to flee from his home to save his life, and that his family were compelled to abandon house and property and seek protection at the hands of the military at Fort Stanton, being compelled to this necessity by a party of murderers, horse thieves and escaped convicts headed by one A. A. McSween."

Peppin's affidavit, according to the complaint, declared "that he had known the McSweens from the day they set foot in Lincoln County, nearly four years ago," and that he knew "Mrs. McSween to be an unprincipled, untruthful woman; one that would not hesitate to use any means in her power to accomplish her ends, even to sacrifice of life;" that Mrs. McSween had told him during the month of June, 1878, that "she would be damned if she would not clean the county of Lincoln out of the parties who opposed her husband's actions if she had to spend twenty five thousand dollars to do it;" that the "daily companions of Mrs. McSween during the last six or eight months have been well known and recognized outlaws, many of whom were positively known by her to be under indictment by the grand jury for murder and other felonies" and that "before and since the death of her husband, Mrs. McSween had shielded, aided and assisted the outlaws to resist by various means the civil authorities in the attempt to arrest such outlaws; that her residence or quarters which she occupied had been a rendezvous for murderers, thieves and escaped convicts" and "that no time since April last had it been considered safe or prudent for any civil posse that could be called on to aid the legally constituted authority of the county to attempt to serve warrants on the outlaws whom she has definitely harbored and protected by violent and unlawful means."

Contending that all of the statements in the affidavits were false and maliciously circulated, Mrs. McSween asked the judgment of the court, and a trial by jury. Mrs. McSween's lawsuit against Dudley was never tried. Insofar as official records of Lincoln County are concerned, the case is still pending on the docket.[3]

Andrew Boyle, one-time British soldier, who had been in the thick of the maneuvering and fighting in Lincoln County on July 19, 1878, and had been an eyewitness to many important events during the preliminary and final stages of the Lincoln County War, wrote a letter to Ira M. Bond, publisher of the Mesilla *News,* from Lincoln, on August 2, 1878, in which he submitted what he described as "a plain, unvarnished statement of facts" relating to the difficulties. Boyle's letter, written in forthright, soldier-like style, with little attention paid to grammar or punctuation, is of considerable probative value. It contains two important statements, one concerning participation by Colonel Dudley's soldiers in scouting maneuvers against the McSween forces in mid-July, 1878, and the other a somewhat detailed description of the part played by John Kinney, a professional gunman of Mesilla and Silver City, in helping to hound McSween to his grave.

Andy Boyle's letter, written within two weeks after Mc-Sween's death, while the events were still fresh in mind, was as follows:

LINCOLN. N. M., AUG. 2nd 1878

IRA M. BOND, ESQ.

DEAR SIR: I have the pleasure of contradicting some of the Mesilla Valley *Independent's* statements regarding the trouble in Lincoln Co.; more so as it has been to the trouble of falsifying many tales in regard to said troubles. Having been hired by A. A. McSween, J. S. Chisum and others to the detriment of law abiding citizens of said Co. To commence: I received a letter from C. H. Brady, one of J. S. Chisum's warriors, dated May 27, 1877 South Spring river viz. Mr. Andrew Boyle; Dear sir, you red headed s— of — b—— if you do not bring them horses back you stole you shall hear the gentle report of my needle gun; that is the kind of a hair pin I am, this thing of being on a Sheriff's posse for a band of horse thieves may do in some places but it has got too thin with me, yours, on the first dark stormy night Chas H. Brady. I received this cheeky epistly on my return from Mesilla court to Seven Rivers July 8 1877; I paid no attention to that, or any of the *Independent's* scurrilous language and back biting letters against my statement, to U. S. Atty. Catron, of the Chisum-Pecos War in April 1877; which everybody knows. I defy any man to face me and say I stole animals or anything else.

Boyle charged that the Chisum-McSween combine tried to ruin Lincoln County, told of Dudley's harangue to Dolan, Sheriff Peppin and John Kinney at Fort Stanton; and disclosed facts indicating that Dudley's sympathies were with the Dolan-Riley contingent:

The Chisum-McSween-*Independent's* "Regulators," have tried to ruin Lincoln Co. by assassinating Maj. Brady Sheriff, deputy sheriff Geo. Hindman, deputy sheriff Morton, Roberts and others; in fact trying to murder the whole Murphy, Dolan and Riley party and everybody that worked for them; and by threats to coerce the Mexican citizens into submission to this band of outlaws, thieves and assassins.

June 20th 1878 J. J. Dolan, Sheriff Geo. W. Peppin, John Kinney, and a posse of 15 men reached Lincoln and Fort Stanton for the purpose of trying to quell said riots; we staid 1 day at Fort Stanton. Gen. Dudley Commanding Officer called the posse to Head Quarters and gave them an harrangue to this effect.

Gentlemen: I have a very unpleasant and thankless duty to perform. It has been reported to me that there are some criminals here in the command of Cap. John Kinney; whether this be true, I am not their judge. Now I want you all distinctly understand, that if one of Sheriff Peppin's posse steals a horse, mule or anything else I will hold the sheriff responsible for said deed, and punish the culprit as I would any of the opposite party for a like offense. I am going to send my soldiers to assist the sheriff to serve legal papers from the District Court, and if any of my men fire the first shot I shall have him court martialed. I hope there will be no trouble.

The Sheriff's posse encountered resistance while attempting to serve warrants on members of the McSween faction in Lincoln and San Patricio. The posse numbered some fifty men, including thirty soldiers and a number of John Kinney's hired gunmen:

Sheriff Peppin, Deputy Sheriff J. Long, Lt. Goodwin and thirty soldiers and Capt. Kinney and 15 of posse proceeded to Lincoln to see if any of the persons were there that the sheriff had warrants for; arrived one hour before day, sheriff going with soldiers into town, deputy Long and posse going below town, waited till one hour after sun rise no person appearing, Long and posse rode into town; no person there sheriff had warrants for so soldiers and posse started back to Stanton.

Several days after hearing McSween and the "Regulators" were in San Patricio, we rode into said Plaza at sun rise, found no person in town except Geo. Washington, colored, who was trying to make his escape. Capt. Kinney called to him, he kept running with his Winchester rifle in his hand. K. then shot over his head and called again to him to halt, he dropped his rifle and surrendered himself, saying if you do not kill me I will tell you all I know about the Regulators.

Previous to this John N. Copeland ex sheriff, on our arrival at Lincoln was in McSween's house deputy Long sent for him and told him, if he would go home and attend to his business no person would interfere with him; he promised faithfully to do so, but in the first fight at San Patricio, Copeland was the leading man, killing two horses, one of Capt. Kinney's and J. Long's mare; no other casualties. Deputy Sheriff Long took a posse of five men to go to Newcomb's ranch to serve warrants on two persons supposed to be there, but not finding them there he was returning down the Ruidoso when they espied eleven men riding up on the other side of the stream, supposing them to be Kinney's men they rode towards them and got within sixty yards before they found out their mistake. When the Regulators fired on the posse shooting deputy sheriff Long's horse in the flank and Roksey's horse in the neck; we heard the shooting at San Patricio when Capt. Kinney called the posse together who were guarding the town, and we rode at full speed to the scene of action, arriving there we found the Regulators on the prominent peak of a mountain, two ravines between and no means of surrounding them unless by direct assault. Capt. Kinney and seven men tried to surround their position we got within 500 yards, they opened a heavy fire on the posse, which we could not resent being too far below; we held them four hours till troops from Stanton came up, when the posse retired to Lincoln; the troops following the Regulators down the Hondo as far as Agua Azul, but were recalled by order from Washington.

Boyle described the events that appeared significant to him between July 2 and July 19, culminating with the death of McSween and others in the fighting in Lincoln:

July 2nd. Sheriff Peppin summoned a posse of fifteen Mexicans under deputy sheriff Baca to go to San Patricio and find out if Regulators were there, if so to send dispatch to Lincoln for help. The Mexican posse rode into San Patricio at early daybreak when they were fired upon by the Regulators; when they at once dispatched a messenger to Lincoln; deputy sheriff Long had fifteen men in as many seconds, and found on entering the town that the Regulators had left. We saw them about a mile below leave the creek and take to the mountains six of us followed them clear up into the peak making them drop a horse on the ascent, they then left for the Pecos where deputy Sheriff Marion Turner, on a request from deputy Sheriff Powell called on sheriff's posse to assist the Seven Rivers posse. We arrived there at noon July 5 found that the Regulators had left for Lincoln. Returning to Lincoln found all quiet, McSween and the Regulators still in the mountains; waited four days, learned forty of them were near the Ruidoso, of twenty four followed their trail, but were misled, because the Regulators entered Lincoln swearing death to Sheriff Peppin and posse, Dolan and party and destruction of their property; they take possession of the town; occupy the premises of McSween, Ellis, Patron and Montana; the fight continues for three days and nights; the McSween party held the sheriff's posse at bay from July 16 to 19th when the tug of war commenced; the house being on fire McSween called out that they would surrender to an officer; deputy Sheriff R. W. Beckwith went forward to receive them and protect those that surrendered, when the treacherous assassins shot him dead. With a shout to "revenge the murder of Beckwith and others," the posse fight desperately resulting in the death of McSween and others; wounding many others and driving the band of Regulators to the mountains; leaving the sheriff and posse in possession of the town of Lincoln. I have tried to give a plain, unvarnished statement of facts; and am responsible for what I say.

The John Kinney referred to in Andrew Boyle's letter was one of the most colorful characters of his day. Few men in the Southwest of the 70's and 80's could rival his experiences and exploits; and subsequent to the 80's, Kinney led a storybook life. Born in Hampshire, Massachusetts, in 1847, John Kinney died in Prescott, Arizona, on August 25, 1919.[4] His body went to the grave with the scars of five major bullet wounds, proof that he had been under fire, at comparatively close range. As a young man Kinney joined the United States Army in the East, and was assigned to New Mexico in 1868 as a trooper of the Third U. S. Cavalry. After serving in several posts in Arizona and New Mexico, he was honorably discharged in 1873 at Camp Bowie, Arizona, with the rank of sergeant in Troop K. Out of the army, Kinney engaged in ranching and cattle raising on a small scale in the Mesilla Valley, and ran a butcher shop in Mesilla. His enemies claimed that he devoted more of his time to "cattle rustling" than to "cattle ranching." While carrying on his meat-marketing activities, Kinney was indicted on several counts by a Doña Ana County grand jury for "larceny of neat cattle." Utilizing in a practical and profitable manner the experience he had gained as a cavalryman, Kinney in 1877 organized a professional force of fighting men in southern New Mexico, and at the urgent call of El Paso officers, hurried to the aid of Texas Rangers, beleaguered in San Elizario, some miles from El Paso; and some months later accepted employment, with his hired gunmen, on the Peppin side in his fight against McSween, Bonney and others in Lincoln County. John Kinney and Bonney were not strangers. They had become acquainted in Georgetown, Grant County, New Mexico, while both men were hiding out from the law because of alleged violations of the criminal code. In the 80's Kinney served as a scout for General Crook in Arizona, in campaigns against the Apache Indians, and in 1890 settled down for a time near Prescott; later becoming interested in mining in Chaparral. Prior to the Spanish-American War of 1898, Kinney, scenting trouble in far off Cuba, went there, and with several companions, became involved in revolutionary difficulties. From these troubles Kinney was extricated through the intercession of Gen. Leonard Wood, whose friendship he had gained in Arizona in the mid-80's, while Kinney was a scout and Wood was helping to capture Geronimo.

The Grant County *Herald* of Saturday, December 22, 1877, told of John Kinney's exploits in an emergency across the border in Texas:

On Monday last, John Kinney received a dispatch from Sheriff Charles Kerber, of El Paso, Texas conferring authority on him to raise a force for the relief of the rangers besieged at San Elizario. Kinney went to work at once and by evening had twenty five names on the muster role. The party started from Mesilla for El Paso the same evening. Traveling all night, Kinney's men reached El Paso, forty miles away in the morning with 27 men, and left that evening for Ysleta to join the forces already there. Ysleta is about eight miles from San Elizario.

The trouble at San Elizario was serious, and threatened for a time to extend across the border into Mexico. The origin of the trouble was obscured in conflicting reports, but it appeared that on December 12, 1877, Judge C. H. Howard, agent and attorney for Col. George B. Zimpelman, with writs and warrants in his hand for service, went to San Elizario, escorted by Texas Rangers, prepared to take formal possession of the Guadalupe salt lakes. The people in the area resisted, claiming that the salt lakes were common property, and that since time immemorial they had taken salt from the lakes and carried it away at will. Prior to Howard's visit to San Elizario, his client, Zimpelman, had gone to Austin, the state capital, and filed papers believed necessary to support a claim on the land covered by the lakes. In the rioting that followed Howard's attempt to exercise dominion over the lakes, he was killed and his body mutilated; and several other men were also killed, among them Charles E. Ellis, a local merchant, George E. Mortimer and John G. Atkinson; and several Rangers were taken prisoner and threatened with death. The trouble at the salt lakes caused much excitement in the vicinity of El Paso, Ysleta and San Elizario; and had repercussions in Mesilla, Silver City, and other places across the border in neighboring New Mexico. Gen. Edward Hatch accompanied a troop of the Ninth Cavalry from Fort Bayard, New Mexico, made a forced march to El Paso, and pitched camp at Ysleta, supplementing troops from Fort Bliss and other Texas forts.

Anxious to get into the fight, the Grant County Light Brigade was mobilized in Silver City, hurried to Mesilla and El Paso, but failed to reach San Elizario before the fighting had subsided. The brigade, made up of officers, included Brig. Gen. Dan Corcoran, Col. Americus Hall, Lt. Col. Alex Mitchell, Major Daniel Keho, Capt. Edward Deadwater, First Lt. Paul W. Keaton, Second Lt. George Cassidy, First Sgt. Frank Mullins, and Master of Transportation, J. M. Williams.

The Grant County *Herald* of January 26, 1878, told of the return of the home guard and the hazards of the trip:

A considerable number of the Silver City contingent to the El Paso Army of Occupation returned to town last Saturday. They expressed themselves as well satisfied with their lark. No expense, plenty of fun and a measure of experience which may be turned to advantage in future campaigns.

Within six months after the trouble in San Elizario, John

Kinney was in Lincoln County with some sixteen fighting men, arrayed at the side of the Dolan-Riley faction. To Kinney the trouble in Lincoln County was just another professional engagement.

The Grant County *Herald* of January 15, 1878, through publication of an article taken from the Las Cruces *Eco,* told of Kinney's prowess, of his growing strength and prestige:

Capt. John Kinney now has an independent command of about 70 men and has issued a call for 30 more well armed and mounted to join him at or near El Paso. Pay $40 per month and forage, by state of Texas. With 100 well armed and mounted men Capt. Kinney is liable soon to have a world wide reputation and lay Lieut. Bullis in the shade.

Although John Kinney had business as a professional gunfighter in Texas and New Mexico in 1877 and 1878, his time was not altogether taken up with other people's troubles. He had been in considerable trouble in New Mexico. Indicted by the Doña Ana County grand jury for the murder of Isabel Barela, at Mesilla on November 2, 1877, Kinney was arrested after having been on the dodge for several months and placed in jail in Mesilla for a brief time. When his lawyer threatened to institute habeas corpus proceedings, Kinney was released on bond, and granted a change of venue to Grant County. The Grant County *Herald* of December 14, 1878, told the final result:

The case of the Territory of New Mexico vs. John Kinney, accused of the murder of Isabel Barela, at Mesilla, on Nov. 2, 1877, occupied the greater part of the day. Col. Rynerson represented the Territory, and the defense was conducted by Judge S. B. Newcomb. The jury was called at about eleven oclock a.m., and but little difficulty was experienced in selecting the twelve competent men. Numerous witnesses were examined, and after able arguments by both attorneys, the jury retired. They were absent but a short time, and returned with a verdict of not guilty. The court then (about 11 P.M.) adjourned.

NOTES AND PROFILES

[1]Within less than a month after the July 19 fighting in Lincoln, in which his son Robert Beckwith was killed, Henry Beckwith became involved in a war of his own. On August 16, 1878, he shot and killed William H. Johnson, his son-in-law, at the Beckwith ranch on Seven Rivers, using a double-barrelled shotgun loaded with slugs and pistol balls. The charge took effect in Johnson's neck and breast, killing him instantly. After killing Johnson, Beckwith quarrelled with his son, John Beckwith. Bystanders interfered and saved John's life. Further complicating the trouble, which was the outgrowth of a family quarrel, Wallace Olinger wounded the elder Beckwith in the cheek and nose with a revolver shot. Olinger, a brother of Bob Olinger, who was killed by William H. Bonney at Lincoln on April 28, 1881, was arrested and taken to jail in Fort Stanton. (LVG, August 31, 1878.)

[2]Details regarding McSween's death emerged slowly from the welter of confusion surrounding the happenings of July 19. On or about May 20, 1879, almost a year after McSween's death, Sheriff Peppin testified before the Court of Inquiry at Fort Stanton that on the morning of July 20 he had sent word to Mrs. McSween that he "would furnish help to dig a grave and bury her husband's body." She sent back word "for me not to touch his body—that she would see to the burial."

On July 7, 1926, in the mellow haze of reconstructing past events, Yginio Salazar, of the McSween forces, was to recall: "McSween's orders were not to fire if Peppin's crowd didn't fire. In five minutes after Col. Dudley arrived in Lincoln on July 19, he was talking with Dolan and others. . . . There would have been no trouble if Dudley had stayed out of Lincoln."

Charles Bowdre commanded the forces in McSween's house during the days of fighting; Mrs. McSween played the piano, and Zebrioen Bates, McSween's Negro servant, played the violin while some of the fighting went on; when McSween went out of the house, at the time Bonney was attempting to escape, McSween wore a white shirt, which made him a target; McSween had refused to take up arms during the fighting because it would invalidate a $10,000 policy on his life. (See Marshall Bond Papers, U.N.M., Albuquerque.) Yginio Salazar, one of the last survivors of the Lincoln County War, was buried in the cemetery in Lincoln. On his tombstone is the inscription: "Yginio Salazar, Born February 14, 1863. D. Jan. 7, 1936 'Pal of Billy the Kid.' "

[3]On June 20, 1880, almost two years after her husband's death, Susan McSween was married to George B. Barber. Barber was born in Fredericksburg, Virginia, May 28, 1854. His parents moved in 1857 to Milwaukee, where their son was educated to be a civil engineer. After leaving school, he went to the Dakotas where he spent some months surveying.

George Barber came to Colfax County, New Mexico, in 1875, and to Lincoln

County in 1877. For several years Barber worked as a surveyor in the Lincoln country, then studied law and was admitted to the New Mexico bar on October 28, 1882. In 1885 Barber organized the Three Rivers Land & Cattle Co., then and later owner of important ranch properties. Barber sold his interest in the company in 1889.

On September 15, 1891, Susan Barber, through Attorney John Y. Hewitt, of White Oaks, filed a suit in the District Court of Lincoln County, asking for a divorce from George B. Barber, alleging that he had never supported her from the time of their marriage, and that he had abandoned her on March 1, 1891. A decree of divorce was entered on October 16, 1891.

For many years after McSween's death and her divorce from Barber, Susan McSween Barber demonstrated her independence and ability to make her own way in the world. On April 21, 1892, the Old Abe *Eagle* of Lincoln reported that she had driven 700 to 800 cattle from her ranch to Engle, the most accessible railroad point, from which place they were shipped "in 38 foot New England cars" to the Jones & Nelson feed lots in Grand Summit and Strong City, Kansas. The Old Abe *Eagle* of September 1, 1892, published an article, copied from the Commercial *Advertiser,* of New York City, which indicated that Mrs. McSween had not only survived the exciting days of the Lincoln County troubles, but had triumphed over them quite nicely. The Commercial *Advertiser* said: "Near the town of White Oaks, N. M., lives one of the most remarkable women of this remarkable age, at the present time a visitor in this city. The house in which she lives, a low, whitewalled adobe building, is covered with green vines and fitted out with rich carpets, artistic hangings, books and pictures, exquisite china and silver, and all the dainty belongings with which a refined woman loves to surround herself. The house was built with her own hands. The huge ranch on which it is located with its 8,000 cattle, is managed entirely by her. It is she who buys or takes up the land, selects and controls the men, buys, sells and transfers the cattle. She is also a skillful and intelligent prospector, and found the valuable silver mine on her territory in which she now owns a half interest. She sings charmingly, accompanying herself on the piano or guitar, and handles a cambric needle or a water color brush as dexterously as she uses an adze or a jack plane. She entertains delightfully at her home, whist parties, little dances, and even an occasional german. Her name is Mrs. Susan E. Barber. A woman who can run a ranch, build a house, manage a mine and engineer a successful german, deserves a prominent place in the ranks of women of genius."

[4] John Kinney's criminal court record in Doña Ana County, New Mexico, was extensive and impressive. On November 16, 1877, a grand jury, with Louis Rosenbaum as foreman, handed up an indictment against him for assault; on November 17, 1877, there was another indictment, this time for assault with intent to murder. On June 24, 1878, with C. P. Crawford as foreman, the grand jury returned an indictment against Kinney for murder. When arraigned,

he pleaded not guilty; the case was transferred for trial to Grant County and Kinney was acquitted by a jury.

During 1883 seventeen cases were docketed against him, all for larceny of cattle, buying stolen cattle or killing cattle. These cases were numbered on the docket as 907, 911, 912, 913, 914, 915, 917, 918, 919, 920, 921, 950, 953, 955, 991, 1013 and 1014. On motion of the district attorney all the cases were nolle prossed excepting No. 953, on which Kinney was tried, convicted for larceny of cattle, sentenced to five years in the penitentiary, and ordered to pay a fine of $500. Kinney appealed his conviction to the Supreme Court of the Territory, which on January 10, 1884, sustained the verdict of the jury. (See Terr. v. Kinney, 3 N. M. 97, 2 Pac. 357.) W. T. Thornton, attorney for Kinney, filed a motion for a rehearing in the Supreme Court, and kept Kinney out of prison until January 30, 1886. (See Terr. vs. Kinney, 3 N. M. 369, 9 Pac. 599.)

The extent to which Kinney, his hired gunfighters, and other New Mexicans, participated in the so-called "salt war" at San Elizario is open to question. Doubt exists as to whether any of the men who surrendered at San Elizario, except Lt. J. B. Tays, was a genuine Texas Ranger. John B. Jones, Major of the Frontier Batallion, swore during the subsequent investigation that upon learning of the formation of the so-called mob, there was "organized a small company of State troops, under the command of Lieut. J. B. Tays, which was stationed at San Elizario." (Ex. Doc. No. 93, H.R. U.S., 55th Congress, 2nd Session.) Sergeant Mortimer, killed before the surrender, was a regular member of the Ranger force. This would account for two trained Rangers in the original party, and only one at the time of surrender.

The same official document contains the affidavit (Exhibit 10, p. 37) of Gregorio Garcia who testified that he "was forced to surrender with five men for want of ammunition." Apparently Major Jones recruited a relatively small number of men at El Paso to support the regular Rangers, Tays and Mortimer, at San Elizario. Concerning the Kinney group, Tays testified (p. 115) that "neither myself or my men . . . had anything to do with the men from Silver City. We didn't stay with them or camp with them, but tried to keep separate from them, and I ordered my men not to mix with them, or have anything to do with them, because I knew a great many of them were bad men, that they were acting badly, and didn't appear to be under any restraint. I didn't consider they were in the service of the State." From all of which it appears that the Kinney contingent went to the aid of a small party of beleagured men, including a few Texas Rangers, many of the latter being fresh recruits.

Through the courtesy of R. Stewart Kilborne of New York City, New York, and his cousin, Mrs. Elizabeth Warner, of Northampton, Massachusetts, it has been established that John Kinney's ancestors lived, died and are buried in Chesterfield, Plainfield, Worthington and nearby towns in Massachusetts. The first recorded John Kinney fought in the Revolutionary War and died in Worthington on September 25, 1788.

CHAPTER EIGHT

LEW. WALLACE, GOVERNOR

FEW NEW MEXICANS, regardless of political affiliation, would deny in 1878 that there had been a complete breakdown of law and order in several parts of the Territory, particularly in Colfax and Lincoln counties, located in opposite portions of New Mexico. Samuel B. Axtell had become governor of New Mexico at a very inopportune time for him. Colfax County, in the northeastern part of the Territory, was in a virtual state of siege, the result of a number of shocking murders and killings which had divided the people of several communities in the county into armed camps. On or about June 1, 1875, some two months before Axtell's arrival, Rev. F. J. Tolby, a Methodist minister, had been murdered in a lonely canyon between Elizabethtown and Cimarron. Three months before the murder, the minister and Chief Justice Joseph G. Palen had quarreled openly on a street corner in Cimarron over the failure of the Colfax County grand jury to return an indictment against Francisco Griego for the murder of two soldiers from Fort Union. Many people professed to believe that the minister had been killed as a direct result of his quarrel with Judge Palen, a belief which had no foundation in fact. On October 30, 1875, some six weeks following the Tolby murder, one Cruz Vega was lynched by a mob which suspected him of the crime. Members of the mob reported that Vega, while being strung up, had whispered the name of Manuel Cardenas; and Cardenas was promptly arrested, given a hearing before a justice of the peace and bound over to await the action of the grand jury. While being returned to the county jail after the preliminary hearing, officers escorting Cardenas were "overpowered." A single shot was fired, according to newspaper accounts of the day, and Cardenas was dead. A coroner's jury returned a verdict that he had "come to his death at the hands of a party or parties unknown."

Clay Allison, alternately a brave man or a bad man, depending on which side he was fighting, continued the death pattern by killing Francisco Griego, the man who had initiated all the trouble, and whom the grand jury had failed to indict. Allison and others theorized that Griego had employed Cruz Vega to murder Tolby, and was primarily responsible for the minister's death. Subsequent developments tended to prove, however, that Vega, Cardenas and Griego were not guilty of any complicity in the Tolby murder.

As a result of the several murders, and the apparent breakdown of law and order that ensued, the Territorial Legislature on January 14, 1876, passed an act annexing Colfax County to Taos County for all judicial purposes. Introduced and enacted by the Legislature on the closing day of the session, the people of Colfax County were not given an opportunity to assert their opposition to the bill. Despite requests that he withhold his signature until a delegation could reach Santa Fe from Cimarron, Governor Axtell signed the bill, and it became law. For this, and many other official acts which displeased them, many prominent citizens of Colfax County never forgave Axtell; and they began and carried on a vigorous, relentless campaign to have the President remove him from office.

Leadership for the fight to remove Axtell was provided by Frank W. Springer, a young attorney of Cimarron. He charged that Axtell had conspired with District Attorney Ben Stevens of the Second Judicial District to have him assassinated, together with William R. Morley, Henry M. Porter and Clay Allison. Springer enlisted the support of his father, Judge Francis Springer, of Wapello, Louisa County, Iowa, who went to Washington, armed with a letter of introduction and explanation to President Hayes signed by United States Senator William Boyd Allison, of Dubuque. In his letter to the President, Senator Allison suggested that Axtell "should not remain in office for a moment longer than the time necessary to appoint his successor." Springer's complaint, coupled with reports of Axtell's inept handling of official business in Lincoln County, prompted the President to act quickly. On or about September 1, 1878, he instructed Secretary Schurz to suspend Axtell from office, and to remove him as governor if he refused to accept the suspension gracefully. Axtell's friends in New Mexico rallied to his defense and forwarded petitions to Washington, signed by hundreds of citizens, asking the President to continue him as governor. The protests were of no avail.

Lewis Wallace, fifty-one years old, of Crawfordsville, Montgomery County, Indiana, became governor of New Mexico on September 30, 1878. Never before had the Territory been honored by having such a noted man become its governor. He succeded Samuel Beach Axtell, who had served as governor since July 30, 1875. The new governor, who invariably used the abbreviated "Lew." in signing his name (complete with a period after the "w"), was one of the nation's most distinguished citizens. He had gained fame and glory in the Mexican and Civil wars. He had won and retained prestige in the literary world. In several national conventions his name had been put forward as Indiana's favorite son for high honors on the Republican ticket.

Wallace took the oath as governor in Santa Fe before Judge Samuel C. Parks, until recently a resident of Logan County, Illinois, now an associate justice of the Territorial Supreme Court. Axtell, the outgoing governor, relinquished the office reluctantly. The years of his administration had been marked by events reflecting the tension and unrest of the times, aggravated by his inclination to participate as a partisan in non-political matters; and by adopting a "plague on both your houses" attitude in administrative affairs demanding his prompt and efficient intervention.

Lew. Wallace, the new governor of New Mexico, had not been overly eager to accept an appointment which could not be considered in any light, for him, to be a political plum. The changeover in the governorship had been accelerated as the result of the election to the Presidency of Rutherford B. Hayes. Wallace had groomed himself for an appointment by Hayes to a position which would enable him to devote most of his working hours to literary work. Disappointed in his hopes, and almost as a last resort, Wallace accepted the governorship of New Mexico, at an annual salary of $2,400, confident that before many months the President would give him a more important post.

Despite efforts to keep the news confined to official Santa Fe, it had been generally known in New Mexico some days before Wallace's arrival that Axtell had been "suspended from office," words which were synonymous in New Mexico with "removed for cause."

The newly appointed governor arrived in Santa Fe unannounced. No committee was on hand to welcome him as he alighted from the stagecoach. Before leaving for New Mexico he had spent some days in Washington, where he was given background information on conditions in the Territory. Leaving Washington for the West, Wallace remained for a short time in Crawfordsville. Riding on courtesy transportation, a practice common enough at the time, Wallace traveled on the railway cars from Crawfordsville to Chicago, and thence to Kansas City, Pueblo and Trinidad, then the end of the railroad. From Trinidad Wallace traveled by stagecoach through Dick Wootton's tollgate, Red River, Crow Creek, Vermejo to Cimarron. He left the stage at Cimarron, where he remained for a day and a night, the guest of Frank W. Springer and William Lee,[1] young attorneys, the latter a friend from his home state. In Cimarron, Wallace was "entertained by Judge William D. Lee, an old Indiana friend, at an elegant dinner, attended by the best and most prominent men and women of the county," according to Cimarron *News and Press* of October 3, 1878. In Washington, Wallace had been told that Axtell had considered Cimarron the greatest plague spot in the Territory, and he was anxious to see the place and to talk to some of the people. Axtell had no love for Cimarron or its residents and when it had become known in Cimarron that Axtell had been suspended from office, the people rejoiced. Dancing in the streets, they celebrated by the free use of six-shooters, shotguns and a fireworks display.

The Cimarron *News and Press* of October 3 published an article which had recently appeared in the Washington *Republic:*

The Cimarron *News & Press* is full of joy that actually gushes over at the removal of Axtell and the appointment of Gen. Lew Wallace as the governor of New Mexico, and the *News and Press* fairly represents the feeling and sentiment on that question. Fifty guns were fired by the people of Cimarron in honor of the event. A sense of relief fell upon that people when it was known that Axtell, who had been tyrannical and oppressive in his administration of affairs has been forced to surrender his position to a manly, just and upright man. So far as we have been able to penetrate the true inwardness of the affairs of New Mexico under Axtell's administration, we come to the conclusion that the people have cause for heartfelt rejoicing. There are now one or two Republicans in this city who have been driven from New Mexico by Axtell's proscriptive policy, and who hope now to return unmolested and enjoy their deserted homes.

By remaining overnight in Cimarron, Wallace did something which Governor Axtell had declared he would not do. For months before Wallace's arrival in New Mexico, Axtell, in the Santa Fe *New Mexican,* and Springer, in the *News and Press* (published in Cimarron on the "northeast corner of the Public Square"), had carried on a duel over Colfax County affairs. Only a few days before Axtell's "resignation," he had attacked Cimarron and its people in an open letter published in the Santa Fe *New Mexican,* accusing Springer of having failed to tell the truth concerning charges he had preferred against the Axtell administration:

But in his very greed of lying, Mr. Springer blunders upon one truth—he swears I would not stay over night at Cimarron but preferred to sleep in the open plains. This is true. I cannot understand how any right minded man could do otherwise; the place is crimson with human blood and polluted with the hourly presence of liars, slanderers and murderers. I have never heard that charges were preferred against Lot because he would not stay in Sodom.[2]

Having learned Springer's version of the alleged breakdown of the Axtell administration, Wallace resumed his stagecoach journey from Cimarron to Santa Fe, passing through Rayado, Sweetwater, Eureka, Sapello Lake and Las Vegas. Riding in a buckboard from Trinidad to Cimarron, and from Cimarron to Santa Fe, over rocky roads proved a trying experience for Wallace. On October 8 he wrote to his wife, Susan E. Wallace, describing the hardships of the journey:

I reached here about 9 o'clock the night of the 29th of September, having ridden on a buckboard from Trinidad. When the vehicle drew up in front of the hotel in this town, and I took a look at it when I jumped, or rather crawled off it at door of the *Fonda* here, I was thankful beyond expression, in truth I do not believe you could have stood it all—you would have been sick in every bone, dead in every muscle. A deadlier instrument of torture was never used in the days of Torquemado.

Had anything the equal of it been resorted to then, there would have been few heretics. It is a low wheeled affair, floored with slats; the springs are under the seats and so weak that with the least jolt they smite together with a horrible blow, which is all the worse if overloaded, as was the case when I rode on them.

Before he could take over as governor, Lew. Wallace was confronted with a somewhat disagreeable task, that of informing Axtell of his suspension from office. Secretary Schurz had given Wallace instructions in writing as to how to proceed:

I transmit herewith an order from the President for the suspension of Samuel B. Axtell, from his office, as Governor of the Territory of New Mexico, together with a designation of yourself, to perform the duties of said suspended office, subject to all provisions of law applicable thereto. You will deliver said order of suspension to Governor Axtell upon your arrival at the capital of New Mexico.

Wallace wrote to Susan Wallace, his wife, in Crawfordsville, on October 8, telling her how he had faced the ordeal:

The Governor was sitting at the table when I entered. He arose to receive me, giving me to see a good looking, gray haired, dark eyed, pleasant featured man, about fifty five years old, and a gentleman. As you may imagine, the interview was not a pleasant one; yet he went through it very well. After the introductions, we shook hands, and I said: "I have come to pay my respects to you, Governor, and to ask when it will be agreeable to you to present my papers." He replied: "I have been expecting you General, and of course know all about your business. It is not my pleasure that is to be consulted, but yours." "Will tomorrow suit you then?" I asked. "Certainly," he replied. "I do not want any ceremony about it." "Well then, Governor, I will write you a note with an enclosure—the President's order —tomorrow. And it shall follow immediately that I have qualified by taking the oath." "Yes," he replied, "when you have qualified, you are governor." He then introduced me to his friends, all of whom received me very politely, and we took seats. "I wish to say to you General," the Governor said, dropping all formalities, "that I am glad the appointment as my successor has fallen to you. I knew there were parties in Washington who were energetic in trying to oust me, and have themselves appointed. I also know you were not one of them; that the place was tendered you without solicitation on your part. If your coming is in the least degree a disappointment to me, it is more than counterbalanced by the fact that your appointment was a defeat to my enemies." Of course, I assured the Governor I had nothing to do with his removal, and added: "Now that I have come and seen you, I am glad that such was the case and that you knew all about it."

In an official report Wallace advised Secretary Schurz that he had qualified as governor:

I have the honor to inform you that, in compliance with your instruction, dated Sept. 4, 1878, I qualified as Governor of New Mexico yesterday (Sept. 30) at 3:15 o'clock P. M. This morning I addressed a note to Gov. S. B. Axtell informing him that I had qualified, and delivering him the order of suspension directed to him by the President.

On my way from Trinidad, I stopped a day and night in Cimarron, Colfax county, one of the localities about which a great deal has been said in connection with disorder. Without reference to the past, there certainly appears to be a good feeling on the part of citizens there, and a decided disposition to keep the peace.

The Santa Fe *New Mexican* of October 5, 1878, told of Wallace's arrival, and something of his background:

General Wallace, the newly appointed Governor of our Territory, arrived Sunday evening. Gen. Wallace is a man of national reputation. In 1861 he resided at Indianapolis and was engaged in the practice of law. When war broke out he raised a regiment for three months service. It was a Zouave regiment and became noted for its proficiency in the Zouave drill. It is said when the regiment was mustered into service Col. Wallace called it to kneel and swear to remember Buena Vista, where Jeff Davis was said to have reflected upon the courage of the Indianians. The regiment saw service in West Virginia. After the expiration of the term of service, Col. Wallace reorganized his regiment for the war and was sent to Missouri, promoted to Brigadier General. He commanded a division at the siege and capture of Fort Donelson, and by his conspicuous gallantry won the commission of Major General. He did good service in the second day's fight at Shiloh and afterwards in command at Memphis and did good service throughout the war. General Wallace is an earnest Republican. We are very favorably impressed by his appearance and conversation. He is apparently in the prime of life, vigorous and active, a man of fine presence, evidently a keen observer, and a thoughtful, self reliant man. We predict that he will make an efficient and popular governor. We understand that Gov. Wallace intends to cast his lot with our people, and become a permanent resident of the Territory.

The *New Mexican's* article introducing the new governor to its readers was conservatively worded and perhaps necessarily brief. Wallace's descent on New Mexico had been sudden and unexpected. Few political leaders had yet had an opportunity to form an opinion about him. It was certain, however, that his accession to the governor's office would not be received with any degree of enthusiasm by members of the Democratic party, particularly by those Democrats who had fought on the Southern side in the Civil War. Every Confederate veteran in New Mexico had long since become reconciled to the fact that Territorial officials were rated in Washington as being eminently qualified for a position of honor and trust if they or an influential political friend had fought under Grant at Shiloh, Buell at Perryville, Rosecrans at Stone River or Chattanooga, Thomas at Mission Ridge; or if they had served in the Army of the Potomac, fought in the battles of the Wilderness or Cold Harbor, or had been fortunate enough to have participated in some equally famous or well-publicized campaign. Nevertheless, without reflecting any political views, the *New Mexican* could well have published a much more detailed biography of the new governor.

Few men in public life in America at the time could equal, and not many could surpass, Lew. Wallace's record of diversified achievements. Born in Brockville, Indiana, April 10, 1827, he had been educated in the common schools of Indiana and for a short time had attended Wabash College. His father, David Wallace, a protege of Gen. William Henry Harrison, was elected governor of Indiana in 1837. Young Wallace reported the proceedings of the Indiana Legislature in 1844-45 for the Indianapolis daily *Journal,* a Whig party newspaper, and studied law until he joined the army at the beginning of the Mexican War in 1846, in which he served as a second lieutenant at twenty years of age. Admitted to the Indiana bar in 1847, Wallace practiced law intermittently for some years thereafter. He was active in politics in Indiana from 1841 to 1861. During the Civil War he served as an officer in the Union army, being discharged with the rank of major general. Immediately after his army service, Wallace spent considerable time in Galveston, Point Isabel, and other places in Texas, on a mission to investigate reports that Mexican Imperialists and Texas Confederates were conspiring to re-annex Texas to Mexico.

On April 15, 1865, while enroute from Mexico to Galveston, Wallace heard of President Lincoln's assassination. Hurrying to Washington, he served as one of nine officers on a court martial which tried several people charged with conspiracy to assassinate Abraham Lincoln. The court convened in Washington on May 10, 1865. Wallace ranked next to Maj. Gen. David Hunter, President of the Court. The trial lasted sixty days. Wallace voted to find Mary Surratt and others guilty of the charge of "Aiding armed rebellion within the United States, cooperating with John Wilkes Booth, and others, to murder Abraham Lincoln, President of the United States." Wallace voted for the death penalty, and for execution on July 7, 1865.

President Johnson subsequently appointed Wallace on the commission which inquired into the conduct of Confederate Captain Henry Wirz, keeper of the prison at Andersonville, Georgia, accused of "starving, mistreating and killing thousands of Union soldiers." Wallace was made president of the commission, which convened in Washington on August 20, 1865. Wirz was found guilty of "combining, confederating, and conspiring with Jefferson Davis" and others, as alleged in the bill of particulars before the commission, and was executed on November 10, 1865, at the Old Capitol Prison, in Washington.

After the Wirz trial, Wallace returned briefly to his home in Crawfordsville, Indiana, and soon became active in Mexican politics, aiding in plans to have Mexico expel Emperor Maximilian. In connection with this work, Wallace carried on negotiations in 1866 and 1867 with New York banks in an effort to float a loan for the Mexican government. He spent considerable time in Monterrey, Chihuahua and elsewhere in Mexico, cooperating with the forces of Benito Juarez. When Maximilian was executed on July 17, 1867, there was no further need for Wallace's services in Mexico, and he returned to Indiana, where he practiced law in a desultory fashion and ran for Congress in 1870 on the Republican ticket. In this race, the Democrats attacked him viciously, claiming among other things that he had speculated in Mexican bonds, and that he had been identified with a ring which had schemed to have the United States assume a part of the Mexican national debt. Wallace failed to win a seat in Congress, but only by 458 votes, demonstrating his ability as a vote-getter.

Lew. Wallace was talented in the fields of art and literature. Eventually the bent for creative writing predominated. He worked off and on after his nineteenth year on *The Fair God,* a historical romance, which he finished in 1870. It was revised and published in 1873. Some critics praised it, others contended it was mediocre; and several accused Wallace of having taken the story from *Malmistic the Toltec,* a book published some years before. Most critics eventually conceded, however, that Wallace had been cleared of the charge of plagiarism. With *The Fair God* published, but a poor success, Wallace began work on another book. He spent many weeks in the Congressional Library in Washington, working on a manuscript which became the famous *Ben Hur.* In order to finance himself while working on his new book, Wallace signed an agreement in 1875 with James Redpath of the Chautauqua Circuit, to lecture on Mexico. After several appearances on the platform, Wallace was convinced that people generally had no interest in Mexico's past, present or future, and gave up lecturing. Wallace placed lecturing in the same category with the legal profession, which he described as "the most detestable of human occupations," and which he abandoned permanently in 1878.

Settled at last in unattractive quarters in the Palace of the Governors, an ancient and honorable building in Santa Fe, Lew. Wallace endeavored to reconcile himself to life in the Territory, so radically different from that of his own Indiana. Wallace found life in Santa Fe greatly unlike the tempo and atmosphere he had known in cities in Mexico. On Sundays in Santa Fe, as had been his custom in Crawfordsville, Wallace attended church services, but was not much inspired by Parson Smith's sermons. Bishop Simpson, in Santa Fe for a church convention, called upon him, but Archbishop John B. Lamy failed to call and pay his respects. On October 20, the Governor wrote to Mrs. Wallace, indicating that he had considered the matter of protocol:

I broke off yesterday to go to church, where I was again intolerably bored by Parson Smith. I don't know whether I can stand it or not. I come out a worse sinner than when I go in. Yet there is no remedy for it except the Catholic Cathedral, and there I will not go, even to gratify my curiosity—not one of the priesthood has called on me. I understand the Bishop is waiting for me to call upon him first.[3] Be sure, my dear, he will wait a long time. When Bishop Simpson was here, he called first. We'll see.[4]

Fortunately for Wallace on this occasion, his thoughts about religion and clergymen were interrupted by the arrival of a visitor, of whom Wallace wrote: "Gen. Atkinson, of the Land Office is at the door with his bay team, come to drive me out."[5] Back from the drive with Atkinson, the Governor continued with his letter to Mrs. Wallace, demonstrating for the first time in New Mexico perhaps, his ability to write beautiful English:

Just returned from the ride. How delicious it was! What perfection of air and sunlight! And what a landscape discovered to show you when you come—a picture to make the fame of an artist, could he only put on canvas as it is! Soft blue sky, vast distance, bounded by purple walls as transparent and summery, it is hard to believe it, and see. Over on the east there is a height crowned by the remains of old Fort Marcy, which from here appears about as far away as from our house to the college—at home, I mean—yet they tell me it is really three miles off; it challenges me every time I look at it, and I'll try it soon. The sun goes down gradually in tinted clouds, which hover over the long purple mountain ranges, for as there are mountains in the east so there are mountains in the west—mountains, understand, not hills, royal mountains, in view of which one knows the delight Ruskin writes about. Upon the going out of the day, the wind dies, leaving the night still and cool, and gradually growing cooler until at midnight if you are out of doors, you would want a heavy shawl, while if you are indoors, a fire is cheery and enjoyable.[6]

Now that he was duly appointed, qualified and acting governor of New Mexico, Lew. Wallace had leisure time in which to review the events and circumstances which had brought him to the Territory. He had not been an active applicant for the governorship. He had gone to Washington primarily to do research work in the Congressional Library on his new book.

Incidentally, and perhaps more important at the moment, Wallace was in the capital, like many other visitors, to attend the inauguration of Rutherford B. Hayes, nineteenth President of the United States, on March 5, 1877. He had an extraordinary interest in the inauguration. For months he had been of counsel for Hayes in connection with proceedings before the canvassing board in the Hayes-Tilden contest, beginning on November 24, 1876, in Tallahassee, Florida. The board, made up of two Republicans and one Democrat, decided that, based upon the available evidence, Florida's vote in the Electoral College belonged to the Republican candidate, a decision followed by storm and strife which for a time threatened to disrupt the orderly processes of national affairs.

On March 9, 1877, five days after Hayes had become President, Lew. Wallace called at the Executive Mansion to pay his respects. Under the circumstances, the meeting between the two men may have been somewhat stiff and formal. No doubt Wallace, in the course of his conversation with the President, had touched upon the possibility for a political appointment, because on the same day he wrote Hayes a note which read :

DEPARTMENT OF STATE
MAR
15
1877
RECEIVED

Washington, March 9. 1877.

His Excellency, President Hayes.

Dear Sir

I avail myself of the request you made me this morning.

It is hardly necessary to give reasons for a preference of the Italian mission over all others of the second class.

The Brazilian embassy would be my next preference One manufactured products ought to command the markets of that country, and it is my opinion that a generous transmission of comparative details, reaching everybody through the State Department would go far to achieve the object by evidencing enterprise

The Spanish mission is over attractive — only I am afraid of the possible complications to which we are momentarily liable in that quarter

Mexico would be my last choice, at the same time my knowledge of the country and people might make me more serviceable there than elsewhere

It is for you to say.

Very truly your friend,

Lew. Wallace

[*The National Archives.*]

Wallace remained in Washington for some days after his meeting with the President, hopeful that he might hear a word about an appointment. After the passage of many days, Wallace became disturbed because he had not heard from Hayes, and he returned to Crawfordsville and discussed the political etiquette of the situation with a brother-in-law, former U. S. Senator Henry S. Lane. On June 3, Lane wrote to Richard Wiggenton Thompson, an influential Indiana political leader,

whom President Hayes had recently appointed to be Secretary
of the Navy, urging him to intercede:

You will pardon me for troubling you in reference to a matter in
which I feel a great interest. My friend, Gen'l. Lewis Wallace, is an
applicant for a foreign mission and when he was in Washington last
spring he spoke to the President on the subject who very kindly and
confidently assured him that his wishes on the subject would be regarded. He had very strong recommendations ready to be filed in
the State Department, but the President assured him it was not necessary & they were not filed. The President asked him to indicate in a
letter his preferences as to an appointment and he named in the order
stated Rome, Spain, Brazil & Mexico. Gen'l Wallace's friends think
his eminent qualifications, his services to the country & to the Republican party entitle him to a recognition by the administration. I fear
that in the hurry of business his application may be overlooked. You
will confer a personal favor on me if you consistently with your sense
of public duty can bring this matter to the attention of the President
& Cabinet & look after it as far as convenient. Gen'l. Wallace's preferences as stated in the letter to the President were not intended to
restrict the President by any means but simply as an expression of his
own wishes in reference to the matter. Please let me know as soon as
practicable how the case stands & what are the General's prospects
for appointment.

Thompson forwarded Lane's letter to the President, together
with a petition signed by a majority of the Indiana Congressional delegation, urging that Wallace be named to a foreign
mission. When nothing appeared to have been accomplished
through the intervention of others, Lew. Wallace on June 15
wrote the President direct:

A few days after your inauguration, you were kind enough to request me to leave with you a written statement of my preferences
among the foreign missions, saying you might not have it in power to
give me my first choice. Thinking to escape imputation of abuse of
your favor, I gave the following as preferences in their order—Italy,
Brazil, Spain and Mexico—all of the second class. After delivering
you the paper, I refrained scrupulously from troubling you with calls,
or letters, or recommendations. In particular, I have declined the ef-

forts of influential friends to wait on you in my behalf. I did not even have communication with Mr. Evarts upon the subject. The reason you will readily see. In the next place, I came home, and disengaged myself from business. The newspapers have now had you dispose of *all* the missions stated. While I do not, of course, believe all the newspapers say, still I begin to think that possibly my expression of preferences may have been overlooked or forgotten by you, or that you may have come to think me indifferent about the matter. In either of these events, there can be no impropriety, I am sure, in setting myself right; and for that purpose I presume to send you this note.

Wallace spent many months in 1877 and 1878 in Crawfordsville, waiting on the President's pleasure. The President, perhaps, was reluctant to give Wallace a lucrative or important appointment because of the political repercussions it might engender. Wallace had just about abandoned hope of any appointment, when the President, through Carl Schurz, Secretary of the Interior, offered him the governorship of New Mexico. Needless to say, Wallace was disappointed. Instead of the assignment to the glamorous far-off country he had envisaged, he was being handed an administrative position in a remote Territory, at a salary of $2,400 a year. But viewing the offer from a realistic standpoint, it had some attractions. Wallace needed money, and the salary, although small, would help tide him over. In considering whether to accept or reject the appointment, Wallace was influenced by the possibility that he might make a fortune in New Mexico through the discovery of a gold or silver mine. There was the possibility too that New Mexico might become a state of the Union, and that he might be elected by the Legislature to the United States Senate. Above all else, Wallace was confident that the governorship would afford him ample time to complete his book, a project close to his heart. After consulting friends in Indiana, Wallace accepted the appointment. The President sent Wallace's name to the Senate on or about September 5, 1878. There were some objections on the floor of the Senate, but these were withdrawn, and the nomination was confirmed on December 16, 1878.

Because of his prominence in the nation, newspapers in many states commented on Wallace's appointment to the governorship. Many editorials expressed surprise that he would consent to accept a mediocre place in the provinces. In general, editorials reflected a day-to-day political policy. Papers supporting the tenets of the Democratic party were quick to claim that the appointment was nothing more nor less than payment of a reward for services rendered in the Hayes-Tilden contest. In this vein, the Philadelphia *Times* of September 10 commented:

Another of the visiting statesmen, one of the very few remaining unprovided for, has got his reward. This time it is General Lew. Wallace, who has been appointed Governor of New Mexico, in place of Axtell, suspended. The trouble with Axtell appears to be that he is, or is supposed to be, a Mormon, and in the peculiar relations of the Mormons to the United States government, it is just as well to select our Territorial Governors from another class. General Wallace is not open to objection on this score, and he has the merit of considerable familiarity with Spanish-American interests and modes of thought. The only thing discreditable about his appointment is its obvious connection with the service rendered the present administration by General Wallace in Florida, where he stood by and countenanced the palpable fraud by which the vote of that state was counted for the Hayes electors.

The Las Vegas *Gazette* of September 14, referring to the background of an investigation conducted prior to Axtell's removal, manifested open hostility to the appointment:

We infer from the action of the President directly after the return of Frank Warren Angel to the capital that the quarrel between him and Gov. Axtell had more to do with the latter's removal than any misdemeanors in office. Mr. Angel is a satrap of Carl Schurz sent out on the European plan, with a wave of the hand like a Bismarck, and instructions that if any one presumed to differ with you, "refer them to me." Angel got mad, went off huffy, reported Axtell, and Schurz at once recommended removal. This remarkable power was vested in the hands of a young fledgling who while here exhibited no signs of ordinary ability. Hayes likewise was ready; he had a man in tow that unless rewarded was likely to give cumulative evidence to McLin. Gen. Lew. Wallace must have a position for services rendered, and this was the opportunity. The President has fulfilled his contract; the Senate may now do its duty, and that is, to reject Wallace if he was knowing to and sanctioned the returning board frauds. These fellows damned themselves forever. They were willing instruments in a corrupt plot and should be shunned by honest men as tainted and dangerous.

A week later, on September 21, the *Gazette* was once more critical of Wallace:

Wallace may be a good enough man under ordinary circumstances; but if the reports are correct about his aid in the Florida vote, the Senate should defeat him. The policy against returning board men should be inexorable. They should never be allowed to hold positions of trust and profit. It was a crime which should never be forgiven, or condoned by repentance. . . . The President should not quarter any more of his returning board friends on New Mexico. They are too good for this Territory. There are no offices here worth enough to be any compensation for the services rendered.

The Terre Haute, Indiana, *Express* of September 24, 1878, praised the appointment:

No man in Indiana, possibly no man in the nation, has filled his high walks of life so well as Lew. Wallace, the newly appointed Governor of New Mexico. He has achieved well deserved fame as a soldier, orator, artist, poet and novelist. He is a well rounded man.

The Milwaukee *Sentinel* offered a realistic comment:

Gen. Lew. Wallace has been appointed Governor of New Mexico. As Gen. Wallace is one of "them literary fellers," he should have had a foreign appointment. There is considerable work to do in New Mexico.

In assuming the governorship of New Mexico, Lew. Wallace was aware that he was taking over responsibilities of major importance. In a general way, he was familiar with the background of the fighting and feuding in some parts of the Territory and the events which had resulted in Axtell's suspension. Before leaving for New Mexico, he had attended a number of conferences in Washington with Frank Warren Angel, special investigator, and with department heads, at which time acute problems in the Territory had been discussed and remedial action proposed and considered.

It is doubtful, however, that the new governor fully understood and appreciated the real nature and extent of New Mexico's difficulties, with all their ramifications. Gen. Edward Hatch, in charge of United States troops in New Mexico, presumably in the Territory for the sole and only purpose of dealing with incipient Indian disturbances, maintained headquarters at Fort Marcy, only a few steps from the governor's office. Although Hatch was available and willing to assist Wallace in any way possible, he was handicapped in offering him disinterested advice, primarily because he had been involved in a long-standing quarrel with Col. N. A. M. Dudley, commanding officer at Fort Stanton. Hatch had learned by experience that Dudley had powerful friends in the War Department in Washington, and that it was practically useless to complain of Dudley's shortcomings as an officer.

NOTES AND PROFILES

[1] William Daily Lee (grandfather of Laurence F. Lee of Raleigh, North Carolina, and Jacksonville, Florida; Chester Lee of Denver, Colorado; Floyd W. Lee of San Mateo, New Mexico; and Margaret Lee McArthur of Wagon Mound, New Mexico), one of the organizers of the Republican party, was born in Indiana on November 8, 1830. He attended De Pauw University at Greencastle; graduated from law at the University of Indiana; served as Captain of Co. E, 135th Indiana Volunteers throughout the Civil War; practiced law in Cimarron and Las Vegas, New Mexico, from 1876 to 1889, in which year President Harrison appointed him to be judge of the Second Judicial District, with residence in Albuquerque, an office he held until 1894. Judge Lee died in Albuquerque on December 23, 1908.

[2] Frank W. Springer (father of Edward Thomas Springer, of Cimarron, Eva Springer and Ada Springer Davis, of Santa Fe, and Laura Springer Caskil, of Wayne, Pennsylvania), one of the most prominent citizens in the New Mexico of his day, was born in Wapello, Louisa County, Iowa, on June 17, 1848, died September 22, 1927. Coming to New Mexico in 1873, he settled in

Cimarron, for some years the county seat of Colfax County, and took an active part in the trouble and excitement inevitable in a frontier community.

Springer became general counsel for the Maxwell Land Grant & Railway Co., owners of the vast Maxwell Land Grant, the major portion of which was located in Colfax County. He argued and won for the company before the lower courts and in the Supreme Court of the United States the famous Maxwell Land Grant case. In the latter years of his life Frank Springer, always a public-spirited man, devoted most of his time to philanthropy and scientific studies. He specialized in crinoids, in which field he became an internationally known authority.

[3] In writing that "I understand the Bishop is waiting for me to call upon him first," Wallace was referring to Bishop John B. Lamy. How the matter of protocol was disposed of is not known, but the two men eventually became acquainted, and established a cordial relationship.

In making a report of his missionary work after nineteen years residence in New Mexico, Bishop Lamy paid high tribute to the assistance given to him by the military. The report was published originally in the Catholic *Mirror*, copied by the Santa Fe *Post*, and by the Albuquerque *Review* of October 29, 1870: "In concluding I must express my gratitude to the officers of the United States army for all the good services I have received from them since the founding of the Santa Fe diocese. I shall confine myself to the most remarkable instances. In the spring of 1851 when I was going for the first time to my diocese, after enduring many delays and even suffering shipwreck, I arrived without means of any sort in Texas, where I had not even an acquaintance. I had the good fortune to meet Gen. Harney, Commander in Chief of that state, who gave me rank as an officer, with privilege of conveyance and rations for myself and six persons who accompanied me in the caravan of 200 wagons which he sent to New Mexico. Our journey across the prairies lasted three months and some days. . . . In the course of my journeys and pastoral visitations, I have administered the sacraments and said mass in the military encampments, and little forts, and I have always been received with the greatest politeness and cordial hospitality. We are allowed full liberty and every facility for the exercise of our sacred ministry among Catholic soldiers who are generally pretty numerous. They always supplied us with provisions to continue our journey, and even gave us an escort when necessary. I deem it a duty to express my grateful feelings toward American officers from whom I have received so much politeness, favors and services during the last nineteen years, on many occasions too numerous to mention, and I am happy to be able to take this opportunity of giving public expression to these sentiments."

[4] The "Bishop Simpson" referred to in the Governor's letter was famed Bishop Matthew Simpson, of the Methodist Episcopal Church. The Bishop was present in Santa Fe to attend the annual missionary meeting of the church on October 7, 1878. Rev. Thomas Harwood, superintendent of the New Mexico mission, presided over the meeting. The missionary work in New Mexico was

under the Bishop's episcopal jurisdiction. On Sunday, October 8, the distinguished churchman preached a sermon in "the old adobe chapel," in Santa Fe, on the subject, "The Christian Victory," from 2 John, 5, 4, "This is the victory that overcometh the world even our faith." After the services, Governor Wallace offered his congratulations: "Bishop, I am delighted with this service. I shall have something new to write home to Mrs. Wallace." (*History of New Mexico Missions*, 1850-1884, Harwood, p. 298.)

Born in Cadiz, Ohio, June 20, 1811, Bishop Simpson died in Philadelphia June 18, 1884. He was for years perhaps the best-known and most influential clergyman in his church. Abraham Lincoln declared him to be the greatest orator he had ever heard. The Bishop reciprocated by officiating at the President's funeral in Springfield. (Appleton, Vol. 5, p. 539.)

Rev. Thomas Harwood, early-day Methodist New Mexico missionary, began his work at La Junta, near Fort Union, on October 1, 1869. As Superintendent of Missions in New Mexico and Arizona, he carried on the work of his church for some forty years. In 1910 Reverend Harwood was elected Chaplain-in-Chief of the Grand Army of the Republic, an honor to which he had long aspired.

[5] Henry Martyn Atkinson was born in Wheeler, Virginia (later West Virginia), September 9, 1838; died in Santa Fe on October 17, 1886. When a child, his parents moved to Ohio. Atkinson was educated in Connecticut, and at Denison University in Ohio. He went to Nebraska in 1857, where he was admitted to the bar in 1861. Enlisting in the Union army in 1862, he served throughout the war as a lieutenant in Co. C., Second Nebraska Cavalry. In 1873, President Grant appointed Atkinson a member of the Mexican Boundary Commission. Later Atkinson served briefly as Commissioner of Pensions in Washington, resigning to become Surveyor-General of New Mexico. General Atkinson came within one vote of election to the United States Senate by the Nebraska Legislature of 1874-75.

[6] Susan E. Wallace, wife of Lew. Wallace, and also a writer of considerable ability, arrived in Santa Fe on February 2, 1879. Governor Wallace met her and Henry L. Wallace, their teenage son, in Trinidad, and escorted them to their new home. Mrs. Wallace was a sister-in-law of Henry Smith Lane (1811-81), one-time U. S. Senator from Indiana, for many years influential nationally in the Republican party.

A candidate for the nomination for the Presidency at the first national convention of the Republican party in 1856, Lane lost by a small margin of votes to John Charles Fremont. In the 1860 convention, Lane was credited to a great extent with influencing the Indiana delegation to cast its vote for Abraham Lincoln. By an odd coincidence, Fremont was governor of Arizona during 1878-81, coinciding roughly with the time Lew. Wallace served as governor of the neighboring Territory of New Mexico.

Susan Wallace wrote *The Storied Sea, Ginevra, The Land of the Pueblos,* and other books, and was a frequent contributor to the *Atlantic Monthly,* and other nationally known magazines. In a foreword to *The Land of the Pueblos,* published in 1888, which was illustrated by some of her husband's pen-and-ink sketches, Mrs. Wallace struck a nostalgic note concerning some of the chapters: "They were written when the Ancient Palace I have tried to describe, was the residence of the Governor of New Mexico; and in turning the leaves after seven years I am touched by the same feeling which then moved me to pipe my little songs. Again I feel the deep solitude of the mountains, taste the all pervading alkali dust, and hear the sandstorm beating like sleet against the window pane."

On June 28, 1877, the Santa Fe *New Mexican* took a dig at the "palace," occupied by the Wallaces while Wallace was governor: "If there ever was a misnomer applied to anything on earth, from what we are led to infer from the word as used in other lands, it is in the name of the long, one story adobe building which fronts the north side of the plaza. Since the year 1600 it has stood there through calm and storm; has seen nations rise and disappear, and if its old walls could only speak, they would unfold a tale that would make a fortune for almost any sprightly historian. With the changes that have taken place in the last few years, and yet going on in the frontage of the "palace," it now looks as speckled and spotted as Joseph's coat or Dave Montgomery's statuary."

CHAPTER NINE

WALLACE'S AMNESTY
PROCLAMATION

WHILE IN WASHINGTON, preparing to leave for New Mexico, Lew. Wallace had been given available information on the administrative difficulties in the Territory which had culminated in Axtell's suspension. For the time being, he was told, things had quieted down in Colfax County; consequently most of the discussions had revolved around conditions in Lincoln County. Wallace conferred with Secretary of War George W. McCrary, who suggested a plan for the use of federal troops in the event of an emergency. Both McCrary and Carl Schurz, Secretary of the Department of the Interior, discussed with Wallace the feasibility and advisability of asking the President to issue a proclamation which would appeal to the people of Lincoln County to end hostilities. A legal question arose as to the power of a Territorial governor to extend amnesty to law violators, and concerning this, Secretary McCrary advised Wallace by letter to Santa Fe on October 2, 1878:

SIR: In accordance with your verbal request I submitted to the President and Cabinet the question as to the extent of your authority as Governor of New Mexico to grant amnesty or pardon to persons charged with offenses. The result of the discussion was the conclusion that you have power to grant pardons and reprieves, and to remit fines and forfeitures for all offenses against the laws of the Territory. Also to grant respites for offenses against the United States until the decision of the President can be known thereon. See Sec. 1841 Revised Statutes.

In order to have something official before him on which he could act, the Governor on October 3, 1878, requested of United

States Marshal John Sherman, Jr., a report on conditions in Lincoln County. On October 5, Sherman submitted such a report to the Governor, in which he outlined the existing situation, and declared in so many words that there had been a complete breakdown of law and order in Lincoln County. Sherman's letter follows:

I have the honor to acknowledge the receipt of your favor of the third inst. requesting a statement of the facts relative to certain information received by you that the terrorism now existing in Lincoln county, N. M., has prevented me from executing certain warrants regularly issued upon indictments found in the proper court against residents of that county and placed in my hands as United States Marshal for official action. In reply I beg to state that I have now such warrants for Charles Bowdre, J. G. Scurlock, Wm. H. Antrim, alias Kid, alias Bonny, Steven Stevens, Serragins, Geo. Coe, John Middleton, Henry Brown and Dash Waite, residents of Lincoln county, charged with the murder of William Roberts, which I am powerless to execute owing to the disturbed condition of affairs in that county, resulting from the acts of a desperate class of men that now control it in such force as wholly to paralyze the efforts of its law abiding citizens in that county. Two contending factions seem to have attracted to their respective standards a lawless body of armed men who by pursuing a merciless system of retaliation and by committing murder in its most revolting form in cold blood and with a reckless disregard of human life that would disgrace savages have either driven out of that country or frightened into abject submission the remaining inhabitants who having had neither sympathy with or interest in the causes that led to the present deplorable condition there have in striving to avoid acting with either faction been alternately the victims of both.

Sherman told of the killing of Sheriff Brady:

One of my deputy marshals William Brady, who was also Sheriff of the county of Lincoln was deliberately assassinated at midday while passing along the public street within fifty yards of the court house of that county and though since then I have personally visited the seat of these outrages and have endeavored by every means in my power both in person and by deputies to execute the processes of

the court I regret to say that I find myself unable to make arrests
there with the civil power under my control. It is impossible for me to
be personally present in that county at all times and since the death
of Brady I have not been able to find a reliable deputy who with the
feeble force I can place at his disposal as a posse will risk his life to
make such arrests in the face of the resistance offered by the well
armed and organized desperadoes who now infest that county. The
militia of New Mexico being wholly without organization, no immediate assistance from that source can be expected and in my judgment there is now no means of enforcing the law in that county
without aid from United States troops.

John Sherman, Jr., United States marshal for New Mexico,
who made the foregoing report to Governor Wallace, was not
a particularly efficient or dependable official at a time of crisis,
when the services of men of courage and capacity were urgently
needed in the Territory. He arrived in Santa Fe on or about
July 27, 1876, to succeed John Pratt, who had served as marshal in the Territory for nearly ten years.

Sherman entered official life in New Mexico accompanied
by unusual political prestige. In Washington he had been engaged in the banking and investment business with Col. Frederick Grant, a son of President Grant. The President had
considered Sherman's appointment a personal matter, and had
seen to it that the Senate confirmed his nomination without delay. Although he had powerful political influence and important social connections, Sherman had no training or experience
which would help him perform the duties of a marshal in a
frontier country.

Young Sherman was a son of Charles Taylor Sherman (of
Sherman & Hedges, attorneys of Mansfield, Ohio), who died
in Cleveland on January 1, 1878; a nephew of Gen. W. T. Sherman, of Civil War fame, and of John Sherman, one-time Congressman and United States Senator from Ohio, and in 1877
Secretary of the Treasury in the cabinet of President Hayes;
and a brother-in-law of Gen. Nelson A. Miles and of United
States Senator James Donald Cameron of Pennsylvania.

After assuming the marshalship in New Mexico, Sherman
was criticized on a number of occasions by the press and scolded
in one instance by a grand jury for alleged incompetency and

gross neglect of official duty. Attorney Singleman M. Ashen-felter, one-time resident of Rock Island, Illinois, publisher of the Grant County *Herald,* of Silver City, made a number of sensational accusations against Sherman in a column-long editorial on June 21, 1879, some six months after the date of Sherman's report to Wallace. Ashenfelter charged, among other things, that Sherman had been guilty of padding the marshal's payrolls; that "he had been stupidly drunk in open court," in Albuquerque. The *Herald* specifically alleged that:

On the last day of the term in Albuquerque, when the United States record was being read, preparatory to final adjournment, Sherman growled out, in plain hearing of the court and its officers: "No use reading the record, United States has no show in this court."

In conclusion, the editorial said:

We advise John Sherman, Jr., to step down and out without delay. Insignificant as we are upon this frontier, we will try to make it apparent to John Sherman, Sr., that he cannot afford to carry so utterly worthless a subject of nepotism—even in New Mexico.

The Doña Ana County Grand Jury, in a report to the Third Judicial District Court, castigated Sherman, according to the Grant County *Herald* of July 4, 1879:

The grand jury find that they are called upon to draw the attention of the court and government, as well as the people, to acts of the U. S. Marshal John Sherman. This officer nearly ever since he has been Marshal for this Territory, has habitually neglected the duties of his office. He has failed and neglected to serve processes when issued, he neglects or refuses to summon material witnesses for the grand jury so as to enable them promptly to conclude their labor and expenses. When indictments are found he will not serve the warrants of arrest and when the parties have been arrested in one or two cases of very serious crimes, he has let them go about the county armed, not being restrained of their liberty, and no sufficient guard over them, and when court comes in has failed to secure their attendance.

Influenced, perhaps, by the grand jury report of neighboring

Doña Ana County, Editor Ashenfelter of the Grant County *Herald* belabored Sherman editorially on July 4, 1879:

Sherman has the reputation of being a scheming trickster against his own political friends, and when not too stupid to control the manipulation of his schemes, has succeeded in helping his enemies and injuring his friends. Sherman is a wart on the nose of New Mexico. His family refuses his presence in Washington and in every part of the states. We cannot conceive why he should be indulged or his vices condoned here.

In connection with his October 5, 1878, report to Governor Wallace, United States Marshal Sherman attached to it a copy of a letter from Judge Warren Bristol, of the Third Judicial District, in which Bristol gave his reasons for not holding court in Lincoln County. Bristol's letter, confirming substantially everything Sherman had written to Wallace, was as follows:

My reasons for not holding October term of court in Lincoln county based on best information I can obtain are as follows: First, the Sheriff has either abandoned or been driven from his office or duty, and taken refuge at Fort Stanton for protection. He refuses to go out. Second, the prosecuting attorney is absent from the Territory. Third, a large part of the better class of the population from which jurors should be drawn have fled from the county. Fourth, the county is completely demoralized. The troubles have arisen from two contending parties both in my opinion equally bad each having in its employ professional assassins whose crimes it seems to shield and if necessary to defend. Fifth, to accomplish the ends witnesses are intimidated, killed or driven from the country. Sixth, it is impossible at present to obtain fair juries whose findings and verdicts will not be tainted with gross partisanship. Seventh, the court can meet only through such subordinate officials as are furnished by election or appointment and juries taken directly from the people. When these from any cause utterly fail in their duties the holding of court for the time being could be but a mockery. Eighth, it is believed by those well informed as to the affairs in that county that during the present state of public feeling and animosity the assemblage of a body of men by attempting to hold court unrestrained by the military or any adequate force as they would be would be more likely to result in serious disturbance than otherwise and do more harm than good. Ninth, there seems to be lacking that degree of force which is necessary to render the execution of the mandates of the court at all.

With the Sherman and Bristol reports before him, the Governor was of the opinion that an extraordinary situation existed which would justify him in communicating with Washington by telegraph instead of by letter. Consequently, Wallace sent a fifteen-hundred-word telegram to Secretary Schurz on October 5, quoting the entire text of the Sherman and Bristol letters. Governor Wallace recommended in the telegram that the President take drastic action:

These papers are all official and disclose plainly the condition of the county with no organized militia in the Territory or arms belonging to it, with the court closed, the Marshal unable to make arrests, the Sheriff shut up in a fort, the good people unable to protect themselves, the regular soldiers fixed to their posts by order necessitated by the act of Congress of June eighteenth, eighteen hundred seventy-eight. I am powerless to maintain the peace and remedy the unhappy state of affairs in the section referred to. In my judgment nothing remains for me to do except call upon the President to exercise his constitutional authority and declare the existence of insurrection in the County of Lincoln, place the county without loss of time under martial law, suspend the writ of habeas corpus therein and appoint a military commission to come and hold sessions there for the trial and punishment of offenders. In no other way can citizens be made safe in person or property.

Wallace wanted the Texas Rangers to cooperate on their side of the line in a plan to stamp out the "robber element":

The Legislature of the Territory is not assembled nor can it be in time to accomplish any quick result; no doubt it would unite with me in this respect. I am loath to put such a mortification upon a high spirited people—at the same time I do not hesitate to charge the necessity for it to the aforesaid law by which the regular army in the Territory is forbidden to cooperate. I suggest obtaining the cooperation of the Texas Rangers on their side of the line. Doubtless the Texas authorities will be glad to join in the movement. Their combination with the regulars on this side will bring permanency of peace by stamping out of the robber element and breaking up their corrals and depots of plunder. The great need is a few rugged examples. I send this by telegraph because to wait on the mail will but give further time for outrage and murder.

Wallace's telegram produced prompt results in Washington. On October 7, 1878, only a few days after Wallace had become governor, President Hayes issued a proclamation, the complete text of which was telegraphed to Wallace in Santa Fe, "admonishing all good citizens of the United States, and especially of the Territory of New Mexico," who had been engaged in law violation "to disperse and return peaceably to their respective abodes on or before noon of the thirteenth of October, instant." The text of the proclamation follows:

BY THE PRESIDENT
OF THE UNITED STATES OF AMERICA:
A PROCLAMATION.

WHEREAS, it is provided in the laws of the United States, that whenever by reason of unlawful obstructions, combinations or assemblages of persons, or rebellion against the authority of the government of the United States, it shall become impracticable in the judgment of the President to enforce by the ordinary course of judicial proceedings, the laws of the United States within any state or locality, it shall be lawful for the President to call forth the militia of any or all the states, and to employ such parts of the land and naval forces of the United States as he may deem necessary to enforce the faithful execution of the laws of the United States, or to suppress such rebellion in whatever state or territory thereof the laws of the United States may be forcibly opposed or the execution thereof forcibly obstructed; and

WHEREAS, it has been made to appear to me, that by reason of unlawful combinations and assemblages of persons in arms, it has become impracticable to enforce by the ordinary course of judicial proceeding the laws of the United States within the Territory of New Mexico, and especially within Lincoln county thereof, and that the laws of the United States have been therein forcibly opposed, and the execution thereof forcibly resisted, and

Whereas, the laws of the United States require that whenever it may be necessary in the judgment of the President to use the military force for the purpose of enforcing the faithful execution of the laws of the United States he shall forthwith by proclamation command such insurgents to disperse and retire peacefully to their respective abodes within a limited time, Now, therefore, I, RUTHERFORD B. HAYES, President of the United States, do hereby admonish all good citizens of the United States, and especially of the Territory of New Mexico, against aiding, countenancing, abetting or taking part in such unlawful proceedings, and I do hereby warn all persons engaged in or connected with said obstruction of the laws to disperse and return peaceably to their respective abodes on or before noon of the thirteenth day of October, instant.

In Witness Whereof I have hereunto set my hand and caused the Seal of the United States to be affixed. Done at the City of Washington this seventh day of October in the year of our Lord eighteen hundred and seventy-eight, and of the Independence of the United States the one hundred and third.

Rutherford B. Hayes.

By the President:

F. W. Seward, Acting Secretary of State.

It had been Wallace's opinion, as expressed in his telegram, that the President would be justified in declaring martial law, suspending the writ of habeas corpus, and in appointing a military commission empowered to try and punish offenders. The proclamation fell far short of complying with Wallace's recommendations. Nevertheless, Wallace promptly carried on the work of placing it in circulation. He wrote to Secretary of State Evarts on October 10, telling him he had accomplished the task:

I have the honor to acknowledge receipt by telegram of the President's proclamation addressed to the people of New Mexico, and dated October 7th inst.

To have the Proclamation posted in Lincoln county speedily as possible I had it telegraphed from this city the day of its receipt to Judge Bristol in Mesilla, with request that he would have it printed there and dispatched thence by courier to the counties of Lincoln and Dona Ana for posting, which was done. Distribution to the other counties was effected from Santa Fe. Enclosed please find copy of the proclamation as printed and distributed. I shall go down to Lincoln immediately that I can get conveyance and escort, the better to report the effect of the proclamation, and the manner in which it is observed.

You may rest assured I shall not use the military unless it be absolutely necessary, then, however, I shall ask and urge the full measure of martial law, with a commission for the trial and punishment of offenders. As such a report is naturally distasteful I hope it may be avoided.

That the United States Army had been prepared to move troops into Lincoln County was apparent from action taken by the War Department. General Sherman sent all commanding officers in New Mexico a copy of the following official bulletin (published in the Las Vegas *Gazette* of October 26) :

WAR DEPARTMENT, WASHINGTON CITY, OCT. 8, 1878 :

To GENERAL W. T. SHERMAN :

The President has issued a proclamation declaring that by reason of unlawful obstructions, combinations and assemblages of persons, the laws of the United States, within the Territory of New Mexico, and especially in Lincoln County therein, cannot be enforced by the ordinary course of judicial proceedings, and commanding persons comprising such combinations or assemblages to disperse and repair peaceably to their respective abodes, before 12 o'clock noon of the 13th inst. The proclamation is preliminary to the appointment of troops of the United States to preserve the peace and enforce the laws in case disturbances and unlawful combinations continue after the time named. The President, therefore, directs that you instruct the proper military officers that after the time above mentioned has expired he will proceed to disperse by military forces such unlawful combinations or assemblages of persons within said Territory, and that he will by use of such force, and so long as resistance to the laws shall continue, aid the Governor and authorities in keeping the peace and enforcing the laws.

GEORGE MCCRARY,
Secretary of War.

In a letter to Secretary Schurz, written from Santa Fe on

October 22, 1878, Wallace expressed the belief that the people of the Territory approved the spirit and purpose of the proclamation:

I have the honor to inform you that since the posting of the President's proclamation of the 7th inst. in Lincoln and Dona Ana counties there has been no report of violence or wrong in those localities. For the time at least the order has had a sufficient effect, and as yet but one paper in the Territory has uttered a word of protest against it, and that one pretends to be Democratic. The better people everywhere have heartily approved the measure. The result will doubtless be gratifying to the President and all his advisers. It certainly is to me.

On October 24, 1878, two days after writing to Schurz, Governor Wallace was somewhat disturbed by the contents of a letter he received from Huston J. Chapman, a Las Vegas lawyer, until recently a resident of Burlington, Iowa. Chapman advised the Governor that Mrs. Sue McSween, "widow of the late Alex A. McSween," had employed him to assist her in settling her husband's affairs in Lincoln County, and charged that Colonel Dudley had been indirectly responsible for McSween's death. Among other things, Chapman wrote:

I desire to call your attention to one person whose actions have been offensive in the extreme to a large number of the best citizens of Lincoln county, and that man is Col. Dudley. I am in possession of facts which make Col. Dudley criminally responsible for the killing of McSween and he has threatened that in case martial law was declared that he would arrest Mrs. McSween and her friends immediately. Through fear of his threats Mrs. McSween left Lincoln and is now residing here until such time as she may with safety return to her home. . . .

On November 8, 1878, almost a full month after the date of President Hayes' proclamation and after he had served as governor barely two months, Lew. Wallace wrote a peculiarly worded letter to Secretary Schurz, saying that the "special mission" to New Mexico had been accomplished, and asking for promotion. In his letter the Governor said:

The task assigned to me, as my special mission here has been accomplished. Do you not think that I am now entitled to promotion? As the field in which your hand has to appear is a very wide one, with much to be done in it, I would be particularly happy if you would entrust me with some fitting part of the work.

A week later, November 13, perhaps by that time in a different frame of mind, Wallace wrote to Schurz in an optimistic vein, expressing the belief that the outlaws had been driven from the Territory:

The opinion expressed in a former communication was well founded. Thirty days have elapsed since the publication of the President's proclamation requiring disturbers of the peace in Lincoln to disperse, and, as show by dispatches of Col. Dudley, commanding at Fort Stanton, there has been no instance of violence in that time.

It was a great point gained to drive the outlaws out of the Territory without bloodshed; the next was to prevent their return. For that purpose, availing myself of the orders of the Hon. Secretary of War and General Sherman, (to whom my hearty acknowledgments are due) issued in connection with the President's proclamation, I addressed a request to General Hatch, commanding the District of New Mexico, to the effect that he send all available force to Lincoln and Dona Ana counties, under certain orders. General Hatch placed me under great obligation by complying promptly. The troops being distributed in the counties as much for the moral effect of their presence as from any expectation that there would be necessity for their use, I waited the expiration of the thirty days; then, there being no report of disturbance or outrage, I concluded the people might be in a state of mind to avail themselves of amnesty for the past, and begin anew. It is easy to see now, without something of the kind, the vendetta spirit which has marked the outbreak might go on indefinitely. Accordingly I have this day issued a proclamation announcing the end of the disturbances, inviting peaceably disposed citizens who have been driven away to return to their homes, and offering a general pardon, the latter carefully worded in expression and limitation.

It is my opinion that if the present status continues thirty days, or sixty, at the furthest, affairs in Lincoln county will settle down and go on in peace. The trouble is ended now, so that I have only to prevent its renewal, and help the people back to quiet control.

On November 23, 1878, Secretary McCrary wrote Wallace:

I acknowledge the receipt of your letter of the 15th inst., giving an account of your proceedings to suppress the disorders lately prevalent in the Territory of New Mexico, accompanied among other papers by the proclamation issued by you, announcing the termination of the disturbances, and offering under certain conditions, amnesty to those who participated in the disturbances. In reply I have the honor to state your action has the approval of the President.

The text of the amnesty proclamation referred to in Wallace's letter of November 13, 1878, was as follows:

For the information of the people of the United States, and of the citizens of the Territory of New Mexico in especial, the undersigned announces that the disorders lately prevalent in Lincoln County in said Territory, have been happily brought to an end. Persons having business and property interests therein and who are themselves peaceably disposed, may go to and from the County without hinderance or molestation. Individuals resident there but who have been driven away, or who from choice sought safety elsewhere, are invited to return, under assurance that ample measures have been taken and are now and will be continued in force, to make them secure in person and property. And that the people of Lincoln County may be helped more speedily to the management of their civil affairs, as contemplated by law, and to induce them to lay aside forever the divisions and feuds which, by national notoriety, have been so prejudicial to their locality and the whole Territory, the undersigned, by virtue of authority in him vested, further proclaims a general pardon for misdemeanors and offenses committed in the said County of Lincoln against the laws of the said Territory in connection with the aforesaid disorders, between the first day of February, 1878, and the date of this proclamation.

And it is expressly understood that the foregoing pardon is upon the conditions and limitations following:

It shall not apply except to officers of the United States Army stationed in the said County during the said disorders, and to persons who, at the time of the commission of the offense or misdemeanor of which they may be accused were with good intent, resident citizens of the said Territory, and who shall have hereafter kept the peace, and conducted themselves in all respects as becomes good citizens.

Neither shall it be pleaded by any person in bar of conviction under indictment now found and returned for any such crimes or misdemeanors, nor operate the release of any party undergoing pains and penalties consequent upon sentence heretofore had for any crime or misdemeanor.

The Governor's amnesty proclamation was published in the Santa Fe *Sentinel* of November 14, 1878, and in other Territorial papers soon thereafter. The *Sentinel* gave the background of the Lincoln County troubles, and praised the Governor for the work he had done in restoring peace in the county:

The thanks of the people of New Mexico are due Governor Wallace for the firm stand and the effective measures taken by him in this matter, his action being worth thousands of dollars to the people at large in quelling the lawlessness that so lately existed in Lincoln county. Peace is ours once again and Governor Wallace has cause to congratulate himself for having brought it about within sixty days as he said he hoped to do when he first came to New Mexico.

Wallace's amnesty proclamation failed to create much excitement among people in Lincoln County. However, officers at Fort Stanton immediately took offense because of the wording of a part of one paragraph which they interpreted as excluding the rank and file of the military from its provisions and inferring that army officers had been guilty of offenses against the law for which they should be pardoned by civil authority. The following words were considered as being particularly objectionable to the military:

And it is expressly understood that the foregoing pardon is upon the conditions and limitations following: It shall not apply except to officers of the United States Army stationed in the said County during the said disorders. . . .

Colonel Dudley,[1] commanding officer at Fort Stanton, on November 30, 1878, wrote an open letter to Governor Wallace, published in the Santa Fe *New Mexican* and other papers, which was highly critical of Wallace's proclamation. In his letter, Dudley served notice on the Governor that he and other officers at Fort Stanton respectfully declined to accept the offer of a pardon for offenses alleged to have been committed by them in connection with Lincoln County affairs. The proclamation charged by inference, Dudley contended, that officers had been guilty of misconduct. The officers, Dudley said in effect, had never departed from the strict line of their duties; and the army had been the only authority that had given the people any protection. Dudley charged in his letter that the Governor had failed to investigate personally the Lincoln County troubles:

Without any intention of criticizing the official course of your Excellency, permit me to state that you have now been more than eight weeks in the Territory, and have never been during this period within nearly two hundred miles of the scene of the terrible death struggles that have been enacted in this county during this time.

Dudley told the Governor that people had been forced to hide in caves, afraid of their lives at the hands of the class of men to which he had extended clemency:

The occasional passing of troops over the public roads, has had the effect to give the poor frightened settlers an opportunity of a few hours of seeming security. Wherever the colored cavalry have made their appearance, doors that have for weeks and months been barred and barricaded, windows have been opened for a few hours, husbands and sons have enjoyed the luxury of a night's rest at their homes, whenever troops have camped a single night near their ranches. For weeks and months, they were compelled to seek safety in the caverns, and mountain fastnesses against the very class of men included with the officers of the United States Army, in the pardon of your Excellency.

Pardon me for saying, it is not to be wondered at, that you have received erroneous views of the exact state of affairs here. I most respectfully ask you to come to Lincoln county, and see and judge for yourself, from personal observation of the facts.

In conclusion, Dudley skinned off the Governor's hide and hung it on the fence to dry:

I am aware that it is not within the province of an officer of the Army, to make suggestions to a civil functionary, occupying the high position held by yourself, much less criticize his official course; but when false and unjust accusations are made, either against myself, or the gallant officers of my command, it becomes my duty to demand for them and myself a hearing, and not allow a general pardon to be promulgated for them or myself, for offenses that we know not of, and of which we feel ourselves guiltless.

The officers at Fort Stanton endorsed Dudley's stand in his opposition to Wallace. On November 30, 1878, they addressed a letter to Dudley from Fort Stanton, which was published in the Grant County *Herald* of December 28:

We the undersigned officers of the U. S. Army stationed at this post during the recent troubles in Lincoln county, have heard read an open letter addressed by you to his Excellency, the Governor of New Mexico, and desire to say that the said letter expresses most fully and spiritedly our feelings upon the subject, thus publicly declining to accept the pardon tendered us by His Excellency.

(Signed) D. M. APPEL, Asst. Post Surgeon
G. W. SMITH, 2d Lieut., 9th Cavalry, Post Adjutant
M. F. GOODWIN, 2d Lieut., 9th Cavalry
SAM S. POGUE, 2d Lieut., 15th Inf. and A.A.M. & A.C.S.
J. H. FRENCH, 2d Lieut., 9th Cav., Comdg. Company M

The Mesilla *News* of December 14, 1878, published a letter from Lincoln, dated November 8, signed "W," which was critical of Wallace's proclamation:

DEAR NEWS: Thinking you are anxious to know how I feel, and all law abiding citizens feel in this section in regard to the governor's proclamation, pardoning all those "whom could not be brought to justice," I wish to state that we look upon it as an insult and an outrage upon society. I also wish to state for the benefit of people who are anxious of knowing, that the governor (Lew. Wallace) issued his proclamation on information received from the files of the Headquarters of the District of New Mexico, on one side; Mrs. A. A.

McSween, John S. Chisum and R. A. Weideman on the other side. I hope Headquarters wont be hot at me for telling the truth.

Huston Chapman, Las Vegas lawyer, differed from Colonel Dudley's views in regard to the conduct of the military in the Lincoln County War. From Lincoln on November 27, 1878, Chapman wrote a letter to the governor which was highly critical of Dudley and his soldiers:

Today this town was thrown into a panic by two hundred deputy sheriffs charging into town on their horses with their guns cocked and directed at the house of Mrs. McSween. A few minutes afterwards a posse of soldiers under command of Lieut. Goodwin came riding into town with three horse thieves who had formerly been of Sheriff Peppin's posse, and were brought in for examination before the justice of the peace. . . . The Sheriff's deputies who were with the military were drunk and had with them a flask of whiskey from which they were continually drinking and their conduct was everything but that of a peace officer. One of the deputies who had accompanied the military, fired his gun into the street to the great danger of peaceable citizens, and in fact there was no disturbance except that made by the military and drunken deputies. . . . Such outrages by the military are becoming too common. . . . Your own proclamation that peace had been restored in Lincoln county supersedes the necessity of further action by the government, and prevents the use of the military to aid the civil authorities in Lincoln county, and I have advised the citizens here to shoot any officer who shall in any manner attempt their arrest, or interfere with their rights. . . . The McSween men are willing to stand their trial in the proper courts of the Territory, or to observe your proclamation, provided the other side or "ring" observe it, but they will never allow themselves to be arrested by murderers like Col. Dudley and Sheriff Peppin, but will peaceably surrender to any decent man who may be sent with a warrant for their arrest. When the courts are held in this county Dudley and Peppin will be arrested and tried for the murder of McSween and others, and the legality of your amnesty proclamation will then be tested. I cannot but think that if you had visited Lincoln county, as you should have done, that you would have acted differently, and would never have pardoned notorious outlaws and murderers. You have been grossly imposed upon by the military, who have lied to you in order to shield themselves from the outrages they have committed.

Lincoln County people took "no stock" in Wallace's amnesty proclamation, according to Chapman's letter:

There is not an honest man in Lincoln who would believe Col. Dudley on oath, yet you rely upon him for all your information and have pardoned him for the murder of an innocent man. I can assure you that the people take no stock in your amnesty proclamation and they think you have been derelict in your duty in not visiting Lincoln County and acquainting yourself with the status of affairs.

There can be little doubt that Governor Wallace was remiss in not visiting Lincoln County and making a first-hand investigation into conditions. On February 24, 1879, some three months after the date of Chapman's first letter to Wallace, J. H. Watts of Santa Fe wrote to the Governor from Fort Stanton, urging him to visit the county:

I am going to Mesilla and El Paso in a few days, but cannot refrain from dropping you a few lines and asking that you look this matter over and see if you cannot adopt some means to put a stop to the lawlessness that prevails. . . . The worst thing is the feeling of insecurity, which everybody has, stopping all business, and making travel and traffic very risky for strangers and impossible for residents. I am thoroughly satisfied that the troops are impartial and doing all they can but they cannot act except to help carry out the civil process, and every one is afraid to put that in proper shape. I am sure you have been misinformed in regard to the status of affairs here, as I find I was myself, and then nothing but a personal visit and stay of some week or ten days will enable you to form a correct idea of the true standing and bearing of the matter. I found that nearly every idea I had was erroneous. These bad men on both sides, who have flocked in here to murder and plunder, taking advantage of the unsettled condition of affairs, should be taken up and tried. But it is of no use to give you my opinions—you must come down here yourself. I have no doubt you will be well received everywhere and then you can tell what to do and how to do it. It is likely that others will get killed and especially about court times, unless something in the interest of law and order should speedily be done.

On November 29, 1878, two days after Huston Chapman had written him a scolding letter from Lincoln, Chapman wrote

Wallace again, accusing him of "quietly sitting in Santa Fe and depending on drunken officers for information." Chapman's letter:

I am now preparing a statement of facts for publication, which I am sorry to say will reflect upon you for not coming here to get a correct idea of the outrages that have been committed here by quietly sitting in Santa Fe and depending on drunken officers for information. A decent respect for the people of this county would have caused you to come here in person and ascertain who was responsible for all the trouble, and then you should have seen that the guilty were punished. I am no believer in making the laws a convenience, or prostituting them for the sake of peace, and the people of this county will not submit to it quietly. Fort Stanton is today and has been during all the troubles the rendezvous of the worst outlaws that have infested Lincoln county, and today the disreputable class who are harbored there is a disgrace to the government. The horse and cattle thieves who are, and have been, depredating throughout the county were deputies, under that notorious murderer, the quasi-sheriff Peppin, and they have always been favored associates of the officers of the Fort.

I desire to retain your friendship but I owe a duty to the people of this county, and will discharge it to the very best of my ability and without fear or favor. I earnestly desire to see your administration as chief executive of the Territory made as popular as possible, but I believe that it can only be done by firmly upholding the supremacy of the law and punishing wrongdoing.

Colonel Dudley's insolent, almost insulting reprimand and repudiation of Governor Wallace's amnesty proclamation of November 13, 1878, resulted in a demand by the Governor that Dudley be relieved of his command. On December 7, 1878, the Governor wrote a letter to General Hatch,[2] praising Dudley for some of his virtues, but asking that a stranger to the people be assigned to Fort Stanton:

I am constrained to request that Lieut. Col. N. A. M. Dudley, commanding at Fort Stanton, be relieved and an officer of equal rank, ability and firmness be ordered to this place. In doing so, I mean no disparagement to Col. Dudley. Not more than once in a lifetime probably is an officer charged with duty more delicate and difficult than has fallen to him of late, and that he has maintained himself so long is the highest and best proof of qualities of exceeding value to the country, and the service. It is, however, apparent that he has excited the animosity of parties in Lincoln to such degree as to embarrass the administration of affairs in that locality. The same result may happen to any other gentleman whom you may assign to succeed him, yet in view of the important part the military are called upon to perform in keeping the status there as at present, I think it better that you send to that command a stranger to the people—at least one who has had no connection whatever with the feuds that have divided them.

General Hatch forwarded the Governor's request through channels to Washington. That Wallace had not yet visited Lincoln County, although he had been governor for nearly three months, was evident from a rather apologetic letter he wrote to Secretary Schurz from Santa Fe on December 21, 1878:

I have the honor to report that affairs of this Territory are moving on quietly, and offering nothing worthy of extended notice.

In Lincoln county the peaceable status continues. The Commandant at Fort Stanton (Lt. Col. Dudley) grew indignant about the clause in my amnesty proclamation which extended its privileges to the officers of the army and he rushed into print to his own detriment. I have requested the military authorities to relieve him. I send you the *New Mexican* containing his paper and the *Sentinel* with an answer to it, although not from me.

An individual by the name of Chapman went to the plaza (town of Lincoln) and tried to get up a disturbance. The burthen of his plaint was that I have not visited the town to get the truth there instead of at the Fort. On the other hand Dudley's grief is that I did not come to the Fort to get the truth there. Now as the two places (Town and Fort) were centers of the two factions, it was not possible for me to go to either without provoking jealousy and hard feelings; so I stayed away from both and am well satisfied that I did so.

General Hatch and Governor Wallace were not kept waiting for any considerable length of time on the Governor's request for Colonel Dudley's removal as commanding officer at Fort

Stanton. On December 26, 1878, Gen. W. T. Sherman, in a curtly worded memorandum, refused to accede to Wallace's request:

I disapprove of this for the reason that it is unjust. In "politics" changes are made to reconcile conflicts of opinion, but in military government, such action implies censure. To relieve Lieut. Col. Dudley now would leave him without recourse. There is no military reason why he should be displaced of his command at Fort Stanton. He is not required to report to, or explain his public acts to the governor of New Mexico, but will promptly do so to his superiors, including the Secretary of War, and the President of the United States if called upon. If Governor Wallace will prefer charges against Lieut. Col. Dudley, they can be thoroughly examined and tried by the law of the land, but if a mere request of the governor of a territory is to damage an officer of the army in his reputation and good name, then there is an end to the system which now enables executives of this nation to interpose the disinterested and impartial action of the army amid conflicting civil factions.

There is a principle involved in this case. Lieut. Col. Dudley, by no action of his own, has been placed between two factions of desperate men on the frontier. These spare no efforts, and resort to any amount of falsehoods to remove any obstacle. This obstacle now seems to be Lieut. Col. Dudley, United States Army, an officer of high repute, sustained in his immediate action by Generals Hatch, Pope and Sheridan. I add my own, asking specific reasons from the governor of New Mexico, that the questions involved may be settled now on the spot.

NOTES AND PROFILES

[1] Nathan Augustus Monroe Dudley, stormy petrol of the military in the Southwest for a decade, was born in Lexington, Massachusetts, on August 20, 1825; died in Roxbury, Massachusetts, on April 29, 1910. Serving his military apprenticeship in the Boston home guard, Dudley was made a first lieutenant in the Tenth U.S. Infantry; participated in expeditions against the Sioux in 1855; served in Utah in 1859 under Albert Sidney Johnston, and as a major officer in the Gulf States throughout the Civil War.

Subsequent to Civil War years, Dudley led a colorful life in Southwest military posts. He was frequently at odds with fellow officers, departmental superiors and civil authorities. However, Dudley enjoyed the personal friendship of a number of high-ranking officers, and had considerable influence in political circles in Washington. As a result he managed to extricate himself from time to time from situations which would have meant disaster for the ordinary officer's career. In old age, anxious to vindicate his name, Dudley spent considerable time and effort in attempting to prove that he had been the victim of malice and jealousy, particularly in connection with his difficulties in New Mexico. On November 14, 1871, Dudley was court martialed at Camp McDowell, Prescott, Arizona, on a number of charges, among them one alleging that he had appeared before the garrison on July 16, 1871, while under the influence of intoxicating liquor. Found guilty of some counts, not guilty of others, Dudley was reprimanded and suspended from rank and the Camp McDowell command for sixty days. The sentence was approved by Col. George Crook in a severely worded order.

Six years later on November 26, 1877, Dudley, then commanding officer at Fort Union, New Mexico, was tried before a general court martial on several charges, including alleged disobedience of orders of Brig. Gen. John Pope, commanding the Department of Missouri; villification of and refusal to cooperate with Capt. A. S. Kimball, when ordered to do so by Col. Edward Hatch, commanding the Ninth Cavalry; drunkenness while on duty on April 27, 1877. Dudley was found guilty of some of the charges, not guilty of others, suspended from rank, relieved of command at Fort Union, and deprived of half-pay for three months. On March 8, 1878, Gen. W. T. Sherman ordered the unexecuted portion of the sentence remitted.

Dudley became commanding officer at Fort Stanton on April 2, 1878, only a few hours after Sheriff William Brady had been ambushed and killed in nearby Lincoln. Four months later, Lew. Wallace became governor of New Mexico, and became friendly with Gen. Edward Hatch, commanding the Military District of New Mexico. Hatch and Dudley were enemies, and Wallace suffered as a result of the failure of the two military men to cooperate with each other in military affairs.

2 Edward Hatch, Commander of the U. S. Military District in New Mexico from 1878 to 1882, was born in Bangor, Maine, December 22, 1832; died April 11, 1889. He enlisted as a volunteer April 5, 1861, to defend the national capital; went to Davenport, Iowa, and served as a camp instructor; was commissioned captain in the Second Iowa Cavalry August 12, 1861; promoted to major, then brigadier general; served with distinction in Grant's Mississippi campaign; brevetted major general of volunteers; mustered out of the volunteer service on January 15, 1866; commissioned a colonel of the Ninth Cavalry on July 7, 1867; saw service in Colorado, Indian Territory, Wyoming and Nebraska before coming to New Mexico.

CHAPTER TEN

THE GOVERNOR AND THE OUTLAW

LAWYER HUSTON CHAPMAN'S insistent and persistent efforts to accelerate a reformation in Lincoln County affairs ended in stark tragedy. About the noon hour on February 18, 1879, while standing in front of the post office in Lincoln, Chapman was shot. With several bullets in his body, any one of which would have caused his death, Chapman died almost instantly. Eyewitnesses claimed that the bullets which killed Chapman had been fired from pistols held in the hands of William Campbell and Jesse Evans, two notorious outlaws, and that William H. Bonney, for once in his life a spectator instead of a participant, had witnessed the killing at close range.

Chapman's body was buried in the Lincoln cemetery, following an informal inquest, which produced the traditional frontier coroner's jury verdict to the effect that "the deceased had come to his death at the hands of a party or parties unknown." Attorney Ira E. Leonard notified Chapman's father, in Portland, Oregon, of his son's death, and received a reply dated March 20, which, among other things, suggested a psychological reason for Huston Chapman's aggressive character:

On account of an accident in his early youth our son lost one arm and he was always an object of our most anxious solicitation. We preferred that he should remain nearer home but his energy and enterprise knew no bounds. He spurned the idea that he could not accomplish with one hand anything that others could do with two.

In Santa Fe Governor Wallace was notified as quickly as possible of Chapman's "assassination," as it was described by adherents of the remnants of the McSween faction in Lincoln.

Shocked and horrified by the news of the killing, the Governor began at once to make arrangements to leave for the scene of the trouble. On March 1, the Governor reported the tragedy to Secretary Schurz, taking advantage in the report of the opportunity to take a dig at Colonel Dudley:

I have information that certain notorious characters, who have long been under indictment, but, by skilful dodging, have managed to escape arrest, have formed an alliance which looks like preparations for raids in Lincoln county. The horrible assassination of H. J. Chapman, lawyer, in front of the Court-House in Lincoln, the night of the 18th. ult., was the commencement of operations for the season. At all events their seizure now will put a quietus upon them.

With that idea, I proposed a plan of campaign—the word may be excused—to take them all in. The plan proposes the untiring use of the troops and Indian scouts. Gen. Hatch, commanding the District of New Mexico, approves, and will go with me and in person direct the military. I rely greatly upon his judgment and energy.

Accordingly I will leave for Lincoln today; and as it is uncertain how long I will be gone, I think best to notify you of my intention and departure, and request official communication to be addressed to me at Fort Stanton, Lincoln County, New Mexico, care of Commandant of Post. This until my return to Santa Fe.

Sometime ago I requested that Lt. Col. Dudley might be relieved from the Command of Fort Stanton. My application was curtly refused by General Sherman, and it was demanded of me that I should make military charges against Col. Dudley. *It will now be developed why I made the request.*

Governor Wallace and General Hatch left Santa Fe on March 2, ready for any emergency, accompanied by an escort of cavalrymen, sixty horses and mules, a supply train of ten wagons, and three ambulances. Traveling over roads that were almost invariably rough, rocky and sandy, the outfit reached Lincoln in four days, arriving on March 6. Governor Wallace, with a detail of seventeen soldiers and a Gatling gun, established headquarters on the outskirts of the town. General Hatch continued on to Fort Stanton.

As soon as his camp tent had been staked down, Wallace wrote a formal note to Hatch requesting him to send a detail of soldiers to assist George Kimball, sheriff of Lincoln County and also a United States deputy marshal, in arresting "J. G. Scurlock and Charles Bowdre, at a ranch called Taiban, about 12 miles east of Fort Sumner, for the murder of Andrew L. Roberts in April, 1878." On the following day, March 7, 1879, Wallace wrote a note to Hatch asking him to relieve Colonel Dudley from the Fort Stanton command, renewing the request he had made on December 7, 1878. Wallace's letter to Hatch:

I have the honor to repeat the request made on a former occasion that Lt. Col. N. A. M. Dudley be relieved of command of Fort Stanton. This is done upon conviction that he is so compromised by connection with the troubles in this county that his usefulness in the effort now making to restore order is utterly gone. The intimidation under which really well disposed people are suffering, and which prevents my securing affidavits as the foundation of legal proceedings against parties already in arrest, results in great part from fear of misdirection of authority by him. . . . I will state in general terms that it is charged here that Lt. Col. Dudley is responsible for the killing of several people in Lincoln county. I have information also connecting him with the recent murder of H. J. Chapman to the effect that he knew the man would be killed, and announced it the day of the night of the killing, and that one of the murderers stated publicly that he had promised Col. Dudley to do the deed.

This time, instead of sending Wallace's request through channels, General Hatch acted promptly on his own initiative. On March 8, 1879, he suspended Dudley from active military duty and ordered him to Fort Union, "there to remain in readiness to answer charges preferred by the Governor of New Mexico." Hatch appointed Capt. Henry Carroll[1] as Dudley's successor at Fort Stanton, and instructed him to cooperate fully with Wallace.

Now that Dudley, for the time being at least, had been replaced by a commander who might be expected to cooperate, Wallace began carrying out his own ideas concerning restoration of law and order in Lincoln County.

With Sheriff Kimball and a posse of soldiers engaged in scouring the hills in search of "Doc" Scurlock and Charlie Bowdre, charged with the killing of Roberts, Wallace's next step was to order the arrest of the men believed to have been responsible for Huston Chapman's death. He wrote to Hatch:

I have information that William Campbell, J. B. Matthews and Jesse Evans were of the party engaged in the killing of the late H. J. Chapman in this place the night of the 18, February ult., and that they are all now with J. J. Dolan at Carisoso Ranch. You will please send a sufficient force to arrest them; and when arrested, have them brought to Fort Stanton, and held securely until their cases can be investigated by the grand jury at the coming session of the Lincoln county court next month. I suggest the detachment be started immediately.

Arresting Campbell, Matthews and Evans proved to be a comparatively easy task. A detachment of soldiers took all three men into custody and placed them in the guardhouse at Fort Stanton. Anxious to have the trio held virtually incommunicado, Wallace sent a note to General Hatch on March 8:

I think, under present circumstances, it would better subserve public interests if the prisoners now in military custody should not be interviewed by persons other than their counsel, who I understand, is Mr. Wilson, of Lincoln. I suggest also that all communications to and from them be examined by a confidential officer before delivery. You will do me a favor by directing these points to be observed.

The Governor was dubious about the advisability of allowing his precious prisoners to remain at Fort Stanton indefinitely. He suspected that most officers at the Fort were either unfriendly or hostile to him personally, and sympathetic and loyal to Dudley. Deciding that he preferred not to risk the possibility of an escape, Wallace requested Captain Carroll on March 10, to have the prisoners transferred to Fort Union:

Under the circumstances, particularly in the absence here of suitable cells for the safekeeping of Jesse Evans, Jacob B. Matthews and William Campbell, charged with the murder of H. J. Chapman, I have to request you to be good enough to send them, securely guarded and with the usual precautions against escape to Fort Union, and there turn them over to the commanding officer. Enclosed find a request to that officer. The sooner they are gone the better.

Having written to Carroll asking that the prisoners be transferred to Fort Union, Wallace made doubly sure of their security by writing on the same day to Major Whittemore, commanding officer at Fort Union:

Jesse Evans, Jacob B. Matthews and William Campbell have been arrested for the murder of H. J. Chapman. Evans and Matthews are also under indictments for the murder of Tunstall. The prison quarters here are so unsafe that I have been compelled to request Capt. Carroll to transfer them for safer custody to Fort Union. Be good enough to receive them, to be held for trial, subject to my call. Place them in separate cells, and forbid communication with them or each other. You cannot be too careful to prevent their escape.

It is very possible that I will have in a few days to make a further call of a similar nature upon you.

With Campbell, Matthews and Evans safely in the guardhouse, Wallace took steps to bring about the arrest of James J. Dolan. The Governor was of the opinion that Dolan, if not a principal in the Chapman murder, was guilty of aiding and abetting the commission of the crime, an accessory before and after the fact. Wallace was in a quandary as to how to handle Dolan. In some respects, he rather liked the smooth-tongued, fast-talking Irishman, who had impressed him as being a strange, contradictory character. The Governor recalled that Dolan, on various occasions, had tried to promote and establish a friendly relationship between Dudley and himself. While in Santa Fe, during the latter part of December, 1878, Dolan had called upon the Governor, and talked about Lincoln County problems. Upon returning to Lincoln, Dolan had apparently told Dudley of his talk with the Governor. On December 31, 1878, Dolan wrote to Wallace saying that he had "repeated your explanation to the Comd'g officer (General Dudley). He seemed much pleased and said that if it was possible that you and him could meet and talk matters over for one hour he was satisfied that you would be fast friends. I also explained matters to Sheriff Peppin and many of our citizens, all of whom were pleased. I am convinced that the explanation has caused a very different feeling from that in evidence before I came down."

After considering the advisability of having Dolan arrested,

the Governor decided to save him any unnecessary embarrass-
ment. Sending for Dolan, he told him that he had intended to
have him arrested, but was willing to trust and take his word
that he would consider himself under arrest, go at once to Fort
Stanton and remain there until he communicated with him
again. On March 7, 1879, a disillusioned Wallace wrote a note
to Hatch, saying:

> I took Dolan's parol, confining him to the limits of the Fort. He
> violated his parol and by my orders, was put in close confinement.

"Close confinement" was apparently a meaningless phrase
at Fort Stanton. Taking advantage of the lack of discipline at
the fort, Dolan went to Lincoln on March 10. Wallace learned
of the visit and promptly wrote to Captain Carroll:

> J. J. Dolan was down here tonight. Arrest him upon his return to
> the Fort and put him in close confinement for the murder of H. J.
> Chapman.

On the same day, Carroll advised Wallace in writing: "J. J.
Dolan is confined. Do you wish him ironed and sent to Fort
Union with the others? Capt. Conrad will go in charge of the
prisoners." Instead of going through with his original plan to
send Campbell, Matthews and Evans to Fort Union, Governor
Wallace wavered, and reconsidered the matter, now that Dudley and Dolan might also be sent there, and, on March 11 coun-
termanded instructions previously given to Captain Carroll:

> Upon reflection I am of the opinion that if Dudley is really going
> to Fort Union, the four prisoners—Evans, Campbell, Matthews and
> Dolan—had better be kept in close confinement in Fort Stanton.
> First, they will be less likely to bother us with habeas corpus. Second:
> the escorts will weaken your detachments for other proposed duties.
> So hold on till you see what the Colonel does—or at least till I can
> see you.

Couriers carried official communications at all hours of the
day and night between Wallace's camp in Lincoln and the military at Fort Stanton. It was inevitable that rumors of plots and

counterplots should spread throughout the area. Placing some credence in a widespread report that friends of the prisoners at Fort Stanton planned to buy the entire supply of firearms and ammunition at the sutler's store and stage a jail break, Wallace relayed his knowledge of the rumors to Captain Carroll, who promptly posted an official notice on the bulletin board at Fort Stanton on March 13: "The Post Trader at Fort Stanton is hereby prohibited from selling arms and ammunition to soldiers or supplies of any description to citizens without an order from the Post Commander."

Even prisoner James Dolan began to sense the tightening-up of the lines of communication. Fearing that his mail might be tampered with, he sent a note to the Postmaster at Fort Stanton: "Please return all letters addressed to me, to the writer, providing the return address is on the envelope, and if not, please hold the time specified in Postoffice Guide, and if not called for within that time forward to the Dead Letter Office and oblige. No one is authorized to receive my mail from your office, or ask for it."

With Campbell, Matthews, Evans and Dolan in custody, and with Colonel Dudley stripped of his command at Fort Stanton, Governor Wallace appeared to be making some headway in his campaign to control the situation in Lincoln County. On March 6, the Governor wrote to General Hatch asking him to send a squad of soldiers to Las Tablas and arrest William H. Bonney, reported to be hiding near there. Bonney, however, managed to keep out of sight of the soldiers.

Every now and then during his stay in Lincoln, the Governor had heard rumors that the notorious Bonney might be willing to surrender to the law, testify before the grand jury concerning what he knew about the Chapman killing, and stand trial for his own misdeeds. The Governor discussed the situation with Justice of the Peace John B. Wilson, who had served with the First Regiment, Illinois Volunteer Infantry during the Mexican War, had been a resident of New Mexico since 1849, and of Lincoln County since 1873. The two men considered ways and means of gaining Bonney's confidence and cooperation. As a result Wallace was not greatly surprised to receive a letter from Bonney, dated March 13, 1879, delivered to him through Judge Wilson, which marked the beginning of an extraordinary correspondence between two men of extreme contrasts in character, personality and disposition. One correspondent was a mature man of great prestige; the governor of a Territory; a man of acknowledged pre-eminence in letters and literature; a gallant soldier, who had been privileged to wear with honor and distinction the shoulder straps of a major general in the army of his country in time of war; a man accepted as a celebrity in the national capital and elsewhere throughout the country. The other party to the correspondence was scarcely of legal voting age; almost illiterate; acquainted with comparatively few people; a desperado, gunman and outlaw; a man who had not hesitated to take human life on more than one occasion, whether justly or unjustly was yet to be determined.

Bonney's letter, with spelling, capitalization and punctuation exactly as in the original, follows:

To his Excellency the Governor,
    Gen. Lew Wallace

Dear sir I have heard that you will give one thousand $dollars for my body which as I can understand it means alive as a Witness. I know it is as a witness against those that Murdered Mr. Chapman. if it was so as that I could appear at Court I could give the desired information, but I have indictments against me for things that happened in the late Lincoln County War and am afraid to give up because my enemies would kill me. the day Mr. Chapman was murdered I was in Lincoln at the request of good Citizens to meet Mr. J. J. Dolan to meet as Friends. so as to be able to lay aside our arms and go to Work. I was present When Mr. Chapman was Murdered and know who did it and if it were not for those indictments I would have made it clear before now. if it is in your power to Anully those indictments I hope you will do so so as to give me a chance to explain. please send me an answer telling me what you can do You can send answer by bearer I have no Wish to fight any more indeed I have not raised an arm since Your proclamation. a's to my Character I refer to any of the Citizens. for the majority of them are my Friends and have been helping me all they could. I am called Kid Antrim but Antrim is my stepfathers name,

                              Waiting an answer I remain

    Your Obedeint Servant

                              W. H. BONNEY

Governor Wallace replied to Bonney's letter on March 15:

Come to the house of old Squire Wilson (not the lawyer) at nine (9) oclock next Monday night alone. I dont mean his office, but his residence. Follow along the foot of the mountain south of the town, come in on that side and knock at the east door. I have authority to exempt you from prosecution if you will testify to what you say you know.

The object of the meeting at Squire Wilson's is to arrange the matter in a way to make your life safe. To do that the utmost secrecy is to be used. *So come alone.* Dont tell anybody—not a living soul— where you are coming or the object. If you could trust Jesse Evans, you can trust me.

Governor Wallace and William H. Bonney met face to face in dramatic fashion in Squire Wilson's home on the night of March 17, 1879. Bonney entered the place of rendezvous alone, as the Governor had requested. He carried a six-shooter in a holster attached to a cartridge belt, and held a rifle in his hands rather carelessly, but ready to pull the trigger at an instant's notice. The Governor was taken aback by Bonney's youthful appearance, and impressed by the fact that he did not seem to be the outlaw he had pictured. In a matter of minutes the men got down to the business in hand. Bonney agreed to submit to arrest and tell the Lincoln County grand jury what he had seen and heard at the time of the Chapman killing, and some of the things he knew about cattle stealing in the Pecos River country. The Governor promised to furnish Bonney protection under the law after his arrest, and explained to him how he could take advantage of the amnesty proclamation of November 13, 1878. The two participants having reached an understanding and agreement, the meeting between the Governor and the outlaw came to an end. The two men went their respective ways, Wallace to his camp in Lincoln, Bonney to his hideout near San Patricio.[2]

Despite Wallace's efforts to keep it secret, news of his meeting with Bonney became public property within a matter of hours after it had taken place. The disclosure was of particular importance to Campbell and Evans, still confined in the guardhouse at Fort Stanton. They knew that Bonney had been a witness to the Chapman killing, and realized that his testimony alone, if given before the grand jury, would result in an indictment against them for first-degree murder, and if repeated before a petit jury might very well justify a conviction and a death sentence. Both Campbell and Evans preferred not to stand trial for the Chapman killing. There had been much talk in and about Lincoln for some days after the Chapman killing that officers at Fort Stanton, including Colonel Dudley, had voiced their approval of the crime. There was even some talk to the effect that some military officers had anticipated the killing and had predicted that it would take place. Consequently, there was no undue surprise or excitement apparent at Fort Stanton when it was discovered that Campbell and Evans had escaped from the guardhouse, and had taken the precaution to take with them in their flight a Texas recruit, who had been on guard duty at the time.

Wallace was awakened before daylight on March 19, in his camp in Lincoln, and told that Campbell and Evans had escaped. The Governor was angered, and greatly disturbed by the news. He had particularly requested General Hatch to see to it "that these prisoners be held securely," until the grand jury could pass on the charges against them. Now they were free, perhaps at that very moment snickering at the thought of his dismay, discomfort, and disappointment. Knowing that it would be a waste of time and effort to ask Fort Stanton for help, the Governor, galvanized into action and somewhat excited, sent a note on March 19 to Juan B. Patron, captain of the Lincoln County Riflemen, which he, Wallace, had organized on March 15, only a few days before. The Governor's note to Patron offered a reward of $1,000 for the two men:

Be good enough to send word to all your men to turn out as soon as possible to join in the hunt for Jesse Evans and William Campbell, who escaped from Fort Stanton last night. Say to your men that, as Governor of New Mexico, I offer a reward of $1000 for Evans and Campbell.[3]

Campbell and Evans escaped at a particularly critical stage of the negotiations between Governor Wallace and William Bonney. That the two outlaws were free, and undoubtedly able, ready and not only willing, but anxious to kill him on sight, was a matter of paramount concern to Bonney. On Thursday, March 20, two days after the escape, Bonney wrote a note to Squire Wilson evidencing apprehension:

Please tell you know who that I do not know what to do, now as those prisoners have escaped, to send word by bearer, a note through you it may be that he has made different arrangements if not and he still wants it the same to send: William Hudgins as Deputy to the Junction tomorrow at three o'clock with some men you know to be all right. Send a note telling me what to do.

W. H. BONNEY

P.S. Do not send soldiers.

Squire Wilson sent Bonney's note to Wallace, who was then at Fort Stanton. Wallace replied immediately. Exactly as written, the letter from the Governor to the outlaw read:

The escape makes no difference in arrangements. I will comply with my part if you will with yours.

To remove all suspicion of arrangement understanding, I think it better to put the arresting party in charge of Sheriff Kimbell, who shall be instructed to see that no violence is used.

This will go to you tonight. If you still insist upon Hudgins, let me know. If I dont get receive other word from you, the party (all citizens) will be at the junction by 3 oclock tomorrow.

Wallace enclosed a note to Wilson in his letter to Bonney:

I enclose a note for Bonney. Read it, and forward at once. I presume the messenger is in waiting. If you know why Kimbell should not go rather than Hudgins, hold on till I get over this evening.

Within a matter of a few hours, Wallace had Bonney's answer, saying that he would keep the appointment. The wording of the letter demonstrated that Bonney was entirely willing and unafraid to risk a fight in the open; that he had a native, inherent shrewdness, and a capacity for intelligent leadership:

SIR: I will keep the appointment I made but be sure and have men come that you can depend on. I am not afraid to die like a man fighting but I would not like to be killed like a dog unarmed. tell Kimbal to let his men be placed around the house and for him to come in alone; and he can arrest us. all I am afraid of is that in the Fort we might be poininered or killed through a window at night. But you can arrange that all right. Tell the commanding officer to watch Lt Goodwin he would not hesitate to do anything There will be danger on the road of somebody waylaying us to kill us on the road to the Fort. You will never catch those fellows on the road. Watch Fritzes, Captain Bacas ranch and the Brewery. They will either go to Seven Rivers or to Jicarilla mountains. They will stay close untill the scouting parties come in give a spy a pair of glasses and let him get on the mountain back of Fritzes and watch and if they are there will be provision carried to them. It is not my place to advise you, but I am anxious to have them caught, and perhaps know how men hide from soldiers better than you. Please excuse me for having so much to say and I still remain

Yours truly

W. H. BONNEY

P.S. I have changed my mind. Send Kimbal to Gutierrz just below San Patricio one mile, because Sanger and Ballard are or were great friends of Conuls. Ballard told me yesterday to leave for you were doing everything to catch me. It was a blind to get me to leave. Tell Kimbal not to come before 3 oclock for I may not be there before.

William H. Bonney on March 23 submitted to a simulated arrest at the hands of George Kimball, who succeeded George W. Peppin as sheriff of Lincoln County on February 1, 1879. Bonney became a prisoner in a makeshift jail in a vacant storeroom, owned by Juan B. Patron, on the main street of Lincoln, and not in the guardhouse at Fort Stanton as he had anticipated.[4]

Being in jail in Lincoln was anything but an ordeal for Bonney. Sheriff Kimball was on his side in the county troubles, and Juan B. Patron, owner of the prison, was a personal friend. Governor Wallace was at a loss to understand Bonney's popularity in the town. Writing to Secretary Schurz from Lincoln on March 31, the Governor, perhaps forgetting for the moment the part he had played in inducing Bonney to become a prisoner, described an occasion on which he had been serenaded:

A precious specimen named "The Kid," whom the Sheriff is holding here in the Plaza, as it is called, is an object of tender regard. I heard singing and music the other night; going to the door, I found the minstrels of the village actually serenading the fellow in his prison.

Referring to the escape of Campbell and Evans, the Governor reported to Schurz:

The only setback in my operation yet sustained was the escape a few nights ago of two of my prisoners, Campbell and Evans. They were helped out of the guardhouse at the Fort by a faithless sentinel, who deserted with them. I have offered $1,000 for their return, and hope to recapture them yet.

Wallace had succeeded in his plan to bring about Bonney's arrest and imprisonment, but had failed ignominiously to cause the rearrest of Campbell and Evans. It was generally accepted as true in Lincoln that both outlaws had long since discontinued the use of their true names and were known only under aliases.

Hopeful of furthering the search, Wallace on March 21 wrote the commanding officer at Fort Stanton, asking him to furnish Crescencio Sanchez, who would hand him the request in person, with five days' rations and sufficient cartridges and ammunition for himself and eight mounted men. The apathy and indifference prevailing at Fort Stanton were indicated in the position taken by Capt. George A. Purington, commanding the Ninth Cavalry, who advised the Governor that he could not honor the requisition without the written approval of superior officers, not presently available.

By March 29, Capt. Juan B. Patron, of the Mounted Rifles, was ready to abandon the chase. He reported to the Governor that the riflemen, led by Lt. Martin Sanchez, had failed to find any trace of the escaped prisoners, and had discontinued the search. Ira E. Leonard, the Governor's personal legal adviser, who had been in Fort Stanton doing what he could to assist in recapturing Campbell and Evans, was entirely disillusioned. He sent a note to Wallace in Lincoln: "I have no faith in the military—too slow and too much red tape. These scoundrels sit on the hills and laugh at them. Dangerous diseases require heroic treatment. That's what is needed now."

Replying to Leonard's note, the Governor said: "You have no idea how pleasant it is to have one hearty assistant and sympathizer in my work. To work trying to do a little good, but with all the world against you, requires the will of a martyr."

By April 1, 1879, Governor Wallace had reluctantly reached the conclusion that prospects for recapturing Campbell and Evans were dim. On that date he wrote a long report to Secretary Schurz advising him of plans he had in mind to break up the widespread cattle-stealing industry in Lincoln and adjoining Doña Ana counties. The Governor outlined for Schurz a somewhat visionary and bizarre scheme which would require the Territory of New Mexico to establish stations, or depots, where lost, strayed or stolen livestock could be impounded until claimed by the lawful owner. Utterly impractical in a vast range country, nevertheless the Governor was serious about undertaking the project. He told Schurz:

I am waiting here for Judge Leonard; when he comes I shall employ him as attorney in behalf of the Territory with this business; then I shall go to Mesilla, over in Dona Ana county, to concert action with the Commandant of Fort Bliss, looking to a thorough cleansing of that county. In all probability the purification will take the whole summer.

Of one thing Governor Wallace was absolutely convinced, and that was that it would take a strong hand to subdue the outlaws in New Mexico. In a closing paragraph in his letter he asked Secretary Schurz to read to the President the following personal message: "The desperadoes in this Territory include some of the most noted of their class in the United States. These outlaws cannot be made to quit except by actual war by guns and pistols, not writs or lectures."

The Governor was fearful that Dolan and other prisoners at Fort Stanton would emulate the example set by Campbell and Evans, and make their escape. From Lincoln, on April 3, he wrote a note to Col. George A. Purington:

I have information that there is being concocted a plan for the escape of the prisoners in military custody. You will do me the favor to take extra precautions in selecting of the guards who may be immediately in charge of them, and especially permit no person to see or converse with Mr. Dolan or any of the prisoners unless it be their attorney, and him only, in the presence of the officer of the day. Be good enough also to forbid communication with the prisoners or any of them in writing, except the communication be brought to you for inspection first, that you may judge of the propriety of delivering it. The same rule should be applied, it seems to me, to all matters addressed to them.[5]

NOTES AND PROFILES

[1] Henry Carroll was born in New York, enlisted in the army as a private January 13, 1859, was promoted through the ranks from corporal and sergeant to brigadier general. While stationed at Fort Stanton, Carroll was seriously wounded on April 7, 1880, fighting Indians in the San Andres Mountains.

[2] The New York *World* of June 8, 1902, published an article, headlined "General Lew Wallace writes a Romance of Billy the Kid, Most Famous Bandit of the Plains," with a subhead, "Thrilling Story of the Midnight Meeting Between Gen. Wallace, then Governor of New Mexico, and the Notorious Outlaw, in a Lonesome Hut in Santa Fe." The article said that Wallace had completed his autobiography, to be published in a few weeks. The article contained so many inaccuracies that it is of no value from the historical standpoint. When published, the biography contained only meager information concerning the meeting between Wallace and Bonney in Lincoln.

[3] Wallace's "Lincoln County Riflemen" were organized to "assist the civil authorities in repressing violence and restoring order." The men were in the field from two to thirty days. Under the provisions of Chapter 39, Laws of 1880, the sum of $2,206.50 was appropriated to pay debts incurred for subsistence for men and animals; Jose Montano received $565.73, Isaac Ellis $144.10, and Sue McSween, widow of A. A. McSween, $43.65, Juan B. Patron $246.52.

The roster of the mounted riflemen is a veritable "Who-Was-Who" of the Territorial forces in the field during part of the Lincoln County War: Captain Juan B. Patron, Ben H. Ellis, Martin Sanchez, Camilo Nunez, Elias Gray, Ramon Montoya, Estelano Sanchez, Trinidad Vigil, Fernando Herrera, Jesus Rodriguez, Juan Pedro Torres, Martin Chavez, Florencio Chavez, Jose Chavez y Chavez, Maximiano Chavez, Romuldo Frezquez, Gregorio Giron, T. B. Longworth, Eugenio Maldonado, Pablo Miranda, Manuel Martin, Santiago Maes, Martin Montoya, Zenon More, Trinidad Romero, Manuel Romero,

Crescencio Sanchez, Jose Marie Sanchez, Esiquio Sanchez, Franco Sanchez y Gonzales, Higinio Salazar, Jose Salazar, J. C. Wilkins, George Washington, Alex Rudder, and Ramon Vigil.

[4] Juan B. Patron was exceptionally well educated for his day. A one-time student in St. Michael's College in Santa Fe, and Notre Dame University at South Bend, Patron was shot and killed by M. E. Maney, alias Mike Manning, of Guadalupe County, Texas, at Puerto de Luna, then in San Miguel County, New Mexico, on April 12, 1884. The apparently unprovoked killing took place in Moore's saloon.

[5] George Augustus Purington, stationed for a time at Fort Stanton, was born in Ohio, enlisted in the U.S. Army April 1, 1861, served with distinction during the Civil War. He was promoted to colonel on March 6, 1867, for gallant and meritorious service in the battle of Cedar Creek, Virginia. He retired on July 17, 1895, and died May 31, 1896.

CHAPTER ELEVEN

CRIMINATION AND RECRIMINATION

S AN ATTEMPT to bring order out of chaos in Lincoln
County, Governor Wallace on several occasions had
recommended the use of a grand jury, an ancient and
honorable instrument of government, used since time
immemorial in Anglo-Saxon communities to ferret out
and punish wrongdoing. In letters to the Secretary of the Interior, to Judge Bristol, and to others in official life, the Governor had contended that a grand jury, properly empanelled and
instructed, would accomplish more than any other single device
to restore peaceful relations between warring factions, and
among the residents of the county.

Judge Bristol had been reluctant to call a grand jury, but
finally complied with Wallace's repeated requests. The grand
jury was convened and began its deliberations in Lincoln on
April 14, 1879, and a Court of Inquiry, convening in Fort Stanton, began to examine Wallace's charges against Colonel Dudley, on April 16. Governor Wallace had been anxious to avoid
concurrent investigations. He wrote to Secretary Schurz on
April 4, complaining of the conflict:

I have official information that a court of inquiry for Colonel Dudley has been ordered to assemble at Fort Stanton April 16th inst.
The time chosen is very unfortunate for me, so far as I am concerned
in that affair, inasmuch as the District Court for the county begins
on the 14th of April, and will require all my attention without any
extraneous distraction. It would really be a great relief to me if the
session of the inquiry could be postponed to a later period. Please
submit the matter to the President and Secretary of War.

Wallace had been busy rounding up criminals:

My work goes forward somewhat slowly, but well enough to keep me in hope. The third detachment of which I spoke in my last is returned, and there are now fifteen prisoners in custody, some of them very desperate characters. Henceforward everything depends on the conduct of jurors and witnesses. I confess to much doubt upon the subject. Still it is my opinion the experiment should be tried; if there is failure, if, on account of intimidation, partiality, prejudice or corruption, there be acquittals grossly wrong, then the last civil resort will have been spent, leaving only martial law. And then the President will be amply justified in taking that last step. The political situation in Washington, as I see it from this distance, requires so much in his behalf.

Wallace's letter of April 4 was referred by Schurz to the Secretary of War, and thereafter ignored.

The court term in Lincoln began as scheduled. Judge Bristol's charge to the grand jury was lengthy, and of necessity dealt with many phases of law violation. The Santa Fe *New Mexican* of May 3, 1879, published that part of the charge in which Judge Bristol referred to the local situation:

Since the last term of court in this county, the most serious disturbances of the public peace have transpired. Murder and robbery and pillage, have run their course without scarcely any restraint. Peaceful citizens knowing that crimes and misdemeanors have been committed, have not dared to take a prominent and decided stand against this lawlessness nor to open their lips to communicate to the proper officials their knowledge of crime, on account of their belief that by doing so their lives would be in peril, or their property stolen or destroyed. Murderers and thieves, if accused and arrested, in their defense, count largely upon this intimidation of the people and the suppression of evidence thereby. If necessary, open violence or threats of violence have been resorted to for the purpose of suppressing evidence of crime. Peaceful citizens very naturally and very properly look to the courts for protection. In this connection I feel it my duty to say to you that while the court has its specific duties to perform under the law, yet the court will be unable to give the needed protection unless the people on their part sufficiently perform their duties under the law in aid of the court. . . .

The court instructed the grand jury on its duty in considering the alleged crimes and misdemeanors:

From the character of the public disturbances in the county one would be led to suppose that the people had abandoned all idea of having their differences settled and their wrongs redressed through the courts, but had resorted to violence for this purpose. Now let me ask any fair and candid man among you if the experiment of redressing wrongs and grievances in Lincoln county by violence—by the rifle and the revolver—by the shedding of blood—has not been pretty thoroughly tested? What are the results of this method? Is any fair minded citizen satisfied with them? Does he expect any better results by continuing this experiment? Take for instance, the survivors of either party who were instrumental in the inauguration of these disturbances, and who at the beginning of the conflict were so eager and active in resorting to deadly weapons to settle actual or pretended grievances, have they bettered their condition? To use a common and homely phrase, "has it paid?"

Judge Bristol cautioned the grand jury against prejudice and partisanship:

We are all aware that partisan feeling has run very high; that it has been very intense and very bitter; and for this reason I warn and admonish you that you cannot permit this partisan feeling to influence your action as grand jurors without violating the solemn oath you have taken as grand jurors that "you will present no person by indictment through malice, hatred or ill will nor leave any unpresented through favor or affection."

The grand jury reported and was discharged on May 1, after having heard the testimony of many witnesses, among them William H. Bonney, who had faithfully kept the promise made to Governor Wallace some weeks before to appear and tell what he knew concerning violation of the law in the county.

Despite the fact that the legal machinery of the grand jury was in the hands of Judge Bristol and District Attorney Rynerson, that body demonstrated its partiality for the McSween faction by returning almost two hundred indictments against men who had been identified with the Dolan and Riley combine.

Among others, Colonel Dudley was indicted for arson incident to the burning of Alex. A. McSween's house on July 19, 1878. When arraigned before Judge Bristol in Lincoln, Dudley pleaded not guilty. The court thereupon granted a motion filed by Dudley's counsel asking for a change of venue, and ordered the case to be tried in Doña Ana County. Bristol first ordered Dudley to furnish a $2,000 bond for his appearance, and then ordered him released on his own recognizance.

Dudley's case was subsequently tried before a jury in Mesilla, with Attorney Rynerson prosecuting and Judge Bristol on the bench. The trial lasted three days. Susan McSween, subpoenaed as a witness for the Territory, at first sent word to Rynerson that she would be unable to appear, but later went to Mesilla and testified. The jury was out two minutes, long enough to elect a foreman, and have him sign a verdict of "not guilty." The Santa Fe *New Mexican* of December 6, 1879, commented: "Thus ends a most infamous prosecution."

The grand jury laid the ghost of speculation as to who had actually killed Alex. A. McSween by returning indictments against Marion Turner and John Jones, charging that they and each of them, on July 19, 1878, "with certain guns then and there loaded and charged with gunpowder and divers leaden bullets, by force and gunpowder shot and sent forth against the said Alexander A. McSween, in and upon the breasts and belly of him, inflicting mortal wounds from which he instantly died."

Upon arraignment before Judge Bristol in Lincoln, a number of men against whom indictments had been returned, through their lawyers filed pleas in bar, claiming immunity from prosecution under Governor Wallace's proclamation of November 13, 1878. Other defendants, spurning the right to ask for immunity and thus escape prosecution, pleaded not guilty and filed motions asking for change of venue. Judge Bristol ruled that the Governor's proclamation was a general amnesty for all offenses coming within its provisions, and with one or two exceptions, discharged all defendants asking for its protection. On or about May 1, 1879, the court granted a change of venue from Lincoln to Socorro County in the cases of the Territory vs. Samuel Perry, George Peppin, John Hurley, Jacob Matthews, John M. Beckwith, Joe Nash, Louis Paxton, Buck Powell, Robert Olinger, John Galvin, Thomas Cochrane,

Charles Kresling, Richard Kelly, Charles Martin, Wallace Olinger, John Mace and W. H. Johnson, all of whom had been indicted for murder, or assault with intent to murder.

The Mesilla *Independent* of May 3 gave a sketchy report of the court proceedings in Lincoln:

Indictments were found against Gen. Dudley and Peppin for the burning of the McSween House, Dolan and Campbell for the Chapman murder, Tom O'Folliard for horse stealing. Quite a number plead the Governor's pardon and were discharged. District Attorney Rynerson would not release "Kid," to turn State's evidence in the case of Dolan and Campbell, and considering the character of the man the action was right in the premises. Dudley took a change of venue to Dona Ana county. Peppin, Dolan and Matthews took a change of venue to Socorro county.

Thirty Four, a weekly newspaper published in Mesilla, made a more complete report of the court proceedings which was republished in the Grant County *Herald* of May 10, 1879:

At the recent term of court in Lincoln, about 200 indictments were found. Among them, Col. Dudley and George W. Peppin for burning McSween's house, Dolan and Campbell for the Chapman murder, in which the Kid is the principal witness; about 25 persons for the murder of McNab; Tom O'Folliard for stealing Fritze's horses. But two criminal cases were tried—that of Lucas Gallegos, for the murder of his nephew. He was found guilty and sentenced to one year; and a case of assault in which the accused was acquitted. No civil case was tried. In nearly all of them, one or the other party was dead. O'Folliard, Jack Long, Marion Turner, and others, plead the governor's pardon, and were discharged. Peppin, Dolan and Matthews took a change of venue to Socorro, and Dudley took a change of venue to Dona Ana county. The District Attorney would not consent to the release of the Kid for turning State's evidence. His case comes to Dona Ana county. The greater portion of persons indicted will probably come forward and plead the governor's pardon. Dolan and Matthews, indicted at last term for the Tunstall murder, also go to Socorro on change of venue. Opinion is divided as to what the result will be. Some think a fresh outbreak is imminent, and others, that the trouble is over. The two opposing factions have about exhausted themselves and future troubles will only arise from bands passing through and plundering. Jesse Evans and Campbell have not been rearrested.

Governor Wallace left for Santa Fe on April 18, 1879, in all probability a discouraged and disillusioned man. He had spent some six weeks in the county, working many hours each day, and occasionally far into the night, trying to restore peace and quiet among the inhabitants of Lincoln. The problems had been many, and vexatious. The Governor, in all probability, would have been the first to admit that he had not contributed greatly to their solution.

While in Lincoln the Governor received a letter from John S. Chisum written from Fort Sumner under date of April 5, outlining a plan Chisum had in mind to cut down on cattle thievery. In his letter, Chisum recommended Pat Garrett as "a very suitable man" to take charge of the work, marking the first mention of Garrett's name in correspondence connected with law enforcement in the Pecos River country. Chisum's letter:

If 10 good men were stationed at a large spring 12 miles east of this place it would prevent robbers from coming in off the plains on to the Pecos and give protection to this place and the citizens below. Roswell is so far below that the robbers can come in and rob as low down as Bosque Grande a distance of 50 miles and get out unmolested before the troops from Roswell can reach them. If 20 men could be stationed at Pope's Crossing on the Pecos, it would prevent them from coming up the Pecos. Having those two points guarded you then have possession of the two main keys to the settlements on the Pecos river. Pat Garrett who resides here would be a very suitable man to take charge of the squad east of this place if authorized to do so.

I hope Gov. you will not think I show any disposition to meddle or dictate. I know the country well, and I am satisfied you are more than anxious to give the citizens protection and I am equally anxious to see the robbers kept out hence I make these suggestions. Robbers cannot very well reach the Pecos by any other route on account of the lack of water.

At the time he received John Chisum's letter, the Governor

had little time to think of devising ways and means of placing Pat Garrett at the head of a squad to round up livestock thieves. For one thing, Wallace was particularly concerned about the Dudley Court of Inquiry, scheduled to begin work on April 21. Wallace had hoped that the grand jury might be allowed to conclude its labors before the Court of Inquiry convened. But the military had refused to agree to any postponement. The Court, composed of Col. G. Pennypacker, of the Sixteenth Infantry; Major Hambright, of the Nineteenth Infantry; Major Osborne and Capt. A. M. Brinkerhoff, both of the Fifteenth Infantry; and others, began the opening session on scheduled time. Dudley was represented by Henry L. Waldo, former Justice of the Supreme Court and judge of the First Judicial District, former attorney general of the Territory, and Wallace by Ira E. Leonard, a recent arrival in New Mexico from Colorado.[1]

The charges instigated against Dudley by Governor Wallace before the Court of Inquiry for its consideration may be summarized as follows: That on July 19, 1878, without legal authority, or by virtue of any right vested in him to so do, Dudley had taken a squad of sixty armed soldiers, with one cannon and one Gatling gun, to the town of Lincoln; that the soldiers, assisted by a gang of armed outlaws, had killed A. A. McSween and set fire to his house; that Dudley had compelled John B. Wilson, a justice of the peace of Lincoln, by threats of ironing and imprisonment, to issue warrants for the arrest of McSween and other citizens; that on July 20, 1878, Dudley accompanied by soldiers, had entered John H. Tunstall's store and had stood by and allowed it to be plundered of more than six thousand dollars worth of goods; that when asked to stop the plundering "Dudley aided the plunderers to consummate their object;" that during November and December, 1878, Dudley had procured "base and wicked men" to make slanderous charges against Susan E. McSween, and caused the same to be filed in the military department of the government "for the purpose of ruining her reputation and destroying her influence in seeking redress for the gross outrages perpetrated by the said Dudley against her;" that during November and December, 1878, in order to subvert the ends of justice and prevent Gov. Lew. Wallace from restoring peace in Lincoln County, Dudley "did ma-

liciously and falsely publish a letter in the *New Mexican* at
Santa Fe, calculated to foment the disturbances then rife in that
county."

One hundred twenty witnesses were summoned to testify before the Court of Inquiry. As the trial dragged on, day after
day, it was apparent that the government was paying out each
day a substantial sum of money for witness fees, mileage and
sustenance. On May 23, 1879, after being in session for several
weeks, the Court summarily excused all witnesses expected to
offer cumulative evidence. In taking this action the Court held,
among other things, that it would be unnecessary for the Court
of Inquiry to examine into the truth or falsity of the charge that
Dudley had been an accessory to the killing of Lawyer Chapman, because the Lincoln County grand jury, "after a continu-
ous session of about eight or ten days and after quite an
exhaustive investigation of criminal matters," had failed to indict him in connection with that crime. An accounting as of
July, 1879, showed that the expense of the Court, up to that
date, had been in excess of $30,000. On June 28, 1879, the Grant
County *Herald* sandwiched in a dig at Wallace: "The Dudley
Court of Inquiry, now in session at Fort Stanton, is a miserable
farce, for which Governor Wallace is mainly responsible. His
intermeddling in Lincoln county matters will never send him
to the United States Senate."

As the trial proceeded it was apparent that Dudley's witnesses were always on hand, prepared to offer persuasive testimony. Many men who might have been expected to testify in
support of Wallace's contentions had either left the country or
were reluctant and unsatisfactory witnesses. Alex. McSween
and Dick Brewer, who would have been important witnesses
against Dudley, were dead and buried. Most of the testimony
introduced before the Inquiry revolved around the fighting in
Lincoln between the decisive days extending from July 15 to
July 19, between the Peppin and McSween forces. Small doubt,
from the evidence before the Court, that great excitement had
prevailed in Lincoln during the days of fighting. But, as always,
eyewitnesses differed in their versions as to just what had taken
place.

Much of the important testimony on Dudley's behalf was
offered by three witnesses—Lieutenant Appel, assistant sur-

geon at Fort Stanton, Sheriff Peppin, and John Long, a Peppin deputy. From a composite of their testimony it appeared that for months Sheriff Peppin held warrants in his hands for the arrest of William H. Bonney and several of Bonney's companions, for the murder, on April 1, 1878, of Sheriff Brady and Deputy Hindman, and for the murder, on April 4, 1878, of Andrew L. ("Buckshot") Roberts. For first one reason and then another, Peppin had been unable to serve the warrants. In late June and the early days of July, reports reached Peppin that McSween, Bonney and others of their crowd, had been seen in and about San Patricio. Peppin then deputized John Long and authorized him to serve the warrants. Long had lived in Lincoln on and off for two years, was considered a good shot, fearless, and resourceful in a crisis.

On July 13, Long went to San Patricio, looking for William H. Bonney, previously known to him, according to Long's testimony, as "Henry Antrim." Approaching San Patricio on the Ruidoso road, John Long's mare stopped quite suddenly. Several hundred feet away Long saw eleven men on horseback, among whom he recognized Bonney, John Copeland and Alex. McSween. The next thing John Long knew, his horse had been shot and disabled. When the shooting began, Long dismounted, made his escape from the range of fire, and returned to Lincoln with the warrants unserved.

Two days later, on July 15, 1878, according to his testimony, while on a scouting trip, John Long saw forty-three mounted McSween men approaching Lincoln from the southeast. Five men rode to McSween's house and entered it. Others went to various houses in Lincoln, as if by pre-arrangement; still others made camp in an arroyo along the banks of the Bonito River. That same evening, Sheriff Peppin's posse, around forty men in all, rode into town and passed by McSween's house, from which several shots were fired at the posse. No one was hit.

After making several trips to Fort Stanton, Sheriff Peppin announced that he proposed to serve warrants on McSween, Bonney and other men quartered in McSween's house, and established headquarters at the Wortley Hotel, several hundred feet away. Peppin placed several deputies at the hotel, others on a hill south of town, and a few on the tower in the plaza. By July 16 most of the McSween forces had been arrayed in battle order. Some were at McSween's home, some at the Ellis home, others at Patron's and Montano's. A half-dozen fighters were placed in Tunstall's building. Firing began, and continued intermittently during many hours of the day and night of July 15, 16, and 17. The plaza in Lincoln was virtually an open-air shooting gallery. A man went outside at his own risk, knowing in advance that he would be obliged to dodge missiles fired from pistol, rifle and shotgun, and might be killed or badly hurt.

Unusual excitement and activity prevailed at Fort Stanton on the afternoon of July 18. Colonel Dudley hastily summoned his staff officers to consider a request from the Baca family that the military protect non-combatant residents of Lincoln. The officers unanimously agreed that protection should be offered. Lieutenant Goodwin, post adjutant, prepared an appropriate resolution, which was endorsed in writing by all officers present.

Bugle calls at daylight readied the soldiers at Fort Stanton for action on July 19. Orders for the day were read; sergeants shouted commands; sixty cavalrymen advanced toward Lincoln. Colonel Dudley brought up the rear. Upon arriving in Lincoln, Dudley went to the Wortley Hotel and talked to Sheriff Peppin. Concerning this conversation, Peppin testified before the Court of Inquiry:

Col. Dudley told me he wanted me and my men to understand that he had not come to Lincoln to assist in any way; that he came there to protect women and children; that if me or any of my men fired on his command, wounded or killed any of his officers or soldiers that he would return the fire.

Only a few minutes after the talk between Dudley and Peppin, a squad of soldiers called for Peppin and marched him to Dudley's camp, located "a little below Montano's place." Dudley told Peppin, in emphatic language, that he wanted him to know where his camp was located, so his men would not fire in that direction. Within the same hour, Dudley sent for Peppin again. Peppin testified:

I told the Sergeant I did not want to go, that I had other business. He said I would have to go, so I went along with him. I arrived at the camp. Col. Dudley repeated the same conversation as before. This time, Isaac Ellis was there. Dudley told us, that if he and his men were fired upon, by either party that he would return the fire. As I started to leave, Col. Dudley said: "———— damn you, understand me; if one of your men wounds one of my men I will blow you above the clouds."

The extraordinary situation that had developed in Lincoln on July 19, 1878, with Colonel Dudley and United States soldiers ostensibly in the role of spectators to the fighting between McSween and Peppin forces, resulted in large part from General Orders No. 49, issued in Washington on July 7, 1878, directing the attention of officers of the army to the Act of Congress of June, 1878, prohibiting the army from acting as a posse comitatus, "or otherwise," for the purpose of executing the laws.

In Colorado, the Pueblo *Chieftain* of August 13, 1878, had commented editorially:

A few days since a riot broke out in our neighboring Territory of New Mexico. Perhaps we should not say a few days since, for this is only a fresh outbreak of an old feud that has been in progress for several months. The town of Lincoln was taken possession of by a band of armed men, whom the Sheriff of the county with a small posse attempted to arrest. A desperate fight ensued in which several men were killed, many wounded and a house burned. A body of United States troops, with artillery, was on the ground and stood as idle spectators of the scene, because the laws of Congress prevent them from interfering at the request of the authorities! Before the troops could be allowed to interfere the Governor of the Territory must apply to the President in due form. As the Governor of New Mexico was from three to four hundred miles away from the scene of the disturbance, and there is no telegraph or railroad communication between Lincoln and Santa Fe, the whole population of that county might have slaughtered one another before the troops could have received orders to interfere. All of this too, in a territory under the fostering care of the government of the United States. When the Congress of the United States passed this wise and wonderful law, they forgot that there are States and Territories located on the fron-

:iers, where railroads are unknown and telegraph lines a thing of the future, and in destroying the fleas they cremated the unfortunate dog.

Sheriff Peppin returned to the Wortley Hotel after his third interview with Dudley, according to his testimony, and handed to Marion Turner, a recently commissioned deputy sheriff, Territorial warrants for the arrest of McSween, "Kid Antrim," Hendry Brown and John Middleton, with instructions to serve them. Deputy Turner, it appeared, was not a regular peace officer. He was a farmer and rancher in the lower Pecos River country, who had been in the country since 1872, and had consistently asked for nothing more than to be allowed to continue his ranch work unmolested. He had been persuaded to become a deputy sheriff under Peppin because he believed that John S. Chisum and Alex. A. McSween were working together, and he had no love for Chisum.

On April 18, 1878, Turner had written a letter expressing his views, and giving his understanding of the background of Lincoln County troubles. Turner's letter, obviously the composition of a man of superior native intelligence and ability, was published in the Las Vegas *Gazette* of May 14, 1878:

In 1875, Alex A. McSween arrived in Lincoln. He came, with his wife, penniless, hauled here in a farmer's wagon by Martin Sanches. He expressed his intention of making his El Dorado in Lincoln and he has accomplished his design. . . . Lawrence G. Murphy & Co. were sutlers at Fort Stanton, beginning in 1870. They controlled the business of the country. No farmer, stockraiser, artisan or mechanic within a radius of 100 miles could secure employment except through this firm, directly or indirectly. . . . The charge to the recent grand jury by Judge Bristol was denunciatory to the action of McSween and laudatory to the opposing party. . . . My firm belief is that although the adherents of these parties (Murphy party and McSween party) have been guilty of "killing their enemies," there is no murder in the matter, but a contest for the "best of the fight," which any man will try to get. Let any man stand in the shoes of any of these men and try to restrain his propensities. . . . I believe that both parties were unscrupulous, and used such means to accomplish their object, that they employed unlawful instruments. . . . The result

has been bloodshed and disaster, costing the lives of good citizens
against whose character the breath of scandal never reached; costing
the lives of citizens who leave behind friends, who before the feud
would have sacrificed their lives to save the lives of the men who have
been killed.

An unscheduled event took place in Lincoln about sundown
on July 18. Peppin and Susan McSween, bitter enemies, met
each other face to face. Concerning this dramatic meeting, Pep
pin testified at the Inquiry:

She was a coming up the street. She hollered at me and says: "Pep
pin what does this mean? What are you going to do?" I told her
that I was going to have those men out of McSween's house that
had warrants for if it cost the life of every one of my posse and mine
too.

By the noon hour of July 19, Peppin's deputies, John Long
and Marion Turner, had not served warrants on any of the Mc
Sween crowd. Sheriff Peppin, Long and Turner reached a de
cision of desperation. They would set fire to McSween's house
and force the inmates either to get outdoors and surrender, be
killed in an attempt to escape, or stay indoors and be burned to
death. At half past one in the afternoon of July 19, 1878, John
Long, helped by "Dummy," a man whose real name Long did
not know, poured coal oil on the kitchen floor of McSween's
house, and started a fire, which burst in flame, then smouldered
and went out. Late in the evening Long made another attempt
to set the house afire. This time he used shavings and pieces of
kindling previously saturated in coal oil. The fire blazed, and
the kitchen was quickly enveloped in flames.

Deputy Sheriff Long had been a busy man during the day
and nights of the fighting in Lincoln. For many hours at a time
he had taken a stand on the round tower, which commanded a
view of the McSween house, the Wortley Hotel, and other stra
tegic points. From time to time J. B. Matthews and Sam
Sperry, of Lincoln, Jim Reese from Spring River, and Jim
McDaniels took their turn on the tower, relieving Long. At the
Court of Inquiry Long testified in regard to the warrants he
held for McSween's men:

I held a number of warrants, one for Kid Antrim, Charles Bowdre, Doc Scurlock, A. A. McSween, Henry Brown, Frank Coe, George Coe, Josefito Chaves, Jesus Rodriguez, others I dont remember. Kid, a murderer, Scurlock, a murderer, Henry Brown, murderer, Bowdre same, Josefito Chaves, horse stealing, I believe. Rodrigues same. That's all I can remember. McSween charged with attempt to assault to kill. I had two warrants for Kid for murder, Henry Brown was 2, Scurlock 2, for murder, Bowdrie 2, I don't remember how many warrants I had that day.

Deputy Long named some of the men who made up the sheriff's posse on July 19:

Pierce was one, Joe Nash, Robert Beckwith, John Beckwith, Robert Ollenger, Wallace Ollenger, Andrew Boyle, John Hurley, J. B. Matthews, James J. Dolan, Buck Waters, Buck Powell, John Chambers, John Kinney, Tom Jones, Jesse Evans, a man by the name of Hart, Collins, Irvin, a Mexican boy they called Luciano, Panaleon Gallegos. That's all I believe. I could not tell where they were all from, some I could tell.

William Bonney testified before the Court of Inquiry on May 28, 1879. Unfortunately, his testimony was brief and failed to throw much light on the happenings during the period July 14 to July 20. Bonney testified that his name was "William Bonnie," and that he resided in Lincoln. When asked by the Recorder: "Are you known or called Kid? Also Antrim?" he replied: "Yes." Bonney denied that he had been known in Lincoln County or elsewhere under the name, "Billy the Kid." Asked to describe movements and actions of the soldiers on July 19, Bonney testified:

I was in Mr. McSween's house in Lincoln, and I seen the soldiers come down from the Fort. The Sheriff's party, that is the Sheriff's posse, joined them a short distance above McSween's house. The soldiers passed on by. The men dropped right off, and surrounded the house, the Sheriff Party. Shortly after three soldiers came back with Peppin, and passed the house twice afterwards. Three soldiers came down and stood in front of the house in front of the windows. Mrs. McSween wrote a note to the officer in charge asking him what the soldiers were placed there for. He replied saying that they had business there—that if a shot was fired over his camp or at Peppin, or any of his men, that he had no objection to his blowing up if he wanted to his own house. I read the note. He handed it to me to read. I read the note myself. I see nothing further of the soldiers until night. I was in the back part of the house, when I escaped from the house. Three soldiers fired at me from the Tunstall store, outside the corner of the store. That is all I know in regard to it.

Bonney testified that he and others had gone to the McSween house with Alex. McSween, and had remained there several days; that he had heard that the Sheriff was trying to arrest him and others in the house; that "about dusk, in the evening of July 19th, a little after dark," after John Long had started a fire with coal oil in the McSween kitchen, he had made his escape from the house. At first he ran toward Tunstall's store, thirty to forty yards away from McSween's house, but when the soldiers fired on him he swerved and ran toward the river. Harvey Morris, a McSween man, according to Bonney, was the first man killed:

We all tried to escape at the same time. In the getaway, Vicente Romero, Francisco Samaro and McSween were killed. I knew also that Bob Beckwith of the Sheriff's posse had been killed.

On May 23, 1879, the fourth day of the Court of Inquiry, Susan E. McSween was called to testify for the prosecution. After qualifying as a witness, and identifying herself as the widow of the late A. A. McSween, she told her story of the happenings in Lincoln on July 19, 1878. Mrs. McSween's testimony, apparently an exchange of rapid-fire questions and answers, indicated that she was a woman of combative disposition, willing to take the initiative in calling at Dudley's camp in Lincoln and demanding that Colonel Dudley give an explanation of his conduct and enmity toward her husband.

The meeting between Mrs. McSween and Colonel Dudley developed into somewhat of a fishwife affair. Mrs. McSween, it seemed, had berated Dudley, and she may have occasionally used a few salty words in her efforts to impress upon him her opinion that his soldiers should protect her husband and their property. When cross-examined, Mrs. McSween denied addressing any improper words to Dudley or engaging, while talking to him, in any "conduct unbecoming a lady." Testifying specifically in regard to the events of the day on which her husband had been killed, Mrs. McSween said:

Well, on the day that my husband was killed, Col. Dudley came into Lincoln in the morning about 10 o'clock, with about 40 or 50 soldiers, as near as I could tell, without counting them. Well, when coming in, he stopped at the Wortley Hotel, occupied by a band of men known as the Sheriff's posse. Dudley stopped there about 5 or 10 minutes, as near as I could tell, then passed on by our place and camped in about the middle of the town. A few minutes afterwards, I saw three soldiers going back with Sheriff Peppin. Well, after seeing this we all became alarmed, that is, all who were in the house, seeing Peppin guarded by the soldiers, and immediately we hung out a black flag in front of our house. Then Mr. McSween wrote a note and sent it to Col. Dudley by a little girl asking him what he intended to do. Well, in a few minutes afterwards, the little girl returned with an answer from Col. Dudley, written by Lt. Goodwin, in which he said Col. Dudley wished to have no correspondence with Mr. McSween. The purpose McSween had in writing to Dudley was to find out what Dudley's intentions were by coming into town, camping there, and guarding Sheriff Peppin with his soldiers—whether he intended to assist Peppin and his posse. Well, before this letter was written Dudley sent us word that if a shot was fired from our house at his soldiers or near them he would turn his cannon loose. That was the expression he used, and he said he would tear the house to the ground, regardless of its inmates. After we received this note from him, Col. Dudley not giving us any satisfaction, I then said to Mr. McSween that I believed I would go down to Dudley's camp and talk with him myself, perhaps I could get some satisfaction from him or could perhaps have some influence with him by talking with him. I then started with Mr. McSween's consent.

Mrs. McSween's own servants were forced into service against her, and ordered to help set fire to the McSween property:

On my way to his camp I saw Bates and Washington, colored servants of mine, standing by a pile of lumber just in the act of picking some up. At the same time, I saw three of these "Murphy men" as I term them, standing by these two colored men with their arms. I then asked those servants of mine what they were doing there. They then said that Peppin and Col. Dudley had sent them to carry lumber to our house to set it on fire. I then asked my servants what these men were doing with the guns, or their arms, who were standing there with them. They said these men were trying to force them to carry the lumber to the house. I then begged them not to do so, if they could possibly get out of it. Then, these armed men, Murphy men, said to me they had got to do this—"we intend to burn your house down, and we will make these men help us. If they dont want to get into trouble they had better not refuse. We were ordered to make them help." I then started again for Col. Dudley's camp, and met Mr. Peppin. I asked him why he was trying to force my servants to help burn down the building. He then said that if I did not want my house burned down, I must make these men who were in the house get out of it—that he was bound to have these men who were inside out today, dead or alive; that he was tired of this, and would give them enough of it today. I then said to him I would go down to Col. Dudley's camp and see if he would not give me protection. When I said that, Peppin appeared to get very angry and said I could go, but I need not think that I would get any protection from Col. Dudley or anyone else when I would harbor such men as were in the house.

Mrs. McSween made an informal call on Colonel Dudley:

I then started again for Col. Dudley's camp. Arriving there, I told Col. Dudley about these men, and Mr. Peppin threatening to burn down the house and asked him if he would not give us some protection and save our house from being burned. He then said he had nothing to do with these troubles—that he had only come there to camp, and did not intend to have anything to do with either party— that he knew nothing about the matter. I then asked him why he camped there in the middle of the town and just on that day when these men were trying to do their duty. The soldiers in camp laughed out loud at that expression, which appeared amusing to Col. Dudley. I then said it looked strange to see his men, or his soldiers I should say, guarding Peppin back and forth through the town and sending soldiers around our house and sending us such word as he had sent s if he had nothing to do with it. He then got very angry, and said that it was none of my business—that he would send his soldiers when he pleased; that I had no business to have such men as Billy Kid, Jim French and others of like character in my house. He then acknowledged, or said, that he had come there to protect women and children. I then asked him why he did not protect myself, my sister, Mrs. Shields, and her children. He then said I had no business or he had no business to be in that house—that he could not give us protection, and that if a shot was fired from our house at any of his soldiers, near them, or over them, near their camp or over it, he would turn his cannon loose and tear the house to the ground regardless of women or children, and if I or my sister did not want to get hurt we had better get out of the house, that they intended to have these men.

Dudley complained that McSween had fired at his soldiers, according to Mrs. McSween's testimony, and made sport of her because she was "Mrs. McSween":

Then I said they were trying to kill Mr. McSween with the pretension of having a warrant. He then said they had a U. S. warrant for him and would have him. I told him I did not see for what reason they could procure a U. S. warrant for him unless it was done falsely, that I did not know him to be guilty of any crime against the U. S. Col. Dudley then said that he was guilty of such a crime—that McSween's men had fired shots at his soldiers the evening before. I told him he must be mistaken, that Mr. McSween had always regarded the military with great esteem and always charged his friends and men not to shoot at soldiers or officers, but give themselves up at any time rather than do anything against the military. Col. Dudley then said: "In a sporting way I am glad to hear this," and then he rather made fun of my remark and said Mr. McSween was a mean man— that he had no principle. He then made sport of me being Mrs. Mc-Sween, as though it was degrading to be called Mrs. McSween. I then told him I was proud to be McSween's wife—that I knew him to be a man of principle, and far better principle than those men who he, Dudley, was assisting; he had not killed any one and I knew it was never his design that any one should be harmed at his house. I told him he was assisting men who I believed were known by everybody to be outlaws; that he could not understand these troubles and assist such men if he intended to do what was right.

Dudley became angry, but Mrs. McSween stood her ground :

Dudley then got very angry with me, used abusive language toward me, threatened my husband. He said that I was not a woman of good character. I told him: "I can see through your whole intention now I expect nothing else than that Mr. McSween will be killed in his own house. Even if they have a warrant for him, they will not arrest him. They want to kill him." I then went back to my house and told Mr. McSween all the conversation that had passed between Col. Dudley and myself—how little encouragement I had received. Not long afterward I saw three soldiers standing near the house on the west side and some of these Murphy men standing close up to the wall of the house. I also met my sister and Mrs. Ely the minister's wife, going to Col. Dudley's camp. I saw one man, Jack Long, pouring coal oil on to the floor of my sister's house. I want to correct that— it was not Jack Long pouring coal oil, it was another man with Jack Long, whose name I do not know, but Jack Long threw something that looked like torpedoes to set the coal oil afire. They then began to shoot into every door and under the house and set fire to a back door near where these soldiers were standing. They then set fire to a window next to that door, to all the windows on that side of the house. I remained with Mr. McSween all that day until 5 o'clock in the afternoon. All the rooms of my own house were burned before I left the house with the exception of one and they continued to shoot into every door and window up to the time I left the house. There were three women and five children in the house when they started to pour coal oil on the house and set it on fire. As soon as the fire started the women and children got out. After that Mr. McSween was killed, also Harvey Morris, Vicente Romero, and Zamora, that is all on our side.[2]

Governor Wallace was on the witness stand before the Court of Inquiry for five consecutive days. He was examined by the recorder and cross-examined by his own personal attorney, and by Dudley's counsel, Judge Waldo. The scope of Wallace's testimony was limited from the very beginning to matters of which he had personal knowledge; and later the Court further restricted his testimony to events directly connected with Dudley's participation in the troubles in Lincoln on July 19, 1878. Because of the limitations imposed, Wallace could not offer

ıuch in the way of evidence not previously introduced into the
:cord. Excused from further attendance, Wallace returned to
anta Fe, leaving Judge Leonard in Fort Stanton to represent
is interests. On May 19, Leonard wrote a letter to Wallace
ıdicating that he had Dudley on the run:

I write to you with pencil because I am laboring for breath and
is less labor than with a pen. We have been dragging along seven
 nd eight hours a day in the Court ever since you left and I tell you
·e are pouring the "hot shot" into Dudley so fiercely that his face
ɔr the last three days has strikingly resembled the wattles of an
ıraged turkey gobbler. . . . He is the most unmitigated old scoun-
rel that ever had an existence.

Leonard wrote to the Governor again on June 6, 1879, warn-
ıg Wallace that the Court was all set to whitewash Dudley:

Dudley commenced on the defense Tuesday afternoon and our
pprehensions as to what the court intend to do was plainly visible.
"hey mean to whitewash and excuse his glaring conduct. They have
:anscended all rules of evidence to allow hearsay coming through
ther channels than direct parties and are allowing liberally to Dud-
:y which they peremptorily refused us. I have no hope of any good
esults. I am thoroughly and completely disgusted with their pro-
eedings. They held yesterday that since the prosecution had closed
·e could not call out from the witnesses on the defense on cross
xamination in matters that had been testified to concerning Dudley's
ulpability. They had Dolan on the stand and cut off my examination
f him by not allowing me to interrogate him even upon what he had
estified to in chief. I had a good notion to show my disgust by aban-
oning the case and let them have it their own way. There is nothing
ɔ be looked or hoped from the tribunal. It is a farce on judicial
ıvestigation and ought to be called and designated "The Mutual
ṭdmiration Inquiry." I hope the evidence may go to the War De-
artment, so that they can see how things are managed. The evidence
gainst Dudley would hang a man in any country where right and
ustice prevailed. . . . I sent you a petition signed by a large number
f citizens asking the removal of Bristol.

From the Territorial capital in Santa Fe on June 11, 1879,

Governor Wallace wrote a long letter to Secretary Schurz i
which he reviewed recent past events, and expressed a belie
that his amnesty proclamation had been a success. The Govei
nor ventured the opinion that the old "Murphy-Dolan" an
"McSween" factions were a thing of the past; urged that troop
then stationed at Fort Stanton, with minor exceptions, be oi
dered to serve elsewhere, and that they be replaced by troop
who would be strangers in the community. Mindful of the diff
culties he had encountered in preferring charges against Colc
nel Dudley, the Governor begged not to be asked to support hi
recommendations with charges against anybody, saying: "The
get me into personal quarrels for which life is too short, whil
in nineteen cases out of twenty 'the game is not worth th
candle.' " The Governor's letter to Schurz follows in part:

Enclosed please find copy of the last report of the Commandai
of Fort Stanton, which justifies me in saying the peace reported i
my last letter still continues in Lincoln County. And I think I may b
pardoned for calling your attention and the President's to the fac
that for quite eight months now there has been in that locality bu
one murder—Mr. Chapman's—with reference to which you kno▾
my procedure.

This leaves me at liberty to repeat for your better understandin
of the present situation there, that the old factions, known respe▪
tively as the "Murphy-Dolan" and the "McSween," are dead as oi
ganizations; to which may be added, that my amnesty proclamatio
has had exactly the effect intended; which was to shear the past o
close, and make present and future all questions claiming my offici:
action. To illustrate, the grand jury empaneled for the recent count
court was, with one or two exceptions, composed of men accounte
of the McSween or anti-Dolan party, making it undeniable tha
nearly all citizens eligible for such position are of that persuasioi
They found nearly 200 indictments, almost altogether accusatory o
Dolan people. Nearly 200 indictments in the county of a voting popu
lation 150 total! You cannot fail to see what would have come o
trials thereunder—how long they would have lasted—the expense t
a county already bankrupt—the heart-burnings, shootings, dispute▪
revivals of old feuds, fights, bush-whacking, and general turmoi
ending doubtless in the re-appearance of the thieves and professiona
murderers now for the most part vanished. As it was, most of th

indicted appeared in open court, and plead the amnesty in bar. *Hereafter the labors of grand-jurors will be confined strictly to offenses subsequent to my proclamation.*

Wallace was resentful of the fact that James J. Dolan was a Dudley favorite at Fort Stanton:

Now, from my saying that the old factions are dead, that peace is prevailing, and that for eight months there has been but one murder in the county, you should not understand me as meaning that the people are relieved from fears of further trouble. On the contrary, there is great disquiet amongst them, and with reason. They know very well that the outlaws who so harried them are waiting in expectation of recall. They go up to Fort Stanton witnesses on one side or the other of the Dudley court of inquiry—called so for want of a better name—and see strange sights; they see Dolan, admittedly the leader of the fiercest refractories, at large and busy in Col. Dudley's behalf, although he is under two indictments for murder, one a murder in the first degree; they know he is not at large by consent or connivance of the Sheriff; they know the commandant of the Fort has my official request in writing to keep Dolan in close confinement; knowing this, and seeing what they see—Dolan free to go and come, a boarder at the trader's store, attended by a gang well understood as ready to do his bidding to any extreme—they are further met by threats of bloody things intended when Col. Dudley is acquitted by his court and restored to command of the post, and are afraid, and so constantly alarmed as to find it impossible to settle down.

You will see from this description that the only disturbing element remaining to be put out of the way is the *confederacy of outlaws and their friends.* That done effectually, I believe a permanently healthful condition can be promised in Lincoln County.

The question is, how best to proceed.

The method which seems to have met with most favor in the Territory is martial law. And I confess at one time I thought it the best and only method. Two months upon the ground, however, and much study and reflection there where the advantages and disadvantages, forecasting probabilities, were directly under eye, have changed my opinion.

Wallace did not think that martial law was the proper remedy:

In the first place, martial law is after all but a temporary expedient. Next, it must in this instance be of limited application; to extend it to the whole Territory would be unjustifiable, while, if applied to the counties of Lincoln and Dona Ana exclusively, it would certainly fail its immediate objects; that is to say, it would fail to bring offenders to quick trial and certain punishment, since they would only have to cross certain near boundary lines to be safe. Yet, further, military commissioners under modern laws of war are governable by fixed procedures, and their findings must be according to rules of evidence, not the will of a captain, leaving it difficult as ever to overcome perjurous combinations. Finally, admitting it would be effective while in force—a point as to which I am by no means assured, since so much would depend upon the officer charged with its execution and the number and zeal of the subordinates and troops helping him—yet it must have end; and then what? It is my judgment, founded upon careful observations, that in this case at least the restoration of civil authority would be the signal for the outlaws, in retreat over in Mexico, Texas, the Staked Plains, and for that matter, the contiguous counties of New Mexico, to return and renew their operations, with the additional incentive of fresh victims to prey upon. To these objections, I have heard but one argument—that under military protection the county would become settled and able to take care of itself. Possibly so, though I doubt it, for the reason that, as a rule, people looking out for new homes find very little attraction in martial law; the strongest ground for a belief is that its prevalence would be almost universally accepted as a warning to stay away. Under martial law contractors would multiply and flourish; men with families would go elsewhere.

The Governor was confident of General Hatch's support:

Not improbably the Honorable Secretary of War and General Sherman, to whom my present recommendation will doubtless be referred, will be satisfied to take the opinion of General Hatch, commanding the District of New Mexico. It gives me pleasure to say General H. has not only aided me promptly and with great intelligence, regardful of his orders; in fact he is the only person with whom I have constantly and freely advised from the beginning. He knows the situation perfectly.

After being in session many weeks, the Court of Inquiry at Fort Stanton adjourned on July 5, 1879. The Court respectfully heard final arguments submitted by the prosecution and defense, noted objections and exceptions. Within a matter of days the Court's decision was announced through Colonel Pennypacker, completely exonerating Colonel Dudley, and finding that a court martial would be unnecessary. The announcement stated:

In view of the evidence adduced the court is of the opinion that Lieut. Colonel N. A. M. Dudley, 9th U. S. Cavalry, has not been guilty of any violation of law or of orders; that the act of proceeding with his command to the town of Lincoln on the 19th day of July, 1878, was prompted by the most humane and worthy motives and of good military judgment under exceptional circumstances. The court is of the opinion that none of the allegations made against Lieut. Colonel Dudley by his Excellency the Governor of New Mexico, or of Ira E. Leonard, have been sustained and that proceedings before a court martial are therefore unnecessary.

In a letter to Secretary Schurz on July 30, 1879, the Governor denounced the Court of Inquiry proceedings, and asked for an opportunity to submit his views at a future time:

The Dudley investigation is at an end. Of course I know nothing of the proceedings personally, except that part of it covering my own testimony. If what I hear to be true, however, it must have been one of the most extraordinary tribunals ever assembled. According to information received from Judge Leonard, who assisted the recorder, the defense was permitted to prosecute me. Witnesses were introduced on that side with whom I never had any conversation materially connected with Lincoln County affairs, against whom, however, I had repeatedly warned Judge Leonard, denouncing them as the associates and aiders and abetters of some of the worst men in that region, who seem to have testified to things which they said I told them, and which were in impeachment of my testimony. When the defense closed, the recorder moved that I be recalled to contradict the fellows; but the court refused the motion. Had I had notice of such proceedings I should have certainly demanded to be heard.

There is consequently no remedy left for me but to request that the record be sent for by the Secretary of War and carefully examined, and that to such matters as may be found affecting my personal honor, I may be furnished an opportunity for denial, explanation, or rebuttal —that is, of course, in case the record leaves a harmful doubt against me in the minds of the President and his advisers.

Notwithstanding the Court's decision, Gen. John Pope, in Fort Leavenworth, on October 15, 1879, after having reviewed the record in the case, expressed his disapproval in the following words:

Having carefully considered the evidence in the foregoing case, the Department Commander disapproves the opinion expressed by the Court of Inquiry.

NOTES AND PROFILES

[1] Henry Lynn Waldo (grandfather of Hon. Waldo H. Rogers, Judge of the United States District Court for the District of New Mexico) was born in Jackson County, Missouri, June 16, 1844, and died in Kansas City, Missouri, on July 9, 1915.

Waldo's father, Lawrence Ludlow Waldo, operated caravans in the Santa Fe trade between Westport, Missouri, Santa Fe and Chihuahua, during the years 1829-47; was captured while enroute from Westport to Santa Fe and executed by Mexican soldiers near Mora, New Mexico, on January 19, 1847.

Henry L. Waldo was educated in the common schools of Missouri, then attended Bethany College in Virginia and the University of Missouri. He left the University in 1862 to accompany a caravan from Westport to Santa Fe. Waldo went to California in 1863, where he taught school and studied law in the office of James T. Farley. He was admitted to the bar of California and in 1867 he was elected district attorney of Amador County.

In 1873 Waldo moved from California to Santa Fe. He practiced law in New Mexico until January 10, 1876, when the United States Senate confirmed President Grant's appointment of Waldo to be Chief Justice of the Supreme Court of the Territory, with the knowledge that he was a Democrat. Judge Waldo served on the Supreme and District courts of the Territory for two years. He resigned on March 3, 1878, and the next day accepted Gov. S. B. Axtell's ppointment as attorney general for the Territory. In 1879 Waldo was counsel or Col. N. A. M. Dudley at the Court of Inquiry in Fort Stanton which heard he evidence in connection with charges preferred against Dudley by Governor Wallace.

Judge Waldo's services were much in demand in civil and criminal cases. He was successful in defending a number of defendants in sensational murder ases. In one murder trial in which a Spanish-American was being tried before Spanish-American jury, the prosecuting witness, a Texan, gave very damaging estimony. Waldo had only a trifling defense. He made a one minute speech to he jury: "Gentlemen of the jury! The only eye witness produced by the Territory in this case is a Texan. I didn't believe one word of his testimony. Did ou?" Waldo sat down. The jury retired, returned in a few moments with a verdict of "not guilty."

With the coming of the Santa Fe railroad to New Mexico, Judge Waldo became its solicitor in the Territory, and later general solicitor with offices in Kansas City.

2 The Mrs. Ealy referred to in Mrs. McSween's testimony was the wife of Rev. T. F. Ealy, a medical missionary. The Ealys and two small children, together with a Miss Susan Gates, a school teacher, were new arrivals in Lincoln through invitation of Alex. McSween. For the Ealy story see the New Mexico Sentinel October 5 and 12, 1937, also "Recollections of Old Lincoln," by Mrs. T. F. Ealy in *New Mexico Magazine,* March, 1954, and "Medical Missionary," by Ruth R. Ealy in *New Mexico Magazine* for March and April, 1954.

CHAPTER TWELVE

FROM GUNS TO DIPLOMACY

T HE MURDER of John Henry Tunstall, accomplished by desperadoes under pretended authority of law at Turkey Springs, Lincoln County, New Mexico, on February 18, 1878, caused repercussions and reverberations at home and abroad. It was generally known in and about Lincoln that Tunstall was not an American citizen, but a British subject. Most of his acquaintances casually referred to him as "the Englishman." Needless to say, some people in Lincoln County looked askance at Tunstall. A "foreigner" in southeastern New Mexico was rare. Apparently none of the men implicated in the conspiracy had stopped to consider the probability that murdering him might result in a demand in high places not only for an explanation, but for indemnity from the American government. Such demands were not long in arriving.

Soon after Tunstall's death, his father John Partridge Tunstall, a prominent merchant in London, a man of prestige and influence, asked Lord Salisbury to assist him in obtaining redress. As a result on April 8, 1878, His Excellency, Sir Edward Thornton, G.C.B., Envoy Extraordinary and Plenipotentiary in Washington, made a formal demand for the British government upon Secretary of State F. W. Seward for a complete investigation into Tunstall's death and a prompt and satisfactory report on the facts and circumstances surrounding it. Secretary Seward referred the request to the Attorney General of the United States, who in turn asked the United States district attorney in New Mexico for a detailed explanation. New Mexico officials resorted to dilatory tactics and evaded complying with the request. Annoyed by the delay, official Washington authorized an independent investigation. Frank Warren Angel, of 62 Liberty Street, New York City, was assigned to the task, as the representative of the State, War and Interior departments. When months passed, and he had heard no word from the State Department, Sir Edward Thornton wrote a letter on November 7, 1878, to the then Secretary, William M. Evarts:

With reference to previous correspondence, and in compliance with an instruction I have received from the Marquis of Salisbury, I have the honor to ask you to let me know for the information of Her Majesty's government, what has been the result of steps taken by the government of the United States with a view to the investigation of the circumstances connected with the murder of John H. Tunstall.

Month after month, and year after year, the State Department declined to assume a forthright position on the Tunstall case, refusing to either admit or deny liability. John Partridge Tunstall proved indefatigable in his efforts to obtain a complete report, contending meanwhile, through diplomatic channels, that the American government should pay him and his family not less than $150,000 as compensation for his son's life and property.

The elder Tunstall carried on a voluminous correspondence with Lord Salisbury, and other British officials in London, from which it appeared that he had invested in his son's enterprises in Lincoln pounds sterling equivalent to $25,000 in American money. John Partridge Tunstall not only wanted a money payment from the government of the United States, but he also wanted the government to see to it that his son's murderers were brought to the bar of justice. Sir Edward advised the State Department that, to the best of his knowledge and belief, three men were present at the time Tunstall was killed, William Morton, Jesse Evans and Tom Hill; that of the three, Morton and Hill had already been killed, leaving only Evans to account for. Sir Edward repeatedly urged the American government to use every effort to pursue and arrest Evans and prosecute him vigorously.

The Tunstall papers, filed in several large folders, officially stamped and sealed, tied together with the traditional red tape, were passed from hand to hand in Washington for several years after Tunstall's death. Finally, on June 1, 1885, after much prodding by British officials, the State Department took a stand

and notified the British government that it had no alternative but to decline to acknowledge any responsibility or liability growing out of Tunstall's death. In a lengthy letter addressed to the Hon. L. S. West (later Lord Sackville), couched in diplomatic language, Secretary of State T. F. Bayard said that the American government owed no duty to the Tunstall heirs because Tunstall had been domiciled in the United States and at the time of his death was actively engaged in business in New Mexico.

Bayard attempted to distinguish the Tunstall case from one in which a British subject might have been killed while on an ordinary visit to the country. Mr. Bayard suggested another point which he considered of considerable importance: Tunstall had been killed in a Territory of the United States, over which the federal government had no jurisdiction. Bayard's letter covered many pages, and cited many precedents in attempting to justify its conclusion. The final paragraph of Bayard's letter summarized the situation:

After a full review of all the facts and circumstances of the case I am constrained to inform you that this Government cannot admit any liability, as alluding to it in the premises, either directly toward the representatives of the murdered man, or internationally toward Her Majesty's government demanding in their behalf.

In an effort to soften the blow, Secretary Bayard wrote a postscript, saying that he did not wish the British to gain the impression that the American government was indifferent:

Sympathizing as I do most fully with the father of the deceased in his bereavement, I would be happy to be able to see a way in which this government might, in consideration of his affliction and loss, make him some suitable compensation in the nature of a pecuniary gratuity, but upon this point also I regret to be obliged to inform you that there is no fund under the control of the Executive Government from which such a gratuity could in accordance with law and proper authority be paid.[1]

Although it declined to assume responsibility for Tunstall's death or to indemnify the deceased's next of kin, the federal government conducted an exhaustive and painstaking investigation into the tragedy. Within a matter of weeks after the killing, Special Investigator Frank Warren Angel was on the ground in Lincoln County, interviewing witnesses, and obtaining affidavits from those who knew, or professed to know, the facts. The Las Vegas *Gazette* of May 18, 1878, noting Angel's arrival in Fort Stanton, somewhat apprehensively offered a bit of sage advice:

If Angel does not get his wings shot off, or take his departure prematurely for the New Jerusalem, all of which he is liable to do if he fools around Lincoln County, we hope he will investigate fully and freely all those officers whose conduct seems to require it. Good officers should have lily white hands and not fear an overhauling of their administrations. United States officials and all others in high places should be investigated about once a year, or oftener, if practicable. It has a tendency to keep men honest, if they are not inherently so.

Proceeding with his investigation, Mr. Angel soon discovered that members of the McSween-Tunstall faction were more inclined to tell what they knew, and to sign affidavits, than those who had been identified with the anti-McSween, anti-Tunstall forces. An interesting and important affidavit was signed by Juan B. Patron, leading Spanish-American citizen in Lincoln County, a strong supporter of the McSween-Tunstall faction. In his affidavit Patron claimed that he had been subjected to persecution at Murphy's hands. Patron's sworn statement reflected his impression that Murphy was a tyrannical, despotic character. He described one occasion on which Murphy had demonstrated his "rule or ruin" policy, by breaking up a political convention. Patron recalled that Murphy had shouted: "You might as well try to stop the waves of the ocean with a fork as to try and oppose me." Patron's affidavit, dated July 1, 1878, giving his version of the trouble in the county, was in part as follows:

Deponent says he had taken out a claim on some land in the Ruidoso, supposing that no one had a claim to it. Dr. Tideman afterwards claimed that it was his land and deponent was abused, arrested and all his acts and movements watched and misinterpreted. The result of all this was that William Brady, who was a tool of L. G. Murphy and a U.S. Commissioner at the instigation of the doctor, and Murphy, began a persecution of deponent and endeavored to influence the people against deponent. The result was that the people were divided into two parties, the Mexican element standing by me, and the Americans, the soldiers and Murphy against me. Before this, L. G. Murphy controlled everything that there was any money in, and dictated who should run for office and who should not, at one time going into a convention of the people who were to select persons who were to run for office which the people had to give, knowing that said convention was opposed to him, overthrew the table, destroyed the stationery and told them: "You might as well try to stop the waves of the ocean with a fork as to try and oppose me." As a result of this determination to put down or out of the way those who opposed Murphy's will, the Harrold War began which was called the Texans against the Mexicans. Murphy & Co. aided and abetted the Harrold party and the result was that the Harrold party left the country leaving, however, all their property in the hands of Murphy, such as cattle, lands, etc. There are people who say that this was one of the ends Murphy was working for. From this on there has been, although not concentrated, opposition, but there has been enough of individuality among some of the people that Murphy, Dolan and Riley have been opposed in their schemes and plots. That in order to dispose and "get out of the way" obnoxious parties, a vigilante committee was attempted to be organized of which Murphy was to be the prime mover, the real object of which was to kill this deponent and others. The farmers had been complaining greatly as to the one sided settlements had with the firm of Murphy & Co., that they had been induced to buy merchandise of them under an agreement that they should be paid a fixed price for their produce, but when a settlement was had the goods were charged at extortionate prices and the produce turned in at prices to suit them. Matters continued to go on this way until Mr. John H. Tunstall came to this county, opened a store and by his straightforward course made friends of the people, who preferred to trade with him rather than with Murphy, Dolan and Riley. This caused the enmity of them against Tunstall and this enmity resulted in the death of Tunstall and the present bloodshed in this county. Sometime ago Murphy told me that he would have to get rid of McSween and Tunstall. I know the reputation of Jessie

Evans, Frank Baker, Tom Hill and George Davis. It is that of notorious horse thieves and murderers. I believe that Murphy, Dolan and Riley and W. Brady, our late sheriff, were friendly with them and assisted them. . . .

On June 26, 1878, Jacob B. Matthews, employee and one-time partner in the Murphy, Dolan and Riley combine, the man who, as deputy sheriff levied an attachment against John H. Tunstall's cattle upon instructions from Sheriff Brady, signed an affidavit in Lincoln. In it he gave his version of the circumstances surrounding the attachment and the events leading up to the killing of Tunstall. Matthews stated in the affidavit that he was a deputy under Brady; that he had assisted Brady in levying the McSween attachment against the contents of the Tunstall store in Lincoln; that he had then gone with a posse to Tunstall's ranch on the Feliz River; that on his first trip to the ranch he had failed to levy the attachment on Tunstall's property, and had sent to the Pecos River for reinforcements. The Matthews affidavit in part:

The names of the posse which went to attach the horses the first time were John Hurley, Manuel Sagalia, George W. Hindman, Pantaleon Gallegos, J. W. Olinger, R. W. Beckwith, Ramon Montoya, W. S. Morton, Thos. Green, Thos. Cockrane, Charles Kruling, George Kitt, Charles Marshall and Sam Perry. On my first trip to Tunstall's ranch I saw 15 horses there. For the second trip I raised a part of the posse in Lincoln, then went to Ham Mill's ranch on the Ruidoso on the 14th of Feb., arriving there at night. The next morning went to Turkey Springs and stayed there. The next day went to Paul's Ranch and reached there Friday afternoon. At this place Evans and Hill came to our camp on Saturday. They were not sent for by me or requested to come there. They came of their own free will. On Sunday, Baker and Rivers came to the camp. None of these men were part of the posse but on the contrary were ordered away by me. We were met here by the party from the Pecos. I had sent Telesfor Lopez to the Pecos to raise a posse. No one went with him to my knowledge. I did not send anyone with him. I or Sheriff Brady did not send anyone with him. On Monday we started for the Felix, Tunstall's ranch. We had been informed by "Dutch Martin," that if it was not for Widemann there would be no trouble as Brewer would make no resistance. We went to the ranch carefully, one party in front of the house and the other from the rear, myself and Roberts being the party in front. We found there was no one there except Gauss and I think "Dutch Martin." The party had left with the horses. I then deputized Morton and selected a party to go with him after the horses and they left, I having instructed them to overtake the horses and bring them back and in case there was any resistance to arrest the men and bring them back too. If he did not overtake them before they reached the Plaza (Lincoln), if he found they were going to Lincoln then to follow them in and have Sheriff Brady attach the horses. Morton returned at about 2 A. M. the next day and reported to me that he caught up with the horses about 30 miles away and that Tunstall resisted and fired at him and that he returned the fire and Tunstall was killed. That the resistance was made by Tunstall while he was reading the attachment to him, and that he notified Tunstall that if he would throw up his hands he would not be hurt, instead of which Tunstall fired at him, that he fired back killing Tunstall. The names of the men in the posse the second time we went to the ranch to attach were myself, John Hurley, Manuel Sagolia, Geo. W. Hindman, Andrew Roberts, Pantaleon Gallegos, James J. Dolan, A. H. Mills, J. W. Olinger, Thomas Moore, R. W. Beckwith, Ramon Montoya, Felipe Mes, E. H. Wakefield, Pablo Pino y Pino, Wm. S. Morton, Thomas Green, Charles Wolz, Thomas Cockrane, Charles Kruling ("Dutch Charley"), George Kitt, Charles Marshall, Samuel Perry.

Godfrey Gauss, an itinerant camp cook and ranch helper, friend and confidante of William H. Bonney, participated in some of the most exciting days of the Lincoln County War. He was employed on the Tunstall ranch as cook and caretaker at the time a sheriff's posse was seeking a pretext to kill Tunstall while using a court paper as a shield. He was also an eyewitness to the events that took place on April 28, 1881, immediately following the killing, by William Bonney, of Bell and Olinger, his guards. On July 1, 1878, Gauss made an affidavit for Special Investigator Angel, in which he recited many of the significant details of the conspiracy to kill Tunstall. On August 22, 1878, seven weeks after he made the affidavit, Gauss wrote to John Partridge Tunstall, in London, and told him: "I am an old man 54 years old, sickly and not able to support myself by hard labor. Without all means as I am, I cant even leave this God forsaken country, and have to look starvation in the face." The object of the Gauss letter was to get Tunstall, Sr., to send him $175, claimed to be due as wages from John H. Tunstall.

In his affidavit of July 1, 1878, Gauss declared under oath the truth of the following:

Besides Widemann and Dick Brewer, I remember Martin Mertz was with me at the ranch and left when the posse did. We told the posse on the first trip that they might attach any cattle here that belonged to McSween, but that there was none here. Matthews, the head of the posse, then replied that I shall have to go to Lincoln for instructions if that was the case. I then gave them something to eat. Matthews told us that when he returned he would bring back only one man. They then left. While they were there Jessie Evans wanted to know if Widemann was agoing to arrest him and Baker. Widemann said "that is my business." Widemann told Dick Brewer in my hearing that he had warrants against them and wanted to arrest them, but Dick said not to do it for if he did we would all surely be killed. Widemann did not arrest them. Alex Rudder was sent by Brewer to the Penasco to get a load of corn and when he returned he said he had been taken prisoner by the Sheriff's posse on the Penasco, and that they told him they were waiting for reinforcements from the Pecos and that as soon as they arrived they were coming to "round us up." Afterwards they let him go and he told us that if we remained we would be killed. On the 17th of February 1878, Mr. Tunstall came to the ranch. He told Widemann that there must be no bloodshed. We must not remain. Let them attach what cattle they please. We will leave Gauss here. He is an old man and they wont touch him. On the next morning after breakfast, Mr. Tunstall, Widemann, Brewer, Henry Brown, Waite, Middleton and Bonney (there was no one left but me) started with all the horses for Lincoln. On the night of the 17th Mr. Tunstall sent McCloskey over to the Penasco to get Martin Mertz to come over to the ranch to help turn over the cattle to the sheriff's posse. The sheriff had been informed by Martin that the levy was made against his (Tunstalls) consent, but there would be no resistance. On the 18th of February, Billy Matthews came up to the ranch and asked where was Brewer and the rest of the party. I told him they had all left this morning. There was a large party with him (Matthews) I should judge at least 30.

I gave them something to eat, or rather they helped themselves to what they wanted. Matthews then said to me—"Why not some one remain to turn over the property?" I said that Mertz would be here to do that. They commenced to shoeing their horses out of Tunstall's property. Three or four horses were shod. Matthews said, "If only Jim (meaning Dolan) was here—I have a notion to send after them and bring them back." I do not know whether they sent for Dolan or whether he came of his own accord. He came about this time and he picked out the men to follow after Tunstall's party to bring them back if they caught them before they reached the Plaza. From their actions I thought that some of the party of Tunstall would be killed. I heard—I think it was Morton cry out "Hurry up boys, my knife is sharp, and I feel like scalping some one." They were all excited and seemed as though they were going to kill some one. The party that remained went into camp about 300 yards from the house. I cannot tell who was there. I saw Matthews and Mills. I did not see Dolan. Dolan did not sleep in the house that night. I am sure of it. There was two or three who slept in the house. I only know one of them, Charley Woolf, who slept in the house. P. Gallegos started to make a list of the posse and started to put down the parties who were with them and had started to write down Davis' name when Matthews stopped him and said, "Dont put them boys down at all," meaning Baker, Evans, Hill and Davis. Some of the posse rounded up the cattle and the rest of the party above mentioned started after Tunstall and his party. I heard no one object to Baker, Evans, Hill and Davis going with the party. I am positive that Matthews and Dolan picked out the men. They would say, "You go, you go," and so on, point out each person, and these persons commenced to examine their arms and horses. I saw Baker, Evans, Hill and Davis at this time getting ready to go with the rest of the party. I heard no one make any objections to their going. I was in the shanty. They might have objected to their going. I did not hear them. I was in and out of the house. The door was open all the time and the party were coming in and out of the house, shouting a great deal. During the night the party who went after Tunstall returned and the next morning I heard that Tunstall had been killed. Baker told me. He gave me no particulars.

Godfrey Gauss had no love for Murphy:

I know L. G. Murphy. He has treated me very badly. I hired his brewery for a year. I wrote him that I wanted it in writing. He wrote me that as long as I held to my bargain he would to his. I thereupon commenced the business of brewing and had been there about two months and at that time I had 400 gallons of beer ready, when Murphy and Dolan and Matthews came with arms and told me I must leave claiming that he had sold the brewery. I was forced to leave and sell him my beer at forty cents a gallon. I could not take the beer away because I had nothing to put it in and that he well knew. I could not take it away, and he told me to come down and settle. My account was made out and then they owed me $160 and they not having the money the next day thereafter they made me another statement, in which they owed me only about $28. I do not believe they had sold the brewery and I believe it still belongs to them.

Samuel R. Perry, a member of the Matthews posse, made an affidavit in Las Cruces on June 17, 1878, narrowing the killers of Tunstall to three men, William S. Morton, Jesse Evans and Tom Hill.

Perry's affidavit contained damaging testimony to the effect that "either Hill or Morton or Davis had fired off Tunstall's pistol." Morton's story, as told to Perry, had been that Tunstall had fired twice at him, Morton. Establishment as a fact, that two shots had been fired from Tunstall's pistol, presumably before his death, was essential for the purpose of attempting to demonstrate and prove that he had been the aggressor, and had been killed under circumstances which would justify his death. The affidavit:

We arrived at the Felix on the morning of the 18th about 8 a.m. We found there Martin Mertz who was in charge of the cattle (he was either there or came before we left I am not positive) and a cook by the name of Gauss. We inquired for the horses and they told us they had gone but did not know where they had gone. They had left about daylight and thought they had gone to Lincoln but did not know. Matthews then gave the attachment papers to Morton and told him to take some men and attach the horses. Morton selected Robert W. Beckwith, Wallace Olinger, Sam Perry, Charley Kruling, Thomas Cochrane, Thomas Green, P. Gallegos, John Hurley, Charles

Marshall, Manuel Sagolia, George Kit, Ramon Montoya and Geo. Hindman, Frank Baker, Jessie Evans, Thomas Hill. The three latter were not called upon. They volunteered saying they had a horse among the horses Tunstall had taken away and that they wished to go after it. I do not remember whether there was any objection made by anyone to their accompanying us except that Dolan said to either Matthews or Morton that they (Baker, Evans and Hill) had better not go. Either Baker, Evans or Hill replied that a person had a right to go for their property or something to that effect. I am positive that Dolan did not go with us, and we with Morton started after the horses. Myself, Hindman and Marshall, having tired horses, brought up the rear. We had gone about thirty miles when Manuel Sagolia appeared in front of us beckoning us to come on. We trotted on and when we were about one half a mile from our party who were ahead and had overtaken Tunstall's property and party Hindman said "I heard a shot." I replied: "I guess not, it was a horse stumbled." "I hear another," he said. When we reached the top of the hill we saw the horses rounded up and some of our party around them. Morton came up and said Tunstall was killed. I said it could not be for I did not believe Tunstall was there. He said he had followed after Tunstall, whereupon Tunstall turned and came riding up to him. He (Morton) commenced to read the warrant, whereupon Tunstall drew his pistol and fired two shots at him. Before Tunstall had fired Jesse Evans called to him to throw up his hands and he would not be hurt. Tunstall disregarded this and fired as above set forth whereupon he (Morton), Jesse Evans and Hill fired at him and the result of the firing was that Tunstall and his horse were killed. After the above statement had been made to me Evans and most of our party being present I went to the place where Tunstall was laying. I found him lying on his face, his horse was close beside him, their heads being in the same direction. The horse was still alive but nearly dead. Tom Hill thereupon to put the horse out of misery shot him with his (Hill's) carbine. I took his blankets and myself, Tom Green, Wallace Olinger, Charles Kruling and George Hindman laid him out by the side of his horse. We did not see his hat nor did anyone put it under the horse's head. Tom Hill had Tunstall's revolver which he had found eight or ten feet from where the horse fell. Tom Hill handed it to Montoya and Montoya handed it to me and I placed it by the side of Tunstall. I did not examine the pistol. Tunstall's face was bruised by his fall, nor was it or his head mutilated by any of our party. We thereupon returned to the Felix with the horses. We found Dolan at the camp about 500 yards from Tunstall's house. I am sure and positive that Dolan was not with our party that went after Tunstall's property, after our return to the Felix. I either heard Baker, Evans or Hill say the death of Tunstall was a small loss, that he ought to have been killed, or something to that effect. I cannot say which one said this of the three, one of the three said that Tunstall had tried to have them killed while they were in jail in Lincoln. Except as above set forth I heard no threats against Tunstall either directly or indirectly. I believe that under the circumstances above set forth that Tunstall met his death while resisting a legal process. Frank Baker was with Rivers when he (Rivers) brought the papers deputizing Morton and I with the other persons on the Pecos were summoned. Dolan told Morton we were starting after Tunstall's property to be very careful and to do nothing but what was according to law. While I was laying out Tunstall I heard two or three shots. I will not be positive. I enquired what they were shooting about and they said they were shooting at *that* tree. There was some talk at this time that either Hill or Morton or Evans had fired off Tunstall's pistol. I thought it a little strange that they were shooting at a mark. I did not think it was an appropriate time to be shooting at a mark. I do not know who were shooting at the mark. I was busy laying Tunstall out.

John Wallace Olinger, whose brother, Robert Olinger, was shot and killed by William H. Bonney in Lincoln on April 28, 1881, made an affidavit in Las Cruces on June 17, 1878, declaring that he had read the affidavit of Samuel R. Perry, and corroborated its contents. Olinger suspected that Tom Hill had fired two shots from Tunstall's revolver, after Tunstall had been killed. The Olinger affidavit:

That he was one of the posse that went from the Pecos, and one of the men that followed after Tunstall's horses. I first saw Tunstall about ¾ of a mile from where he was killed or at least his party. I never saw Tunstall to know who he was until after I saw him dead, assisted in laying him out. I examined his pistol and found two loads out of it. It was reported that he (Tunstall) had shot it off at Morton. The empty shells were in the chambers of the revolver and were left there by deponent and his party. The revolver was placed by the side of Tunstall. I heard I think two shots fired about this time. I heard the shots before I examined the revolver. I think that Hill fired those two shots. I do not know positively whether he did or not or whether they were fired out of a pistol or a carbine. There might have been three shots. I thought at first that perhaps the Tunstall party was firing at us, then I thought the shots were fired to collect our party. Baker, Evans and Hill were informed at the Felix that they were not part of the posse and that we did not want outlaws with the party, and that Widemann had warrants for their arrest. I did not see Tunstall's hat. I did not nor did any of our party put his hat under his horse's head to my knowledge. I would have been likely to have heard of it if they had. We thought it was a very serious matter. Tunstall's head was not mutilated. It was badly broken by the fall.

Pantaleon Gallegos, an employee of Dolan, Riley & Co. who accompanied the Matthews posse on its second trip to Tunstall's ranch, made an affidavit in Santa Fe on July 1, 1878, in which he gave his recollection of the events preceding the Tunstall killing. Gallegos was not an eyewitness to the killing, but heard William Morton tell his story within a few moments after Tunstall had been killed. The Gallegos affidavit:

I went to Tunstall's ranch with the posse and there made a levy on some cattle, but found no horses. Deputy Matthews and Mr. Dolan, A. H. Mills, Thomas Moore, Andrew Roberts, E. H. Wakefield, Pablo Pino y Pino, Juan Andres Silva, Felipe Mes and Pablo Pino y Pino's son, I do not recall any others now, were left with the cattle, and Wm. S. Morton, your deponent, George Hindman, John Hurley, Thomas Cochran, R. W. Beckwith, George W. Kitt, Thomas Green, Ramon Montoya, Juan Segolia, Wallace Olinger, Charles Kruling ("Dutch Charley") and Charles Marshall—Frank Baker and Jessie Evans following behind—started off for Tunstall who had gone off with the horses, as we were informed by Martin and Gauss, who were in charge of the cattle at the time of the levy. We rode about thirty miles before we came up to Tunstall and his party with the horses. Morton was ahead and the rest of us were riding behind as near as possible, there was only a trail through the mountains and it would not permit of our riding close together. Billy Morton and I first saw a man ahead riding a grey horse, who upon seeing us, called out to the men driving the horses ahead of him. It was too far to distinguish what he said. Thereupon Tunstall and his men left, the horses ran and scattered. Morton and John Hurley followed after them. Myself, Robert Beckwith, Kitt and Thomas Green, went after the horses. I do not now remember sufficiently to name any other persons that were with either me or Morton. The next thing that occurred was my hearing shots fired in quick succession. I did not see the shooting because it took place in the bushes. It was all over in a moment. There might have been others with me or Morton. There was so much excitement at the time I cannot tell exactly who was with me or who was with Morton.

Afterwards Morton returned and said that a man had been shot and killed. I asked who, and he said Tunstall. I asked how it occurred. He said "I rode after Tunstall calling to him to halt and waiving at him the attachment. Suddenly Tunstall wheeled his horse around and came towards me (Morton) on a jog trot with his hand on his revolver. I (Morton) asked him to halt again, as I (Morton) desired to serve a writ and to throw up his hands and he would not be hurt. In place of which he, Tunstall, pulled out his six shooter and fired at me (Morton.) Whereupon I (Morton) and those with me returned the fire. The rest of Tunstall's party were not near him at the time he was shot. Tunstall was shot about one hundred yards off the trail just upon the top of the hill." Morton was going northwest at the time of the shooting. That about the time Tunstall fell, his (Tunstall's) horse fell too. All this was told me by Morton. Hurley at the same time, told me and the rest of our party the same story and the above was told deponent immediately after the shooting—not over five or ten minutes thereafter.

Deponent further says that he desires to explain how Baker and Evans appear to have been part of the posse. At the Rio Penasco we met Baker and Evans for the first time and afterwards at Rio Felix a cow camp of Tunstall's, I heard Billy Morton tell them he did not want them along and that they could not go with the posse. Then Jessie said: "We are not going with you. We are here on our own business. We are after our horses which had been loaned to 'Kid Antrim' (Wm. H. Antrim), they tell us they have been taken away by Tunstall with the other horses." They continued to follow behind us although told not to, and were not a part of the posse.

Deponent further says that at Tunstall's ranch I saw sandbags before the doors of the house and port holes cut between the bags.

The sand bags looked new and the port holes looked as though they had been recently cut.

Robert A. Widenmann, at one time a clerk in Tunstall's store in Lincoln, and on occasion a United States deputy marshal, made a statement on June 6, 1878, verified before Juan B. Patron, Deputy Probate Clerk of Lincoln County, in which he covered, from his viewpoint, the background of events leading up to the killing of Tunstall. In his statement Widenmann unwittingly disclosed that he was not a fighting man in any sense of the word, and that he was not favored by inheritance with the nerve and fearlessness essential to a frontier law officer. As a United States deputy marshal he had held in his hands on one occasion federal warrants for the arrest of several desperadoes, among them Jesse Evans and Frank Baker. Both Evans and Baker, in separate, isolated encounters described in Widenmann's affidavit, bluffed him out at Tunstall's ranch. Widenmann's narrative, disclosing that he was an observant witness, but at the same time pretty much of a "scared kid," is as follows:

Some time during September, 1877, horses and mules of J. H. Tunstall and others, then at the ranch of R. M. Brewer, were stolen by Jessie Evans, Tom Hill, and I think Frank Baker. R. M. Brewer, Charles Bowdre, and J. G. Scurlock started after the thieves and at Shed's ranch (also called San Augustine) the party parted, Brewer going to Mesilla while Bowdre and Scurlock remained at Shed's ranch. Brewer obtained warrants for the arrest of the thieves, sworn out, I think, before Justice Rosencrance. In the meantime the thieves arrived with the horses at Shed's ranch. Bowdre and Scurlock asked them to return the horses and mules, especially those of Brewer, he being a poor man, to which they answered they would do no such thing, that they had been to too much trouble to get the horses to return them again and the thieves went to Las Cruces where they arrived with the horses while Brewer was still there. Brewer could not induce the Sheriff to arrest them because he had not the force to do so. All the above was told me by Brewer when I met him near Tularosa on his way back. He was in company with Bowdre and Scurlock. I was with F. T. Waite who heard the above facts stated to me by Brewer. Waite returned with Brewer and his party while I went on to Mesilla in company with Lieut. Pogue.

Subsequently Baker, Evans, Hill and Davis were arrested by Sheriff Brady and posse at Seven Rivers at Beckwith's and brought to Lincoln and lodged in jail from which they afterwards escaped. Mr. Tunstall took an active part in having them pursued and arrested. He furnished funds, horses, saddles and arms and the thieves knew that he did it. That subsequently deponent was appointed a Deputy U. S. Marshal and warrants were placed in his hands for the arrest of Evans, Hill, Davis and Nicholas Provencia for stealing government mules. In trying to execute these warrants I tracked them to the ranch of L. G. Murphy at the Caresosa Spring. I was informed by Mr. Murphy personally that they were not at his ranch; that they had been there but once when they sold a horse to Matthews. Deponent further says that the horse referred to above was sold to Matthews prior to their arrest last above mentioned and this conversation with said Murphy was referred to above. Afterwards and on or about Feb. 13, 1878, Evans admitted to deponent that at the time he was at Murphy's ranch he was in the hills near the ranch sleeping there nights and being at the ranch during the day time and that he saw me when I left the ranch. That on or about the 9th day of February, 1878, Sheriff Brady entered the business house of J. H. Tunstall, of which I was then in charge, and read to me a writ of attachment attaching the property of A. A. McSween. I told him that the property belonged to J. H. Tunstall, that I protested against any attachment and would hold him and his bondsmen responsible for any loss or damage. Sheriff Brady said that he knew better, that the property belonged to A. A. McSween and he would attach it as such. He proceeded to take an inventory without placing a value on any article he attached. He demanded the keys of different doors leading from the store and upon my refusal to deliver the same, had me arrested and searched without warrant or legal process and finally took the keys from me. He was at the time accompanied by G. W. Peppin, Jack Long, James Longwell and T. G. Christie.

On the 10th of February, 1878, Mr. Tunstall and McSween arrived in Lincoln from Mesilla. On the 11th of February, Mr. Tunstall and I came to the store which was then in possession of the sheriff and again protested against the attachment. We succeeded in getting all the horses released (2 mules and 6 horses) and at once started a man named G. Gauss with three horses for the ranch, I think, and on the afternoon of the same day started Wm. McCloskey and John Middleton for the ranch on two other horses, and subsequently I followed in company with F. T. Waite, and Wm. Bonnie and arrived at the ranch the morning of the 12th. R. M. Brewer was there in charge of the ranch as well as the above named persons who had been sent on and who were employed at the ranch then and prior to this.

On the morning of the 13 of February J. B. Matthews (claiming to be a Deputy Sheriff) rode up to the ranch of Tunstall's on the Rio Feliz in company with George Hindman, John Hurley, an Indian, Roberts, Evans, Baker and Hill. Seeing the last three in the party and knowing they had themselves threatened to kill me on sight I stepped out and asked the party to stop where they were (which was about fifty yards from the house) and asked Matthews to come forward and state his business. Matthews said he was a deputy sheriff and had come to attach the cattle of A. A. McSween to which I answered that McSween had no cattle there but if there were any he might take them. I offered no resistance nor did the people with me, nor did we make any threats. R. M. Brewer told Matthews in my presence and the rest of the party that he could round up the cattle and if he (Matthews) claimed that Brewer's cattle (there being some of Brewer's cattle on the range) belonged to McSween he could leave a man there to take care of them until the courts could settle the question. I then told Brewer I was going to arrest Evans, Baker and Hill under my U. S. warrants whereupon Brewer and the rest of the party that were at the ranch with me said it could not be done, that they were all ranch men, and living at their places and if they assisted in arresting Evans, Baker and Hill—Dolan, Riley and Murphy would have them killed as soon as they got back to their ranches, and positively refused to aid me in the arrest. Brewer then asked the party up to get something to eat and Evans advanced toward me swinging his carbine holding it at full cock towards me, and asked me if I was looking for him; I told him that he would find out when I was looking for him. He asked if I had any warrant for him to which I answered that was my business. He then said if you ever come after me you are the first man I am going to shoot at to which I said that it was all right that I could also play a hand at that game too. He also told me in the presence of Brewer that Murphy, Dolan and Riley were the only ones in this section who paid them money. Matthews told me that Evans had come over to see me to find out if I had any warrant for him. He said this in the presence of all. While Matthews was saying this, I heard Baker say to Roberts, "What the hell's the use of talking, pitch in, and fight and kill the son of a b————." I asked Evans what he came over here for and he said that Matthews wanted him to come along and that besides that he wished to see me. This was said to me alone. During part of the conversation which the others heard Baker walked up in front of me with a pistol in his hand as though handing it to me, swung it on his finger, cocking it at the same time, pointing the muzzle towards me. After most of the party had eaten Matthews said he would go back to town to get further instructions as to holding Brewer's cattle and would come back with one man. On the way to town I rode with them several miles (I mean by them Matthews, Hurley and the Indian) the rest of Matthew's party said they were going to the Penasco to the ranch of Paul's, and while riding with Matthews he asked me if they attached Tunstall's cattle too whether we would object. I told him not if they left them, but that if they intended to drive the cattle to the Indian Agency as they had said they would do in order to kill them for beef that we would do all that was in our power to defeat them since if the cattle were driven there and killed we could not collect a cent from Sheriff Brady's bondsmen who were known to be insolvent. On my journey to the town I had Waite and Bonney with me part of the time. Matthews and his party last above mentioned rode ahead. Deponent further says that Brewer and Middleton were employed at the ranch continually. McCloskey had been employed there and was then employed as he had been for several weeks previous at rounding up and branding cattle and had made arrangements to work a ranch. Wait had been in the employ of Tunstall. He went out with me as company and from Tunstall's ranch he and Bonney were going to the upper Penasco to work a ranch. We had about 400 or 500 head of cattle at Tunstall's ranch.

I arrived at the town (Lincoln) on the night of the 13th and left on the morning of the 14th to be there when Matthews rounded up the cattle and to count them. Wait & Bonney and others returned with me. In meantime Mr. Tunstall had heard that Matthews with a large party were going to the ranch. The Mexicans were to round up the cattle while the rest of the party were to kill all of us. He at once started for the ranch alone and arrived there the night of the 17th. We decided upon his informing us all of this than risk the lives of the men, we would leave everything as it was, send Mc-

Closkey over to the Penasco to inform Matthews and his posse that they could take the cattle and that we would seek our remedy by the law. We did this because we did not wish trouble and to show them that no resistance would be made. We sent McCloskey because he was a friend of a great number of the party that was reported to be with Matthews. McCloskey left the ranch at three oclock in the morning and he had orders to tell Mr. Martin on the Penasco to come over and stay at Tunstall's to count the cattle with the Deputy Sheriff and to stay at the ranch with party the Deputy Sheriff left at it until the matter could be arranged through the courts. Tunstall, Brewer, Middleton, Bonney, Waite and myself started for the Plaza about 8 o'clock of the 18th, Waite driving the wagon, the rest of us driving about eight horses besides those we were riding. The horses were the property of Mr. Tunstall, R. M. Brewer and myself. None of the horses then or ever belonged to A. A. McSween and all but three had been released by the Sheriff and of these three horses one belonged to Brewer, one to Bonney and the third horse was traded by Brewer to Tunstall for one of the horses the Sheriff had not attached here.

About ten miles from the ranch Waite took the road with the wagon while the rest of the party took the trail passing by Pajarito Spring. About 5 oclock in the evening of the 18th Brewer, Tunstall and I were riding along driving the horses, Middleton and Bonney being about 500 yards in the rear and we three had just come over the brow of the hill when a flock of turkeys rose to the left of the trail. I offered Tunstall my gun, he having none with him, to shoot some of them, but he declined the use of it saying that I was a better shot than he was. Brewer and I started off for the turkeys leaving Tunstall with the horses and had got about three hundred yards from the trail when I heard a noise behind me. Turning in my saddle I saw a party of men come over the brow of the hill on a gallop. I said "look there Dick," and hardly spoken the words when a ball whizzed between me and Brewer and the attacking party all commenced shooting at us without speaking a word to us. I said to Brewer "we cant hold this place," it being a perfectly barren and rocky hillside, "let us ride to the hill over there and make a stand," the hill being covered with trees and large boulders. We rode towards the hill, the whole party coming after us until they had reached the hillside we had been on, continually firing at us. When they reached the hillside they evidently saw Tunstall for they all turned down to where he was. In going to the hill we were met by Bonney and Middleton who had partly rode around us to get away from the attacking party. When we were very near the top of the hill we heard two or three solitary shots, Middleton then remarking to me that they had killed Tunstall. From the time the party turned from us and towards Tunstall and the firing of the shots last mentioned must have been from five to ten minutes. Not one of us fired a shot against the attacking party nor had we or did we or either of us fire our guns off.

I was riding on a bay horse. Brewer was riding a bay. Tunstall was riding a bay horse. Middleton was riding a bay. Bonney was riding a gray. We rode to the top of the hill covered with trees for shelter and stopped and the other party rode upon the hill we had just left. That was after the shots which we believed had killed Tunstall. They then rode around us on the top of said hill in full view of us and then disappeared. I recognized Evans riding a bay, Baker riding a grey, Dolan riding a sort of sorrel, P. Gallegos riding a bay. Hinman, Hurley, Hill, Morton, these are all that I can now recall by name as seeing on the top of last mentioned hill. There were altogether nineteen with the sheriff's posse as I have been informed by Wm. McCloskey who rode with the party from Tunstall's ranch (and was with them from the Penasco) towards us about fifteen miles when his horse gave out and he remained behind, he being on his way to join Tunstall and the rest of us. The following are the names given by McCloskey to me as being with the sheriff's posse and were taken down by me at the time he gave them to me. I now read from the original entry made by me in my memorandum book Sam Corbet being present, viz: William Morton (since killed) Jessie Evans (now at Fort Stanton under arrest) Tom Hill, (since killed) Frank Baker (since killed), Tom Green (now in the employ of Charles Woolse at the Pecos) George Hinman (since killed) John Hurley (now with Riley) Ponciacho, (being one of the murderers of Benito Cruz, for the murderers of whom a reward of $500 is offered by Gov. Axtell) Pantaleon Gallegos (now at Santa Fe) Charles Marshal (now in charge of Catron's or Riley's cattle herd at the Pecos) Sam Perry (I do not know where he is) Tom Cochran (now with Riley) Rivers (I do not know where he is, I think in Arizona) Robert Beckwith (now at Seven Rivers with his father) Charles Kruling alias "Dutch Charley," (now in hospital at Fort Stanton) Kitt, (now I think in Arizona) J. J. Dolan (now at Lincoln) and the Indian (since killed).

We had intended before Mr. Tunstall had come the last time to the ranch that if the Sheriff's party rounding up the cattle should attempt to attack us to resist and for that purpose had cut port holes in the house and had sand bags before the door—they were to be used in no other case.

Deponent further says warrants were sworn out by Brewer, Middleton and I think Bonney, I being absent at the fort, before J. B. Wilson, Justice of the Peace, but against whom the warrants were made out I am unable to say never having examined them. There was only one warrant; all the persons were mentioned in it, I believe.

On the 21st of Feb., 1878, I think, I will not be positive of the date, new warrants were issued by J. B. Wilson, Justice of the Peace and placed in the hands of Atanacio Martinez, Constable, to serve them. The parties wanted under said warrants or most of them were at the house of J. J. Dolan & Co. at Lincoln. Martinez went to serve them, after summoning Waite and Bonney to aid him, to the house of J. J. Dolan & Co., where the murderers were with the Sheriff. I saw them go there and am informed by said Martinez, Waite and Bonney, that as soon as they got to J. J. Dolan & Co.'s store they were covered by guns in the hands of the Sheriff and Tunstall's murderers, disarmed, Waite and Bonney taken prisoners by the Sheriff Brady without warrant or legal process and held prisoners. Martinez was told by the Sheriff that J. B. Wilson had no power as Justice of the Peace, that his warrants would not be recognized by him and that he (Brady) would not allow anyone to be arrested in the house, and then, he, Martinez, was allowed to depart but without his arms.

It was left for Alexander A. McSween, however, to make the most detailed statement of any witness interviewed by Special Investigator Angel. On or about June 1, 1878, McSween made an affidavit, which, coupled with other contemporaneous writings, left for posterity much of McSween's side of the difficulties known as the Lincoln County War. It is apparent that McSween, although living in a frontier community, refused to conform to many of its customs and traditions, and suffered the consequences. Only a few weeks before making the affidavit, on April 17, 1878, McSween wrote to John Partridge Tunstall, in London, to say that he had never carried a gun, an extraordinary statement from a person living in a place where almost every man went armed: "I have never carried a fire arm in my life—dont now—dont expect to. I have lived thirty five years without them and without drinking whiskey and I can, I hope, get along the balance of my days without."

On June 5, 1878, McSween wrote to Tunstall, Sr., to tell him that he had heard that James J. Dolan had offered $1,000 to get him killed: "Parties for years in the employ of Murphy have testified that the sentence of death had been passed on your son and myself long before he was killed. It is notorious that I have never used or carried a more formidable weapon than a pen knife, and it would be an easy matter to kill me." In his affidavit, McSween gave names and dates, and exhibited an ability to describe and evaluate situations. In many ways his valedictory, for he was killed soon after, McSween's affidavit stated:

I have resided in Lincoln County since the 3rd day of March 1875, and since that time I am conversant with the state of affairs that has existed in that county and I am acquainted with the people in that county. I am a lawyer by profession and have been and am now engaged in the practice of my profession. I have given the subject of what has caused the trouble in Lincoln county considerable attention and study, and have inquired and talked with a great number of persons as to the causes which have produced this state of affairs which has resulted in the death of John H. Tunstall and as to the general lawlessness that exists in said county.

From this examination and inquiry of the matter I am informed that Laurence G. Murphy and Emil Fritz, doing business under the style of L. G. Murphy & Co., had the monopoly for the sale of merchandise in this county and used their power to oppress and grind out all they could from the farmers and force those who were opposed to them to leave the country. For instance, the farmers would buy merchandise of them at exorbitant prices, and were compelled to turn in their produce in payment thereof at prices that suited L. G. Murphy & Co., and if a farmer refused so to do, they were subject to litigation and the whole judicial machinery was used unwittingly to accomplish that object. The results of these proceedings were that L. G. Murphy & Co. were absolute monarchs of Lincoln County and ruled their subjects, the farmers and others, with an oppressive iron heel. This state of affairs has existed for some time, at least ten years and was carried out either by L. G. Murphy & Co., or their successors. The said L. G. Murphy in carrying out their schemes would drive out a settler who had opposed them or who would not follow their beck and call, and without a particle of right, title or claim, take possession of such person's real estate and claim that it belonged to them and then rented it to some other person who was led to believe that it belonged to them, and if such person should afterwards find out they had no right, title or interest in the property, and refused to pay them for the rental thereof, a system of persecution would be instituted which resulted in either the appeasing party giving in or leaving the county. This rule of Murphy & Co. and their successors continued until the matter was precipitated by the event of the killing of John H. Tunstall—and that in order to support the monarchy it is reported that L. G. Murphy & Co. and their successors had lately surrounded themselves and were employing the most desperate characters in the country and affairs were carried by such a high hand after deponent came to this county and Murphy desiring to regain lost power and obtain control over the people desired and wished to organize a vigilance committee ostensibly to put down horse stealing but really as after facts show to kill persons who were opposed to him and among other persons to be disposed of he named to me that he was going to have this vigilance committee kill were Hon. J. B. Patron, Stephen Stanley and Richard M. Brewer, since deceased, and he informed me inasmuch as I appeared to support them I would have to leave the county.

Deponent further says that he discountenanced in every way this measure and used his influence to prevent this state of affairs wishing rather that the courts be resorted to and that the people would stand by and see the laws enforced.

McSween heard Murphy assert that he "controlled not only courts and juries, but that he could cause the death of any person who opposed him":

These facts and the further fact that the people were determined to throw off the burden of Murphy & Co., and the fact that Murphy & Co. found that the power to influence courts, juries and even to kill persons was being lost, rendered more desperate and compelled them to resort to more desperate measures which culminated in the death of John H. Tunstall. Deponent has heard L. G. Murphy assert that he controlled not only the courts and juries, but that he could cause the death of any person who opposed him. Deponent verily believes that so far as the courts are concerned that they were made unknowingly the tools in his hands to work out his schemes and revenge. The foregoing facts are I believe the primitive cause of the troubles in Lincoln County at the present time. The direct and immediate cause or the event that precipitated the matter was the death of John H. Tunstall which occurred as hereinafter stated.

In November, 1876, John H. Tunstall came to this county for the purpose, as he said, of going into the stock raising business, and took steps to secure four thousand acres of land for that purpose and invested about $25,000 in his business of stock raising and in merchandise for a store which he opened at Lincoln. At this time the firm of J. J. Dolan & Co. comprised of J. J. Dolan and John H. Riley seemed to be friends of his and knowing that he had considerable money to invest, they tried to have him as far away from Lincoln as they could and also to get his money away so he would be financially crippled and for that purpose tried to have him purchase L. G. Murphy's ranch at Fairview about 35 miles from Lincoln and knowing that I was a friend of Tunstall they tried to induce me to use my influence with Tunstall to have him buy it and promised me if I would induce Tunstall to buy it that they would give me $5,000. I informed Tunstall of this offer and told him that they had no good title to the land and Tunstall refused to buy—this was the beginning of the enmity of Murphy, Dolan and Riley against Tunstall.

During the month of August 1877 horses were stolen from Tunstall and myself by Jessie Evans and Tom Hill. The said Evans and Hill afterwards admitted to me, Mr. Tunstall, Harwood and others that they had taken the horses. They were afterwards arrested at Beckwith's on the Seven Rivers by Sheriff Brady and lodged in jail under an indictment for stealing said horses. That on or about the 7th day of November 1877 I was informed by J. B. Patron that Evans, Baker, Hill and Davis had filed off their shackles and cut the logs in their cell and were ready to make their escape. I told him to inform Sheriff Brady who was the jailer by virtue of his office which he did as he (Patron) subsequently informed me. Whereupon Brady, Patron & Shields went and examined the said prisoners and the jail and found Patron's statement to be true and correct. The Sheriff, however, took no precautionary steps to better secure their confinement. A few days afterwards Sheriff Brady came into Tunstall's store in an half intoxicated condition and indirectly accused Mr.

Tunstall of giving the credit of the arrest of said outlaws to R. M. Brewer (now deceased) and had considerable talk with Mr. Tunstall and among other things accused Mr. Tunstall of having tried to aid Baker, Evans, Hill and Davis to escape. Mr. Tunstall told him "You know their shackles are filed & there are holes cut in the logs and take no pains to secure them, and do you dare accuse me who have aided in the arrest of these persons, who have threatened my life with assisting them to escape?" Sheriff Brady thereupon put his hand upon his revolver as though he was going to draw it and I stepped between them and placing my hand on his shoulder and said "It ill becomes you, as a peace officer, to violate the law by shooting." Brady replied "I wont shoot you now, you haven't long to run. I aint always going to be Sheriff," and then left the store. There were several present besides myself during the conversation. I now recall Atanacio Martinez and Rafael Gutierrez as being present. A day or so after the prisoners referred to made their escape during the night. Upon learning of the escape J. B. Patron, J. H. Tunstall and myself went to the jail from which they had escaped and found several sacks to which rocks weighing 20 or 25 pounds were tied augers and files. Upon further investigation I found that no one had been left in charge of the jail that night, and that the doors had not even been locked, though Brady was at Murphy's house where he made his headquarters. I am informed and verily believe that the augers and files referred to above were packed in goods bought in the store of J. J. Dolan & Co., where Murphy resided, and by one of their employees (Pantaleon Gallegos) delivered to the prisoners.

I am also informed that they went to Brewer's ranch and took horses, saddles & guns by force belonging to Tunstall and Brewer. After their escape it was reported at Lincoln that Brewer had been killed and I went to Sheriff Brady and offered to raise twenty men to go and recapture the escaped prisoners. Brady replied "I arrested them once and I will be d———— if I am agoing to do it again; hereafter I am going to look after Brady's interest," and declined the offer. Subsequently some of the escaped prisoners to wit Davis were seen with Brady at the store of J. J. Dolan & Co. as I am informed by George Washington, and he did not arrest them or offer or try to do so.

Individual loans, tax money, and the Emil Fritz estate further complicated an already involved situation:

About the 29th of September 1877 J. J. Dolan & Co. borrowed from Mr. Tunstall through me one thousand dollars. I had before this taken up a note for Mr. Richard M. Brewer held by J. J. Dolan & Co. for about $2,300 in order to protect said Brewer, who had incurred the anger of J. J. Dolan & Co. and who had determined to ruin him. About this time it was reported that J. J. Dolan & Co. were using the Territorial tax money which Sheriff Brady had collected and not paid over to the Treasurer, in order to help them out of their financial troubles, and being very anxious to find out if there was any truth in the report, and in order to see if they were endeavoring to ruin the County in their own interests against the wishes of all law abiding citizens, I inquired of them after I had agreed to furnish as aforesaid the $1000 why they did not get the tax money from Brady, and to this question Dolan said that Riley had already got it. Subsequent facts show that that was the fact as will more fully appear by the check given by me to the sheriff. About June 24, 1874, Emil Fritz died in Germany. At this time his partner L. G. Murphy was probate judge. No steps were taken to administer on the estate of Fritz until about April 20, 1875, when one William Brady, the late sheriff of Lincoln County was appointed administrator by said Murphy. At that time Dolan, who had been clerk for L. G. Murphy & Co. and afterwards partner of L. G. Murphy, and the said L. G. Murphy admitted to me that according to the books of the firm Emil Fritz had an interest in the business at the time of his death to the amount of about $48,000, as John Watts, who had examined their books as an expert, had informed them, and that they desired that Charles Fritz and Emilie Scholand (brother and sister of the deceased) should have whatever interest Emil Fritz had in the business. About this time I was employed by Brady, administrator, to make collections for the estate and instructed by him that Dolan & Murphy should receive all moneys collected. Among the assets of the estate was a life insurance policy on the life of Fritz in the Merchants Life Insurance Company of New York for $10,000. Mr. Brady, administrator, informed deponent that this policy had been placed in the hands of Levi Spiegelberg, of New York City, a member of the firm of Spiegelberg Brothers of Santa Fe, New Mexico, by Mr. L. G. Murphy, without consulting him (Brady).

About the month of February 1876 I went in company with Mr. Brady to Santa Fe. During our journey we became quite confidential with each other. Brady told me among other things that he was in the power of L. G. Murphy. After we got to Santa Fe he informed me that J. J. Dolan, the junior partner of said Murphy had compelled him to give an order on Levi Spiegelberg to place the money received on the Fritz policy to the crèdit of L. G. Murphy & Co. with Spiegelberg & Bros. of Santa Fe, New Mexico, with whom at that time said L. G. Murphy & Co. were greatly indebted for goods and merchandise.

At this critical point there is a hiatus in the narrative which jumps ahead to McSween's version of circumstances revolving around the attachment sued out against him, culminating in John H. Tunstall's death. McSween and his associates had been in Mesilla trying to straighten out McSween's affairs, which had become tangled as the result of his arrest in Las Vegas on an embezzlement charge. Switching to the difficulties growing out of a meeting with Jesse Evans, Frank Baker, James J. Dolan and others at San Augustine Springs, and describing the events leading up to the attachment, McSween's affidavit continued:

On or about the 5th day of February 1878 I started for Lincoln in charge of Deputy Sheriff Barrier and in company with D. P. Shields, J. B. Wilson and J. H. Tunstall. On the evening of the same day we camped at San Augustine, and shortly after going into camp Jessie Evans, Frank Baker, Long, alias Rivers, notorious outlaws, came into our camp and inquired of us if we had passed J. J. Dolan on the road. Whereupon D. P. Shields replied that we had not; that he understood that Mr. Dolan would not leave until tomorrow morning (the 6th). Baker said that they had found Jimmie, (meaning J. J. Dolan) very punctual in their engagements with them and that Dolan had made an appointment with them to meet them here and that they believed he would come. Deponent further says that it was a notorious fact that this Evans, Baker, Rivers and others, had determined to take J. H. Tunstall's and my life owing to our activity in having them previously arrested for horse stealing.

Deponent further says that about one or two oclock of the morning of the 6th of February 1878, said J. J. Dolan reached San Augustine aforesaid. About 8 or 9 oclock in the morning of the said day whilst Tunstall, D. P. Shields, J. B. Wilson and this deponent were eating breakfast at their camping place at the east end of the San Augustine corral, deponent saw J. J. Dolan with gun in hand and another man descending a house occupied by Mr. Shedd, said house being situated about 70 or 80 yards due south of where deponent, Tunstall, Wilson, Shield and Barrier were camped. Said J. J. Dolan and the person accompanying him appeared to be going in a westerly direction thus hiding themselves from us by the southeast corner of said corral. In a few minutes said J. J. Dolan and Jessie Evans came around the southeast corner of said corral. Mr. Dolan drew his Winchester carbine on Mr. Tunstall and asked him if he was ready to fight and settle their difficulties. Mr. Tunstall asked him if he asked him to fight a duel. Mr. Dolan replied "You d————d coward I want you to fight and settle our difficulties." Dolan drew his gun cocked on Mr. Tunstall three times. Mr. Barrier placed himself between or in line with Dolan and Evans and saved as I believe the lives of Tunstall and myself. When Mr. Dolan was leaving he used these words "You wont fight this morning, you d————d coward, but I'll get you soon." After he had gone off about 20 yards he turned around and said to Tunstall "When you write the Independent again say I am with the boys," the term "the boys," being used in Lincoln & neighborhood to denote notorious thieves and murderers such as Evans, Baker, Hill and Davis and the reason that he mentioned the "Independent," was because Tunstall had written said newspaper published at Mesilla a letter dated Jan. 18, 1878, which letter was published in said newspaper in its issue of the 26th of January 1878, charging Wm. Brady, Sheriff as aforesaid with having allowed said J. J. Dolan & Co. to use the Territorial funds collected by said Brady as Ex officio Collector of said Lincoln County and the Governor of said Territory in his message to the Legislature having reported that said Brady was in default in the payment of the money collected by him (said Brady). Deponent further says that said letter elicited a reply from said J. J. Dolan which was published in said Independent on or about the 2d of February 1878.

Deponent further says that after the occurrence of the attempted killing of Tunstall and myself related above we started for Lincoln. After traveling about 20 miles we were passed on the road by said J. J. Dolan, Evans, Baker, Hill and Long alias Rivers. Evans and Baker rode with Mr. Dolan in his ambulance. It was known to Mr. Dolan at this time that all of these men were highwaymen and escaped prisoners.

Riley, Dolan, Murphy and Brady anticipated celebrating McSween's imprisonment in Lincoln:

Deponent further says that when he arrived at the town of Lincoln he was informed that a courier had preceded me from Mesilla with a writ of attachment. That Riley, Dolan and Murphy and Sheriff Brady were in ecstasy over deponent's prospective confinement in the county jail and I was informed that Sheriff Brady was making the occasion a subject of merriment by making contracts to grind corn in the Mexican mills to make gruel for my maintenance; that said Riley had swept out the jail in order that he might in future have it to say that he swept out the room in which I was incarcerated; that said Brady expressed himself in the presence of E. A. Dow and others to the effect that Tunstall and I had reported that he (Brady) was a defaulter to the Territory but that he meant to show us that he would not make a default in confining this deponent in jail and taking the spirit out of him; that he may have allowed Baker or Evans & Hill to escape, and that he would not allow deponent to do so.

Deponent further says that he found a writ of attachment had been issued out of the Third Judicial District Court in which the said Emilie Scholand and Charles Fritz were plaintiffs, that it was dated the 7th of February 1878 and that the Sheriff commenced to attach thereunder on the 8th, it having been sent a distance of about 154 miles in an almost unprecedented short time for this Territory; that he not only attached my personal property but also my real estate together with the property of J. H. Tunstall and others, even pictures of the family of the latter, as also a notarial seal of D. P. Shields. He, (the Sheriff,) was commanded to attach and safely keep so much property as would secure the sum of $8,000 but he attached property both real and personal, worth over $110,000. At this time I was not Mr. Tunstall's partner although I was to become such by articles of agreement in May, 1878. I was his attorney and took an active part in the management of his business. For this I was to have one half of the profits of the business up to May 1878 after the deduction of 8 per cent on the capital invested. In May 1878 Articles of Copartnership were to be signed by which Mr. Tunstall was to furnish the capital, I to pay 8 per cent interest per annum for my share. At the time (February 1878) Mr. Tunstall owed me over $4,000 as appears by the copy of the available account, the same being a true and full account of all money transactions had by and between us from the time indicated until his death. Other than I have stated I had no other financial interest in Mr. Tunstall's business. He had done business in the name of J. H. Tunstall only. No resistance of any kind or character was offered by deponent to the Sheriff Brady in the execution of said writ of attachment nor by any other person so far as this deponent knows.

Deponent further says that on or about the 14th of February, 1878, Mr. Tunstall was informed that one J. B. Matthews (who was in the employ of Murphy and attended to anything that Dolan and Riley desired done,) was at his (Tunstall's) ranch with said Baker, Evans, Hill and Davis as a sheriff's posse to attach Tunstall's cattle and horses as the property of this deponent. That said J. B. Matthews, as Sheriff Brady's deputy, was informed that deponent had neither cattle or horses there but they could "round up" and if he found any he could take them; that he could not take Tunstall's properties without an order from him or process against him; that said Matthews then and there stated that he would return to Lincoln and report to Brady, that he would return in a day or so probably but that he would bring only one man with him. R. M. Brewer, who was Tunstall's foreman, told him that when he came he would "round up" the cattle and horses and he could see if there were any of McSween's horses or cattle there. On or about the 14th of February Robert Widemann came in from Tunstall's ranch and informed Tunstall in my hearing of what had taken place as heretofore related, that he was satisfied that Matthews intended to raise a large posse and take the cattle by force, that for that purpose said Baker had gone down to Dolan's camp on the Pecos with instructions to William Morton, their foreman, to raise all the men he could and meet Matthews with his posse at Turkey Springs, a few miles from Tunstall's ranch on the morning of the 16th of February 1878. Mr. Tunstall was informed in my hearing by George Washington, that Murphy, Riley & Dolan had helped Matthews raise a force to the number of 43 men, that said Riley informed him (Washington) that there was no use in McSween's and Tunstall's trying to get away from them this time, as they had them completely in their power, that they could not possibly be beat as they had the District Attorney (meaning Rynerson) the Court and all the power in Santa Fe to back them, that their plan was to take the cattle from Tunstall's ranch and by sending two Mexicans they had in the posse to make a sham round up of the cattle and horses, so as to draw the men in Tunstall's house out of it, then the balance of the posse were to take possession of the house and "get" Tunstall's men. Upon this information Mr. Tunstall concluded to go to the ranch and induce his men to leave and allow Matthews and posse to take the property and seek his remedy in the courts. For this purpose as he informed me, he left Lincoln on the night of the 16th. This was the last time I saw Tunstall alive.

I have been informed by R. M. Brewer (deceased) John Middleton, Mr. Bonney, R. A. Widemann, F. T. Wait and Henry Brown that Mr. Tunstall reached his cattle ranch on the night of the 17th and commanded them all to leave the ranch and come to Lincoln which they did. McCloskey (deceased) informed me that Tunstall sent him to get one Martin who was a good cattleman to come to the ranch to turn the cattle over to Deputy Sheriff J. B. Matthews and posse who were now said to be at Turkey Springs numbering 43 men and see that the cattle were properly tallied, and that he (Tunstall) would seek his remedy at law, that he would not sacrifice the life of one of his men for all the cattle, for they would all be killed if they remained on the ranch. Said McCloskey informed me further that he not only delivered that verbal message to said Martin but told the same to J. B. Matthews and informed him that Mr. Tunstall would offer no resistance to the taking of the property though none of it belonged to this deponent. Deponent further says that on the night of the 18th of February 1878 he was informed by R. M. Brewer, W. Bonney, J. Middleton and R. A. Widemann that said J. H. Tunstall was murdered on the road to Lincoln about 30 miles from his cattle ranch by Jessie Evans, Frank Baker, J. J. Dolan, W. Morton, T. Corcoran, P. Gallegos, O. L. Roberts, Tom Hill, George Davis, Robert W. Beckwith, Tom Green, George Hinman, J. Hurley and others to the number of 18 men. My informants further stated that at the time of the murder they were some distance from Mr. Tunstall but that he endeavored to make his escape, but failed to do so. I am informed that Tom Green who was present when the murder was committed said that Morton, who was acting as Deputy under orders from said Deputy Matthews called out to Tunstall to stop that he wanted to see him and that they did not want to hurt him, and that thereupon Mr. Tunstall dismounted and walked towards Morton and delivered him a Colt's pistol carried by Tunstall and that a few minutes thereafter Jessie Evans aforesaid took aim at

Mr. Tunstall and shot him, the ball taking effect in his breast, and that as he (Tunstall) fell on his face, said Morton fired another shot at Mr. Tunstall out of Tunstall's revolver, the ball entering the back of the head and coming out in the forehead and that thereafter Morton walked to Tunstall's horse and shot another shot out of Tunstall's pistol at said horse, whereupon the horse dropped dead and that then the murderers carried the corpse of said Tunstall and laid him close by the side of said horse, putting his hat under his dead horse's head.

On the night last above mentioned this deponent wrote a note to John Newcomb requesting him to go where Tunstall's body was and bring it to Lincoln that it might have a decent burial. That on the night of February 19th 1878 said John Newcomb with others brought into Lincoln the lifeless body of Tunstall. Said Newcomb informed me then and there that he found said Tunstall dead at the place indicated by me, that when he found the body it was lying close by the side of a dead horse belonging to said Tunstall and that Tunstall's hat was lying under the head of said dead horse. That on the night of the day last above mentioned a coroner's inquest was held on the body of said Tunstall. That on or about the 20 I caused the body of said Tunstall to be embalmed and a post mortem examination made by Drs. Ealy and Appel. That not only was the body shot as already stated, but the skull was broken in pieces by a blow from some instrument after being shot as aforesaid. That on the 19th day of February 1878 I caused affidavits to be filed before J. B. Wilson, Justice of the Peace within the said Town of Lincoln charging the murder of Mr. Tunstall on the parties named, upon which affidavits a warrant of arrest for such parties was duly issued and placed in the hands of Atanacio Martinez, Constable in and for said town of Lincoln for execution.

That upon the 20 day of February 1878, said Constable Martinez called upon W. Bonney and F. T. Waite to help him serve said warrant. That it was well known that ten or twelve of the murderers of Mr. Tunstall were then in the house of L. G. Murphy, Dolan and Riley aforesaid. That as this deponent is informed by said constable, he proceeded to the house of Murphy, Dolan and Riley to make arrests as directed. That at said house he met the said Sheriff Brady who without any warrant or authority of law, took the said constable, the said Bonney and Waite prisoners and refused to aid or allow them to arrest any one though the majority of said murderers were then and there with said Sheriff. That on the evening of the day last mentioned said constable was released and Bonney and Waite retained for two days more. That after the burial of Mr. Tunstall on the 22nd day of February, 1878, a meeting of the citizens of Lincoln County was held to prevent further bloodshed, if possible. That at such meeting Hon. Florencio Gonzales, Probate Judge of said county, Isaac Ellis, merchant, Jose Martino, merchant and John Newcomb, farmer, were appointed a committee to wait upon said Sheriff Brady to ascertain why he prevented the said constable from executing said warrant and making arrests as therein directed and took said constable and posse as prisoners as aforesaid and still held Bonney and Waite as such. They informed me on their return that Sheriff Brady said he held both the constable and posse as prisoners because he had the power. They further informed me that they asked Sheriff Brady to set a value upon the property (he having failed to appraise the property attached) and that deponent would give a bond to be approved by said Brady; that the property so attached would be forthcoming to answer any order or decree that might be made in the premises by the Hon. District Court for said Lincoln County, and that if this deponent failed to give such bond then he (Brady) could do with the property aforesaid as he thought fit; and they informed me that Brady replied that he would not take a bond of any kind from deponent for said property.

Deponent further says that five or six deputies were put by Brady in charge of the store of J. H. Tunstall, deceased, with its stock of general merchandise attached as the property of deponent and that three of that number were non residents of this county, to-wit: W. Morton, J. Long and J. Longwill, and all irresponsible and notorious tools of Murphy, Dolan and Riley. That said Brady acknowledged to this deponent in the hearing of several persons that his deputies last above mentioned had abstracted goods from said store and appropriated the same to their own use. That on or about the 18th day of February 1878 said Sheriff Brady had a detachment of United States soldiers from Fort Stanton stationed at the house of Murphy, Dolan and Riley aforesaid, and that he caused to be issued for the horses belonging to such detachment the hay belonging to Mr. Tunstall in his lifetime without authority or permission other than the fact that he had attached it as the property of this deponent. That at the time of such issue as aforesaid, the said Brady refused as I am informed by S. Corbett, to allow any of the hay so attached to be fed to Mr. Tunstall's horses, and that in consequence of this refusal Mr. Tunstall's horses had to be fed elsewhere at great expense.

That on the 19th day of February 1878 an affidavit was filed with J. B. Wilson, Justice of the Peace, charging said Sheriff Brady's deputies as aforesaid with the appropriation of goods, etc., as aforesaid and that as a result of an examination on said matter, they were held to await the action of the Lincoln County grand jury.

McSween's enemies put pressure on those willing to become a surety on his appearance bond:

Deponent further says that on the 11th day of February 1878 he made and executed an appearance bond as required by Judge Bristol and sent the same by registered letter to W. L. Rynerson, District Attorney as aforesaid, which bond was refused. Jose Montano, merchant of the town of Lincoln volunteered to become one of my bondsmen as aforesaid. Subsequently he informed deponent that he was threatened with ruin by J. J. Dolan & Co. if he became one of my bondsmen. The said Sheriff as said Montano informed deponent, used all his influence with said Montano to prevent me from giving bond and to oblige me to go to jail. Subsequently said Montano became one of my bondsmen. Joseph H. Blazer informed me that J. J. Dolan had also threatened that if he became one of my bondsmen they would have him prosecuted for cutting timber on the public lands, as I understand, in U. S. courts by T. B. Catron, U. S. District Attorney at Santa Fe. A few days after the execution of said bond said Sheriff Brady called upon said Jose Montano as the latter informed me, with a letter purporting to be from said W. L. Rynerson to the effect that though a friend to said Montano he could not accept him on bond of this deponent and requesting that he withdraw his name from said bond. After such representations and coaxing by said Sheriff said Montano signed a letter complying with said request of withdrawal written by said Brady. The sureties on said bond justified in different sums amounting in the aggregate to $34,500. Deponent was informed by G. Washington that he heard Brady and Riley aforesaid say that there was no use in deponent trying to give bonds as W. L. Rynerson, the District Attorney, would not approve any that he (deponent) would give and he would have to go to jail.

In many respects, Alex. McSween's deposition of on or about the first of June, 1878, was an ante-mortem statement. In fifty days he was dead, his body torn by five bullets fired at close range.

NOTES AND PROFILES

[1] The State Department file on the Tunstall case is in the National Archives. The case is also reported in John Bassett Moore's *A Digest of International Law* (Washington, Government Printing Office, 1906), Vol. VI, pages 662-66, and in *Foreign Relations of the United States, 1885* (Washington, Government Printing Office, 1886), pages 449-59. For the British viewpoint of the Tunstall case, with particular reference to the indemnity claim, see "A Sidelight on the Tunstall Murder," by Frederick W. Nolan, of New Brighton, Cheshire, England, in *New Mexico Historical Review*, July 1956, pp. 206-22.

CHAPTER THIRTEEN

THE BONNEY TRAIL

THREE OUTLAWS—William Bonney, William Wilson and David Rudabaugh—rode nonchalantly into White Oaks at dusk on November 28, 1880. The three men, thrown together by chance and circumstance, were fugitives from justice, but were not joint companions in crime. Each one, entirely independent of the other, had transgressed the law. Their only bond was the common tie of a desire to escape prosecution, and to avoid punishment for their respective misdeeds.

Bonney was wanted by officers of the law for the murder of Sheriff Brady and Deputy Hindman in Lincoln on April 1, 1878, and for the murder of "Buckshot" Roberts at Blazer's Mill on April 4, 1878.

Billy Wilson was scarcely a desperado at all, but a young man who had believed he could attain wealth by a short cut through the use and manipulation of counterfeit United States currency, with the result that he was now in trouble with the federal government.

In many respects, David Rudabaugh was the most hardened criminal and most desperate character of the trio. When he became a resident of Las Vegas in 1879, it did not take officers long to classify him as an undesirable citizen. When the Trinidad-Santa Fe stagecoach, on one of its last runs prior to being supplanted by the railway, was robbed on August 30, 1879, at a point between Tecolote and Las Vegas, law officers strongly suspected that Rudabaugh had engineered the job, but there was no proof to back up their suspicion.[1]

When four masked men, late at night, climbed aboard a Santa Fe passenger train as it was pulling out of Las Vegas on November 14, 1879, and robbed the express and mail car at the "big cut," three miles south of town, suspicion again pointed to Rudabaugh as one of the robbers. And once again Rudabaugh was prepared to establish his innocence by means of an apparently invincible alibi.

Successful in evading prosecution on the stagecoach and railway mail car robberies, Rudabaugh continued to hang about in Las Vegas until he got into serious trouble. On March 2, 1880, John J. Webb, one-time resident of Deadwood and Cheyenne, shot and killed Michael Kelliher in Goodlet and Robinson's saloon in Las Vegas. Within a matter of days the San Miguel County grand jury indicted Webb for murder. He was convicted by a jury, and on April 9, 1880, was sentenced by Judge L. Bradford Prince to be hanged. On April 30, three weeks after pronouncement of the death sentence, Dave Rudabaugh attempted to rescue Webb from the county jail. When Deputy Sheriff Antonio Lino Valdez courageously resisted the jail delivery, Rudabaugh shot and killed him, and made his way to Fort Sumner, where he became acquainted with William Bonney and joined him as a fellow outlaw.[2]

Regardless of previous relationships and affiliations, Bonney, Rudabaugh and Wilson were now partners in crime as they rode into White Oaks on November 28, 1880. They were driving ahead of them a bunch of stolen horses. Most outlaws looked down on horse stealing, considering it a risky, undignified operation, and a sorry way of raising money. Bonney and his companions, however, had no apologies to offer. They were badly in need of flour, salt, sugar, coffee, bacon and smoking tobacco, and were willing to stoop to stealing horses to obtain them. The outlaws drove the horses into the corral of Sam Dedrick's livery stable in White Oaks. Their title to the animals was defective, but this deficiency could be overlooked in the bustling, gold-mining camp, established some two years before, about forty-five miles by wagon road from Lincoln.

Soon after arriving in White Oaks, the outlaws learned that a posse was being organized to arrest them. Prudence dictated that they should not tarry in the town; and they quickly arranged with Sam Dedrick to sell the horses at the best price obtainable, and use the money to buy provisions. There was a strong demand for horses in White Oaks. Dedrick sold several of them overnight to anxious purchasers, willing to overlook the niceties of pedigree, title of ownership, and right to possession.

Early next day, following instructions left by the outlaws, Sam Dedrick's brother Mose started for their hideout with a load of supplies. Fairly certain of Mose Dedrick's errand and destination, Deputy Sheriff Will Hudgin and a posse of eight men trailed along, following hoofprints and wagon tracks. When Mose guided his team away from the White Oaks-Las Vegas road and struck out across country, the possemen knew that fighting might be imminent. The shooting began the instant the outlaws caught sight of the posse. In the exchange of shots, Bonney's horse and Wilson's horse were shot down, forcing their riders to run for their lives. The outlaws escaped, and the posse returned, empty-handed, to White Oaks. (LVG, November 30, 1880.)

Apparently in a spirit of bravado and daring, Bonney, Rudabaugh and Wilson returned to White Oaks on November 30, the day immediately following their encounter with the posse. Deputy Sheriff James Redman, standing in front of the Hudgin store, watched the outlaws parade into town. Just for luck, one of them took a shot at him, and he ran for cover. Attracted by the shooting, a crowd of thirty or forty men, armed with Winchester rifles and six-shooters, rushed into the main street, anxious to participate in the excitement. The outlaws galloped out of town.

At daybreak the next morning, a posse of twelve men, headed by Deputy Sheriff James Carlyle, left White Oaks and trailed the outlaws to the Kuch and Greathouse ranch house, "forty miles from White Oaks, on the Las Vegas Road." The posse surrounded the ranch house. Posse-leader Carlyle demanded that the outlaws surrender to the law. Billy Wilson shouted a reply, and a parley followed which had tragic results. During the talk Wilson promised Carlyle that they would all surrender if Rudabaugh could be assured that he would not be mobbed in Las Vegas.

Carlyle was enticed into the house after Jim Greathouse had offered himself as hostage to ensure his safe return. Hour after hour passed away, evening came, then dark night. The outlaws had not yet surrendered and Carlyle was still in the house. Finally, about midnight, the possemen heard loud talk and shouting, then the noise of shattered window glass, accompanied by the sharp report of pistol shots. Then they saw Carlyle stagger from the house, and slump to the ground, a dead man.

Some nine years later, Joe Steck, an eyewitness to the events which preceded Carlyle's death, wrote his recollections of the trouble, which were published in the Lincoln County *Leader* of December 7, 1889. Summarized, Steck's recollections were as follows: He had been employed by Greathouse and Kuch, who "kept a store and camphouse for travelers on the Las Vegas and White Oaks road," to cook and haul logs and water at their ranch. Travelers came and went at all hours of the day and night. Steck was kept busy from dawn until after dark each day. Just after daybreak on one particular day, while Steck was harnessing a team of horses, two men suddenly appeared in front of him. They commanded him, with guns pointed at his head, to lie flat on the ground, which he did quickly and without question.

Describing Bonney, Wilson and Rudabaugh, one of the two men asked Steck if he had seen them. Steck told them that three such men, whose names he did not know, were stopping at the house. The spokesman for the pair then told Steck that they had the house surrounded by a posse and proposed to arrest the three men they had described, or get killed trying. Steck then carried a note from Carlyle, the posse leader, to William Bonney, demanding immediate surrender. According to Steck, Bonney "read the paper to his compadres, who all laughed at the idea of surrender."

Acting as a go-between, Steck relayed several messages between the posse and the outlaws: "The Kid's party sent me out with a note demanding to know who the leader of the party was, and invited him into the house to talk the matter over. Carlyle, the leader of the White Oaks crowd, at first objected, but Greathouse, putting himself as hostage for his safety while he was in there, he took off his arms and walked into the trap." At eleven o'clock that night Steck went into the house: "I found Carlyle getting under the influence of liquor, and insisting on going out, while the others insisted on his staying." Steck decided to leave the house: "I went outside myself. After being out a moment—I stopped and turned when crash a man came through a window, bong, bang, the man's dying yell, and poor Carlyle tumbled to the ground with three bullets in him—dead."

Steck and Kuch spent the remaining hours of the night at a ranch three miles away, but returned to their place at daylight: "We found poor Carlyle frozen stiff where he fell. We tied a blanket around him and buried him the best we could. He was afterwards taken up and put in a box by the Sheriff's posse."

With Carlyle dead, the posse, for the time being, abandoned any further attempt to arrest the outlaws. As soon as the posse started for White Oaks, Bonney, Rudabaugh and Wilson left for the open country. A few hours later, the ranch house was burned to the ground.

Annoyed by the newspaper reports of the Carlyle shooting, James Greathouse called upon the editor of the Las Vegas *Gazette,* and entered upon a recital of his grievances. Apparently impressed by Greathouse's story, the *Gazette,* on December 11, 1880, published his version of the incident:

Jim Greathouse, owner of the ranch where the brush between the White Oaks boys and members of "the Kid's" gang recently took place, is in Las Vegas. He reports that his ranch was burned during the affair and that he lost $2000 by the conflagration, including ranch property and general merchandise. He disclaims any thought of harboring desperadoes and says the fact that they were there is wholly due to their demanding accommodations. As he kept a public hostelry, he could not refuse. He had seen Billy the Kid several times, but did not know either Rudabaugh or Wilson. The loss cripples him and is certainly unfortunate as he was entirely blameless of any attempt to throw obstacles in the way of the White Oaks boys. As we understand the case, he does not know positively who burned his ranch, but presumes that it was done as an act of retribution by the Oaks party to avenge the death of Jim Carlyle, one of their number, who was shot down by "the Kid."

In an interview published in the Las Vegas *Gazette* of December 24, 1880, Pat Garrett claimed that "Jim Greathouse had been an outlaw; that he had been with Billy Wilson on the Buffalo Range in the Panhandle country." Notwithstanding his published defense of December 11, 1880, Greathouse was arrested on March 21, 1881, at Anton Chico, and taken to White Oaks, where he was arraigned before Justice of the Peace Lea, charged with being an accessory to the Carlyle murder. Lea heard the evidence and bound Greathouse over to the grand jury under a $3,000 bond. Anton Chico property owners signed a bond and Greathouse was released, according to the Santa Fe *New Mexican* of March 23, 1881.

Although the Las Vegas *Gazette* had advised its readers on June 1, 1878, to "ignore all correspondence from, and concerning Lincoln County," and had ventured the opinion that the existing difficulties there would "sink to rest," that newspaper, some thirty months later, adopted a different viewpoint. On December 3, 1880, the *Gazette* published a two-column editorial, which was a clarion call to the good people of San Miguel County. There was a duty, the editorial said, "which the people of San Miguel county should immediately discharge"; which was "to arrest a powerful gang of outlaws harassing the stockmen of the Pecos and Panhandle country, and terrorizing the people of Fort Sumner and vicinity."

"Billy the Kid," Rudabaugh, Bowdre, and other fugitives from justice were members of the gang:

The gang includes from forty to fifty men, all hard characters, the off scouring of society, fugitives from justice, and desperadoes by profession. Among them are men, with whose names and deeds the people of Las Vegas are perfectly familiar, such as "Billy the Kid, Dave Rudabaugh, Charles Bowdre, and others of equally unsavory reputation.

When J. J. Webb, who was convicted of the murder of Kelliher, made his escape from the Las Vegas jail a few weeks since, he made a break for Portales, and is now reckoned as one of the fold.

The band is well armed and have plenty of ammunition, and as they have no hankering to be "pulled in" are very determined.

One circumstance, however, has made them very incautious, which inspires the hope that if a well organized raid is made on them, they may yet be brought to justice. The bivouac of the desperadoes is on what may be termed disputed territory. Lying on or near the boundaries of Valencia, Lincoln and San Miguel counties, it is yet held by many that it is included within the limits of the former county.

From this very uncertainty, officials of the three counties have made it an excuse for hesitating about raiding them, each claiming that it is outside their jurisdiction. This the raiders are perfectly aware of, as they are equally all informed of all matters going on in the neighborhood, which leads to the belief that there are others in league with them, who are never engaged in action.

If the truth were known, it is safe to say that men right here in Las Vegas would be called before the bar of justice to answer to the charge of complicity in this nefarious calling.

Although the band has been organized for some time, it was never so strong as it is today, and the party of old offenders who have been obliged to change their quarters many times, are the nucleus of the present organization.

The time during which they have committed depredations extends over a period of a number of months, but each time they have changed base they have attracted to them others of the same ilk.

Lincoln County people who have been made the victims of their depredations, at last rose in their might and making it too hot for them, finally and forever drove them from their territory.

"Billy the Kid" was the leader:

The gang is under the leadership of "Billy the Kid," a desperate cuss, who is eligible for the post of captain of any crowd, no matter how mean and lawless. They spend considerable time in enjoying themselves at the Portales, keeping guards out and scouting the country for miles around before turning in for the night. Whenever there is a good opportunity to make a haul they split up in gangs and scour the country, always leaving behind a detachment to guard their roost and whatever plunder they may have stored there.

Another resort is the old ranch at Canaditas, ten or twelve miles from Fort Sumner, about which they hover, before swooping down on the ranges and ranches in the Pecos country. Whenever the caprice seizes them they flock into Fort Sumner and take possession, running things to suit themselves, drinking, carousing, rowing and giving balls.

They run stock from the Panhandle country into the White Oaks and from the Pecos country into the Panhandle, equalizing the herds, but in true middlemen style always make heavily by the transaction. Only a short time ago, a considerable amount of stock was found at the Oaks, which it is positively known was stolen from the Panhandle.

Are the people of San Miguel county to stand this any longer? Shall we suffer this horde of outcasts and the scum of society, who are outlawed by a multitude of crimes, to continue their way on the very border of our county?

We believe the citizens of San Miguel County to be order loving people, and call upon them to unite in forever wiping out this band to the east of us. Now is the time to act, for every storm enriches them by driving to their rendezvous large herds from which they make their selection. If anything is done, reinforcements in plenty could be secured from the Panhandle country, and resolute men from the association could be drafted into the army of vengeance.

William H. Bonney read the *Gazette* editorial of December 3, and like many people before and since, he could not resist the urge to reply. But instead of writing direct to the *Gazette,* Bonney addressed his letter to Governor Wallace, from Fort Sumner on December 12, 1880. In the letter Bonney denied many of the *Gazette's* accusations, and specifically disclaimed responsibility for Carlyle's death. With spelling, capitalization and punctuation exactly as in the original, the letter follows:

I noticed in the Las Vegas Gazette a piece which stated that Billy "the," Kid, the name by which I am known in the country was the captain of a band of outlaws who hold Forth at the Portales. There is no such organization in existence. So the gentleman must have drawn very heavily on his imagination My business at the White Oaks the time I was waylaid and my horse killed was to see Judge Leonard who has my case in hand. he had written to me to come up, that he thought he could get everything straighened up I did not find him at the Oaks & should have gone to Lincoln if I had met with no accident. After mine and Billie Wilsons horses were killed we both made our way to a station, forty miles from the Oaks kept by Mr. Greathouse. When I got up next morning the house was surrounded by an outfit led by one Carlyle, who came into the house and demanded a surrender. I asked for their papers and they had none. So I concluded it amounted to nothing more than a mob and told Carlyle that he would have to stay in the house and lead the way out that night. Soon after a note was brought in stating that if Carlyle did not come out inside of five minutes they would kill the station keeper (Greathouse) who had left the house and was with them.

in a short time a shot was fired on the outside and Carlyle thinking Greathouse was killed jumped through the window breaking the sash as he went and was killed by his own Party they think it was me trying to make my escape. the Party then withdrew.

They returned the next day and burned an old man Spencer's house and Greathouses also. I made my way to this place afoot and During my absence Deputy Sheriff Garrett acting under Chisums orders went to Portales and found nothing. on his way back he went by Mr. Yerberys ranch and took a pair of mules of mine which I had left with Mr. Bowdre who is in charge of Mr. Yerbys cattle he (Garret) claimed that they were stolen and even if they were not he had a right to confiscate any outlaws property.

I have been at Sumner since I left Lincoln making my living gambling The mules were bought by me the truth of which I can prove by the best citizens around Sumner. J. S. Chisum is the man who got me into trouble and was benefited Thousands by it and is now doing all he can against me There is no Doubt but what there is a great deal of stealing going on in the Territory and a great deal of the property is taken across the Plains as it is a good outlet but so far as my being at the head of a band there is nothing of it in several instances I have recovered stolen property when there was no chance to get an officer to do it.

One instance for Hugo Zuber post office Puerto de Luna another for Pablo Analla same place

if some impartial party were to investigate this matter they would find it far different from the impression put out by Chisum and his tools

When Bonney's letter to Governor Wallace was published, the Las Vegas *Gazette* commented on December 22, 1880:

The Kid's band showed very good taste in reading the *Gazette* religiously, and thus learn what is stirring in the outside world, from which they are practically outlawed. On numerous occasions we have sought to rouse the people of the county to the east of us to organize a brisk company so that the gang might be captured or driven out of the country.

While Bonney, perhaps with the assistance of Billy Wilson, was laboriously composing his letter to Governor Wallace of

December 12, 1880, officers of the law, well mounted, heavily armed and abundantly provisioned, were on their way to his hiding place, prepared for a showdown.

On Friday, December 10, Frank Stewart, employed as a detective by a Panhandle cattle growers' association, left Las Vegas with twenty men, provisioned and equipped to remain on Bonney's trail at least two weeks. Stewart would have been on his way sooner but had been kept waiting in Las Vegas pending the arrival of corn for his horses. As of Saturday, December 11, Deputy Sheriff Pat Garrett[3] of Lincoln County was in the Fort Sumner country with a posse, ready and waiting to cooperate with Stewart and his posse.

Demonstrating his willingness to cooperate with the law officers in the drive to round up Bonney, Governor Wallace offered a reward of $500 for his capture. The reward notice was as follows:

$500 Reward.
Notice Is Hereby Given that Five Hundred Dollars Reward Will Be Paid for the Delivery of Bonney Alias "The Kid," to the Sheriff of Lincoln County.

Lew. Wallace
Governor of New Mexico
Santa Fe, Dec. 15th, 1880.[4]

In view of his past relationship with "the Kid," particularly the cooperative negotiations carried on between them in Lincoln in mid-March, 1879, Governor Wallace may have been reluctant to offer any reward at all for Bonney's capture. It was noticeable that the words "dead or alive," usually inserted in reward notices, were omitted. In any event, the Las Vegas *Gazette* of December 15 complained about the amount of the reward, and suggested that a purse of $5,000 be raised in the area:

This executive act is good as far as it goes, but the amount offered is too small. But perhaps he has done all the law permits. In that case his judgment is good in setting the price on "the Kid's" head at the highest sum allowed. Surely some recompense should be made the brave fellows who take their lives in their hands to hunt down the outlaws. It is no jack rabbit hunt that Garrett and his band, Frank Stewart and his Panhandle boys and the White Oaks rangers are engaged in, but a determined campaign against lawless fellows who have nothing to fear, as the remainder of their lives will be passed behind the bars, to pay the penalty of their crimes if they are ever caught. What should be done by the people of this and neighboring counties is to raise a purse of $5,000 to be paid the men engaged in this campaign providing they drive the desperadoes from our borders.

Late at night on Sunday, December 19, 1880, William Bonney's pal, Tom O'Folliard (described in after years by Susan E. McSween as a "good natured, rollicking, singing fellow"), was shot and killed, and Tom Pickett, one-time Las Vegas police officer, was wounded as they rode horseback into Fort Sumner, accompanied by Bonney, Charlie Bowdre, Dave Rudabaugh and William Wilson. O'Folliard and his companions had chosen a most inopportune time to go to Fort Sumner. The town was filled with officers, including Pat Garrett and Barney Mason, his brother-in-law; Frank Stewart; James H. East; Lon Chambers and others from the Panhandle law enforcement agencies; making up a combined posse of more than twenty men, all willing, some of them even anxious, to pull a trigger that would mean death for the fugitives.

Surprised on the outskirts of Fort Sumner, O'Folliard was shot immediately following a posse command of "hands up," and died within thirty minutes. The identity of the officer who fired the shot that killed O'Folliard was not definitely established. It was believed that at least two members of the posse fired at him at the same time. Friends gave O'Folliard's age as twenty-two, and said that he was from southwest Texas. Officers who viewed the body after death estimated that his height was five feet eight inches, and that he weighed about 175 pounds.

Bonney, Bowdre, Pickett, Rudabaugh and Wilson escaped during the excitement of the O'Folliard shooting. Rudabaugh's horse was shot and killed in the getaway, but he managed to mount Wilson's horse, and the two men rode double out of danger. The outlaws made their way to Wilcox's ranch, where

they obtained food and water, and Rudabaugh commandeered
a horse. From Wilcox's ranch the fugitives rode three miles to
shelter in an abandoned rock house at Stinking Springs (later
Wilcox Springs) in Arroyo Taiban (not far from present-day
Taiban). Four of the outlaws tied their horses outside the
house, but Bonney, probably because he had in mind that he
might try to escape, led his mare into the house with him.

Pat Garrett and Frank Stewart and their possemen, in hot
pursuit of the outlaws, stationed themselves in Arroyo Taiban,
within rifle-range of the rock house. Charlie Bowdre stepped
outside the door for an instant and proved a perfect target. Two
bullets whizzed through the air. Bowdre, the man who, in all
probability, had fired the shot that killed "Buckshot" Roberts
at Blazer's Mill on April 4, 1878; who had been a leader for
the McSween forces in Lincoln during the three-day battle ending July 19, 1878; a man considered by many to be friendly and
fearless, died within a matter of moments. The next day
Bowdre's body was taken to Fort Sumner for burial.

Having penned themselves up in a house in open country
at Stinking Springs, the four remaining outlaws found themselves in a precarious situation. Perhaps the desperadoes had
little choice in selecting a spot in which to make a stand. All
the surrounding country was blanketed with deep snow, making
it impossible to attempt to escape without exposing themselves
to the certainty of being tracked down. Excepting the Wilcox
ranch, now in the posse's control, there was no shelter for man
or beast for many miles in any direction. With a grim and determined posse maintaining a death watch on the outside of the
rock house, the besieged outlaws were fully aware of the hopelessness of their position. They all knew that the posse to a man
would prefer to kill them in the taking, rather than have them
surrender. In the late afternoon of a cloudy day, on December
23, 1880, just two days before Christmas, following the cus-
tomary preliminary parleys, the four outlaws bowed to the inevitable, threw their guns outside the door, and submitted to
arrest.

Several possemen, captained by Pat Garrett, took Bonney,
Rudabaugh, Wilson and Pickett from Stinking Springs to Fort
Sumner, up the Pecos River to Puerto de Luna, Santa Rosa,
through Anton Chico, and on into Las Vegas.

William Bonney had good reason to feel discouraged. Within a space of several days, two of his close friends, Tom O'Folliard and Charlie Bowdre, had been shot and killed and he had been taken prisoner. Although Bonney, riding in Pat Garrett's commandeered carry-all from Fort Sumner to Las Vegas, might have had reason to feel downhearted, he had no particular reason to be alarmed or apprehensive.

As to Tom Pickett, the fourth prisoner, Pat Garrett said in a Las Vegas *Gazette* interview of December 28, 1880, that Pickett had been a member of a gang that had stolen cattle from Pete Maxwell's Fort Sumner ranch, that he did not consider him an important catch. Garrett recommended that Pickett be left in jail until a formal charge of livestock stealing could be filed against him.

The arrest and imprisonment of Bonney, Wilson, Rudabaugh and Pickett was enough of a sensation to cause the Las Vegas *Gazette* to publish a midnight extra on Sunday, December 27, 1880. That such an extra was published and that a *Gazette* reporter interviewed Bonney the next day were facts of unusual interest unearthed by George Fitzpatrick, editor of *New Mexico Magazine,* in the summer of 1954. While browsing among old newspapers, hopeful of finding elusive bits of New Mexicana, Fitzpatrick ran across a copy of the *Gazette* of December 28, 1880, containing the Bonney interview, and a reference to the previous night's extra. The *Gazette* interview of 1880 was published in *New Mexico Magazine* for September, 1954, almost seventy-five years after its original publication, as the feature of George Fitzpatrick's article, "Interview with Billy the Kid." The long-mislaid interview follows:

With its accustomed enterprise, the *Gazette* was the first paper to give the story of the capture of Billy Bonney, who has risen to notoriety under the sobriquet of "the Kid," Billy Wilson, Dave Rudabaugh and Tom Pickett. Just at this time everything of interest about the men is especially interesting, and after damning the party in general and "The Kid," in particular through the columns of this paper we considered it the correct thing to give them a show.

Through the kindness of Sheriff Romero, a representative of the *Gazette* was admitted to the jail yesterday morning.

Mike Cosgrove, the obliging mail contractor, who has met the boys frequently while on business down the Pecos, had just gone in with four large bundles. The doors at the entrance stood open, and a large crowd strained their necks to get a glimpse of the prisoners, who stood in the passageway like children waiting for a Christmas tree distribution. One by one the bundles were unpacked disclosing a good suit of clothes for each man. Mr. Cosgrove remarked that he wanted "to see the boys go away in style."

"Billy the Kid," and Billy Wilson who were shackled together stood patiently up while a blacksmith took off their shackles and bracelets to allow them an opportunity to make a change of clothing. Both prisoners watched the operation which was to set them free for a short while, but Wilson scarcely raised his eyes, and spoke but once or twice to his compadres. Bonney on the other hand, was light and chipper, and was very communicative, laughing, joking and chatting with the bystanders.

"You appear to take it easy," the reporter said.

"Yes! What's the use of looking on the gloomy side of everything. The laugh's on me this time," he said. Then looking about the placita, he asked: "Is the jail at Santa Fe any better than this?"

This seemed to trouble him considerably, for as he explained, "this is a terrible place to put a fellow in." He put the same question to every one who came near him and when he learned that there was nothing better in store for him, he shrugged his shoulders and said something about putting up with what he had to.

He was the attraction of the show, and as he stood there, lightly kicking the toes of his boots on the stone pavement to keep his feet warm, one would scarcely mistrust that he was the hero of "Forty Thieves," romance which this paper has been running in serial form for six weeks or more.

"There was a big crowd gazing at me wasnt there?" he exclaimed, and then smiling continued: "Well, perhaps some of them will think me half a man now; everyone seems to think I was some kind of an animal."

He did look human, indeed, but there was nothing very mannish about him in appearance, for he looked and acted a mere boy. He is about five feet, eight or nine inches tall, slightly built and lithe, weighing about 140; a frank and open countenance, looking like a school boy, with the traditional silky fuzz on his upper lip, clear blue eyes, with a roguish snap about them, light hair and complexion. He is, in all, quite a handsome looking fellow, the only imperfection being two prominent front teeth, slightly protruding like squirrels' teeth, and he has agreeable and winning ways.

A cloud came over his face when he made some allusion to his being made the hero of fabulous yarns, and something like indignation was expressed when he said that our Extra misrepresented him in saying that he called his associates cowards. "I never said any such a thing," he pouted, "I know they ain't cowards."

Billy Wilson was glum and sober, but from underneath his broad-brimmed hat, we saw a face that had a by no means bad look. He is light complexioned, light hair, bluish gray eyes, is a little stouter than Bonney, and far quieter. He appeared ashamed and in not very good spirits.

United States Deputy Marshal J. F. Morrissey of Santa Fe went to Las Vegas, and surveyed the situation. Soon after his arrival, Morrissey learned that Rudabaugh had recently voluntarily confessed to officers that he, and others whom he implicated, had taken part in the stagecoach robbery on August 30, and in the railway train robbery on November 14, 1879. Rudabaugh confirmed the suspicions of officers at the time the robberies had occurred that U. S. mail sacks had been rifled. As a result, a federal warrant was sworn out, charging Rudabaugh with two offenses against the United States, and he automatically became a federal as well as a Territorial prisoner.

Rudabaugh's eleventh-hour confession placed officers of the law in a quandary. They strongly suspected that he had a definite plan in mind when expressing a willingness to plead guilty to complicity on the mail robbery charges. By such strategy he might avoid an immediate trial in San Miguel County on the charge of having murdered Deputy Sheriff Valdez. Assuming he could plead guilty to the federal offenses on the United States side of the court and begin to serve his sentence in a federal penitentiary, time might dull the eagerness of the district attorney to prosecute the murder case; witnesses might die or disappear. In any event, as Rudabaugh saw it, the strategy was worth a trial.

Recalling previous jail breaks in San Miguel County, Deputy Morrissey decided to take Bonney, Rudabaugh and Wilson to Santa Fe for safekeeping, and made arrangements accordingly. Word got about of Morrissey's plans for removing the prisoners from Las Vegas, and a "warlike" mob gathered at the railway depot. Relatives and friends of Antonio Lino Valdez, the deputy sheriff who had been killed by Rudabaugh, protested against his removal from Las Vegas. Some excitement resulted from threats and protests, but in the end, riding in the cab of the engine with a six-shooter in his hand, Morrissey got the prisoners out of town and on the way to Santa Fe without serious opposition. (LVG, January 1, 1881.) On the train the prisoners were guarded by Pat Garrett and Barney Mason, United States Deputy Marshal J. W. Bell, and by James East and Tom Emory.

Shortly before the train left for Santa Fe, the Las Vegas *Gazette* reporter talked to Bonney for a second time that day. To quote from the *Gazette* interview of December 28, 1880, as reproduced in George Fitzpatrick's article:

We saw him again at the depot when the crowd presented a really war like appearance. Standing by the car, out of one of the windows of which he was leaning, he talked freely with us of the whole affair:

"I dont blame you for writing of me as you have. You had to believe others' stories; but then I dont know as anyone would believe anything good of me, anyway," he said. "I really wasnt the leader of any gang. I was for Billy all the time. About that Portales business, I owned the ranch with Charlie Bowdre. I took it up and was holding it because I knew that some time a stage line would run by there, and I wanted to keep it for a station. But I found that there were certain men who wouldnt let me live in the country and so I was going to leave. We had all our grub in the house when they took us in, and we were going to a place about six miles away in the morning to cook it and then light out. I havent stolen any stock. I made my living by gambling, but that was the only way I could live. They wouldnt let me settle down; if they had I wouldnt be here today," and he held up his right arm on which was the bracelet. "Chisum got me into all this trouble and then wouldnt help me out. I went up to Lincoln to stand my trial on the warrant that was out for me, but the Territory took a change of venue to Dona Ana, and I knew I had no show, and so I skinned out. When I was up to White Oaks the last time, I went there to consult with a lawyer, who had sent for me to come up. But I knew I wouldnt stay there either. . . ."

As the train rolled out, he lifted his hat and invited us to call and see him in Santa Fe, calling out *"adios."*

In a matter of hours after leaving Las Vegas, Bonney, Rudabaugh and Wilson were federal prisoners in the Santa Fe County jail in Santa Fe. Rudabaugh was taken to the courthouse and arraigned before a United States Commissioner on December 28, 1880. Pleading guilty to a complaint charging robbery of the mails on August 30 and November 14, 1879, he was remanded to the custody of the United States Marshal and was returned to jail. On January 3, 1881, Rudabaugh was arraigned before Judge Prince, sitting on the United States side of the court. He pleaded guilty to the charge of robbing the United States mails and was sentenced to life imprisonment in a federal penitentiary. Having sentenced Rudabaugh to life imprisonment, Judge Prince entered a stay of the beginning of the sentence until Rudabaugh could be tried in San Miguel County on the Valdez murder charge. On or about March 9, 1881, Rudabaugh was taken to Las Vegas, where he was once again arraigned before Judge Prince, this time sitting as a Territorial judge. When asked to plead guilty or not guilty, Rudabaugh refused, saying that he had no attorney and no money with which to employ one. Thereupon the court ordered the clerk to enter a plea of not guilty on the defendant's behalf, and appointed W. H. Whiteman and Edgar Caypless as defense attorneys.

Whiteman and Caypless filed a motion for change of venue, supported by affidavits alleging that Rudabaugh could not be given a fair and impartial trial in San Miguel County because of the prejudice and hostility against him throughout the county. The court granted the motion and Rudabaugh was tried before a jury in Santa Fe County. The evidence against him was substantial and conclusive. The jury found him guilty of murder in the first degree, and Judge Prince sentenced him to be hanged. Rudabaugh's lawyers appealed to the Supreme Court, seeking a reversal on technical grounds. The Supreme Court affirmed the decision of the lower court (2 N. M. 223).

On Monday, September 19, 1881, six months after Rudabaugh's conviction, Rudabaugh, John J. Webb, convicted of the Kelliher killing, Thomas Duffy and H. S. Wilson, all desperate prisoners, attempted to break out of the San Miguel County jail. Rudabaugh had managed to get hold of a loaded pistol, and took two shots at Florencio Mares, the jailer. Assistant Jailer Herculano Chavez shot and killed the prisoner Duffy, held on a charge of having murdered Thomas Bishop, a clerk in Gillerman's Store at Liberty, New Mexico. (LVG, September 20, 1881.)

Almost two months later, on December 3, 1881, Rudabaugh, Webb, and five other desperadoes—Tom Quinlan, Frank Kearney, Jack Kelly, William Goodman and S. Schroeder—escaped from the jail. The escape was not discovered until seven o'clock the following morning. The Las Vegas *Gazette* of December 4, 1881, said that the escape "had been accomplished through a hole dug in the wall with a pick, case knife and iron poker; the guards claimed they heard no noise during the night."

Tom Quinlan, one of the escaped prisoners, had been in jail only three days. Pat Garrett had arrested him in Santa Fe on a warrant charging him with the murder of a deputy sheriff in Clay County, Texas. Quinlan was being held in jail in Las Vegas awaiting the arrival of a requisition for extradition from the governor of Texas. The Las Vegas *Gazette* of December 14, 1881, published the editorial comment of the nearby Mora County *Pioneer:*

It is strange that no provision was made for the safekeeping of such notorious characters as Rudabaugh and Webb beyond confining them in a place that could be dug through in one night with a case knife, an iron bar and a pick ax. The arrest and conviction of these men has cost the Territory no small sum, and it would seem but right that extra precaution should have been taken to prevent their escape. It is just such breaks as these that induce law abiding citizens to take the law into their own hands, and we have no word of fault to find when a captured murderer is executed by the mob without going through the farce of a trial in the most of our courts, and then taking the chance of escape of the guilty ones, if convicted of their crimes. The Territory must get rid of this class of lawless men and the quickest and cheapest is the one to enforce.

Gov. Lionel A. Sheldon offered a $500 reward for the recapture of Rudabaugh and Webb. The Las Vegas *Gazette* of December 7, 1881, quipped that the two men "thought it best to make tracks when the nights were long and the moon was full." Rudabaugh and Webb, after the jail break, made their way to Texas and Mexico. Webb disappeared. Rudabaugh was reported to have been killed in a brawl with Mexicans in a town in Sonora, Mexico.

William Wilson, confined in the Santa Fe jail on a counterfeiting charge, having the foresight and the required funds, employed as his counsel the Hon. W. T. Thornton, of Catron & Thornton. Attorney Thornton found it possible in many ways to alleviate the tediousness of Wilson's imprisonment. When Wilson was arraigned before Judge Bristol in Santa Fe on January 26, 1881, Thornton waived a preliminary hearing. Wilson's bond was fixed at $5,000 and as he was unable to furnish it, he was remanded to jail. John S. Chisum and William Robert, witnesses for the government, present at the arraignment, were placed under $250 bond each to appear and testify at the next term of court in Mesilla. (LVG, February 26, 1881.)

William Bonney had no money for counsel fees, but he was acquainted with a man occupying a high position in Santa Fe who might possibly come to his rescue. The acquaintance was none other than Lew. Wallace, governor of the Territory. On many occasions Bonney had recalled the meeting between the Governor and himself in Squire Wilson's house in Lincoln on March 13, 1879, and the Governor's talk about the benefits that might be available to criminals under the terms of his amnesty proclamation. No doubt Bonney had also recalled that he had not lived an altogether upright life since his last conversation with the Governor, some eighteen months before. But to counteract any wrong impression the Governor might have received, he had written him a long letter from Fort Sumner on December 12, 1880, denying that he had killed Carlyle at the Greathouse ranch, although frankly admitting that he had been making his living by gambling. Bonney had not received an acknowledgment from the Governor of his letter of December 12. Instead, Wallace had posted a reward of $500 "for the delivery of Bonney alias 'The Kid,' to the Sheriff of Lincoln County."

Many things had happened since his first face-to-face meeting with the Governor. Then the Governor had been anxious to see Bonney. Now, Bonney was anxious to see the Governor. On January 1, 1881, Bonney wrote a modestly-worded note to Lew. Wallace:

Santa Fe
Jan 1st, 1881

Gov. LEW WALLACE

DEAR SIR

I would like to see you for a few moments if you can spare time

Yours Respect.

W. H. BONNEY

Governor Wallace was in the East on January 1, 1881, the date of Bonney's note, and for some days thereafter. Presumably his attention was directed to it upon his return to Santa Fe. In any event, there is nothing to show that Wallace acknowledged the communication or replied to it.

Some sixty days later, on March 2, 1881, at a date when Wallace was in Santa Fe, Bonney wrote a second note, which contained words which might be construed as a threat:

Santa Fe New Mex
March 2d 1881

Gov LEW WALLACE

DEAR SIR:

I wish you would come down to the jail to see me. It will be to your interest to come and see me. I have some letters which date back two years and there are Parties who are very anxious to get them but I shall not dispose of them until I see you. that is if you will come immediately

Yours Respect—

WM H BONNEY

In all probability the Governor, usually a most punctilious correspondent, ignored Bonney's second communication. With time running against him, Bonney became a bit desperate. He wrote still another letter to Wallace on March 4. In the third letter Bonney indicated that he was fast reaching the stage of utter disllusionment. The Governor had not answered his letter of two days before. The Governor had failed to keep the promise he had made two years before. If given the opportunity Bonney would offer to "explain everything." It looked to Bonney as if his attorney, Judge Leonard, had failed him; United States Marshal Sherman was mistreating him. It appeared to Bonney as if they were going to send him up "without giving me any show but they will have a nice time doing it."

Subsequent events demonstrated the strength of Bonney's mental resolution, as expressed in the letter, that he would fight with every available resource against "being sent up." Following is the text of Bonney's third letter, revealing some of his innermost thoughts, as he waited in jail for some evidence that the Governor might interfere, intervene, or come to his rescue:

> Santa Fe in jail
> March 4th 1881

Gov Lew Wallace

Dear sir

I wrote you a little note the day before yesterday but have received no answer I expect you have forgotten what you promised me this month two years ago, but I have not; and I think you had ought to have come and seen me as I have requested you to. I have done everything that I promised you I would and you have done nothing that you promised me I think when you think the matter over you will come down and see me, as I can explain everything to you.

Judge Leonard passed through here on his way east in January and promised to come and see me on his way back but he did not fulfill his Promise. it looks to me like I am getting left in the cold. I am not treated right by Sherman. he lets every stranger that comes to see me through curiousity in to see me, but will not let a single one of my friends in, not even an attorney. I guess they mean to send me up without giving me any show but they will have a nice time doing it. I am not entirely without friends. I shall expect to see you some time today

> Patiently waiting
> I am very truly yours Respect.
> WM. H. BONNEY

No word from Governor Wallace filtered through the bars of Bonney's cell as the result of his letter of March 4, but on March 18, he heard that the San Miguel County grand jury on March 15, 1881, had indicted him for cattle stealing. News of this indictment was of no particular impoftance to Bonney at the time. He was more concerned with the Governor's attitude. He clung hopefully to the thought that he might yet hear from him. Hearing nothing from Wallace, Bonney scrawled a last desperate, pathetic appeal to him on March 27:

Santa Fe New Mexico
March 27 1881

Gov Lew. Wallace

Dear sir
for the last time I ask. Will you keep your promise. I start below tomorrow. send answer by bearer.

Yours Resp.
W. Bonney

Bonney's attempts to interest the Governor in his predicament, extending from January 1 to March 27, a period spanning ninety days, proved futile. Although perhaps Bonney was not aware of it, the Governor was no longer particularly interested in New Mexico's future or in the fate of one of its citizens who had chosen to live outside the law. Wallace's life had been affected by the turn of events in the national political arena. Even as William Bonney laboriously wrote communications asking his help, it was a matter of common knowledge in the Territory and elsewhere that Wallace's days as governor were about to end. James Abram Garfield had been elected President of the United States on November 2, 1880, and had been inaugurated on March 4, 1881. Garfield's election touched the lives of many people in the nation, including Lew. Wallace, and through him, William H. Bonney.

NOTES AND PROFILES

[1] Holdups were common in New Mexico stagecoach days. A typical robbery occurred on April 28, 1877, when highwaymen held up the Southern Express coach carrying United States mail at Alamillo, Socorro County. Numa Raymond, owner of the line promptly paid $510 to the U. S. Collector for the government loss. Governor Axtell offered a reward for capture of the robbers "dead or alive": "Whereas, the coach containing the U. S. mails and express was robbed on April 28, 1877 near Alamillo, in Socorro county; and whereas, it is known that three persons were engaged in that robbery who are believed to be desperate men: Now therefore, I, S. B. Axtell, Governor of the Territory of New Mexico, do hereby offer a reward of $500 for the apprehension of said men to be taken alive if possible and delivered to the Sheriff of Socorro County; but as the emergency is great, all good citizens are hereby requested to aid in their pursuit and capture, and this proclamation will be their warrant to do so, and to use all force necessary to arrest said robbers. Upon proof made to me that they or either or any of them have been arrested, whether dead or alive, I will cause an equal proportion of five hundred dollars to be paid for each one."

[2] Webb appealed from his conviction to the Territorial Supreme Court, and it was affirmed. See *Webb* vs. *Territory of New Mexico,* 2 N. M. 148. On March 4, 1881, Governor Wallace, finding that "extenuating circumstances" existed, commuted Webb's sentence to life imprisonment. Both Webb and Rudabaugh escaped from the San Miguel County jail on December 3, 1881, and were never rearrested.

That New Mexico was a haven for criminals in the early 80's was indicated by an editorial in the Las Vegas *Gazette* on November 10, 1880: "It is a self evident truth that New Mexico has been for years the asylum of desperadoes. Mingled with as good people as are to be found anywhere on the continent is the scum of society from all states. We jostle against murderers, bank robbers, forgers, and other fugitives from justice in the post office and on the platform at the depot."

[3] Patrick Floyd Garrett was born in Chambers County, Alabama, June 5, 1850, reared in Claiborne Parish, Louisiana. Going to Dallas County, Texas, in 1869, he worked for several years as a cowhand on Texas ranches. During the winters of 1875, 1876 and 1877 Garrett hunted buffalo in the Texas Panhandle. In 1878 he went to Tascosa, and from there to Fort Sumner.

On November 7, 1880, Garrett was elected sheriff of Lincoln County. On July 14, 1881, he shot and killed William Bonney ("Billy the Kid") in the Lucien B. Maxwell residence at Fort Sumner. On or about December 1, 1901, Garrett was appointed Collector of Customs at El Paso, Texas.

On February 29, 1908, he was shot and killed on the road leading from his ranch in the Organ Mountains to Las Cruces. Wayne Brazil, who was with Garrett at the time, confessed that he had killed him; pleaded self-defense when tried for murder; and was acquitted by a Doña Ana County jury. Prior and subsequent to the trial, there was talk in southeastern New Mexico that Jim Miller, a professional killer, and not Wayne Brazil, had killed Garrett. Jim Miller was hanged by a mob in Ada, Oklahoma, on April 19, 1909, accused of having murdered A. A. Bobbitt, a farmer and cattle grower of Ada, a short time before. James M. Hervey of Roswell, attorney general of New Mexico at the time of Garrett's death, investigated the circumstances and reached the conclusion that Wayne Brazil had not told the truth about the killing.

In his boyhood, Hervey lived in Lincoln, where he knew Emerson Hough, (1857-1923), then practicing law in Lincoln County, later author of *Heart's Desire, The Covered Wagon, The Story of the Outlaw, North of 36,* and other books.

Concerned about the conflicting stories, Hervey went to Chicago where he urged Hough to offer a $1000 reward to any person willing to talk and tell the truth about the Brazil-Garrett trouble. Hough advised Hervey: "Jimmie, I know that outfit around the Organ mountains. Garrett got killed trying to find out who killed Col. Fountain, and if you don't watch out you will get killed trying to find out who killed Garrett. I advise you to forget about the whole thing." Hervey acted on Hough's advice and returned to Santa Fe and Roswell, although as long as he lived he never lost interest in what he believed to have been an unsolved criminal case.

⁴ Pat Garrett and Frank Stewart called at the Governor's office in Santa Fe to claim the $500 reward offered for Bonney's arrest. Governor Wallace was not in Santa Fe at the time. Acting Governor W. G. Ritch did not believe he had the authority to request the Territorial Auditor to draw a warrant on the Treasury for the amount of the reward. Marcus Brunswick of Las Vegas and W. T. Thornton of Santa Fe, paid Garrett and took an assignment of the claim.

On or about January 13, 1881, Wallace issued the necessary requisition and Brunswick and Thornton got the money on their assignment. The indignation manifested by press and public following Ritch's refusal to expedite payment of the claim redounded to Garrett's benefit. A subscription list was circulated in Las Vegas, under the sponsorship of Marcus Brunswick. Dr. Knauer handed Garrett one hundred dollars in gold for his "heroic action in capturing William Bonney, the dangerous desperado." Among other $100 contributors: Brown, Manzanares Co.; Gross, Blackwell & Co.; Otero, Sellar & Co.; First National Bank; J. A. La Rue. Contributors of $50 included Marcus Brunswick, Charles Ilfeld, and San Miguel National Bank; among $25 contributors: Charles Blanchard, T. Romero & Sons, Lorenzo Lopez, Hilty Bros; among $15 and $10 contributors C. E. Wesche, Isidor Stern, Joe Rosenwald, Hilario Romero, R. G. McDonald, Yetta Kohn, Margarito Romero, J. Graaf & Co., F. E. Herbert & Co., Theo. Rulenbeck, O. L. Houghton, Winfield Scott Moore.

Lew. Wallace in the uniform of a Major-General, taken soon after the close of the Civil War. *Courtesy of the National Archives.*

Photostat of the verdict of the Coroner's Jury which held the inquest on July 15, 1881, on the body of William H. Bonney. The blank space shown on the first page has been attributed to a rat chewing on a corner of the original document.

mi cama en mi cuarto a cosa de media noche
El dia 14 de Julio entró á mi cuarto Pat. F.
Garrett y se sentó en la orilla de mi cama á
platicar conmigo. A poco rato que Garrett
se sentó entró William Bonney y se arrimó
á mi cama con una pistola en la mano y
me preguntó "Who is it? who is it" y entónces
Pat. F. Garrett le tiró dos balazos á dicho
William Bonney y se cayó el dicho Bonney
en un lado de mi fogón y yo salí del cuarto
cuando volví á entrar ya en tres ó cuatro
minutos despues de los balazos estaba muerto dicho Bonney."
El jurado ha hallado el siguiente
dictámen "Nosotros los del jurado uná-
nimamente hallamos que William Bonney ha sido muerto por un balazo en el
pecho y izquierdo en la region del corazon
tirado de una pistola en la mano de Pat.
F. Garrett y nuestro dictámen es que
el hecho de dicho Garrett fué homicidio
justificable y estamos unánimes en
opinion que la gratitud de toda la

Milnor Rudulph, foreman of the Coroner's Jury. *Photograph courtesy of Phillip Sanchez, Mora, New Mexico.*

Charles Bowdre, comrade of Billy the Kid, and his wife.

James J. Dolan

John H. Riley

Photographs of Dolan, Riley, Fritz, Murphy and Tunstall Courtesy of the Old Lincoln County Memorial Commission.

Maj. Emil Fritz

Maj. Lawrence G. Murphy

John H. Tunstall

Deluvina Maxwell. *Courtesy
Mrs. Adelina J. Welborn, Fort
Sumner, New Mexico.*

The Palace of the Governors in Santa Fe as it appeared in 1878. *Photograph by E. Montfort of Albuquerque.*

CHAPTER FOURTEEN

IN OLD MESILLA

O N MARCH 28, 1881, federal prisoners William Bonney and William Wilson were taken from jail in Santa Fe and transported some two hundred fifty miles by Santa Fe railway train to Las Cruces. From the Las Cruces station, the two men were taken in a hack to nearby Mesilla, county seat of Doña Ana County, for arraignment before Judge Bristol,[1] of the Third Judicial District Court.

Bonney was perhaps in a dejected mood as he entered the Mesilla jail. He had counted heavily on receiving help, or some assurance of help, from Governor Wallace before leaving Santa Fe. However, the Governor had seen fit to ignore his pleas for an interview, and Bonney was now reconciled to the fact that he could expect no help from him. Bonney and Wilson had been spirited out of Santa Fe, according to the *New Mexican* of April 2, 1881:

"The Kid," and Billy Wilson have been sent south for trial at La Mesilla. There was some fear on the part of the United States Marshal who had them in charge that if it was known in the south that the two men were coming an effort would be made to lynch them, and to avoid this, their removal from the Santa Fe jail was kept as quiet as possible. Hence no mention has been made before of their departure.

The town of Mesilla, one-time county seat of Doña Ana County, with a population of 2,000 in 1881, is pleasantly situated near the banks of the Rio Grande, in the fertile Mesilla valley. Mesilla and adjacent territory, before becoming the property of the United States, had been considered of great value by the Mexican government, not so much for sentimental reasons, but as a pawn in the bargaining in connection with the Gadsden Purchase.

In 1881, old-time residents still retained vivid recollections of the excitement that had prevailed in the town and valley some twenty years before when Col. John R. Baylor, a colorful, dashing cavalry leader, had occupied Mesilla with Texas troops and had captured nearby Fort Fillmore; and how the Stars and Bars had flown from a flagstaff in the plaza, symbolic of the claimed establishment of the Confederate Territory of Arizona. The completion of the Santa Fe railroad to Las Cruces, with a population in 1881 of 1,500, had spelled ultimate doom for Mesilla, a proud town, reveling in its importance as an overnight stage stop.

Regardless of its fast-waning prestige and importance as a transportation center, Mesilla managed, for the time being, to continue as the county seat of Doña Ana County. The courtroom was located on the Plaza, in an unpretentious one-story adobe building. Hon. Warren Henry Bristol, the judge of the district, made his home in Mesilla. He was fifty-eight years of age on March 30, 1881, when he took his place on the bench to preside over the spring term of court. As of 1881, Judge Bristol had been on the bench in New Mexico nine years. He had held court in Lincoln County on many occasions and was familiar, perhaps too familiar, with the background of the Lincoln County War. In fact, he had been in Tularosa, enroute to Lincoln on April 1, 1878, when word arrived of the killing of Sheriff Brady; and had learned with alarm that the man who had shot the Sheriff had threatened to kill him and District Attorney Rynerson. Despite the threats, Bristol continued on his way toward Lincoln. He stopped at Fort Stanton, where he was given an escort of soldiers into Lincoln.

Judge Bristol's record on the bench had not been entirely free from attack. Political enemies had attempted to oust him from the bench in 1876, according to the Grant County *Herald* and the Las Vegas *Gazette* of February 12, 1876. A petition signed by 250 Grant County citizens had been sent to Washington, demanding his removal. Among other things, the signers of the petition charged that in 1876 Bristol had been guilty of secretly informing attorneys on one side of a lawsuit then pending before him, the decision he proposed to render several days before announcing it from the bench. It was further charged that Bristol had "actually refused in an important murder trial, after the prisoner's arraignment at the first term to grant a continuance, although proper affidavits were filed according to law, for the procurement of absent material witnesses, and had forced the prisoner to trial, which resulted in his conviction and execution;" that in two murder trials "he had refused to allow the defendants the right of compulsory process to procure witnesses in their behalf, or to allow them the full number of peremptory challenges;" that he "frequently consulted and advised with attorneys about causes pending before him, such attorneys being interested in the outcome of the litigation."

Finally it was charged "that Judge Bristol is ignorant of the fundamental rules and principles of law with which every tyro should be conversant; that he is indolent and not disposed to study; that he constantly changes his rulings during the course of important trials, and orders the clerk to expunge the record in order to hide his ignorance, and thus deprives parties litigant of the proper recorded history of causes."

Soon after the petition to oust Bristol had been forwarded to Washington, a meeting of 200 citizens was held in Silver City, at which United States Attorney T. B. Catron appeared and submitted a statement denying the truth of the charges, and generally defending the Judge's conduct. Under Catron's leadership, a counter petition was drawn up and signed by 50 men, which praised Bristol for his honesty, ability and integrity. The signers urged that he be retained on the bench.

Some ten months later, on December 22, 1877, the Grant County *Herald* criticized Judge Bristol severely for alleged shortcomings in conducting court in Silver City. Bristol opened court there on December 10, 1877, according to the *Herald,* and immediately announced that it was his intention to finish all the business of the term within eight days. At the end of six days, Bristol abruptly announced that court was adjourned. The *Herald* commented:

It is almost the universal testimony of those who were in regular attendance throughout the term, that business was crowded through with unseemly haste. In civil cases especially, attorneys were given no time to examine into or even consider important points developed by the pleadings, or arising in the course of argument. The rights of litigants were disregarded; witnesses were thrown into a state of bewilderment by the constant interpolations of the judge, the clerk was compelled to labor into the small hours of each morning in order to complete his record of cases hurriedly concluded, important points of law and questions of evidence were passed upon without being duly weighed, and altogether a feeling of nervous uncertainty was kept up, no less among the spectators than the members of the bar. . . . Is Judge Bristol aware that he is a public servant, and not an autocrat? Has he forgotten that he is paid a salary to do his duty rather than to neglect it?

Regardless of the attacks made upon him from time to time Bristol managed to weather the storms, and March 30, 1881, found him presiding over the United States court, with a most interesting calendar of cases before him for disposition. The clerk of the court called the first case on the docket, *United States of America* vs. *William Wilson,* indicted for having "uttered and passed" counterfeit United States currency, knowing that it was worthless. Wilson was represented in court by William T. Thornton, an able and influential lawyer of Santa Fe. When Wilson's case was called, Thornton pleaded not guilty for his client and asked to have the case go over until the next term of court. There being no objection by the United States attorney, the case was continued as requested.[2]

William H. Bonney was before the court and a jury in Mesilla as the sole remaining available defendant in the case of *United States of America* vs. *Charles Bowdry, Dock Scurlock, Hendry Brown,*[3] *Henry Antrim, alias Kid, John Middleton,*[4] *Stephen Stevens, John Scroggins, George Coe*[5] *and Frederick Wait.* The nine men had been indicted by a United States grand jury for the murder of A. L. ("Buckshot") Roberts at Blazer's Mill on the Mescalero Indian reservation, on April 4, 1878.

Charles Bowdre, the first man named in the indictment, was not present in court for the good and sufficient reason that he was dead. He had been shot and killed at Stinking Springs on December 20, 1880.

Scurlock, the second defendant named in the indictment, had disappeared for a time after the Roberts killing, but had been seen in Lincoln on several occasions during the succeeding year. Not too much was known of Scurlock's background. He was known as "Doc" because a belief prevailed that he had studied medicine for a time before moving to Lincoln County. There was a report also that he had taught a village school briefly in the Ruidoso country.

The Santa Fe *New Mexican* of September 11, 1876, told of a fatality in which Scurlock had been involved. Josiah G. Scurlock and Mike G. Harkins, reputed to be close friends, were examining a self-cocking revolver in the L. G. Murphy & Co. carpenter shop in Lincoln. The pistol was discharged. The ball struck Harkins under the left nipple, killing him instantly. A coroner's jury held an inquest, conducted by Justice of the Peace J. B. Silon, and returned a verdict holding that the killing was accidental. Embalmed under the direction of Dr. Carbello and Dr. McLean the body of Harkins was buried in Lawrence G. Murphy's burial ground in Lincoln. Because no clergyman was available, Major Murphy conducted the funeral service. He read the Church of England commitment prayers at the grave. Harkins had been a member of the Episcopal Church. For some months prior to his death, Harkins had looked after a bunch of John H. Riley's cattle, grazing in the vicinity of Blazer's Mill.

About a year after the Harkins killing, Sheriff Brady arrested Scurlock on the Ruidoso on August 12, 1877, on a warrant charging him with having stolen horses in his possession, with knowledge that they had been stolen. Apparently, no serious attempt had been made to arrest him for the Roberts murder while the opportunity offered. On May 3, 1879, from Fort Stanton, Capt. George A. Purington wrote a letter to Governor Wallace complaining about the slipshod methods of handling Scurlock and Bonney:

"Doc" Scurlock and the "Kid," the two most notorious murderers of the county, have been in custody of the sheriff at Lincoln. The grand jury did not indict them. The sheriff, (who is also a U.S. Deputy Marshal) released them, although he knew there were indictments against them for murder in the U. S. Court, and the warrants for their arrest are said to be in his hands.

Time has demonstrated William H. Bonney, otherwise known as Henry McCarty and Henry Antrim, to be one of the two most enigmatic characters in New Mexico's history, the other shadowy and elusive personality being Manuel Armijo, last governor of New Mexico under Mexican rule. There is no known official record of the date or place of Bonney's birth, or satisfactory evidence as to the name of his father or mother. Little is known of his childhood or boyhood years.

It was left for Robert N. Mullin, one-time resident of Las Vegas, New Mexico, and of El Paso, Texas, now of Chicago, Illinois, to unearth a most important piece of information concerning the marriage of Catherine McCarty, believed to be Bonney's mother, to William H. Antrim, born December 1, 1842, near Anderson, Indiana. Antrim and Catherine McCarty were married by Rev. D. F. McFarland, pastor of the Presbyterian Church in Santa Fe, on March 1, 1873, according to official records in the church parsonage and in the county clerk's office in Santa Fe. The witnesses to the marriage were Henry McCarty and Joseph McCarty, presumed to be sons of the bride; and Harvey Edwards, Mrs. A. R. McFarland and Miss Katie McFarland.

The discovery of the record of the marriage effectually disposed of the claim, accepted without challenge for many years, that Antrim and Mrs. McCarty had been married some place in Kansas. The Antrims and the two McCarty boys went from Santa Fe to Silver City. Here the boys were known as Henry and Joe Antrim. Catherine McCarty Antrim died on September 13, 1875. Two years later, one Henry Antrim committed a serious crime, according to an article published in the Grant County *Herald* on September 1, 1877, which the *Herald* had copied from the Tucson *Citizen:*

Henry Antrim shot F. P. Cahill near Camp Grant on the 17th inst., and the latter died on the 18th. Cahill made a statement before death to the effect that he had some trouble with Antrim during which the shooting was done. Bad names were applied to each other. Deceased has a sister—Margaret Flanagan in Cambridge, Mass., and another—Kate Conlon in San Francisco. He was born in Galway, Ireland, and was aged about 32. The coroner's jury found that the shooting "was criminal and unjustifiable, and that Henry

Antrim, alias Kid, is guilty thereof." The inquest was held by M. L. Wood, J. P., and the jurors were M. McDowell, Geo. Teague, T. McClery, B. E. Norton, Jas. L. Hunt and T. H. Smith.

Fort Grant, scene of the Cahill murder, was in Pima County, Arizona, bounded on the east by Grant County, New Mexico. The "Henry Antrim, alias Kid," accused of unjustifiable murder by a coroner's jury, ran away from Fort Grant and went to Georgetown, then a thriving silver-mining camp, some twenty miles west of Silver City. On Georgetown's outskirts, Henry Antrim, traveling on foot, met Sigmund Lindauer (1851-1935), pioneer merchant of Georgetown and Silver City, a resident of Grant County since May 23, 1872. The travelers recognized each other and stopped to pass the time of day. Antrim cautiously asked: "Is the way clear to Georgetown?" Upon being assured that it was, Antrim told Sigmund Lindauer that he was going there to see his brother, and walked on.

There was no question in Lindauer's mind, questioning in later years disclosed, that Antrim and McCarty were one and the same identical person. (In 1908, Sigmund Lindauer was in Denver, attending the Democratic national convention which nominated William Jennings Bryan for the Presidency. While in the Albany Hotel in Denver, Lindauer met and positively identified Joseph McCarty, otherwise known as Joseph Antrim, brother of William H. McCarty, alias Antrim, alias Bonney, whom Lindauer had known as a boy in Silver City. Sigmund Lindauer and Joe McCarty talked about old times in Georgetown and Silver City. When Lindauer asked McCarty what he was doing in Denver, McCarty told him that he had a job as runner for a poker game in a gambling house.)

After his arrival from Fort Grant, Henry Antrim remained in and about Georgetown for several weeks, during which time he became acquainted with John P. Kinney, destined later to fight against him in Lincoln. Henry Antrim emerged from his Georgetown hideout as William H. Bonney. An alias was not at all uncommon at the time. Southwestern New Mexico, with its vast cattle ranches, its mining camps that sprang up almost overnight, and its boomtown life in general, adhered to the code of the day: "Never dig too deeply into another man's past, never try to find out where he came from, or ask him what his

name was before he came." On one occasion, a New Mexican'
curiosity prompted him to inquire into a newcomer's back
ground. The rather vague and indefinite answer : "I was borne(
in a kivered wagon a-comin from Tennessee to New Mexico
and I bin here ever sence."

Why McCarty-Antrim assumed the name "Bonney" is no
known for certain. Perhaps his mother's name was Bonney, a
some have surmised. The question of Antrim's identity wa
bothersome, beginning with the time he assumed the name o
Bonney. As a result, any clue, regardless of how slight, whicl
might help confirm a supposition, is of some value. Such a clu·
was provided in the Grant County *Herald* of August 3, 1878
which ran an eight-word squib in its "Local News" column
which read : " 'Kid' Antrim's real name is W. H. McCarty."

Bonney, after leaving Georgetown in Grant County, mad·
his way across the Territory to the Lincoln country, where h
got to know many people, among them Dick Brewer, Georg·
W. Coe, John H. Tunstall, the McSweens, and others on the re
spectable side of the law, as well as Jesse Evans, Doc Scurlock
Charles Bowdre, Tom O'Folliard, and others, who at time
would have been pleased if the courts had varied the statute
somewhat to suit the peculiar circumstances in which the
found themselves.

Only a skeleton record of the legal difficulties in which Wil
liam H. Bonney was involved in Mesilla is available. The no·
tations concerning his day-to-day appearances are set forth i
Books "A" and "B" of the records of Third Judicial Distric
of the Territory of New Mexico, now filed away in Santa F·
in the office of the Clerk of the United States District Court fo
the District of New Mexico. From such records it appears tha
on March 30, 1881, with the Hon. Warren H. Bristol presidin
as United States judge, the clerk called case No. 411, *Unite*
States of America vs. *Charles Bowdry, et al.* This was the cas·
in which each of the defendants had been indicted for the mur
der of "one Roberts, against whom they had shot bullets, wil
fully, deliberately and in a premeditated manner, causing hi
death, on the Mescalero Indian reservation, then and there be
ing property belonging to the United States of America."

On the official record for the day it was written: "The de·
fendant Henry Antrim alias 'Kid,' appeared in his own prope

erson, and it appearing to the court that he has no attorney and
o means to employ one, the court now appoints Ira E. Leon-
rd, Esq., an attorney of this court to defend said defendants,
nd the said Leonard being in court accepted said appoint-
ent." Thereupon the indictment was read to Antrim by
Jnited States Attorney Sidney M. Barnes, appointed to that
ffice on or about December 20, 1878, as successor to Thomas
. Catron of Santa Fe. The defendant Antrim was given until
ie next day to consult with his court-appointed attorney and to
lead to the indictment. Little was known of Barnes, the new
Jnited States district attorney. Soon after his appointment, the
,as Vegas *Gazette* commented:

Col. S. M. Barnes has been appointed United States District
ttorney for New Mexico. He is a resident of Little Rock, Arkansas.
'ol. Barnes may be all hunkydory; but as a general rule, the pre-
umption is against Arkansas Republicans.

The Grant County *Herald* of January 18, 1879, said:

Col. Barnes, of Little Rock, Arkansas, appointed U. S. Attorney
or New Mexico, is said to be an able lawyer. He is six feet high,
erging on sixty years, and intends to try the climate of this Territory
or his health.[6]

William H. Bonney and his attorney, Leonard, lived in en-
rely different worlds. Bonney had lived a life of crime. Judge
,eonard was a man of high ideals, inclined to the religious life.
On February 15, 1880, only a year before he was in court
efending Bonney in Mesilla, Leonard had been converted to
hristianity by Evangelist Dwight Moody. While in St. Louis
eceiving medical treatment, Judge Leonard attended Moody's
evival meetings every night for two weeks. He made a public
rofession of faith, in the course of which he exhibited a small
ook to the audience. This prompted Mr. Moody to ask:
What is that priceless jewel? Hold it up." Leonard then said:
It is the New Testament; and I want to say I have read it
hrough twice within the last two weeks, and it seems to me I
ever knew anything about it before. Why, it scintillates with
eauty; it is a sparkling jewel. Every time I open it there is

something that strikes my heart, that gives me joy and satisfac
tion, comfort and peace." Mr. Moody then told the audience
"Let us pray that when Judge Leonard goes back to New Mex
ico that he may go to preaching. I would like to have the Judge
preach the Gospel."[7] (LVG, February 24, 1880, based on re
port in St. Louis Globe *Democrat.*)

On March 31, 1881, Judge Leonard, on behalf of his client
Bonney, pleaded not guilty to the Roberts murder, and the
court recessed until the following day. On April 5, 1881, Case
No. 411 was again before the court. Antrim was allowed to
withdraw the plea of not guilty entered on March 31, and inter
pose a plea to the jurisdiction. Judge Leonard thereupon filed
a pleading alleging that the court had no jurisdiction be
cause the crime, if any, had been committed on property known
as Blazer's Mill, which was not on the Mescalero Indian
reservation.

On April 6, 1881, Judge Bristol sustained Leonard's plea to
the jurisdiction and signed an order which gave Antrim and his
co-defendants their freedom from further prosecution in the
Roberts case in the United States court. The Santa Fe *New
Mexican* was disappointed because Judge Bristol had sustained
the plea to the jurisdiction of the court. On April 10, the *New
Mexican* commented editorially:

It is hard to see what difference it makes either to the country
or the prisoner whether he is hung by the Territory or the federal
government. All the indictments are for murder. Legal technicalities
ought not to be allowed to stand between the Kid's neck and hemp.

On April 13, the *New Mexican* said:

At last accounts from Mesilla the question as to the jurisdiction
of the United States in the case of Billy the Kid was being discussed
by counsel, the attorneys for the defense holding that the United
States had no right to punish the prisoner for the murder of Roberts.
In such a case the accused must be turned over to the Territorial
authorities for trial. The discussion has no particular bearing as far
as the outsider can see upon the fate of the prisoner, as the Terri
torial Court is as apt to convict him as the United States court, and
even if it should not find him guilty in the case it is almost certain

o do so in one or two others, which it has against him, so that con-
iction stares the Kid in the face at every turn.

In sustaining Judge Leonard's plea to the jurisdiction, in
Case No. 411, Judge Bristol signed a carefully prepared order,
quashing the indictment, and allowing Antrim "to go hence
without day," but providing that the United States Marshal
hould surrender him to the Sheriff of Doña Ana County.

William H. Bonney, alias Antrim, alias Kid, was free from
prosecution for the time being in the Roberts case, but faced
immediate trial before Judge Bristol in the case of the *Territory of New Mexico* vs. *John Middleton, Hendry Brown, William Bonney, alias Kid, alias William Antrim*. The indictment,
on which he was to stand trial, charged that the defendants, and
each of them "had unlawfully, feloniously and with malice
aforethought," shot bullets into William Brady, at Lincoln, on
April 1, 1878, thereby causing his death. The Brady case had
been on the docket for a long time. The indictment had been
returned by the grand jury of Lincoln County on April 18,
1878. One year later, on April 22, 1879, Judge Bristol had
granted District Attorney Rynerson's motion for a change of
venue, and the case had been removed to Doña Ana County.

William Bonney was in a serious predicament, obliged to go
to trial in a hostile atmosphere, before a judge with an intimate
knowledge of his reputation in Lincoln County, a Dolan-Riley
partisan, who had been a strong personal friend of Sheriff
Brady in his lifetime. The case would be tried to a jury of
twelve men, every one a stranger to Bonney. Could Judge Bristol try the case fairly and impartially? Bonney knew that he
could not expect leniency or mercy. He was totally unprepared
for trial. Even if the court would consent to delay the trial a
few days to allow him time to summon witnesses, Bonney would
have been put to trumps to furnish his lawyers with the name of
even one witness who would or could testify on his behalf.

Although he had represented Bonney in the early stages of
the case, Judge Leonard did not represent him in the trial of the
Brady case at Mesilla. The court appointed Attorneys John D.
Bail[8] and A. J. Fountain[9] to defend him. On April 8, 1881, the
clerk of the court of the Third Judicial District for the Territory of New Mexico called the case of the *Territory* vs. *Mid-*

dleton, Brown and Bonney, charged with the murder of Sheri
Brady. Only one defendant, William H. Bonney, was preser
in the courtroom.

The jury was empanelled and sworn, twelve good men an
true, all Spanish-Americans. The jury: Refugio Bernal, Jesu
Telles, Felipe Lopez, Merced Lucero, Pedro Serna, Pedr
Martinez, Crescensio Bustillos, Luis Sedillo, Pedro Onopc
Jesus Silva, Hilario Moreno and Benito Montoya. The testi
mony and all proceedings in court were interpreted, as require
by the necessities of the occasion, from English into Spanisł
and from Spanish into English.

William L. Rynerson, who had fought the McSween crow
which included the defendant Bonney, was no longer distric
attorney. Simon B. Newcomb had succeeded him and prose
cuted the case for the Territory[10] offering the testimony of thre
principal witnesses, Isaac Ellis, B. F. Baca and J. B. Mai
thews,[11] all to the same effect, that the defendant, Bonney, Joh
Middleton and Hendry Brown, had fired at Sheriff Brady o
April 1, 1878, from behind a wall while the Sheriff walke
down the street in Lincoln; that bullets fired from the vicinit
of the ambuscade had caused his death. Whether or not Bonne
took the witness stand is an open question, although it was per
missible at the time in New Mexico for a defendant in a crim
inal case to testify in his own behalf. (*Territory* vs. *Romin*
2 N. M. 114.)

On April 9, 1881, the second day of the trial, Bonney's cas
was ready to be submitted to the jury. Both Bail and Fountai
were capable and resourceful lawyers. Their theory of the cas
was submitted to Judge Bristol in the following requeste
instructions:

1. Under the evidence the jury must either find the defendant guilt
of murder in the 1st degree or acquit him.
2nd. The jury will not be justified in finding the defendant guilty o
murder in the first degree unless they are satisfied from the evidenc
to the exclusion of all reasonable doubt, that the defendant actuall
fired the shot that caused the death of the deceased Brady, and tha
such shot was fired by the defendant with a premeditated design t
effect the death of the deceased, or that the defendant was presen

nd actually assisted in firing the fatal shot or shots that caused the
eath of the deceased, and that he was present and in a position
o render such assistance and actually rendered such assistance from
premeditated design to effect the death of the deceased.

rd. If the jury are satisfied from the evidence to the exclusion of
ll reasonable doubt that the defendant was present at the time of
he firing of the shot or shots that caused the death of the deceased
Brady, yet, before they will be justified in finding the defendant
uilty, they must be further satisfied from the evidence and the evi-
lence alone, to the exclusion of all reasonable doubt, that the de-
endant either fired the shots that killed the deceased, or some of
hem, or that he assisted in firing said shot or shots, and that he fired
aid shot or shots, or assisted in firing the same, or assisted the parties
vho fired the same either by his advice, encouragement or procure-
nent or command from a premeditated design to effect the death of
Brady. If the jury entertain any reasonable doubt upon any of these
oints they must find a verdict of acquittal.

Judge Bristol refused to give the requested instructions, but
rave his own handwritten instructions, on nine pages of fools-
ap, under which the jury might find Bonney guilty of murder
n the first, second or third degree, or find him not guilty. Bris-
ol made a preliminary statement of the case to the jury:

GENTLEMEN OF THE JURY: The defendant in this case, William
Bonney, alias Kid, alias William Antrim, is charged in and by the
ndictment against him with having committed in connection with
ertain other persons the crime of murder in the county of Lincoln,
n the Third Judicial District of the Territory of New Mexico in
he month of April 1878, by then and there unlawfully killing one
William Brady, by inflicting upon his body certain fatal gunshot
vounds from a premeditated design to effect his death. The case is
ere for trial by a change of venue from the said county of Lincoln.

Having heard the testimony of the witnesses, arguments of
counsel, and the instructions of the court, the jury on April 9,
881, retired to deliberate on its verdict, "accompanied by two
worn officers." The court record recited: "After due delibera-
ion the said jury returned into court and upon their oaths

found as follows: 'We the jury do find the defendant guilty of murder in the first degree and do assess his punishment at death.'"[12]

For the first time in his life of crime and violence, William Bonney had been tried and convicted. He was fully aware of the penalty, and expected no mercy from the trial judge. On April 13, at 5 P.M., Bonney was arraigned before Judge Bristol to be sentenced. When asked if he had anything to say why sentence should not be passed upon him, Bonney replied, according to the record, that he had nothing to say. The court thereupon sentenced him to die on Friday, May 13, 1881, between 9 A.M. and 3 P.M., in Lincoln County.

The judgment of the court read that "the defendant should be confined in prison in said county of Lincoln, by the Sheriff of said county until on Friday the 13th day of May in the year of Our Lord Eighteen Hundred and Eighty one, that on the day aforesaid between the hours of nine of the clock in the forenoon and three of the clock in the afternoon, he the said William Bonney, alias Kid, alias William Antrim, be taken from such prison to some suitable and convenient place of execution within said county of Lincoln, by the Sheriff of such county and that then and there, on that day and between the aforesaid hours thereof, by the sheriff of said county of Lincoln, he, the said William Bonney, alias Kid, alias William Antrim, be hanged by the neck until his body be dead."

On April 15, two days after Bonney had been convicted and sentenced to die, the Santa Fe *New Mexican* predicted:

When the Kid's execution comes off it will probably attract more people than any similar event that ever occurred in the Territory. Certainly this consideration ought to flatter and console the young gentleman.

On April 15, a reporter for the Mesilla *News* interviewed Bonney. The interview was brief, being interrupted by the sheriff after a few moments of conversation. At first reluctant to say anything at all, Bonney finally said a few words. The *News* of April 16 published the interview:

Well I had intended at one time not to say a word in my own

behalf because persons would say, "Oh he lied." Newman, editor of the *Semi-Weekly,* gave me a rough deal; he created prejudice against me, and is trying to incite a mob to lynch me. He sent me a paper which showed it; I think it a dirty mean advantage to take of me, considering my situation and knowing I could not defend myself by word or act. But I suppose he thought he would give me a kick down hill. Newman came to see me the other day. I refused to talk to him or tell him anything. But I believe the *News* is always willing to give its readers both sides of a question. If mob law is going to rule, better dismiss judge and sheriff and let all take chances alike. I expect to be lynched in going to Lincoln. Advise persons never to engage in killing.

In answer to a question as to whether or not he expected a pardon, Bonney told the *News* reporter:

Considering the active part Governor Wallace took on our side and the friendly relations that existed between him and me, and the promise he made me, I think he ought to pardon me. Don't know that he will do it. When I was arrested for that murder he let me out and gave me the freedom of the town, and let me go about with my arms. When I got ready to leave Lincoln in June, 1879, I left. I think it hard that I should be the only one to suffer the extreme penalty of the law.

While confined in the Mesilla jail William Bonney had odds and ends of business to look after. He was particularly anxious to dispose of a controversy over ownership of a horse, which had troubled him since his arrest at Stinking Springs on December 23, 1880. On that occasion, the arresting posse had found Bonney's mare inside the rock house occupied by Bonney, Rudabaugh, Pickett and Wilson. Frank Stewart, a member of the posse, took Bonney's mare to Las Vegas and presented her as a gift to Mrs. Minnie Moore, wife of Winfield Scott Moore, proprietor of the Adobe Hotel at Las Vegas Hot Springs. Stewart reported in Las Vegas that Bonney had given him the mare. Mrs. Moore renamed it "Kid Stewart Moore," according to the Las Vegas *Gazette,* January 7, 1881. Bonney had a different understanding of the transaction. The *Gazette* of March 12, 1881, reported:

Edgar Caypless Esq. has brought a suit of replevin against W. Scott Moore for the little bay mare belonging to the "Kid." It is claimed the "Kid" had given the mare to Frank Stewart, and the latter had made a present of it to Mrs. Moore. The "Kid" on reaching Santa Fe and desiring legal services, sold the mare to Caypless, who now brings an action for her possession. The suit will be warmly contested.

On December 23, 1880, when Bonney, Rudabaugh, Wilson and Pickett were surrounded by Pat Garrett and other officers at Stinking Springs, Garrett shot and killed a horse belonging to one of the outlaws. When shot, the horse fell, and sprawled out on all fours, blocking the doorway to the house in which the four men were confined. In an interview with Bonney, published in the Las Vegas *Gazette* of December 28, 1880 (the subject of an article written by Editor George Fitzpatrick for the September, 1954, *New Mexico Magazine*), Bonney told of the dead horse incident:

If it had not been for the dead horse in the doorway I wouldn't be here in Las Vegas. I would have ridden out on my bay mare and taken my chances of escaping. But I couldn't ride over that for she would have jumped back and I would have got it in the head.

Evidently much concerned about the fate of his mare, William Bonney wrote a rather remarkable letter from his jail cell in Mesilla on April 15, 1881, to Attorney Caypless, in Santa Fe. Bonney's letter to Caypless, strong evidence of Bonney's courage in extremity and of his willingness to do the right thing under the circumstances, is as follows:

I would have written before this but could get no paper. My United States case was thrown out of court and I was rushed to trial on my Territorial charge. Was convicted of murder in the first degree and am to be hanged on the 13th day of May. Mr. A. J. Fountain was appointed to defend me and has done the best he could for me. He is willing to carry the case further if I can raise the money to bear his expense. The mare is about all I can depend on at present, so hope you will settle the case right away and give him the money you get for her. If you do not settle the matter with Scott Moore

and have to go to court about it, either give him the mare or sell
her at auction and give him the money. Please do as he wishes in
the matter. I know you will do the best you can for me in this. I shall
be taken to Lincoln tomorrow. Please write and direct care of Garrett, sheriff. Excuse bad writing. I have my handcuffs on. I remain
as ever,

> Yours respectfully,
> W. H. Bonney[13]

Now that Judge Bristol had condemned William Bonney to
die, the court's officers took the necessary preliminary steps to
see that the sentence was duly executed. Doña Ana County's
Sheriff James W. Southwick gave a deputy sheriff's commission to Robert Olinger on April 15, 1881, and then delivered
the prisoner to him for safekeeping. Southwick's commission
to Olinger, somewhat deficient from a schoolteacher's standpoint, was as follows:

TERRITORY OF NE MEX.   COUNTY OF DONA ANA:

TO ALL WHOM IT MAY CONCERN: BE IT KNOWN THAT I HAVE THIS
DAY APPOINTED ROBERT OLINGER A DEBUTY SHERIFF IN AND FOR
THE COUNTY OF DONA ANA AND HE IS HEREBY CHARGED WITH
THE SPECIAL TRUST OF TAKING WILLIAM BONY ALIAS THE KID
ELIAS HENRY ANTRIM FROM THE COUNTY SEAT OF DONA ANA CO.
AND DELIVERING HIM TO THE SHERIFF OF LINCON COUNTY WITH
FULL POWER AND AUTHORITY TO SUMMONS POSSY OR TO DO ANY AND
ALL THINGS NECISSARY FOR THE SAFE DELIVERY OF SAID PRISONER
IN THE HANDS OF THE ABOVE NAMED AUTHORITY.

The court having fixed May 13 as the date and Lincoln as
the place for the hanging, there was no reason for detaining
William Bonney in Mesilla. On April 15, 1881, he was taken
from the Doña Ana County jail, seated in a conveyance drawn
by four horses, and started on the journey to Lincoln, a distance
of 150 miles. Elaborate precautions had been taken to guard
against any possibility of escape. Special Deputy Olinger was
in charge of the party of seven selected to guard the prisoner.
Among Olinger's fellow officers were J. B. Matthews, chief
deputy of the posse which killed Tunstall, and who had narrowly escaped death on April 1, 1878, while walking with

Sheriff Brady in Lincoln; and John Kinney, who had fought on Sheriff Peppin's side in the McSween round up in mid-July, 1878.

Newman's *Semi-Weekly,* of April 17, described Bonney's departure:

On Saturday night about 10 o'clock Deputy U. S. Marshal Robt. Ollinger with Deputy Sheriff David Woods and a posse of five men (Tom Williams, Billy Mathews, John Kinney, D. M. Reade and W. A. Lockhart) started for Lincoln with Henry Antrim alias the Kid. The fact that they intended to leave at that time had been purposely concealed and the report circulated that they would not leave before the middle of the week in order to avoid any possibility of trouble, it having been rumored that the Kid's band would attempt a rescue. They stopped in front of the Semi-Weekly office while we talked to them, and we handed the Kid an addressed envelope and some paper and he said he would write us some things he wanted to make public. He appeared quite cheerful and remarked that he wanted to stay with the boys until their whiskey gave out, anyway. Said he was sure his guard would not hurt him unless a rescue should be attempted and he was certain that would not be done unless perhaps "those fellows over at White Oaks come out to take me," meaning to kill him. It was, he said, about a stand-off whether he was hanged or killed in the wagon. The Mesilla jail was the worst place he had ever struck. The sheriff wanted him to say something good about it when he left but he had not done so. He wanted to say something about John Chisum and it was some satisfaction to him to know that some men would be punished after he had been hung. He was handcuffed and shackled and chained to the back seat of the ambulance. Kinney sat beside him; Olinger on seat facing him. Mathews faced Kinney; Lockhart driving, and Reade, Woods and Williams riding along on horseback on each side and armed to the teeth, and any one who knows these men of whom it was composed will admit that a rescue would be a hazardous undertaking. Kid was informed that if any trouble should occur he would be shot first and the attacking party attended to afterwards.

NOTES AND PROFILES

[1] Born in Stafford, Genessee County, New York, March 19, 1823, Warren H. Bristol died in Deming, New Mexico, on January 12, 1890. He attended Yates Academy, the Lima Seminary and the Wilson Collegiate Institute in western New York, studied law, taught school, went to St. Paul and Redwing, Minnesota, practicing law in both places.

Selected district attorney and then probate judge of Goodhue County, Bristol later served two terms in the Minnesota House and Senate. President Grant appointed him an associate justice of the Supreme Court and Ex-officio district judge of New Mexico, in which position he served from June 6, 1872, until December 31, 1885. Bristol's district comprised Grant, Doña Ana and Lincoln counties. While in Redwing, Minnesota, Mesilla and Deming, New Mexico, Bristol officiated as a vestryman in the Episcopal Church.

The work of a trial judge in New Mexico at the time was anything but a sinecure. Throughout his term of service in the Territory, Bristol suffered from attacks by lawyers and newspaper editors holding contrary political opinions. Bristol's place in New Mexico is secure not only because it was his fate to be on the bench during the exciting months of the Lincoln County War, but because he was the trial judge in the famous case of the *Territory of New Mexico* vs. *William Bonney, alias Antrim, alias Kid, et al*, on the indictment charging the defendants with the murder of Sheriff William Brady, in Lincoln, on April 1, 1878.

[2] Like many another criminal proceeding in New Mexico in the 70's and 80's, William Wilson's case had a bizarre ending. Granted a continuance by Judge Bristol in Mesilla on March 30, 1881, Wilson was returned to jail in Santa Fe. He was subsequently tried and convicted by a jury in Judge L. Bradford Prince's court. Following time-honored custom, Wilson "escaped" from jail in Santa Fe, and went to Texas, where he was known as D. L. Anderson. He was married, reared two children, became an upright and respected citizen.

More than ten years after Wilson's escape from jail in Santa Fe, his true identity was discovered. For a time it appeared as if he would be compelled to serve out his prison sentence in New Mexico. However, W. T. Thornton, who had been his attorney, was now governor of New Mexico. Governor Thornton filed a petition with the Attorney General of the United States asking him to recommend a presidential pardon. Thornton supplied the Attorney General with the background of the case: Wilson had been a cowboy in Texas. When about eighteen years old, he went to White Oaks, where he bought a livery stable. Several months later, he sold the stable to a man named West, who paid him in several $100 greenbacks, which he took to Dolan's store in Lincoln, cashing one of them. Later Wilson passed some of the bills on Jose Montano and others. It was soon discovered that the bills were counterfeit. Wilson hid out in the Pecos River country, joining William Bonney.

Governor Thornton submitted some twenty-five letters to the Attorney General on Wilson's behalf, including letters from Judge L. Bradford Prince, the trial judge and Ex-officio Chief Justice of the Supreme Court of the Territory, James J. Dolan, of Lincoln, and Deputy Sheriff Pat Garrett, of Doña Ana County. Garrett's letter was written from Las Cruces on May 24, 1896. Wilson received a presidential pardon dated July 24, 1896.

[3] Considerable confusion and speculation have surrounded attempts to identify Hendry Brown (sometimes called Henry Brown), reported to have been with William Bonney at the time Sheriff Brady was killed on April 1, 1878. Some writers have claimed that *the* Hendry Brown who was Bonney's companion went to Caldwell, Kansas, after the Brady killing, and became town marshal there; that while marshal he helped two men rob a bank in Medicine Lodge, Kansas; and was captured and hanged to a cottonwood tree.

The Lincoln County *Leader* of November 11, 1882, contributed this item: "James Bean, a noted Texas desperado who was captured in that state not long since after a desperate fight and taken to Kansas, for killing City Marshal Brown of Caldwell, last summer, has died in jail at Wellington. He had twelve shots in his body, including two Winchester balls. The post mortem examination showed his death directly due to a No. 2 shot which took him in the forehead, entering the brain, and others in the body; he lived for thirty days and talked of his recovery up to within twenty-four hours of his death. He had been a desperate man, having been engaged in deeds of atrocity since he was twenty years old, and carried besides the wounds he received at his capture, marks of ten other balls and many scars."

On May 17, 1884, the *Leader* ran an article clipped from the Las Vegas *Optic*: "Readers of the daily papers are familiar with the facts of the attempted bank robbery at Medicine Lodge, Kansas, and the killing of the president and cashier of the institution by four men whose names were Henry N. Brown, Marshal of Caldwell, Kansas, Ben Wheeler, his assistant, Wm. Smith, and a man by the name of Wesley, both cowboys. The citizens gave pursuit, and the quartette of robbers were caught and lynched. The man Brown had been married but six weeks. He was a native of Rolla, Phelps county, Mo., and was a member of Billy the Kid's gang in the Lincoln County War. . . . While acting as City Marshal of Caldwell, he killed two men. Better for the world that he has gone."

The late Lucius Dills, long-time resident of Roswell, who made his home in Lincoln County in the early 80's, gave the present writer, on February 15, 1940, his written appraisal of Bonney, in which he referred to Hendry Brown. Lucius Dills claimed: That Hendry Brown left Bonney's crowd in 1879, and went to Tascosa, Texas, that he served for some months as a deputy under Cape B. Willingham, the first sheriff of Oldham County, Texas, after its organization in 1880; that Brown served as a deputy under Sheriff Fred Higgins of Chaves County, New Mexico, during the years 1907 and 1908.

To quote Dills: "Brown was personally known to a number of the old residents, both in Roswell and in Old Lincoln County. He knew every dim trail in the entire section and made an efficient officer. At the end of Higgins' term as sheriff, Hendry Brown faded from the picture, and left the country as quietly as he had entered it."

4 Writing to his parents in London on November 29, 1877, John H. Tunstall described John Middleton as follows: "Middleton is about the most desperate looking man I ever set eyes on (& that is not saying a little.) I could fancy him doing anything ruffianly that I ever heard of, that is from his appearance, but he is as mild & composed as any man can be, but his arms are never out of his reach."

Although Middleton was associated with the McSween faction, he did not measure up as a fighting man in the same category with Dick Brewer, Charles Bowdre or William Bonney. Middleton was indicted for the murder of Sheriff Brady on April 1, and of "Buckshot" Roberts on April 4, 1878. After the shooting at Blazer's Mill, in which Roberts was killed, Middleton "cleared out" of Lincoln County, and went to Fort Sumner. After remaining there a short time he went to Sun City, Barber County, Kansas, where he had a small grocery store.

Later Middleton gave his post office addresses as Mule Creek, Spring Ranch, Painted Post, Rancho Grande, Evansville, and other places in Kansas. While living in Kansas, Middleton corresponded regularly for three years with J. P. Tunstall in London. In letter after letter, Middleton, posing as a close friend of John H. Tunstall, tried, without apparent success, to wheedle various sums of money out of the elder Tunstall.

5 George Washington Coe, an associate on occasion of William H. Bonney, was born in Brighton, Washington County, Iowa, December 13, 1856, came to the Ruidoso Valley, Lincoln County, on March 18, 1876. Coe was not in any sense of the word an outlaw. Coe vouched for the good citizenship of Dick Brewer, a neighboring rancher, killed at Blazer's Mill on April 5, 1878. Both Coe and Brewer became involved in the Lincoln County War in order to defend their lives and property.

After the trouble at Blazer's Mill, Coe went to San Juan County, New Mexico, where outlaws were also on the loose. Remaining in San Juan County until things quieted down in Lincoln County, he returned there in 1881. Enroute to Lincoln, Coe stopped in Santa Fe and obtained a letter from Governor Wallace certifying that he came within the terms of his amnesty proclamation. In 1933 George W. Coe told his life story to Nan Hilary Harrison, and it was published in 1934 by Houghton, Mifflin Co., with the title, *Frontier Fighter, Autobiography of George W. Coe.*

6 Sidney M. Barnes was born in Estill County, Kentucky, on May 10, 1821, and was admitted to the Kentucky bar at the age of twenty-one. At twenty-five he was elected to the Kentucky State Legislature.

Barnes was commissioned a colonel at the outbreak of the Civil War and recruited and organized a regiment of twelve hundred men which became known as the Eighth Kentucky Infantry. He participated in many of the battles of the Cumberland, including Chickamauga and Lookout Mountain, in each of which he commanded a brigade. His regiment was given credit for first planting the Union flag on Lookout Mountain.

In 1868 Barnes was the Republican nominee for governor of Kentucky. In February, 1871, he moved from Kentucky to Little Rock, Arkansas, where he practiced law for a number of years. In 1874 he was a member of the Convention that helped draft the Constitution of the State of Arkansas. In 1879 he was appointed United States district attorney, by President Hayes, for the Territory of New Mexico. Late in his life Barnes moved from Arkansas to Carthage, Missouri, where he died on May 19, 1890. His remains were buried in the National Cemetery in Fort Smith with military honors.

[7] Judge Ira E. Leonard died in Socorro on July 10, 1889. He had practiced law, and served as postmaster in Socorro for some months prior to his death.

At one time Governor Wallace attempted to force Judge Warren H. Bristol off the bench in the Third Judicial District, and to have Ira E. Leonard appointed to succeed him. On July 23, 1880, Wallace wrote Secretary Schurz: "I regret to say that I found a somewhat unsettled condition of affairs in Lincoln County, signalized by several atrocious murders. There was no difficulty in tracing out the cause, viz. a failure to hold court in that county for two successive terms. It is not necessary, I am sure, to point out to you the result if such failure continues. I prefer, as a simple precaution against a renewal of outlawry, to urge the appointment immediately of some one who will take the judgeship in the 3rd Judicial District, and attend to it. I may be excused for saying further upon this subject that that office requires in the appointee a man of unusual courage and great experience in frontier life, each quite as much as learning in the law. Such an appointee, in my judgment, cannot be easily found amongst lawyers in the east and west; if one could be found, I doubt if he would come and stick. There is now a gentleman living in Lincoln (the county seat of the county of that name) driven there from Missouri for health, his complaint being asthma, who is a good lawyer, a true Republican, thoroughly acquainted with the peculiarities of the people, the enemy of the old 'ring,' and a most respectable gentleman in every way. If the President has not made a selection for the judgeship in question, I beg to present for his consideration, Hon. Ira E. Leonard, the party alluded to, whom I think just at this time the fittest man in all my acquaintance for the appointment. At all events, the coming term of court in that county should be held; if it is not, I beg not to be held responsible for the consequences. The judge's place will be taken by men behind a pistol."

[8] John D. Bail, one of Bonney's court-appointed attorneys, was known in New Mexico as "a man of strong convictions, fearless in expressing them under all proper circumstances, a man of absolute honesty and uprighteousness."

Born in Ross County, Ohio, July 4, 1825, he served in the Mexican War of

1846. In 1849 Bail studied law in the office of Stuard & Edwards of Springfield, Illinois, where he became acquainted with Abraham Lincoln. In 1852 Bail crossed the plains to California. Locating in Placerville, he mined for gold until 1856, when he returned to Springfield by way of the Isthmus of Panama. From Springfield, Bail went to New York City, practicing law there until 1861, when he enlisted in the Union army, serving throughout the war, part of the time with the Eleventh Missouri Infantry.

In 1866, Bail came to New Mexico, and engaged in mining in the Piños Altos district. Elected as the first representative to the New Mexico Legislature from Grant County after its establishment, Bail later served a term in the Territorial Council as representative of Grant and Doña Ana counties. Admitted to the Bar of the Territory in 1869, Bail practiced law in Mesilla from that year until 1885, when he moved to Silver City, where he practiced until his death on June 20, 1903.

⁹ Albert J. Fountain, appointed by the court along with John D. Bail to defend Bonney, one of the most colorful characters in New Mexico history, was born on Staten Island, New York, October 23, 1838. He came to New Mexico with Carleton's California Column in 1862. After being mustered out of the military service in Mesilla, Fountain became a resident of El Paso County, Texas, and for a time represented the county in the Texas state senate.

Describing Fountain as a printer, the Santa Fe *New Mexican* of October 3, 1870, published an interview in which he expressed himself as being very much gratified on account of the progress of reconstruction in Texas," and "confident that the Texas electoral vote in 1872 would be given to the Republican ticket." Tossing a pinch of salt on the still smarting wounds of proud Texans, Fountain told the *New Mexican*: "Everywhere throughout the State of Texas, the beneficent results of the infusion of a strong, intelligent and enterprising northern element into its population, resulting from the overthrow of slavery by the war, are clearly visible and even the dullest and most prejudiced of the ex-Confederates are beginning to see that the inevitable Yankee is a person to be welcomed and not repelled."

Returning to New Mexico, Fountain practiced law in Mesilla. Although not learned in the law, Fountain was industrious, energetic and ambitious; and his services as an attorney were constantly in demand. In and out of the court-room, Fountain was inclined toward swashbuckling and dramatizing himself. Employed as a special prosecutor in cattle-stealing cases in southeastern New Mexico, Fountain made life miserable for livestock thieves by his aggressive, relentless tactics.

On January 31, 1896, Fountain and Henry, his nine-year old son, left Lincoln for Las Cruces, riding in a buckboard drawn by a team of horses. Within a matter of hours man and boy disappeared, as it turned out, forever. Their bodies were never recovered. No clue was ever discovered which satisfactorily accounted for their disappearance. To this day the Fountain case, a great sensation of sixty-odd years ago, remains New Mexico's outstanding unsolved mystery.

Fountain was never willing to stand aside and watch the parade of events as a spectator. He was always anxious to be a participant in any melee. From Mesilla, on April 3, 1880, a year before Bonney's trial, Fountain wrote a letter to the New York *Sun*, strongly criticizing army operations in the field: "I start tonight for the Mescalero Indian reservation. They are having a terrible time over there. General Hatch, after having been whipped all over the country by Victorio, has gone to the Mescalero agency and driven away all the Indians who were behaving themselves. My old friends, Caballero Gonzales and San Juan, the principal chiefs of the Mescaleros, have fled from the reservation, and it is feared that they will take the warpath. I am sent for to go out and try to induce them to return. The whole country east of us is up in arms. Victorio, with not less than two hundred warriors, has whipped over eight hundred troops. A battle occurred a few days ago in which there were four hundred troops and not over sixty Indians under Nana. The troops claimed a victory and pretended that they had killed Indians, when in fact, they were badly defeated, and came near being annihilated. They lost one captain and seven men, and killed one squaw, and Gen. Hatch makes a big blow about it in the papers and claims a great victory. I predicted this thing months ago. Of all the wretched mismanagement that uniformly characterized the conduct of Indian affairs on this frontier, there has been none equal to this last, and I feel that hundreds of lives will be sacrificed by the imbecility and criminal stupidity of all our officials." (Las Vegas *Gazette*, May 9, 1880.)

[10] Simon Bolivar Newcomb, who prosecuted Bonney for Brady's murder, was born in Wallace, Nova Scotia, March 9, 1838; died in Las Cruces on May 23, 1901. Educated in Canada, he practiced as an attorney and barrister in Nova Scotia from 1861 to 1869, in which year he moved to Toledo, Ohio.

In 1871 through the influence of an uncle, James Newcomb, Secretary of State of Texas, Newcomb was appointed district judge in El Paso, Texas. On April 1, 1875, Newcomb moved to Las Cruces, where he practiced law for more than twenty years. In 1880, Newcomb was elected to the Council in the Territorial Legislature. In the same year he was appointed district attorney for Lincoln, Doña Ana and Grant counties, a position he held for eight years.

[11] J. B. Matthews was born in Woodbury, Cannon County, Tennessee, May 5, 1847. He died in Roswell, New Mexico, June 3, 1903.

Matthews served with Company M, Fifth Tennessee Cavalry throughout the Civil War. In 1867 he went to Elizabethtown, then in Taos County, New Mexico, and engaged in mining for five years. In 1873, Matthews went to Lincoln, was employed by the Murphy & Dolan interests; later he became a partner in Dolan, Riley & Co. While associated in the Dolan business, Matthews was deputized by Sheriff Brady to levy an attachment against the interest of Alex. A. McSween in Tunstall & Co., which culminated in the death of Tunstall and Brady.

Matthews moved to Roswell in 1893. President McKinley appointed him postmaster in Roswell in 1898, and President Theodore Roosevelt reappointed him in 1902.

[12] Some seventy-five years have come and gone since William H. Bonney was convicted of first-degree murder for killing Sheriff William Brady. Bail and Fountain, attorneys for Bonney, failed in their attempt to have the trial judge instruct the jury on the only legal theory on which it might have found Bonney either guilty, or guilty of a lesser degree than first-degree murder. If Bonney had been tried in Lincoln County, he would in all probability have been acquitted. If tried on a change of venue in the adjoining county of Socorro, the chances are he would have been either acquitted, or the jury would have disagreed, and been discharged for failure to reach a verdict. Over the years many people have contended that Bonney was justified in killing, or participating in the killing of Sheriff Brady, the argument being that to all intents and purposes a state of war existed in Lincoln County, and that in war, men who kill other men are not prosecuted, or questioned as to the how or why of the killing. On the other hand, many people have contended that Bonney killed Brady in cold blood, and that hanging would have been too good for him. Some people have argued that in the killing, Bonney acted impulsively when he was confronted with a sudden opportunity for revenge, with a decision to be made almost instantly, to kill or not to kill.

On August 9, 1943, Andrew H. Hudspeth, long-time practicing lawyer of White Oaks, then living in Carrizozo, told the writer: That many years before he had talked about Bonney to George W. Coe, who told him how he happened to fight on Bonney's side; that Bonney rode into Coe's place one day, and Coe gave him a meal and talked to him while Bonney's horse rested. The next day Sheriff Brady came along and asked Coe if he had seen Bonney. Coe told Brady that he had seen him, and explained how the meeting came about. Brady's deputies ordered Coe to bridle, saddle and mount his horse, after which they tied his wrists together with rope and roped his legs under the horse's belly. Brady and his deputies then started for Lincoln, with Coe as their prisoner. On the way to Lincoln the ropes sawed into Coe's wrists and legs. He begged Brady to unfasten the ropes, but Brady refused. Upon reaching Lincoln, Coe was released on bond, returned home, and went to Bonney's hiding place and told him: "From now on out, I'm with you."

Not long after Brady was killed, Bonney met Coe and said: "George, I know you would like to have killed Brady, and I don't blame you; I had a chance to kill him and I thought I'd better do it while I had the chance." Unfortunately for Bonney and a number of his contemporaries, no appeal was taken in the Brady murder case to the Supreme Court of the Territory. It is idle to speculate on what the Supreme Court might have done with the case on appeal, but if an appeal had been taken, a transcript of the testimony would have been filed which would have been of considerable interest to posterity.

[13] Edgar Caypless practiced law in New Mexico from 1880 to 1882, moving

to Denver in the latter year. The Cimarron *Press* of January 15, 1880, published a professional card: "Edgar Caypless, Attorney & Counsellor at Law, Cimarron, N. M., Notary Public."

The letter from Bonney to Caypless, omitting the addressee's name, was published in Griggs' *History of the Mesilla Valley*, 1930. George Griggs, publisher of the *History*, was born in Mesilla, May 2, 1870, died November 2, 1939. He established the "Billy the Kid" museum in Mesilla. The Caypless letter is also mentioned in *History of Colorado*, Vol. 3, p. 258.

What became of Bonney's dog? The Las Vegas *Gazette* of October 7, 1882 noted: "C. B. Smith, of Internal Revenue fame, has shipped his noted canine 'Kid,' to Illinois. This dog has a romantic history, having belonged at one time to 'Billy the Kid.' "

CHAPTER FIFTEEN

BONNEY BECOMES THE AGGRESSOR

T HE BONNEY ENTOURAGE traveled from Mesilla east to the Organ Mountains, and stopped the first night at San Augustine Springs, a place of historic interest dating back to Civil War days. It was at nearby San Augustine Pass that Major Isaac Lynde, on July 27, 1861, "without firing a shot," had surrendered several hundred Union soldiers to Col. John R. Baylor, head of invading Confederate forces. The second night was spent near the Tularosa, home of Pat Coghlan,[1] friend and acquaintance of the prisoner and most of the guards. By April 21, 1881, Bonney was in Lincoln, an event which Olinger carefully noted on his return on the warrant of authority given to him by Sheriff Southwick:

> I hereby certify that I have completed the performance of the servises herein required this the 21st day of April 1881.
>
> ROBERT OLINGER, Special Deputy Sheriff.

William Bonney was once again in familiar surroundings. He had always felt at home in Lincoln, perhaps more so even than in Fort Sumner. Lincoln was his old stomping ground. He knew almost every foot of the country within a hundred miles in all directions. At one time, not so long since, he had known by name, or sight, every man, woman and child, even every stray dog in town. Although a prisoner, Bonney in all probability still believed, as he had written Governor Wallace in Santa Fe on March 4, 1881, that he was "not entirely without friends." On two or three previous occasions, Bonney had been in jail in Lincoln, but on such occasions he had not been particularly concerned, realizing that he could walk away to freedom, almost at will. This time, it appeared, times had changed; things were different.

Bonney's prison was a room on the second floor of a two-story adobe building, occupied in previous years by the Murphy-Dolan-Riley mercantile establishment, only recently remodeled into a makeshift courthouse. Sheriff Garrett assigned two deputies, Bob Olinger and J. W. Bell, to guard Bonney day and night. Olinger was a Texan, 6 feet, 3 inches in height. He had lived in the Three Rivers country for several years, and had the reputation of being a "killer." U. S. Marshal John Sherman, Jr., had given him a commission as U. S. Deputy Marshal, dated January 1, 1881. Bell, known in the Lincoln country as "Long Bell," was a Marylander, about thirty years old. Bell had been a close friend of James Carlyle, killed at the Greathouse ranch on or about November 30, 1880, in the skirmish in which Bonney had taken a leading role.

In Santa Fe, on April 30, 1881, complying with the law in effect at the time, Governor Wallace signed the death warrant, which made it mandatory upon the Sheriff of Lincoln County to execute "William Bonny, alias Kid, alias William Antrim, on Friday, May 13, 1881." An excellent penman, the Governor wrote the warrant in its entirety, in a firm and steady hand, with no recognizable indication of nervousness, which might have been excusable because of the presence of some slight twinge of conscience resulting from a recollection of the negotiations carried on with Bonney in the vicinity of Lincoln in mid-March, 1879.

The Governor's warrant, containing the requisite legal phraseology, set forth that "William Bonny," under stated aliases, had been tried and convicted of the crime of first-degree murder at La Mesilla, Doña Ana County, in the Third Judicial District of the Territory of New Mexico; that on April 13, 1881, he had been sentenced "to be hanged by the neck until dead by the Sheriff of Lincoln county; and that the sentence of the court should be carried out." Following the preamble, the death warrant recited:

Therefore you, the Sheriff of the said county of Lincoln, are hereby commanded that on Friday, the thirteenth day of May A.D. 1881, pursuant to the said judgment and sentence of the said court, you take the said William Bonny, alias Kid, alias William Antrim, from the county jail of the county of Lincoln, where he is now confined, to some safe and convenient place within the said county, and there, between the hours of ten o'clock A.M., and three o'clock, P.M., of said day, you hang the said William Bonny, alias Kid, Alias William Antrim, by the neck until he is dead. And make due return of your acts hereunder.

In the late afternoon of April 28, 1881, two days before the Governor had written out his death warrant, William Bonney, gambling for his life, in a series of daring, panther-like moves, shot and killed his guards, Bell and Olinger, and escaped from the Lincoln County jail. A crowd quickly gathered about the courthouse following the shooting. Bonney's coolness and demonstration of generalship proved most impressive. Onlookers witnessed with amazement the unfolding of an exciting drama. No man in the crowd said one word in opposition to the proceeding or raised a hand in an attempt to prevent Bonney's escape.

Details of the double murder and escape were slow to reach the outside world. The Las Vegas *Gazette* of May 1 published a brief dispatch concerning the affair based on information contained in a telegram sent over railroad telegraph wires from San Marcial to Santa Fe. The *Gazette* of May 3 gave a more extensive outline of what had taken place. By some unknown means, Bonney had snatched Bell's six-shooter and shot him. Olinger, on the opposite side of the street from the courthouse, heard the shot and ran toward the jail. In anticipation of Olinger's appearance, Bonney had made his way into a room "where they kept the guns and ammunition," took a shotgun, loaded it and shot Olinger, killing him instantly. According to the *Gazette:*

Bonney when leaving was armed with two six shooters, a Winchester rifle, his favorite weapon, and had a belt of cartridges.

By May 10, after the initial excitement over the escape had somewhat subsided, the *Gazette* published further details:

As time passes, and further facts concerning the Kid's escape come in, the more wonderful and daring it appears—The handcuffs had been taken from his left hand, to allow him to eat supper. Watching an opportunity, he dealt J. W. Bell a blow with the irons on his right hand. This broke his skull and as he fell, the Kid grabbed his pistol and finished the work. Billy then obtained a double barrelled shotgun and took a position at an open window. He saw Olinger coming across the street and laconically remarked, "hello Bob," and fired both barrels, the contents taking effect in the head and neck of the victim. He then ordered a man to bring him a good horse. While the horse was forthcoming, a file was obtained and the shackles were removed from his feet. Someone started to tell the man not to get the horse, but Bonney told him to go back; that he did not want to kill him. "I am fighting for my life and must be obeyed." He then mounted his horse and started off. He returned soon and said he had forgotten his blankets, which were soon obtained and the daring highwayman left Lincoln forever.

At the time of the shooting and escape, Sheriff Garrett was in White Oaks, forty-one miles northwest of Lincoln. He subsequently accounted for his absence from Lincoln by saying that he had gone to White Oaks on business connected with the tax collection duties of his office.[2] Others claimed that Garrett had gone to White Oaks to get carpenters to build a scaffold for the Bonney hanging. Upon learning of the triple criminal play in Lincoln, Garrett at once deputized William Goodlett and several other White Oaks citizens, and sent them riding fast to Lincoln, with orders to arrest Bonney or kill him in the attempt. Garrett also sent a note by a deputy mounted on a fleet horse to Deputy Sheriff Eaton[3] in Socorro, more than one hundred miles to the west, asking him to be on the lookout for Bonney and to shoot him on sight if necessary. Upon receiving the news, Eaton went to the A. T. & S. F. depot in Socorro, and asked the telegraph operator to tell the train dispatcher in San Marcial of the trouble. The San Marcial dispatcher got an emergency message through direct to Governor Wallace in Santa Fe via Albuquerque and Lamy.

The bodies of Bell and Olinger were left lying undisturbed in a shed in the corral of the courthouse in Lincoln pending Sheriff Garrett's return from White Oaks. On April 29, a coroner's jury viewed the bodies and returned the following verdict:

We, the undersigned, Justice of the Peace and jury who sat upon the inquest held at the courthouse in Lincoln in said county of Lincoln and Territory of New Mexico on the 29th day of April, 1881, on the bodies of Robert Olinger and J. W. Bell found in Precinct No. 1 of the County of Lincoln, find that the said deceased Robt. Olinger and J. W. Bell both came to their death by reason of gun shot wounds inflicted on them by William Bonney alias Kid on the 28th day of April A.D. 1881 at the Court House in Lincoln while the said William Bonney alias "Kid," was being held in custody for the murder of William Brady and was awaiting his execution upon conviction for that crime and that said Olinger & Bell who were guarding him was murdered by said Bonney alias Kid in making his escape from custody.

Jesus Lueras,
Justice of the Peace.

Ysidoro Chavez
Ramon Lujan
Juan Chavez y Montolla
Gabriel Marquez (mark)
Bernabe Mes (mark)

Governor Wallace, on April 30, 1881, offered a reward of $500 for Bonney's "capture." The words, "dead or alive," frequently used in reward notices, were omitted:

BILLY THE KID

$500 Reward

I will pay $500 reward to any person or persons who will capture William Bonny, alias the Kid, and deliver him to any sheriff of New Mexico. Satisfactory proofs of identity will be required.

Lew. Wallace
Governor of New Mexico

That Governor Wallace had considered pardoning Bonney for his offenses, but had decided not to do so, was indicated in an interview given by the Governor in Las Vegas on April 27. Ironically enough the interview was published in the Las Vegas *Gazette* of April 28, the day of Bonney's escape. That part of the interview relevant to Bonney follows:

The conversation drifted into the sentence of "The Kid." "It looks as though he would hang, Governor." "Yes, the chances seem good that the 13th of May would finish him." "He appears to look to you to save his neck." "Yes," said Governor Wallace smiling, "but I cant see how a fellow like him should expect any clemency from me." Although not committing himself, the general tenor of the governor's remarks indicated that he would resolutely refuse to grant "The Kid" a pardon. It would seem as though "the Kid" had undertaken to bulldoze the governor, which has not helped his chances in the slightest.

News of Bonney's escape was the sole topic of the day for many days in Lincoln and elsewhere in the Territory. Many people professed to be shocked by the double murder, and amazed at Bonney's audacity in making the escape. Others contended that they had not been taken by surprise. Several had expressed the opinion, so they now said, that Bonney would not sit idly by in jail, meekly waiting for Pat Garrett to lead him out, tie his hands behind his back, ask him if he had anything to say before being hanged, then adjust a noose around his neck, put a black cap on his head, and give a signal to an executioner to spring the trap. Some men, particularly those who professed to know something of his ability to emerge unscathed from tight places, predicted that Bonney would not submit, that he would not be present at the scaffold on execution day; that he would either escape or die in the attempt.

Newman's *Semi-Weekly,* of Las Cruces, always pessimistic about Bonney and unfriendly to him, had sounded a note of warning on April 7, 1881, while he was still a prisoner in Mesilla:

We expect every day to hear of Bonney's escape. He is a notoriously dangerous character, has on several occasions before escaped justice where escape appeared even more improbable than now, and has made his brags that he only wants to get free in order to kill three more men—one of them being Governor Wallace. Should he break jail now, there is no doubt that he would immediately proceed to execute his threat.

By May 24, 1881, Sheriff Garrett had given up any hope of capturing Bonney in the near future. On that date he made in Lincoln his return on the Governor's death warrant: "I hereby certify that the within warrant was not served owing to the fact that the within named prisoner escaped before the day set for serving said warrant." Garrett's return was filed with Territorial Secretary W. G. Ritch in Santa Fe on June 3, 1881.

Many versions of Bonney's escape from jail on April 28, 1881, were published in newspapers and circulated by word of mouth. To this very day, there is serious disagreement over the maneuvering which preceded the shooting of the two guards; how Bonney managed to get hold of the firearms used to kill them; and the details surrounding his getaway from Lincoln. The Pat Garrett version, based on hearsay, gained wide circulation, and was generally accepted as gospel truth.

Among those in a position to have known about the events surrounding the murders and escape was Godfrey Gauss. Why did Sheriff Garrett allow Gauss to remain around the courthouse, puttering about in a vegetable garden, while Bonney was in jail? Did Gauss play a more important part in the escape than he was willing to admit? These questions have never been satisfactorily answered. Gauss and Bonney were well acquainted with each other. Both men had been employed on the Tunstall ranch at the time of the Tunstall killing, Gauss as a cook and caretaker, Bonney as a sort of horse wrangler.[4] It was not until eight years after Bonney's escape that Gauss consented to write his recollections of the tragic happenings of April 28, 1881. The Lincoln County *Leader* prevailed upon Gauss to tell his story, and it was published in that paper on January 15, 1890. In the telling, Gauss confessed that he had been an accessory to the escape, by disclosing that he threw "a little prospecting pick" through the window for Bonney's use in loosening a leg iron:

Once upon a time, it was, if I mistake not, in the month of April 1880, 1881, or perhaps 1882, whilst Sam Wortley and myself, were raising a vegetable garden behind the court house at Lincoln, that Billy the Kid was brought back from Dona Ana County, where he was traced, for murder, and sentenced to be hanged in Lincoln. About a week after the date I am writing about, he killed his two keepers and escaped. As the County had no jail then he was kept under guard in the upper story of the courthouse. Sam and myself lived in a house together, behind the courthouse. That memorable day I came out of my room, whence I had gone to light my pipe, and was crossing the yard behind the courthouse, somebody hurrying down stairs, and deputy-sheriff Bell emerging from the door running toward me. He ran right into my arms, expired the same moment, and I laid him down, dead. That I was in a hurry to secure assistance, or perhaps to save myself, everybody will believe.

When I arrived at the garden gate leading to the street, in front of the court house, I saw the other deputy sheriff, Olinger, coming out of the hotel opposite, with the other four or five county prisoners where they had taken their dinner. I called to him to come quick. He did so, leaving his prisoners in front of the hotel. When he had come close up to me, and while standing not more than a yard apart, I told him that I was just after laying Bell dead on the ground in the yard behind. Before he could reply, he was struck by a well directed shot fired from a window above us, and fell dead at my feet. I ran for my life to reach my room and safety, when Billy the Kid called to me: "Don't run, I wouldn't hurt you—I am alone, and master not only of the court-house, but also of the town, for I will allow nobody to come near us." "You go," he said, "and saddle one of Judge Leonard's horses, and I will clear out as soon as I can have the shackles loosened from my legs." With a little prospecting pick I had thrown to him through the window he was working for at least an hour, and could not accomplish more than to free one leg. He came to the conclusion to await a better chance, tie one shackle to his waist-belt, and start out. Meanwhile I had saddled a small skittish pony belonging to Billy Burt, as there was no other horse available, and had also, by Billy's command, tied a pair of red blankets behind the saddle. I came near forgetting to say, that whilst I was busy saddling, and Mr. Billy Kid trying hard to get his shackles off, my partner, Sam Wortley, appeared in the door leading from the garden where he had been at work, into the yard, and that when he saw the two sheriffs lying dead he did not know whether to go in or retreat, but on the assurance of Billy the Kid that he would not hurt him he went in and made himself generally useful.

Bonney was sorry that he had to kill Bell, but had no compunction about having killed Olinger:

When Billy went down stairs at last, on passing the body of Bell, he said, "I'm sorry I had to kill him but couldn't help it." On passing the body of Olinger he gave him a tip with his boot, saying "You are not going to round me up again." We went out together where I had tied up the pony, and he told me to tell the owner of same, Billy Burt, that he would send it back next day. I, for my part, didn't much believe in his promise, but, sure enough, next morning, the pony arrived safe and sound, trailing a long lariat, at the court-house in Lincoln. And so Billy the Kid started out that evening, after he had shaken hands with everybody around and after having had a little difficulty in mounting on account of the shackle on his leg, he went on his way rejoicing. That he was afterwards killed at Ft. Sumner by Pat Garrett is known by everybody. . . . In regard to the guilt or innocence of Billy the Kid I will here state, that Billy himself, in many conversations I had with him during the two or three years I was acquainted with him prior to his death, never denied that he was in the habit of stealing cattle from John Chisum, of Roswell, against whom he professed to have a claim, for wages I believe, which Chisum refused to pay, and hence he was determined to secure himself. He always said to me that he had never killed anybody, and never would do so except in self defense. A couple of years before his tragic end he told me that during the time he was an outlaw in the Capitan Mountains all of Pat Garrett's deputies who tried to round him up were once in partnership with him stealing cattle from John Chisum.

Regardless of the methods he employed to escape, William H. Bonney was a free man once again, although more at outs with the law than ever before. Bonney rode east down the road from Lincoln on Billy Burt's mare, until he reached the home of Higinio Salazar, a trusted friend. With a file and other tools furnished by Salazar, Bonney removed the remaining irons from his legs and feet, said *adios,* and struck out across country toward the Pecos River and Fort Sumner, a pathway known ever since as "Bonney's Escape Trail." As he rode along, Bonney undoubtedly experienced a fleeting sensation of exhilaration because of his success in outmaneuvering Pat Garrett, and a feeling of relief that, for the time being at least, he had cheated the gallows.

While waiting in the Lincoln jail for the coming of May 13, friends had relayed to Bonney bits of conversations alleged to have taken place between Garrett and some of his cronies. Garrett was reported to have drawn rough sketches for the making of a scaffold; estimated Bonney's weight; asked advice about the proper length of allowance for the drop; made out tentative lists of those who were to be invited to witness the hanging; employed a man to dig Bonney's grave; decided on the deputy who would do the actual hanging; and talked about the arrangements for burial of the body after hanging.

Two years before, almost to the day, Bonney had said his goodbyes to friends in Lincoln, after testifying before the Lincoln County grand jury (as he had promised Governor Wallace he would do) and before the Court of Inquiry at Fort Stanton. On that occasion, two years before, Bonney had been faced with an important decision. He had the choice of riding westward to the Rio Grande and starting life all over again among strangers, or of going to Fort Sumner, where he would be sure to find friends and boon companions. At that time he had to answer to society and before the law for the commission of one major crime, the killing of Sheriff Brady on April 1, 1878. Bonney's decision then was against going to the Rio Grande, and following it downstream into Mexico, as some of his best friends had advised him to do. In the alternative, he had gone into the Pecos country, a fatal mistake as time was to demonstrate. The following two years were replete with tragedy.

Killing a man in Fort Sumner in the 70's and early 80's had come to be accepted as a somewhat casual and inevitable occurrence. On December 29, 1879, Barney Mason, a not-too-highly-esteemed brother-in-law of Pat Garrett, shot and killed John Faris; and Bonney, in an impulsive moment, on January 10, 1880, shot and killed Joe Grant, in a saloon brawl in Fort Sumner. Barney Mason's killing of Faris, and Bonney's killing

of Grant failed to receive much attention from law enforcement officers in San Miguel County, in which Fort Sumner
was located. The sheriff of that county had his hands full with
killings of more importance and significance.

Between December 25, 1879, and January 25, 1880, a period
of less than thirty days, nine men died by violence in San Miguel County, among them Town Marshal Joe Carson, of Las
Vegas, who was shot and killed on January 22, 1880. The Santa
Fe *New Mexican* piously called attention to the fact that during the same thirty-day period only three murders had been
committed in Santa Fe County. (LVG, January 28, 1880.)

On his way toward the Pecos River on April 28, 1881, Bonney realized that he had now no choice as to the direction he
might travel as he had two years before. He knew for certain
that Garrett and his deputies would be on the lookout for him
south and west of White Oaks, and that officers in adjoining
counties would be asked to scour the county for him toward the
Rio Grande. On May 12, some two weeks after Bonney's escape, The Las Vegas *Gazette* published the first report of his
recent movements, incidentally striking a prophetic note of
warning:

It is reported that William Bonney, alias Kid, has been seen near
Fort Sumner, riding a horse stolen from Bell's ranch. It is believed
Billy is on the lookout for Barney Mason, who was then in Fort
Sumner. The Kid never had any great love for Barney, and especially
since he assisted in the capture of Billy and party at Stinking Springs.

If Bonney remains much longer in Lincoln County, hovering about
to pay off old scores, he is likely to be shot when he is not prepared
to do his best shooting.

William Bonney lived the life of a hunted man after April
28, 1881. He was on the dodge, riding here and there in the
Pecos River country, most of the time on stolen horses, cadging
food, always relying on the occasional bounty of his friends,
always alert, apprehensive that the law would catch up with
him.

Worn out with dodging and hiding, Bonney went to Fort
Sumner on July 13, 1881. Here, in a settlement conditioned to
crime and criminals, Bonney knew he had loyal friends. At a

late hour, perhaps just after midnight, on July 14, 1881, William H. Bonney was shot and killed by Sheriff Pat Garrett. The killing took place in Peter Maxwell's bedroom in the Lucien B. Maxwell residence, at one time occupied by United States Army officers.[5] Garrett and Maxwell were the only eyewitnesses to the killing. Bonney's departure from life was sudden, dramatic and unexpected, probably as astonishing an event to Garrett and Maxwell as it was to Bonney. The news of Bonney's death was sent by a messenger from Fort Sumner to Las Vegas, the nearest railroad and telegraph station, reaching there late Monday night on July 17. The Associated Press correspondent in Las Vegas filed a brief dispatch in the Western Union telegraph office at 8 A.M. Monday, July 18, 1881, which told of the killing.

Pat Garrett's official report of the killing was forwarded from Fort Sumner on July 15, 1881, to Acting Governor W. G. Ritch in Santa Fe. Garrett's version was the first detailed report to reach the public:

I have the honor to inform your Excellency that I had received several communications from persons in and about Fort Sumner, that William Bonny, alias Kid, had been there, or in that vicinity for some time.

In view of these reports I deemed it my duty to go there, and ascertain if there was any truth in them or not, all the time doubting their accuracy; but on Monday, July 11, I left home, taking with me John W. Poe[6] and T. L. McKinney,[7] men in whose courage and sagacity I relied implicitly, and arrived just below Fort Sumner, on Wednesday, the 13th. I remained concealed near the houses until night, and then entered the fort about midnight and went to Mr. P. Maxwell's room. I found him in bed, and had just commenced talking to him about the object of my visit at such an unusual hour, when a man entered the room in stockinged feet, with a pistol in one hand, a knife in the other. He came and placed his hand on the bed just beside me, and in a low whisper, "who is it?" (and repeated the question,) he asked of Mr. Maxwell.

I at once recognized the man, and knew he was the Kid, and reached behind me for my pistol, feeling almost certain of receiving a ball from his at the moment of doing so, as I felt sure he had now recognized me, but fortunately he drew back from the bed at noticing my movement, and, although he had his pistol pointed at my breast, he delayed to fire, and asked in Spanish, "Quien es, Quien es?" This gave me time to bring mine to bear on him, and the moment I did so I pulled the trigger and he received his death wound, for the ball struck him in the left breast and pierced his heart. He never spoke, but died in a minute. It was my desire to have been able to take him alive, but his coming upon me so suddenly and unexpectedly leads me to believe that he had seen me enter the room, or had been informed by some one of the fact; and that he came there armed with pistol and knife expressly to kill me if he could. Under that impression I had no alternative but to kill him or to suffer death at his hands.

I herewith annex a copy of the verdict rendered by the jury called in by the justice of the peace (ex officio coroner) the original of which is in the hands of the prosecuting attorney of the first judicial district.

An English translation of a portion of the verdict of the coroner's jury, the original of which was written in Spanish, was attached to Garrett's report. The original verdict of the coroner's jury, which held the inquest over Bonney's body on July 15, 1881, disappeared, and for many years could not be located, either in San Miguel County, or in the capital in Santa Fe. Fortunately, in the early 30's, while the late Harold Abbott, of the office of the Commissioner of Public Lands was classifying old records in the basement of the Capitol building, he found the long-missing document. The writer is indebted to George Abbott, Harold's brother, long-time resident of Otero County, for a photostat of the original. The full text of the verdict, translated for this work from Spanish into English by Gilberto Espinosa, of Albuquerque, a distinguished scholar and noted authority in both languages, is as follows:

TERRITORY OF NEW MEXICO
SAN MIGUEL COUNTY   PRECINCT NO. 27

To the Attorney of the First Judicial District of the Territory of New Mexico:

Greeting:

This 15th day of July, 1881, A.D., I, the Justice of the Peace of the Precinct above written, received the information that there had been a killing in Ft. Sumner in said precinct and said place and named Milnor Rudulph, Jose Silva, Antonio Saavedra, Pedro Antonio Lucero, Lorenzo Jaramillo and Sabal Gutierres as jurors to investigate the matter and the said jury meeting at the house of Luz B. Maxwell, they proceeded to a room in said house where they found the body of William Bonney alias "Kid," with a bullet wound in the breast on the left side of the breast and, having examined the body, they examined the evidence of Peter Maxwell which was as follows:

"As I was lying down on my bed in my room at about midnight the fourteenth (14th) of July, Pat F. Garrett came in my room and he sat on the side of my bed to talk with me. In a little while after Garrett sat down, William Bonney came in, and approached my bed with a pistol in his hand and he asked me, 'Who is it? who is it?' And then Pat F. Garrett fired two shots at William Bonney and the said Bonney fell at one side of my fireplace, and I went out of the room. When I returned 3 or 4 minutes after the shots, the said Bonney was dead."

The jury gives the following verdict: "We, the jury named find unanimously that William Bonney has been killed by a bullet in the left breast in the region of the heart, fired from a pistol in the hand of Pat F. Garrett, and our verdict is that the act of Garrett was justifiable homicide and we are unanimously of the opinion that the gratitude of all the community is due to said Garrett for his deed and that it is worthy of being compensated."

M. Rudulph
Presidente[8]

Antio Sabedra
Pedro Anta Lucero
Jose X Silba[9]
Sabal X Gutierrez
Lorenso X Jaramillo

All which information I put at your disposal.

Alejandro Seguro
Jues de Paz.

Deluvina Maxwell, a colorful character indeed, who died in Albuquerque on November 27, 1927, was in Pete Maxwell's house on the night William Bonney was killed. Born of Navajo

parents in Cañon de Chelly, in the Navajo country, Deluvina
was taken as a slave by the Apaches when she was nine or ten
years old and traded to Lucien B. Maxwell in Cimarron for
ten head of horses. Odelia Bernice Finley Johnson, of Albuquerque, great-granddaughter of Lucien B. Maxwell, heard
Deluvina tell on many occasions her version of the Bonney
shooting. Deluvina's story, in substance, as told to Lucien B.
Maxwell's grandchildren in Fort Sumner more than fifty years
ago, follows:

Deluvina could not remember just how she became acquainted
with William Bonney. She had never been his sweetheart, as she
had often heard it rumored, but she thought a great deal of him,
and was always glad to wash and iron his clothes. Billy Bonney was
very kind and friendly to all the people in and about Fort Sumner.
Not once, but many times, he offered to give himself up to any one
who wanted to collect the rewards that had been offered for his
arrest, but no one would betray him because they liked him so much.
Deluvina disliked Pat Garrett, claiming that he had been one of
Bonney's gang, and had left it to double cross Bonney and collect
a reward offered for his arrest. Pat Garrett heard that Bonney was
in town and went to Pete Maxwell's house on the night he was killed,
to question Pete. It was around 9 p. m., a bright moonlight night.
Pete was already in bed. A door went straight into Pete's bedroom
from an outside porch. Pat Garrett had two deputies with him. They
stayed out on the porch while Garrett went in to talk to Pete Maxwell. There was no light from lamp or candle. Garrett sat on the
edge of the bed to talk to Maxwell. Bonney had been across the
street at the house of Celsa Gutierrez. Bonney had asked Celsa to
cook supper for him. He told Celsa he had seen fresh meat hanging
on the Maxwell porch that afternoon and was sure Pete would let
him have a chunk of it. Taking a small knife Bonney went across
the street to Maxwell's house. He had removed his boots and was
in his stocking feet. Bonney passed the two deputies on the porch
and he spoke to them politely, saying "Buena Noches," probably
thinking they were Pete's work hands. The deputies must not have
recognized Billy Bonney. He walked right into Pete Maxwell's bedroom before finding out that Pete had company. Pat Garrett was
as much surprised as Bonney, so they both asked about the same
time: "Pedro, quien es?" Pete replied softly, "El Es" and Pat Gar-

rett shot twice. At the same time Pete jumped out of bed and ran from the room, followed instantly by Garrett. Garrett and the two deputies were afraid to go back into the room themselves, thinking Bonney was only wounded and waiting to shoot back. In all the excitement, Deluvina took a few drinks and then cursed Pat Garrett, using strong language. Having vented her anger on Garrett, she grabbed a lighted candle and walked into Pete Maxwell's room, not to help Garrett, who was asking that somebody volunteer to go in there, because he was afraid to go himself, but to help Bonney if he had only been wounded and was in need of help. Garrett had shot twice. The first shot had killed Bonney. There was a washstand with a marble top in Pete Maxwell's bedroom, which Garrett had seen in the moonlight and shot at, thinking it was Bonney trying to get up. It was an old Spanish custom that the night before the burial of a person, people would take turns staying with the body and reciting prayers. William Bonney had a proper funeral. The people took turns and stayed with the remains all during the night. He was buried in the old government cemetery in Fort Sumner. For many years Deluvina left flowers on his grave in the summer time.[10]

NOTES AND PROFILES

[1] Patrick Coghlan, a fabulous character of his day in the Sacramento Mountain country, was born in Ireland, March 15, 1822, came to the United States in 1848. Like many other Irish immigrants of the time, he served for several years in the United States Army, including a hitch in the cavalry at Fort Stanton in 1872.

Coghlan settled in the Tularosa country in 1874, engaging in fruit growing, ranching and cattle raising, until his death on January 27, 1911, at the age of eighty-nine. A powerfully-built man, 6 feet 1 inch in height, Coghlan was a noted foot racer in young manhood, both in Ireland and America. It was his boast that he had never lost a race.

[2] Pat Garrett, appointed administrator of Olinger's estate in the Probate Court of Lincoln County, filed a final report on April 2, 1883, which stated that the only asset he could find belonging to the estate was a $50 account due Olinger from Lincoln County. Among the papers filed in the estate was an official request dated April 29, 1881, addressed to Justice of the Peace Jose

Lueras, Precinct No. 1, Lincoln County, "to hold an inquest over the dead bodies of Robt. Olinger and J. W. Bell who are now lying in a room in the correll of the courthouse in the town of Lincoln and ascertain by means of a coroner's investigation how the said deceased came to their death."

Appointed a United States deputy marshal by United States Marshal John Sherman, Jr., in Santa Fe, on January 21, 1881, Olinger was arrested in Las Vegas on March 11, 1881, by Deputy Sheriff Segura on a charge of carrying arms. He was released from jail on order of Judge Prince. Found on Olinger's body when killed, and later filed with the estate papers, was a notebook in which he had written his version of the incident: "The first time I was in jail March the 11th 1881. Arrested by order of L. Bradford Prince Chief Justice of the supreme court of N.M. and judge of the first judicial court charged with being a deputy u. s. marshal and carrying deadly weapons disarmed and sent to jail afterwards discharged from custody and allowed to carry arms."

[3] Ethan W. Eaton, deputy sheriff of Socorro County in 1881, was one of the best known old-timers of Anglo ancestry in the Territory. Born in Montgomery County, New York, October 10, 1827, of New England parentage, Eaton attended school in Sharon Center and Amesville, New York.

Joining a California gold rush party Eaton reached Santa Fe in 1849. He decided to remain in New Mexico. His companions continued on west toward the Pacific Coast, and were never heard from again. In Santa Fe on April 26, 1822, Citizen Domingo Fernandez was granted a tract of land in the vicinity of Galisteo. Fernandez conveyed his interest to Eaton on January 20, 1851. The grant was confirmed to Eaton by the surveyor general of New Mexico on September 18, 1857.

On July 29, 1861, Eaton, commissioned a captain, organized Company F of the New Mexico Volunteers, which served under Canby and Carleton during the Civil War. He was mustered out as a colonel. During the Navajo Indian campaign, Eaton was at one time commanding officer at Fort Wingate.

Moving to Socorro in 1875, Eaton remained there until his death on September 15, 1913. Colonel Eaton took an active part in community affairs. When things got out of hand in Socorro in 1880, he organized the Vigilantes, who quickly restored law and order. While serving as a deputy sheriff, and attempting to quiet down a row in a Socorro saloon, a desperado shot Eaton in the arm, inflicting a serious injury. When his assailant resisted arrest, Eaton shot and killed him.

[4] Godfrey Gauss emigrated from Germany to the United States in 1853. He enlisted in the U. S. Army and was stationed at Fort Union and Fort Stanton, New Mexico. After Bonney escaped from jail Gauss worked as a cook for J. A. Alcock, an Englishman, on the Carrizo ranch, bought from T. B. Catron of Santa Fe in 1882 for $170,000.

[5] Peter Menard Maxwell was the only surviving son of Lucian B. Maxwell (1818-75), one-time owner of the fabulous Maxwell Land Grant. Born April

27, 1848, Pete Maxwell died on June 21, 1898, and was buried in Fort Sumner.

[6] Born near Maysville, Mason County, Kentucky, October 17, 1850, John W. Poe died in Roswell, New Mexico, on July 17, 1923. In 1872, Poe went to Fort Griffin, Texas, where he worked for a time with cattle. He became a buffalo hunter in 1875. He and his associates reported that they had killed 20,000 buffalo, and had found it to be a profitable business.

Poe was appointed town marshal of Fort Griffin in 1877 and served one year, during which time he made the acquaintance either in person or by reputation of many cattle rustlers, desperadoes and outlaws. In 1879 Poe went to Fort Elliott, Wheeler County, Texas, where he was employed by the Canadian River Cattle Association, which furnished him money and authority to protect the interests of Association members.

Poe came to New Mexico in the spring of 1881, and soon met Pat Garrett at a time when William Bonney was hiding from the law. George Gwynn told Poe in White Oaks that he had heard that Bonney was at Fort Sumner. Poe then told the story to Garrett. Garrett was reluctant to place any credence in the report, but at Poe's insistence, started up the Pecos River from Roswell with Poe and Deputy Thomas L. McKinney.

Poe, being a stranger in the country, went to Fort Sumner with a note from Garrett to Milnor Rudulph. Garrett and McKinney remained on the outskirts of the town. Poe arrived in Fort Sumner about one o'clock on the afternoon of the night on which Bonney was killed. Poe waited a few steps away at the time Garrett killed Bonney.

Poe was Garrett's opposite in build, character, temperament and disposition. Garrett was a tall, lanky, hail-fellow-well-met type of a man, inclined to be easy going, fond of playing cards, not very businesslike. John Poe was about 5 feet 8 inches in height, against Garrett's 6 feet several inches. Poe was heavy-set, built like an athlete. Friendly enough with intimates, a cool, calculating sort of an individual, Poe was inclined to be quite reserved with casual acquaintances and strangers, a hard-headed man, with a keen business sense. Poe never claimed to be a gunman, but was successful in rounding up criminals when he succeeded Garrett as sheriff of Lincoln County in 1883 and 1884, due in large part to the work of Jim Brent, his chief deputy.

Garrett and Poe became involved in a dispute over a land transaction in 1882, which resulted in termination of their friendship. The two men pitted their political strength and popularity in an election held in Lincoln County on November 7, 1882. Garrett, a candidate for the Territorial Council, was defeated by John A. Miller. Poe, a candidate for sheriff, was elected.

When Chaves County was carved out of Lincoln County in 1889, Garrett was ambitious to be elected the county's first sheriff. Poe opposed his candidacy, backed a man who was nominated and elected. Poe resigned as sheriff of Lincoln County on December 31, 1885, and thereafter devoted most of his time to ranching, livestock and banking.

On many occasions John Poe was asked about his recollection of the Bonney
shooting. The present writer discussed the incident with him in 1910. John
Poe's recollections of the killing, edited by E. A. Brinninstool, were published
in the *Wide World* magazine for December, 1919, and published in booklet
form as *Billy the Kid, Notorious New Mexico Outlaw*, July 17, 1923. Houghton Mifflin Co. published John W. Poe's book, *The Death of Billy the Kid*,
in 1933. In 1936 Poe's widow, Sophie A. Poe, wrote *Buckboard Days*, edited
by Eugene Cunningham.

[7] On May 8, 1881, some two months before Bonney was killed, Deputy
Sheriff Thomas L. (Tip) McKinney, of Roswell, holding a commission under
Sheriff Garrett, shot and killed Bob Edwards, described as "a notorious horse
thief from southwest Texas." Edwards had a ranch in the Peñasco country,
which officers claimed was a blind for large scale horse-stealing operations. It
was claimed that Edwards, with four others, had stolen twenty-one horses from
John Slaughter, of Tombstone, Arizona, and had driven them to Seven Rivers.

The fight between Deputy Sheriff McKinney and Edwards took place at
Harrison's ranch, near Rattlesnake Springs, on Black River. McKinney reported that Edwards opened fire on him with a Winchester at close range. In
the exchange of shots, McKinney put a bullet through Edwards' head. (LVG,
May 17, 1881.)

Tip McKinney, scion of a noted Texas family, was a grandson of Collin
McKinney, one of the signers of the Texas Declaration of Independence in
1836. Robert McKinney, one of Collin McKinney's sons, was killed in the
defense of the Alamo. In the late 70's, Tip McKinney's father, John McKinney,
drove a herd of horses from east Texas to Palo Pinto County, where he traded
it for a bunch of cattle, which he and Tip drove straight west to the Seven
Rivers country in New Mexico, reaching there in time to become involved in
the fighting between and among the "Seven Rivers Warriors," described by
James M. Miller in a series of articles published in the Roswell *Record* on
July 19, 20 and 21, 1932.

Tip McKinney's father, John McKinney, was a brother of William Henry
McKinney, father of Edward S. McKinney (born in Marlin, Falls County,
Texas, on September 5, 1876), whose son, Robert Moody McKinney (a grandson of Robert Moody, who freighted on the Santa Fe Trail between Santa Fe
and Westport Landing between 1858 and 1865), is the owner and publisher
of the Santa Fe *New Mexican*. Some twenty years ago, Robert Moody McKinney wrote a play based on the Lincoln County War, which was being considered
for production in New York when Pearl Harbor intervened and he went off
to war.

[8] Milnor Rudulph, foreman of the coroner's jury which held the inquest over
the body of Bonney at Fort Sumner on July 15, 1881, was widely known
throughout New Mexico in his day and respected for his ability, honor and
integrity. Through the courtesy and cooperation of Phillip Sanchez, of Mora,

New Mexico, and William S. Wallace, Associate Librarian and Archivist of New Mexico Highlands University, Las Vegas, New Mexico, it is now possible to rescue from obscurity a colorful figure in New Mexico history.

In his early years in New Mexico, Rudulph spelled his surname "Rudolph." In later years, wishing to become disassociated from a brother from whom he had become estranged, he changed the spelling to "Rudulph." Born in northeastern Maryland near the banks of the Potomac on August 25, 1826, Rudulph (a Wallington on his mother's side) died in Rociada, a tranquil, picturesque Spanish-American village in Mora County, New Mexico, on November 8, 1887. (Las Vegas *Optic,* November 12, 15, 1887.)

Rudulph was educated in the common schools in Maryland and then moved to Philadelphia, where he studied mathematics and the classics. When sixteen years old, he went to Memphis, Tennessee, where he lived four years, teaching school and working in mercantile establishments. Early in 1849 he left Memphis with a wagon train, intending to go to the gold fields in California. Upon reaching Santa Fe, Rudulph decided to remain in New Mexico. On October 1, 1861, Rudulph signed the muster rolls of the Third Regiment, New Mexico Volunteers; was assigned duty as Regimental Quartermaster and placed in charge of Hatch's Ranch.

On March 27, 1862, Rudulph submitted in distinctive handwriting a petition for membership in the Masonic Lodge at Fort Union, stating that he was a resident of Fort Union and "by occupation an officer of the Army." S. L. Pratt and Frank Phelps joined in the petition and recommended him for membership. Initiated into Chapman Lodge in 1862, Rudulph retained his membership throughout his life.

Elected to the New Mexico Legislature in 1870, Rudulph was chosen as Speaker of the House. During the years of his residence in the Mora valley, Rudulph rendered community service as justice of the peace and postmaster in Rociada; he taught school and engaged in farming. In 1878, seeking the proverbial greener pastures, Rudulph sold his Rociada property to John Pendaries and moved to Sunnyside, near Fort Sumner, on the Pecos River.

While a resident of Sunnyside, on July 15, 1881, Rudulph was summoned to become a member of the coroner's jury empanelled and sworn to inquire truthfully into the death of William H. Bonney. No doubt Rudulph, fluent in both the English and Spanish languages, and well prepared by education, training and experience, played a leading role in investigating the facts and circumstances surrounding the killing and had much to do with the findings contained in the verdict. (A comparison of Milnor Rudulph's signature in the petition for Masonic membership in Fort Union with the "Milnor Rudulph" signature affixed some nineteen years later to the verdict following the William H. Bonney inquest, leaves no room for doubting that the signatures were written by one and the same person.)

In 1882, a year after the Bonney killing, Milnor Rudulph reached the conclusion, as had Lucien B. Maxwell of neighboring Maxwell Land Grant fame some years before, that the Fort Sumner country was inferior in many respects to the high mountain country of northeastern New Mexico. As a result, he retraced his steps and returned to the Mora valley, repurchased from John Pendaries his old residence and a small tract of land surrounding it. The district school directors welcomed his return, and re-employed him to teach in the Rociada school.

Once each year, in early spring, when the first mountain flowers of the season appeared in the Mora valley, Milnor Rudulph would suspend lessons and tell his pupils about his boyhood years along the Potomac in Maryland; and of a most important occasion when his father took him to Washington as a small child and introduced him to Henry Clay (1777-1852), a most famous statesman of the day, and would describe in detail how Mr. Clay shook his hand, patted him on the head and used kind and affectionate words in talking to him. In the later years, Rudulph had a new story to tell his pupils, about an important day in his life in 1880 on which he received a letter from James A. Garfield, President of the United States, inviting him and Mrs. Rudulph to go to Washington and be the guests of the President and Mrs. Garfield. The invitation, which they had been unable to accept, had been extended, Rudulph would always carefully explain, not through political influence, but because he and the President's wife, Lucretia Rudolph Garfield, were second cousins, and had spent many happy hours together in their childhood.

After Milnor Rudulph's death, a public meeting was held at Rincon del Tecolote on November 10, 1887, attended by all the countryside and presided over by Ramon Maestas, chairman, and Jesus M. Sanchez, secretary. A committee composed of Manuel Gonzales, Felipe Sanchez and Juan Sanchez submitted resolutions of condolence, which were adopted. Milnor Rudulph and his wife, Maria Candelaria Trujillo de Rudulph (who died February 5, 1904, at the age of fifty-nine), are buried side by side in the village cemetery in Rociada, their graves marked by suitable monuments.

[9] Three of the jurors, Jose Silba (Silva), Sabal Gutierrez and Lorenzo Jaramillo, signed the verdict of the coroner's jury by mark, an indication they were unable to write. Strangely enough, in the verdict, the words, "who is it? who is it?," quoted from Peter Maxwell's testimony, were in the English language in an otherwise all-Spanish verdict, evidence that Bonney may have spoken in English in asking about the identity of the stranger in Maxwell's bedroom. Pat Garrett's report of July 15, 1881, however, stated that Bonney asked the question in Spanish.

Sabal (Savalla) Gutierrez was Pat Garrett's brother-in-law.

Several days after Bonney's death, Manuel Moraga (father of A. S. Moraga, seventy-five years old, of 312 Mountain Road East, Albuquerque) was in Fort Sumner and talked with Gutierrez about the killing. Gutierrez told Moraga that Bonney had been in hiding, and had ridden into Fort Sumner tired and hungry. He went to the Gutierrez home, borrowed a butcher knife, and went across the street to Pete Maxwell's meathouse, where he helped himself to part of a butchered sheep, expecting to take it back to the Gutierrez house to have it cooked. Later Bonney went to tell Maxwell that he had taken the meat, so that Maxwell would not suspect that it had been taken by some one else. Bonney encountered Garrett, while looking for Maxwell, and was killed.

Manuel Moraga owned a traveling circus which played the Pecos River towns for many years and was well acquainted with Bonney. On one occasion Bonney wanted to see the circus at Anton Chico, but had no money for a ticket. Moraga admitted him free. Later the same day, because Bonney was poorly dressed, and the weather was cold, Moraga gave him a red flannel shirt and an overcoat. Next year when the circus again played in Anton Chico, Bonney showed up, bought a ticket, and handed Moraga seventy-five dollars in payment for the clothing he had given him the year before.

[10] On April 30, 1881, Governor Wallace issued the following notice: "I will pay five hundred dollars reward to any person or persons who will capture William Bonney, alias 'The Kid,' and deliver him to any sheriff of New Mexico. Satisfactory proof of identity will be required."

The use of the word "capture" in the reward notice hampered Pat Garrett in his efforts to collect the reward. On February 2, 1882, the Legislature passed an act authorizing the Territorial Treasurer to pay him the reward money. After quoting the reward notice, the Act provided: "And Whereas, Pat Garrett was at the time Sheriff of Lincoln County, and did, on or about the month of August (sic) 1881, in pursuance of the above reward and by virtue of a warrant placed in his hands for that purpose, attempt to arrest said William Bonney, and in said attempt did kill said William Bonney at Fort Sumner, in the County of San Miguel, in the Territory of New Mexico, and wherefore, said Garrett is justly entitled to the above reward, and payment thereof has been refused upon a technicality, now, therefore, etc." (See Chap. 101 of 1882 Session Laws.)

New Mexico and Missouri had something in common in outlawry in the 80's. On July 15, 1881, the day after Garrett killed Bonney, a gang of desperadoes, captained by Jesse Woodson James, held up a Rock Island train at Winslow Station, near Cameron Junction, Missouri, killed Conductor Westfall, robbed the passengers, rifled the mail and express cars. Gov. T. T. Crittenden, on July 26, offered a reward of $5,000 for the arrest or capture of Jesse or Frank James, dead or alive.

CHAPTER SIXTEEN

END OF AN ERA

ISOLATION for central New Mexico came to an end as the result of the construction of railroad and telegraph lines in the Territory during the years 1879, 1880 and 1881. The end of isolation spelled the beginning of the end for outlawry in the Territory. Desperadoes on horseback could not compete with law officers riding railroad trains and using the telegraph in connection with their work.

Having obtained from the Congress of the United States additional time to meet federal grant requirements, the Atchison, Topeka and Santa Fe railway penetrated country that had always been the exclusive domain of the man on foot or horseback, the passenger in an animal-drawn vehicle. Brushing aside a host of difficulties, the Santa Fe began a new era for New Mexico by building from Colorado through the Raton Pass and on to Las Vegas, by-passing Cimarron, to the profound regret of William R. Morley, H. M. Porter and Frank W. Springer, who had envisaged a Cimarron City, after the coming of a main-line railroad, which would rival Pittsburgh as an industrial center.

The decision to by-pass Cimarron was a difficult one for the builders of the road to make. By-passing Santa Fe, a namesake of the project, was doubly difficult because of Santa Fe's insistence on being served by the main line. In the end, however, engineers for the road pacified the people of Santa Fe by showing them that the hills and mountains which protected their town from summer heat and wintry blasts, were stumbling blocks to main line construction because of excessive grades and prohibitive costs. Consequently Santa Fe was obliged to surrender its dreams of being an important railroad town, and be content with branch line transportation.

As the Santa Fe railroad built south and west, through Las Vegas, and on to Albuquerque and San Marcial along the Rio Grande, ten thousand Chinese coolies toiled and sweated, grading the road bed, laying ties and track for the Southern Pacific Railroad building east from the Colorado River. The Santa Fe from the east and Southern Pacific from the west were striving to reach a tentative junction point in southwestern New Mexico, eventually named Deming.

The Las Vegas *Gazette* of March 20, 1881, told of the confusion and excitement which prevailed as construction work neared completion, which would afford for the first time in New Mexico's history through railway transportation from the Atlantic to the Pacific:

When it was thought that the junction of the two railroads would be made at Rio Mimbres Station on the Southern Pacific, 230 miles east of Tucson, and ten miles east of the old temporary station of Deming, a motley crowd made preparations for emigrating to what they were pleased to consider the coming hurrah town. Some of the worst characters in southwestern New Mexico and southeastern Arizona banded together, and taking up a tract of land adjacent to the section house and water tank of the Southern Pacific, announced their intention of holding it and laying it off in town lots. Notices of warning were posted up in all quarters, marked by the significant symbols of skull and cross bones, ordering all persons to keep off. A saloon town sprang up in a night almost, tents and rough buildings rolling up mushroom like where the vilest of all vile liquor was sold for whiskey. . . . "Six Shooter" Smith, one of the gang of San Simon valley cowboys, who had terrorized that region, circulated a petition to get himself appointed a deputy sheriff, and secured many signatures. Smith was boss of the Rio Mimbres settlement, partly because of his fondness for shooting at people to see how close he could come to killing them without actually doing so. While waiting for his appointment as a deputy "Six Shooter" Smith abrogated to himself the duties of an officer of the law and terrorized the place. Fortunately, the junction of the railroads was not made in the immediate vicinity of Smith's realm.

The *Gazette* of April 16, 1881, reported that United States troops had been sent from Fort Cummings to Deming to evict

Smith and his "land jumpers." The army was used, the *Gazette* explained, "because the land is part of a land grant to the railroad, and the government is responsible that no squatters take it up."[1]

The Las Vegas *Gazette* of March 22, 1881, described the wonders of through travel following the Santa Fe-Southern Pacific connection at Deming:

There were forty-two through passengers from the Pacific coast on the train that passed east through Las Vegas yesterday noon! It is not merely the novelty of traveling by the new overland route that is the explanation of the heavy train, but is an index of the great travel that is likely to pass over the A. T. & S. F. and Southern Pacific roads. Emigrant trains will be put on as soon as they can be arranged for, so that express trains will carry only those holding first class passenger tickets. The Southern Pacific owns its own sleeping cars, which are vastly inferior to those of the A. T. & S. F. Railroad. They are painted a bright yellow color, as are the passenger coaches. A train thus made presents a fine appearance from the distance as it goes skimming along on the iron roadway The interior of the sleeping cars is fitted up in light woods, but there is a lack of that luxuriousness so noticeable in the Pullman cars of this road. This comparison may be extended to the passenger coaches. The distance from Kansas City to San Francisco is 2,358 miles, and requires five days in transit, three nights and two days from Kansas City to Deming, and three days and two nights from Deming to San Francisco.

According to the *Gazette,* Deming had brighter future prospects than El Paso:

The new railway town of Deming is just now commanding a deal of attention, being the junction of the two great overland routes, the A. T. & S. F., and Southern Pacific railroads. . . . There is much comment as to the relative merits of El Paso and Deming as the future coming great city of the southwest, in which El Paso suffers greatly by comparison.

As two great transcontinental railroads pushed their projects to completion in New Mexico, Governor Lew. Wallace, in his study in the Palace of the Governors in Santa Fe, wrestled with a major task of his own—the completion of the novel *Ben-Hur*. In response to a letter written to him by A. J. Wissler, inquiring as to how much work he had done on the book in Santa Fe, Wallace replied from Crawfordsville on May 6, 1890, saying in substance and effect: That at the time he was appointed governor of New Mexico the book had been finished down to the sixth volume; that he took the uncompleted story with him to Santa Fe, and there wrote the sixth, seventh and eighth books. Among other things, Wallace wrote Wissler: "When in the city it was my habit to shut myself after night in the bedroom back of the executive office proper and write until after 12 o'clock. That room has ever since been associated in my mind with the Crucifixion."

Despite interruptions by day and by night, resulting from political quibbling, Indian raids and uprisings, the doings of desperadoes and outlaws, quarrelling among the military, and a host of other difficulties, Lew. Wallace managed to complete his novel.

By midsummer 1880, Wallace sent the final sheets of the manuscript to Harper & Brothers, Franklin Square, New York City. On October 9, the publishers wrote Wallace:

In pursuance of your request, we send you herewith a copy of Ben-Hur in sheets, and also a copy of the cover.

We can publish the book about the 22nd of this month. It has occurred to us, however, that the interests of the book would be hazarded if published before the holidays. The pressure of books intended for the holiday season absorbs the attention of the trade and drives from their counters books not specially suited for gifts. In addition, the newspapers are apt to pay less attention at that time to books of a general character. We think that it would be better for the book, if the publication were deferred until after a New Year's. What do you think of the suggestion? We sent the sheets of the book to our London agent with instructions to endeavor to secure a sale in England. We trust he may be successful and that the book may have a successful sale there.

Wallace preferred not to defer publication of his cherished work. He was anxious to see it in print and before the public. The Harpers acquiesced and wrote him on November 13:

We published "Ben Hur" yesterday. . . . We have ordered bound a dozen copies in plain cloth following your suggestions as to lettering, etc. We have also ordered to be bound in full morocco as requested ten copies of "Ben Hur" which we will forward to you shortly.

Now that his book had been published, Wallace turned his attention to the development of the mining properties in which he had been interested from time to time during his residence in the Territory. Like most New Mexico governors during Territorial days, Wallace was almost always in need of ready cash. On December 15, 1880, he wrote to his son, Henry, in Crawfordsville, asking him for $150 to do assessment work in the Chloride district in southwestern New Mexico, assuring him that with that sum advanced he could get along until his "quarter's salary comes in."[2]

Lew. Wallace had not been idle during Garfield's campaign for the Presidency. He made speeches for him in Indiana and elsewhere at the request of the National Committee. He had kept in touch with influential friends, among them, William Wade Dudley (1842-1909) of Indianapolis, one-time United States Marshal in Indiana, later Commissioner of Pensions in Washington. On March 5, 1881, the day after Garfield's inauguration, Dudley wrote the President a letter urging him to appoint Wallace to an important post in Rome:

It has grown, I believe, into a rule, for the Nation to select as its representatives abroad, especially in those places noted for antiquity or learning, American citizens who have carved themselves a name in literature. General Lew. Wallace of Indiana is a man eminently qualified by life and education as well as by his efforts in the field of literature, to take honors to a foreign power—and I hope his gallant service to our country in her time of need—and his scholarly attainments and success as an American author, will ensure him appointment at your hands, as Envoy Extraordinary and Minister Plen. to the Italian Court at Rome. Should it accord with your idea of the fitness of things—that so noted a soldier, so ever true an American, and so representative a citizen of this Republic, withal so gifted and successful an author, as Major General Lew. Wallace shall be sent to represent us abroad—Indianans will feel honored and signify their endorsement of your action.

On March 9, four days after Dudley's letter to Garfield, Wallace wrote to the Secretary of the Interior:

You will do me the favor to take notice of the accompanying paper, and submit it to the President.

It gives me pleasure to report New Mexico in a state of quiet. A large immigration is pouring into it under inducement of rich mineral discoveries and increased railroad facilities. If nothing untoward happens, it will be in condition to become a State before the expiration of the administration just inaugurated. If you have views touching the management of its affairs, I will be happy to receive them and, while in office, diligent in carrying them into effect.

The enclosure in Wallace's letter, for the attention of the President, was a tentative resignation:

The newspapers report quite a number of gentlemen from different sections of the Union as applicants for the office of Governor of New Mexico. It may serve your policy, not to speak of your personal preference, to appoint one of them in my place. To leave you perfectly free to do so, I respectfully offer you my resignation; remarking that if it should be your pleasure to continue me in the office, I will do my best, as heretofore, to discharge its duties satisfactorily.

It may be proper to say in explanation, and speaking from experience, that whoever your appointee may be, the conditions of the Territory are so peculiar that his administration cannot be successful without some affirmative act in assurance to the public of your confidence in him, and your determination to give him hearty support.

President Garfield accepted Wallace's resignation as governor of New Mexico on March 17, 1881, and appointed Lionel A. Sheldon, personal friend and fellow Ohioan, to succeed him.[3]

On March 24, President Garfield sent Wallace's name to the Senate for confirmation as charge d'affaires in Paraguay and Uruguay, but withdrew it when Wallace declined to accept the post. While Wallace marked time pending the arrival of Sheldon, his successor, and of word from Washington about an appointment, the newspapers of the Territory expressed their views of his departure. The Las Vegas *Optic,* which had been critical of Wallace when he assumed the governorship in 1879, praised him on March 23, 1881:

It is observable to all our readers who are familiar with passing events that a determined effort is being made by hungry politicians to remove Gen. Lew Wallace from his official position as governor of New Mexico—indeed it is semi officially stated that that gentleman has already tendered his resignation, which has not yet been accepted. It is not difficult to comprehend that two forces have combined to accomplish this purpose. The only class who are seeking it is composed of those people who have not found him, like his predecessors, their pliant and yielding tool. These parties, to a very great extent, compose what is known as the "Santa Fe Ring," and are men who have prostituted nearly every official and gubernatorial position, as well as the legislatures, through a long series of years, for selfish purposes, purely personal to themselves. We believe Governor Wallace to be almost the only respectable and worthy gentleman who was ever appointed to a Federal office in New Mexico. He is a man distinguished in arms, in law, in literature, able in politics, and honest, just and incorruptible in the performance of the functions of his office. He is incapable of being used by any coterie, clique or faction, and only approachable as governor by an appeal to his intellect, his reason and his cultured sense of justice. . . . The other force that seeks to remove Governor Wallace is the office seeker, who is now on hand, demanding his compensation from the President for services rendered in the late campaign. These men must be provided for, and are constantly being given places to the disgust and detriment of the people of the Territories. Unlike Governor Wallace, the offices do not seek them—in fact, if the offices themselves had a grain of discrimination, very few of the men who have occupied Federal positions in this Territory would ever have been sought by them. Whether this combination will cause President Garfield to belittle himself in the eyes of our people by the removal of our worthy governor, remains to be seen.

We can only hope against it—a hope mingled with grave apprehensions, for such a course would be a sad blow to the future of New

Mexico. The bad element in our Territorial affairs should not be permitted to prevail any longer. If our people can do anything to prevent it, they owe it to themselves and to Governor Wallace to take steps in the matter at once. That a man from Ohio, or any other state, should be appointed Governor of New Mexico on account of party service, or religious convictions, is too disgraceful a proposition to argue or confute. In conclusion, we say to President Garfield in all earnestness and candor, let Governor Wallace alone. The people are satisfied—yes, pleased, with his administration and there is no need for a change.

The Las Cruces *Semi-Weekly* eulogized Lew. Wallace on March 30:

Governor Wallace who it appears is soon to be succeeded as governor by General Sheldon, has made the best executive New Mexico has had for many years. We are politically opposed to him and think that in some instances, both during his residence among us, and before, he has acted unwisely, but we cannot withhold the meed of praise which we think is due him. His administration, when compared with those of Giddings and Axtell, has certainly been a most admirable one. He has done fearlessly whatever he has considered himself called upon to do and has kept himself entirely free from all entangling alliances with rings and cliques. He has done good service against that vampire of political corruption which had fastened upon the life of blood sucked from its veins; and however unwisely he may have in our judgment at times exercised his power he has never done so at the behest of any man or group of men. He has been the governor during his entire term, and we honor him for it. His place is more likely to be filled by a less able and fearless man than by any one who is his equal; and for that reason his resignation is to be regretted. As a cultured gentleman and scholar, known throughout the length and breadth of the land, he has with his pen done much to attract attention to the boundless resources of New Mexico. He has made friends of the people and. should he leave the Territory, on the arrival of his successor, his loss will be one to be regretted.

Wallace's final days in Santa Fe were made memorable by the favorable newspaper reviews of *Ben-Hur,* and the many

etters of congratulations and commendations on the book
vhich he received. He had sent a copy of the book soon after
ublication to Archbishop Lamy; and on March 17, 1881, the
hurchman had written him a note of thanks and appreciation:

HIS EXCELLENCY, GOVERNOR WALLACE:
ermit me to thank you for your fine book (Ben-Hur, a Tale of
Christ.) I have read it all through and found it very interesting.
think it is written in good Christian spirit.

Yours truly,
J. B. LAMY, Abp. of Sta. Fe.

A month later the Governor received a letter of appreciation
rom President Garfield, which to a considerable extent com-
ensated him for all the time and effort invested in the book:

EXECUTIVE MANSION   WASHINGTON   April 19, 1881
DEAR GENERAL: I have this morning finished reading "Ben Hur"
nd I must thank you for the pleasure it has given me. The theme
as difficult; but you have handled it with great delicacy and power.
everal of the scenes, such as the Wise Men in the desert, the sea
ght, the chariot race, will I am sure take a permanent place in
terature. With this beautiful and reverent book you have lightened
he burden of my daily life, and renewed our acquaintance which
egan at Shiloh.

Naturally elated because of the President's praise, Wallace
vrote on April 29 to Mrs. Wallace in Crawfordsville, enclos-
ng a copy of the letter:

There now, my dear, what do you think of that? I think a great
eal of it, partly because the writer is a man of literary taste, partly
ecause it must be honest, judging from the fact that he could have no
notive to deceive or even be polite.

On May 21, 1881, the President sent Wallace's name to the
enate for confirmation as minister to Turkey. Wallace left
anta Fe on May 30 for Crawfordsville, where he consulted
ith friends, and then telegraphed Washington his acceptance

of the appointment to Turkey. The Senate confirmed the ap
pointment within a matter of days. Wallace went to Wash
ington, then sailed from New York on his foreign mission
delighted with the prospects of visiting the Holy Land anc
seeing with his own eyes the places that he had seen only
through the eyes of others in writing *Ben-Hur.*

In leaving New Mexico, Lew. Wallace bequeathed to hi
successor many problems, some of which he had attempted to
solve during his administration. The Indians, particularly the
Utes, Apaches and Navajos, ugly and dissatisfied when he came
to the Territory, were still smarting under the injustices they
had suffered, and threatening to retaliate. With so many othe
things to do, Wallace had been unable to offer more than token
assistance toward alleviation of their complaints. He had no
accomplished anything of significance toward a restoration o
their tribal rights. The outlaws were still a major problem, jus
as they had been on the first day of his arrival. William H. Bon
ney, who had caused him many sleepless nights, was still a
large. Desperadoes were running amuck in the San Juan Rive.
country, in Rio Arriba (now San Juan) County.

The Governor had been a witness to many stirring events i
a frontier Territory—the Wild West—as it had never been be
fore or since. He had elected to observe in his capacity as ;
government official, and not as a writer. During the rest of hi
life few words came from his pen descriptive of the stirrin
days he had spent in New Mexico. He had apparently live
comparatively unimpressed through the final years of ;
significant era in the Territory.

Under ordinary circumstances, the events of those year
might have found first place in his thoughts. Both before anc
after Wallace's arrival in New Mexico, however, the firs
fruits of his thoughts had been dedicated to, and belonged to
a time and country remote from New Mexico; he was enam
ored with places and personalities in far-off Judea and Jeru
salem of two thousand years before; with the tenets of th
Jewish religion; with the Christ and Christian teachings an
philosophy; about a hero named Judah Ben-Hur; over th
inherent possibilities of drama in a chariot race. With hi
thoughts dedicated to and dominated by the demands of a stor
which became *Ben-Hur,* Wallace found himself in New Mex

ico figuratively riding two horses, one carrying him toward a flaming country known as Lincoln County, four days' journey from Santa Fe; the other carrying him toward a country he saw only in his mind's eye, a land beyond the sea, along the river Jordan, the Sea of Galilee, the hills of Judea. In the struggle for the mastery of Wallace's mind, the novel *Ben-Hur* won out over the demands for attention of the actors holding the stage in the aftermath of the Lincoln County War.

In leaving the governorship of New Mexico, Wallace had the satisfaction of knowing that his novel had been finished and published; and he had some faint glimmering, perhaps, that it might become of great importance in the literary world. He had crossed swords with Colonel Dudley of the military; he had sat down and talked things over with William H. Bonney, and then, ironically enough, had been obliged to write out with his own hand and sign his name to a paper which authorized the outlaw's death by hanging. He had no doubt done his best to put out the fires of violence and hatred that had blazed in many parts of New Mexico, ignited and fanned to flame in his time and before his time, by bold and defiant men, bent on destruction of life and property, determined to have things their own way or perish in the attempt. He had come to verbal blows with smart and conniving politicians of his own and of opposite political faiths. He had stood his ground stubbornly in opposing proposed legislative enactments which he believed would be detrimental to the interests of the people of the Territory. He had arrived in New Mexico riding in a horse-drawn stagecoach; he left riding in a steam-drawn railroad Pullman car. He had been a participant in New Mexico's history; but he had never been able to reconcile himself to becoming a New Mexican at heart. His eyes had ever been focused on far horizons, watching for the coming of the Lord from another direction.

Sailing away from the United States to become minister to Turkey, it must have been that his thoughts were of mosques, spires and minarets of a far-off country, rather than the adobe houses, ranches and out-of-the-way places in New Mexico. He already had in mind, perhaps, an outline for another story, which became *The Prince of India* (published in 1893); and when the time came for Lew. Wallace to write his autobiog-

raphy (published in 1906), the story of his days in New Mexico received only brief attention.

When Lew. Wallace left Santa Fe forever, as it turned out
on May 30, 1881, the Santa Fe *New Mexican,* always a bitter
critic, spoke kindly of him:

> Wallace made hosts of friends here, and was as good a governor
> as the Territory has had.

By the year 1881 there were many reasons to justify the belief
that the people of New Mexico could look forward to a new
era in politics and business. The crack of Pat Garrett's pistol
shot, which ended the life of a notorious outlaw at Fort Sumner
on July 14, 1881, had the salutary effect of notifying the criminal element that the heyday of the law violator had passed.

There was every promise that economic conditions would be
gradually improved as the result of the completion by the Santa
Fe railroad of some six hundred miles of railway extending
through the heart of the Territory, from Raton Pass to Deming. Of course, some dislocation in business was caused by avail-
ability of railroad transportation. Bullwhackers, hostlers and
stage drivers found themselves out of work. Owners of horses,
mules and oxen, stagecoaches and freight wagons, previously
used in overland transportation, were obliged to move their
animals and equipment elsewhere or dispose of their property
in a depressed market.

Railroad transportation was of primary benefit to central
New Mexico, and affected Lincoln County only remotely and
indirectly. The town of Lincoln, still the official and business
center of a vast area of southeastern New Mexico, was almost
one hundred miles from San Antonio, a station on the Santa
Fe line below Socorro. After the completion of the Santa Fe
railroad it was no longer necessary or profitable to drive cattle
overland from the Pecos River country to markets in Abilene
or Dodge City, since they could now be driven to rail transportation in Las Vegas, San Antonio or Engle, and shipped on
the cars.

The completion of railroad transportation resulted in greatly
increased emigration to the Territory. Men traveled to New
Mexico from all parts of the country, some of them seeking

employment and business opportunities, others anxious to locate a homestead on free government land. Many newcomers
came to the Territory in the 1880's in their own conveyances,
accompanied by their families, a few head of livestock, and
odds and ends of personal belongings. The prairie schooner,
which had disappeared from the scene in southeastern New
Mexico in the late 70's as a result of the fighting in Lincoln
County, once again became a familiar sight.

However, the homeseeker and the man in the covered wagon
were not the only emigrants of the period. In the early 80's
many business and professional men came to the Territory
from the states, not a few of them endowed with ambition and
characteristics which, when devoted to public affairs, hastened
the "dawn of a new day" for New Mexico.

Beginning with the year 1881 there was a realignment in the
political field in the Territory. In the fifteen years from 1865
to 1881, the affairs of the Territory at large and of Lincoln
County in particular had been in the hands of Civil War veterans, appointed to office by a Republican President.

Grand Army of the Republic posts in Fort Union, Santa Fe,
Albuquerque, Fort Stanton, Mesilla and elsewhere in the Territory, had for many years been suspected of serving as listen-
ing posts for Union veterans and helping old comrades to be
appointed to and retained in political offices. The post Civil
War influence, which had been an important factor in political
maneuvering in the Territory since 1865, was most certainly
on the way out, beginning with the year 1881.

Grover Cleveland, elected President in 1884, hastened the
political realignment in New Mexico by appointing on May 1,
1885, E. G. Ross, one-time Republican United States senator
from Kansas, to be governor of New Mexico. The appointment
of Ross, a convert to the Democratic party, resulted in a political upheaval throughout the Territory. Democrats, long-de-
nied federal office, made the most of the changeover in the
national administration. In a matter of months, all Republican
office holders had resigned, and their places were taken by
Democrats.

Outstanding among the business and professional men who
reached southeastern New Mexico in the 80's and contributed
in a major way to good government and development of the

country were Harvey Butler Fergusson,[4] William C. McDonald,[5] John Y. Hewitt[6] and James Field Hinkle,[7] all of whom were Democrats, and active in the Democratic party. Participation in political affairs by Fergusson, McDonald, Hewitt, Hinkle, and other men who rallied to their support, resulted in the breaking down of old political ties and prejudices. Men who had fought in the Confederate army, and who had been for years subjected to real or imaginary indignities at the hands of G. A. R. politicians, were particularly responsive to the new leadership.

The names of Murphy, Dolan, Riley and Brady; of McSween, Tunstall and Bonney; of John S. Chisum; of Dudley and Lew. Wallace, among others, loomed large in the history of Lincoln County during an exciting and important era. One by one these men, and others of like stature, dropped out of the ranks, either voluntarily or otherwise, and were no longer important factors in public life.

By 1881 other men were ready to assume leadership and take a hand in the conduct of private business and official affairs. For their efforts in helping to achieve good government, the people of New Mexico bestowed high honors upon them. Fergusson was destined to be elected time and again to Congress; McDonald was destined to be first governor of the State of New Mexico; Hinkle was destined to be governor of the state; Hewitt, refusing all major political honors, was to live to be ninety-five years old, confident to the end that his Old Abe Mine in White Oaks would once again yield a vast golden treasure.

In days to come, someone endowed with a true feeling and affection for southeastern New Mexico and its pioneers will write definitively about the trials, tribulations and triumphs of Fergusson, McDonald, Hinkle and Hewitt, and other leaders of their day, who paved the way politically to the Promised Land in New Mexico; will tell of the partitioning of the vast and sprawling original Lincoln County, initiated by the establishment in 1889 of Chaves and Eddy counties. Of necessity, such a writer will tell of the discovery and almost incredible development of gas, oil and potash in territory that was once a part of old Lincoln County; of experiments of world-wide significance in rockets and guided missiles in the

White Sands country; of the increase in population and expansion in industry; of the cotton production and the all-important progress generally in agriculture and livestock. In the telling, such a writer will undoubtedly pay appropriate tribute to the memories of the many beloved old-timers of the frontier in eastern New Mexico, who now walk upon "that further shore," among them, Capt. J. C. Lea, the true father of Roswell, George Curry, Granville A. Richardson, Lucius Dills, Elza White, J. P. White, Edward A. Cahoon, James John Hagerman, Charles B. Eddy, Robert Kellahin, John W. Poe, Will Robinson, Nathan Jaffa, Andrew H. Hudspeth, James M. Hervey, William C. Reid, Dr. Austin D. Crile, and a host of other courageous men who devoted their time, talents and capital, and dedicated their lives to help make men's dreams come true in the Pecos River country.

NOTES AND PROFILES

[1] In 1910 Owen Wister, author of "The Virginian," told the present writer that he had visited in Deming for three weeks in the early 80's going in and out of saloons and gambling houses, "gathering local material." In response to a question, Wister said that the "Virginian" was a composite figure; that he did not have in mind any particular character while writing the book.

[2] On March 19, 1881, Wallace wrote to his son Henry: "As you have doubtless seen by the papers the President has appointed a General Sheldon or some other person to be Governor of New Mexico. . . . I have held the office until I have accomplished what I wanted—the acquirement of what I consider as good mining property as there is in the Territory."

Wallace wrote to his son again on March 29: "It is my intention to go down to San Simon, pitch a tent, live as the miners do, watch where every dollar goes, and every item of property, where every pick is struck, and keep the time of my hands paying them by the hour. That way I can make a $1000 go a long way." None of Wallace's mining ventures proved successful. He filed on a number of prospects, among them claims in the Dolores district near Cerrillos, and in the Black Range country in Grant County. The San Simon district, in which Wallace worked a prospect, was in Grant County.

[3] Like several other governors of New Mexico during Territorial days, Lionel Allen Sheldon was a Civil War veteran and former congressman. Born

in Worcester, Otsego County, New York, August 30, 1828, Sheldon moved with his parents to Lagrange, Ohio; attended the district school and Oberlin College; was graduated from the Fowler Law School, Poughkeepsie, New York, in 1853; was admitted to the Ohio bar in the same year; elected probate judge of Lorain County, Ohio, in 1856 and 1857; was a delegate to the Republican national convention at Philadelphia in 1856; served throughout the Civil War with Ohio troops; brevetted brigadier general of Volunteers on March 13, 1865.

Sheldon lived in Louisiana after the war, practicing in New Orleans from 1865 to 1869; elected as a Republican to the Forty-First, Forty-Second and Forty-Third Congresses, serving from 1869 to 1875. He was defeated for re-election in 1874. Sheldon returned to Ohio in 1879, and was elected a delegate to the national Republican convention in 1880. Sheldon was active in the campaign which resulted in Garfield's election as President, and was offered the place as his secretary, but declined, in order to accept the appointment as governor of New Mexico, on the supposition, it was reported at the time, that New Mexico would soon become a state, and he would be elected by the Legislature to the United States Senate.

After serving as governor of the Territory from 1881 to 1885, Sheldon served as one of the receivers of the Texas and Pacific railway from 1885 to 1887. He died in Pasadena, California, on January 17, 1917. When appointed governor of New Mexico, one Territorial paper noted that "Sheldon has the reputation of being one of the best poker players that ever came to the Territory."

[4] Harvey Butler Fergusson was born near Pickensville, Pickens County, Alabama, on September 9, 1848, and died in Albuquerque on June 10, 1915. He was graduated from Washington and Lee University with B.A. and LL.B. degrees; practiced law in Wheeling, West Virginia, for several years before coming to White Oaks, New Mexico, in 1882 to represent the heirs of John V. Winters in litigation over the ownership of the Homestake, a gold-mining property in which James J. Dolan and others owned fractional interests.

Winters died on or about March 1, 1881. His heirs became involved in a lawsuit which required nearly two years for final disposition. Fergusson lost the case in the Lincoln County District Court, but won out over famed Tom Catron on appeal to the Supreme Court. (See Brunswick v. Winters' Heirs, 3 N. M. 241, 5 Pac. 706. See also Baxter Mountain Gold Mining Co. vs. Patterson, 3 N. M. 179, 5 Pac. 741, litigation involving a gold-mining claim near the Homestake property, of interest principally because Emerson Hough, later a famous writer, then a resident of White Oaks, was one of the attorneys.)

Elected delegate from New Mexico to the Fifty-Fifth Congress (March 4, 1897-March 3, 1899), Fergusson pushed through Congress the so-called "Fergusson Act" of June 21, 1898, which set aside Sections 16 and 36 in every public domain township in the Territory, some four million acres in all, for the use and benefit of public schools, unquestionably the most important single

egislative enactment in New Mexico's history. In 1910 Fergusson was elected
o the Constitutional Convention as a delegate from Bernalillo County; and
upon the admission of New Mexico as a state, he was elected to the Sixty-Second
and Sixty-Third Congresses, serving from January 8, 1912, to March 3, 1915.
Three of Harvey Fergusson's four children became noted writers: Erna Fergusson *(Dancing Gods)*, Harvey B. Fergusson *(The Blood of the Conquerors)*,
and Francis Fergusson *(The Idea of a Theatre)*.

⁵ William C. McDonald, New Mexico's first governor after statehood (January 15, 1912—December 31, 1916), was born in Jordanville, New York, on
July 25, 1858; died on April 11, 1918; was buried in Cedarvale Cemetery,
White Oaks, not far from the graves of John Y. Hewitt, Andrew H. Hudspeth
and other old-timers of his day.

Arriving in New Mexico in 1880 with a background of business and professional experience in law, civil and mining engineering, McDonald became
a lifelong resident of Lincoln County, in which he was elected assessor, member
of the board of county commissioners, and to other offices. He managed for
many years the Carrizozo Cattle Ranch Co. and El Capitan Livestock Co.
During his five-year term as governor, McDonald demonstrated that he was
a capable administrator, with the courage to say "no" to friends and "yes" to
enemies in matters affecting public welfare.

⁶ John Y. Hewitt was born in West Farmington, Trumbull County, Ohio,
on October 11, 1836. He died in White Oaks, on January 5, 1932. He was
educated in the common schools and Western Reserve Seminary in West
Farmington.

At the age of twenty, Hewitt started on his own, going to Franklin County,
Kansas, where he began business.

On October 14, 1861, he entered the Union army, fought in the battles of
Fort Wayne, Canehill and Prairie Grove. Hewitt was mustered out of military
service September 1, 1865. He settled in Ottawa, Kansas, after the war, taught
school, studied law, and engaged in business. Wiped out by the panic of 1873,
Hewitt went to the Black Hills of the Dakotas. Learning of the discovery of
gold in Lincoln County, Hewitt arrived in White Oaks in 1880 with ten dollars in his pocket. He prospected for gold, worked in the mines, continued his
law studies, and was admitted to the New Mexico bar on August 1, 1881. A
successful lawyer, Hewitt bought an interest in the Old Abe and Little Mac
mines in White Oaks and a half interest in the White Oaks *Eagle,* and became
its editor. Believing that White Oaks was destined to be a great gold-mining
camp, Hewitt invested every dollar he could spare in that town, erected two
business buildings, helped to organize the Exchange Bank of White Oaks and
became its first president. Although a Republican in his early manhood, Hewitt
became a Democrat in New Mexico, and for many years took a prominent part
in the affairs of that party.

Regardless of the fact that the pockets of gold carrying ore became more and more difficult to find, Hewitt clung tenaciously to the belief that White Oaks would eventually become a great town. At an advanced age Hewitt transferred his dreams and White Oaks property to Andrew H. Hudspeth, a long-time protégé, who served as the first United States Marshal for New Mexico after statehood, and Justice of the Supreme Court for two terms beginning in 1931. After Hewitt's death, Hudspeth was faithful to the trust imposed upon him by his benefactor. He continued to do assessment work on many mining claims, paid taxes on all the Hewitt property, and carried on until his death with the hope that White Oaks would one day stage a comeback. The hopes and expectations of Hewitt and Hudspeth failed to materialize. White Oaks has been a ghost town for many years.

Judge Hudspeth, seventy-four years old, died in the Huntington Memorial Hospital, Pasadena, California, on March 9, 1948. His ashes were scattered over the White Oaks Mines, most of which he owned.

[7] James F. Hinkle, who began life in New Mexico in 1885 as a cowboy on the Peñasco, a tributary of the Pecos River, was for decades prominent in livestock, banking and public affairs. Born in Franklin County, Missouri, on October 20, 1864, Hinkle was educated in the common schools of that state and at the University of Missouri.

When scarcely twenty years old, he left Missouri and went to Texas, where he became a cowboy for the CA Bar outfit near Colorado City. In 1937 Hinkle told the fascinating story of his life in "Early Days of a Cowboy on the Pecos," a thirty-three page, modestly worded composition, distributed among old-time friends.

When the CA Bar bought a ranch on the Peñasco in New Mexico in 1885, young Jim Hinkle was placed in charge. He ran the outfit in good years and bad, until 1901. In that year the owners liquidated their interests, and Hinkle moved to Roswell. Elected to the Legislature from Lincoln County in 1888, Hinkle helped to enact a law on February 25, 1889, creating the counties of Chaves and Eddy which were carved out of Lincoln County; and served on a commission of three men to settle the business and financial affairs between and among the three counties.

In subsequent years Hinkle was repeatedly elected to the Legislature from Chaves County; was elected mayor of Roswell in 1905; elected governor of New Mexico in 1923, declining to run for re-election, although assured of election.

To this writer the Governor gave a cogent reason for not again becoming a candidate: "It's costing me $125.00 a month more to be governor than the salary I'm getting; it isn't worth it; I'm not going to run again." In the second state election in 1916, Jim Hinkle sent a telegram to his friend, Neill B. Field of Albuquerque, candidate on the Democratic ticket for the Supreme Court, inviting him to be his guest at the Chaves County Apple Carnival in Roswell, where he would be given an opportunity to meet the voters and do some hand-to-hand campaigning. Field promptly telegraphed Hinkle: "I thank you for the invitation, but I have yet to see the day when I will allow myself as a candidate for public office to be exhibited like a stud horse at a county fair." Governor Hinkle died at Roswell on March 26, 1951, survived by his widow, Lillian Roberts Hinkle, and four children: Rolla R. Hinkle, Clarence Hinkle, authority on New Mexico oil and gas law, Vera Hinkle Farnsworth, and Lillian Hinkle Coll, all of Roswell.

THE END

INDEX

N